NARRATIVE

OF AN

EXPLORING VOYAGE.

THE "PLEIAD" EXPLORING VESSEL, BUILT BY MESSRS. LAIRD.

NARRATIVE

OF AN

EXPLORING VOYAGE

UP THE RIVERS KWO'RA AND BI'NUE

(COMMONLY KNOWN AS THE NIGER AND TSÁDDA)

IN 1854.

WITH A MAP AND APPENDICES.

PUBLISHED WITH THE SANCTION OF HER MAJESTY'S GOVERNMENT.

BY

WILLIAM BALFOUR BALKIE,

M.D.R.N., F.R.G.S., F.S.A. SCOT., ETC. IN COMMAND OF THE EXPEDITION.

Rediscovery Books

Reproduced by kind permission of the
Royal Geographical Society

Published by
Rediscovery Books Ltd
Unit 10, Ridgewood Industrial Park,
Uckfield, East Sussex,
TN22 5QE England
Tel: +44 (0) 1825 749494
Fax: +44 (0) 1825 765701

This edition © Rediscovery Books Ltd 2006

To find out more about Rediscovery Books
and its range of titles visit
www.rediscoverybooks.com

Published in association with

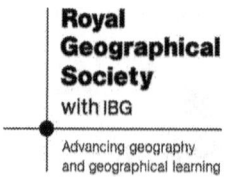

Advancing geography
and geographical learning

The **Royal Geographical Society with IBG** was founded in 1830 to advance geographical science. Today it supports geographical research, promotes geography in schools and through outdoor learning, in society and to policy makers. Geography connects us to the world's people, places and environments.
The **Rediscovery Books** series allow us to see how previous geographers and travellers understood and recorded the world.

In reprinting in facsimile from the original, any imperfections are inevitably reproduced and the quality may fall short of modern type and cartographic standards.

Printed and bound by Lightning Source

PREFACE.

THE following " Narrative," which has been considerably delayed by various unlooked-for interruptions, and which has been compiled during leisure intervals snatched from professional and other pursuits, is simply a record of the observations and results of the exploring expedition up the rivers Kwóra and Bínue in 1854. In addition to what came actually under our notice, I have endeavoured to record any interesting or useful information obtained regarding the little known regions of Central Africa. In an Appendix will be found various tables, lists, and documents, not of general interest, and therefore excluded from the body of the work, but at hand to be referred to by those concerned in such topics. I have been careful to note any traditions regarding the early history of the different tribes, as though at present they are of comparatively little value, the time will come when these apparently trifling stories will be sought after with as much avidity, as the historical antiquary of our-own country eagerly culls any legends or tales relating to those ages when our Teutonic or Keltic progenitors, barbarous and unlettered, were not a whit more advanced than many of the Ethiopian races of the present day.

All native proper names throughout the volume have been written in conformity with the alphabet printed in the Appendix, every letter being sounded, and the vowels having the powers given to them in Italian. To prevent confusion the only mark employed has been simply one over the accented syllable.

In computing distances two very different reckonings are employed. One is the long day's journey, from sunrise to sunset, or from fifteen to twenty-five miles, twenty being an average, equal to about fifteen or sixteen miles made good on horizontal space. The other is the short day's journey, from sunrise to about noon, or from eight to twelve or fourteen miles, ten being perhaps the nearest average, which may represent eight miles of actual progress.

PREFACE.

I have felt obliged often to be more personal than I could have desired, and to allude to disputes and to differences over which I would gladly have thrown a veil; but as these matters have lately been made the subject of judicial proceedings, I have mentioned them, partly in my own defence, partly to show why the success of the Expedition was not more complete than it was, and also that future exploring parties might be aware of and so avoid the various stumbling-blocks which so often tended to impede our progress.

Two works have already appeared regarding our Voyage. One, proceeding from a most estimable individual, is in the form of a short journal, referring more especially to the prospects for missionary efforts, while the other seems rather to relate the private opinions and individual experiences of a member of the party, than to contain an account of the Expedition. It is hoped that the present one, which aims at being more detailed than its predecessors, will satisfy any anxiety which may be felt about the once dreaded "Niger," or concerning the rude natives around; and if it serves in any degree to excite a warmer feeling towards the ill-treated African, to claim a small degree of attention for rich but neglected regions, or to stimulate further enquiries and explorations, the writer will consider his labours not to have been altogether in vain.

HASLAR HOSPITAL,
 26th May, 1856.

TABLE OF CONTENTS.

CHAPTER I.

INTRODUCTORY.

PAGE

THEORIES regarding the course of the Kwóra—African explorers—Dr. Barth's discovery of the Upper Bínuë—The "Pleiad"—Mr. Beecroft . . . . 1—6

CHAPTER II.

THE VOYAGE OUT.

Departure from Plymouth—Bay of Biscay—Towing nets—Oceanic captures—Funchal—Quarantine—Santa Cruz—Torch Fishing—Peak of Teneriffe—North East Trades—Flying-fishes—Petrels—Cape de Verde—Gorée—Wolofs—Bathurst—Tornado—Sierra Leone—Inhabitants—The "Pleiad"—Monrovia—Southern Cross—Cape Coast Castle—A marriage—Mr. Beecroft's death—Akrá—Lagos—Surf—Sharks—Mr. Crowther—Old Kalabár—Cameroon—Fernando Po—New arrangements—Mr. May—Arrival of the "Pleiad"—Dr. Bleek—Preparations . . . . 7—30

CHAPTER III.

THE LAUNCH OF THE EXPEDITION.

Leave Clarence—Nun Mouth—Sea on the bar—Repairs—Alburkah Islands—Mangroves—Richard's Creek—Sunday Island—Orú Villages—Angiáma—Again aground—Wári branch—Abó—Alihéli—Tshúkuma—Visits—Presents—Natives alarmed—Ladies' ornaments—Kola Nuts . . . . 31—50

CHAPTER IV.

I'GBO AND IGA'RA.

Bullock Island—Ossamaró—Hippopotami—Onitshá and Asabá—Sandbank—Ada-Mugú—Round huts—Iddá cliffs—A'boko's party—Iddá politics—Camp on English Island—Court of the Attá—Reception ceremonies—Visitors—Igára—Language—Edó—Ivory—Volcanic blocks—Bird-Rock—Okíri—Moonlight at Iróko—Mounts Franklin and Crozier—Igbógbe—A'ma A'boko—The Confluence—The "Dark Water"—Odokódo—Háusa—Binue—Adamáwa—Model-farm—Sacrifice-Rock—Visit to Mount Páte—Panorama—Trade—Despatches—Baobabs—O'gbe's jug—White Ants' nests—Leave the Confluence—A'tipo—Purchase wood—A'ma-A'boko's messengers—Harriet Island—Lander's Seat—Mount Vidal—Oldfield Range—Yimahá—I'gbira—Pánda—Fulútas—Plague of Flies—Kónde—Sets of observations—Continuance of health—Dispute with a Crocodile—A'batsho—Pánda refugees—Difficulties—Soundings—Consultation—Changes in the Ministry . . . . . 51—93

CHAPTER V.

THE NEW ADMINISTRATION.

Early start—Off Erúko—Dágbo—Admiralty Archipelago—Dóma Hills—A'kpoko—Royal Interview—Sir John Richardson's Islands—Isabella Island—Troublesome Navigation—O'jogo—Two White Strangers?—Embassy to Keána—Wood-cutting—Mitshi—Rejected friendship—Mr. May alarms the Court—Deputations—Dóma Cookery—New Lights—Fresh Plans—Wooden Leg—Dóma History—O'jogo Habits—Iron Money—Juvenile Game—False Gavial—Trade canoe sent to the Confluence—Dearth in the Sugar-Market—Rógan-Kóto—Clarendon Island—Mount Beecroft—Washington Island—Ellesmere Range—Mounts Latham and Christison—Mount Adams—Mount Trénabie—Mount Traill—Nú—Korórofa—Terror of the Natives—Martial Meeting—Alarm of Krúboys—Gándiko—Púlbe—Djúku—Zhibú—Grand Procession—Distinguished Reception—Moslemin—Fáro—Abundance of Ivory . . . 94—134

CHAPTER VI.

THE UPPER BI'NUE.

Mount Humboldt—Temporary Sails—Evening Meeting with Hippopotami—Mount Forbes—Albemarle Range—Akám—Strong Current—Green Wood—Direction of Tornadoes—Attack on a huge tree—Interruption by a Leopard—Mosquitoes—Fumbína Mountains—

TABLE OF CONTENTS. xiii

PAGE

Zhirú—Rise of the River—Zoological Treasures—Sáraki 'n Háusa—
Cut Wood under difficulties—An Embassy Despatched—Gúrowa—
Múri Mountains—Bak 'n Dútshi — *Wa*—Mr. Crowther's Return—
The Sultan's Letter—Start for Hamarúwa—Arrival—Congratulations
—Supper—Heavy Dew—Rain—Púlbe—Dress and Ornaments—
Henna—Geographical Examination—Written Charms—The Sultan's
Palace—Grand Interview—Reciprocity of Sentiment—Attired in
Tobes—Return—March in Detachments—Arboreal Night Quarters
—Feline Attendants and Feathered Companions—Astronomical
Studies—Bad Roads—Breakfast at Wúzu—Trade—Eccentric Rainbow—Scurvy—Struck by Lightning—Boat Cruise—Tshómo—
Hunting Relics—Búibai—Surprise an Elephant—Flooded Banks—
Sunset at Láu—Mount Laird—Pleiad Island—Wild Hunters—
River Horses—Djín—Cause a Sensation—Too Pressing Attentions—
Night-melodies — Fishing Station — Fresh Breeze — Mountainous
Country—Mount Gabriel—Dúlti—Village under Water—Astonishment of the Natives—People become curious—*Ruse de Guerre*—
Rapid Retreat—Dúlti Regatta—Terror of the Krúmen—The Race
Won   .   .   .   . 135—200

CHAPTER VII.

THE RETURN.

Apology for Dúlti—" Ne plus ultra "—Anticipated Cannibalism—Djín
again—Fluviatile bo-peep !—Bándawa—Magnificent Thunder-storm
—Fortunate Position—Morning Exploit—Mount Eleanor—"Pleiad"
again Missing—Farewell to Gúrowa—Take Stock—Regrets—Resume
the Survey—Fan Palms—River still Rising—Devious Channels—
Submerged Country—Genuine Exploring Trip—No Land in Sight
—Dead Lioness—Signs of a Deluge—Amphibious Aborigines?—
Regain the River—" Dere de Ship "—" Pleiad " hard and fast—Successful efforts—Báutshi Slaver—" Kantai "—Prices of Slaves and of
Horses—Scurvy Continues—Measures—Causes   .   .   . 201—222

CHAPTER VIII.

FURTHER DISAPPOINTMENTS.

Zhibú—King surly—The Monarch bearded in his Hall—Diplomacy—
Prevented from visiting Wukári—The Galadíma—Sáraki 'n Dóki—
River falling—*Polypterus*—Crowther Island—Gándiko—Varieties of
Corn—*Kigelia*—A'nyishi—Rapid Current—Route to Wukári—Leadore—Mútshi—Rógan-Kóto—Onúse — Good Fuel—Irihú—O'jogo—

TABLE OF CONTENTS.

Pick up the Messengers—No Dr. Barth—Zúri troublesome—Recompence to O'rabo—Suspected Slave—Visit from King of A'kpoko—White Cock—Dágbo—Extreme Heat—Zózo—Bloodthirsty Mosquitoes—Erúko—Palm-nut Oil—Magnificent Palisade—Architectural Remains—Huge Pipes—Alihóli's Friend—Púlbe Attack—Mr. May visits Ikóreku—A'batsho—Detection and Ransom of a Slave Boy—Amarán—Hear of our Canoe—Sun's Meridian Altitude—Yimahá—Call on the new King—Blacksmith's Forge—I'gbira History—Redeeming Captives—Monkey Bread-fruit—"Big-man of O'gba"—Duck Islands . . . . 223—264

CHAPTER IX.

THE CONFLUENCE.

Changes—Sickness in the Canoe—A'ma-A'boko rather cool—Explanations—Núpe—Kakánda—Bása—Bonú—Ishábe—Brisk Trade—Large Market—Zúri's felonious attempt—Grand "palaver" at the Palace—Anti-slavery Lecture—Mr. May's Ascent of Mount Páte—Huge yams—Agricultural implements—Gigantic Baobab—Arabic MSS.—Stamboul—Symbolical letter—Departure—Pyrotechnic phenomenon—Beaufort Island—Ehimodína and Okéyin—More ivory—I'gbira-Shíma—Iddá—Threatened Tornado—Alihóli's story—Promised bullock—Wild festival—Iddá declining—Igára traditions—I'gbo cloth—Musical band—Adó river—A'da-mugú—Muskets—Signs of confidence—Commercial transactions—A'ra mats—Utó . . . . 265—292

CHAPTER X.

I'GBO.

Inám—Nsúgbe—Prices of muskets—Asabá—Acoustic instruments—Palm wine—Warrior's tokens—Onitshá—E'lugu—Ossamaré—Isuáma—Lilliputian canoes—Muddy town—Ndóni—Abó—Simon Jonas—Stray tea-chest—Mr. Carr's murder—Dásaba's march—Alihóli paid off—Visit from Ajé and most of the royal family—Crowded decks—Animated discussion—Shower bath—Health improving—Provisions nearly consumed—Farewell to Ajé—Malaghetta pepper—I'gbo divisions—'Itshi or Mbrítshi—A'ro—Shrine of Tshúku—Religion—Orísa—Rites—Djú-dju trees—Kamállo—Igwikálla—Funeral ceremonies—I'gbo week—Food—Price of slaves—Agbóri—Pilgrim from A'ro—Recognition of a mosquito—Mist among the trees—Angiáma—Sickly stench—Buy

TABLE OF CONTENTS. xv

PAGE

wood—Advise the King—Doctor's shop—Attack on Lander—
Anchor off Baracoon Point—Prepare for sea—Mr. May's visit to the
Brass river—Distressed British subjects—Nímbe—Kwóra hygiene—
Quinine . . . . 293—328

CHAPTER XI.

FERNANDO PO.

Palm Point—No breakers—Crossing the Bar—Three passages—Meet
a schooner—First news—Round Cape Bullen—Fire a salute—Hear
of the Battle of Alma—Krúboys' rejoicings—Leave the "Pleiad"—
King Peppel—Bonny news—New Kalabár—Rio Formoso—Bíni—
Oedo—Agáto—Belzoni's papers—Sóbo—Tshékeri—Ijebús—Jó-
men—Salt-wood—Baión—Báti—Yála—Value of Fernando Po—
Invasion of Spanish priests . . . . 329—349

CHAPTER XII.

THE VOYAGE HOME.

Leave Clarence—Aground in the Cameroons—Duke Town—Mr.
Anderson—E'fik—Kwá—Mbrúkim—Ordeal bean—Captain Lewis—
Kantóro—Okúloma—King Dappa—Cannibalism—Trust system—
Commercial association—Different modes of reckoning—Disturb-
ances at Bonny—Mr. Crowther's return to Yóruba—Joined by the
Bishop and Archdeacon—Abadayígi—Ashánti—Conversation with
Bishop Vidal—Mítshi boy—Akrá—Cape Coast Castle—Governor
Hill—Cape Palmas—Krú country—Monrovia—Illness and death
of the Bishop—Sad Christmas—Water-spout—Sierra Leone—
Repairs—Interviews with natives—Coffee—Exports—Vexatious
regulations—Bathurst official—Gorée—Snowclad Peak of Teneriffe
—Trophies in the Cathedral at Santa Cruz—Rough weather—Fun-
chal—Gale of wind—Arrival at Plymouth . . . . 350—384

CHAPTER XIII.

CONCLUSION.

Results of the voyage—Slave trade—African squadron—Piracy—
Púlo alliance—Further expeditions—African languages—Late
travellers—Incentives to renewed exertions . . . . 385—397

TABLE OF CONTENTS.

PAGE
APPENDIX A.—Description of the "Pleiad"—Admiralty Instructions —Mr. Laird's Instructions—Correspondence—Native African Treaty 399
APPENDIX B.—Various Forms of Currency . . . . 416—417
APPENDIX C.—Philological . . . . 417—425
APPENDIX D.—Geographical . . . . 425—450
APPENDIX E.—Ethnological . . . . 450—452
APPENDIX F.—Natural History 452
APPENDIX G.—Medical . . . . 452—455
APPENDIX H.—Commercial . . . . 455—456

ILLUSTRATIONS.

VIEW OF THE "PLEIAD" . . . . Frontispiece.
PRINCE TSHÚKUMA . . . . On Title-page.
PLANS OF THE "PLEIAD" . . . . . . To face p. 399.
MAP . . . . At the end.

NARRATIVE

OF AN

EXPLORING VOYAGE.

CHAPTER I.

INTRODUCTORY.

FROM the days of Herodotus to very recent times the theories which have been brought forward regarding the course and distribution of the Kwóra, or Niger, have been alike numerous and varied. Geographers, both ancient and modern, have exerted their utmost ingenuity in endeavouring to solve the mystery; and, according as they believed in the westward or eastward course of the river, ranged themselves into two parties, the one pointing to the Senegal and the Gambia as the mouths of this mighty stream, while the other either conducted it through Lake Tsad to join the Nile, or else led it by a long and dreary route to be identified with the Congo. It certainly appears singular that, until a comparatively recent date, no one even hinted at its real termination. The numerous large bodies of fresh water falling into the bights of Benin and Biafra have for long been familiarly known, yet their source was never enquired after; and although very slight consideration would have shown that, evidently closely connected as all these are, they must flow from some great river in the interior, it was not until 1808, that Reichard, judging from the vast amount of alluvial deposits, first suggested the Rio Formoso as the outlet of the Kwóra, an idea since proved to be partially true. Major Laing and Captain Clapperton also believed in the discharge of its waters into the Bight of Benin, the former selecting the Rio Volta for the purpose, while the latter hypothesised an opening to the eastward of Lagos. But by no one was the enquiry pursued more zealously or more shrewdly than by Mr. Macqueen, who, having collected a vast amount of evidence on the subject, recommended, in 1829, a careful examination of the rivers between the Rio Formoso and Old Kalabar. It must have been highly gratifying to this veteran geographer, whose knowledge of Central Africa is probably unsurpassed, to find only two years afterwards his supposition verified by the splendid exploit of the Landers, who, at the expense of so much risk and suffering, navigated the Kwóra from Yaúri to the sea, thereby proving the existence of an available water communication with the heart of the African continent. Their discovery was quickly seized on in England, and the enterprise of Liverpool merchants speedily fitted out a small expedition for commercial and geographical purposes. This attempt, chiefly from climacteric causes, ended unfortunately: a spirited and graphic account of its discoveries and its disasters was published by two of the survivors, Mr. Macgregor Laird and Mr. Oldfield, while their companion, Captain (then Lieutenant) W. Allen, surveyed and compiled a chart of their adventurous route, which extended along the main stream as far as Rábba, and likewise upwards of eighty miles up a previously unknown large affluent, the Tsádda. The misfortunes met with by these pioneers did not afford much encouragement for further trials, and no attempt of any magnitude was made until 1841, when the Government fitted out three steamers, specially built for the purpose. This expedition was intended to carry out, besides extended research, various philanthropic but ill-matured schemes. Its ill success, with its fearful amount of sickness and loss of life, still fresh in our memories, tended greatly to confirm the conviction of the deadly nature of the climate. The Kwóra was also ascended by the late Mr. Beecroft, in one of the steamers of the West African Company, in 1836, and again by the same gentleman in the "Æthiope," a steam vessel belonging to Mr. Jamieson of Liverpool, in 1840 and in 1845, on one of which occasions he entered and explored the branch running by Wári.

Such is a brief outline of the previous efforts to investigate and explore this river, and though inducements to perseverance were far from wanting, still no one, reflecting on the great probable sacrifice of European life, cared about taking the responsibility of advising another attempt. But in 1852 the question was again started, in consequence of intelligence received from Dr. Barth, who, the sole but still undaunted survivor of a party which had two years before crossed the Great Desert, had boldly journeyed to the southward, to endeavour to reach the province of Adamáwa. On the 18th of June, 1851, he crossed a large stream, named the Bínue, which, from the information he received from the natives, he conjectured to be the upper part of the river hitherto known to Europeans as the Tsádda. To ascertain this point, the present expedition was principally destined, the two objects specially mentioned in the Admiralty instructions being, first to explore the river Tsádda from Dágbo, the point reached by Allen and Oldfield in 1833, as far to the eastward as possible : secondly, to endeavour to "meet and afford assistance" to Drs. Barth and Vogel. To promote these designs, the Admiralty entered into a contract with Mr. Macgregor Laird, to build and equip a suitable vessel. Mr. Laird, having, as already mentioned, been himself up the Kwóra, and having always been closely connected with African trade, and taken a most lively interest in everything tending to improve or benefit this region, was on these accounts, as well as on that of his great general experience and foresight, the very person best suited for planning and giving effect to such an undertaking. Accordingly an iron screw schooner was built at Birkenhead, in the yard of Mr. John Laird, and, on being launched, received the name of the "Pleiad." She was of 260 tons measurement, 100 feet in length, with 24 feet beam, and her engine was of 60 horse-power. Her draught of water when laden was 7 feet, or 6 feet when in ordinary trim. A sailing-master, surgeon, officers, and crew were provided for her by Mr. Laird, and it was arranged that she should be sent to Fernando Po, where the officers appointed by government should join. The peculiar features of this expedition were, first, the employment of as few white men as possible; secondly, entering and ascending the river with the rising waters, or during the rainy season; and lastly, it was anticipated that the use of quinine, as a prophylactic or preventive, would enable the Europeans to withstand the influence of the climate. Mr. Laird, being permitted by his agreement with the Admiralty to trade with the natives whenever it was practicable, provided a well-assorted cargo, and sent out persons specially to attend to this branch. The "Pleiad" having made a very satisfactory trial trip across the Irish Channel, finally took her departure from Dublin on the 20th of May, 1854.

The conduct of the expedition was entrusted to Mr. Beecroft, Her Majesty's Consul at Fernando Po, than whom no one had more experience of African exploration, or could be in all respects better adapted for such a responsible post. I was appointed medical officer and naturalist, and was to have been accompanied by another assistant-surgeon, Mr. J. W. D. Brown, but on the breaking out of the war, his services were required in the Baltic. Subsequently it was arranged that Dr. W. Bleek, a German ethnologist, who had paid much attention to African philology, should proceed with me; and having received our instructions, and being amply provided with instruments and other appliances by the Hydrographical Office, we hurried our preparations for leaving England by the African mail packet.

CHAPTER II.

THE VOYAGE OUT.

ACCOMPANIED by Dr. Bleek and a young man whom I took with me as zoological assistant, I left Plymouth by the "Forerunner" packet on the 24th of May, 1854, and with moderate weather, and a tolerably fair wind, soon crossed the Channel, and reached the Bay of Biscay. The "Forerunner" being a very fast screw vessel, we made rapid progress, while from our complement of passengers being full, our time on board passed away very agreeably. I had the pleasure of making the acquaintance of several "Africans,"* among whom was Mr. Louis Fraser, one of the survivors of the expedition in 1841. On two occasions, tempted by the smoothness of the water, I threw my towing-nets overboard, hoping to waylay some rare pelagian voyager, but from the rate at which we were going, from eight to nine knots, nearly lost all my gear. One evening, when about a hundred miles to the northward of Madeira, something went wrong with the machinery, to repair which

---

* A name familiarly given to all engaged in African trade, or who have resided much on the west coast of Africa.

the engines had to be stopped for some hours. The wind being very light, we did not go under sail more than two knots, so I remained up most of the night with my towing-net, in expectation of intercepting some crepuscular pteropod or other oceanic resident, but only succeeded in capturing some minute tunicaries and acalephs. Many of the latter were highly phosphorescent, so much so, that by holding three or four near my watch, I was enabled to see the hour. Herds of sportive porpoises playing around us clearly intimated that we were approaching warmer latitudes, and, at length, on the morning of the 30th, we came in sight of Porto Santo, and shortly afterwards of Madeira. By the forenoon, after a quick passage of less than six days, we were at anchor in Funchal roads, admiring the steep acclivities and ravines so beautifully clad with verdure, and wondering at the strange contrast between the bright sea and sunny scenes near us, with the dark clouds settling over the top of the island, and frowning ominously upon us. No sooner was the anchor down than all the passengers, many of whom had never previously performed such a lengthened sea-voyage, or been so long out of sight of land, prepared for an excursion on shore, and anxiously waited for the moment when the vessel should be admitted to pratique. But to our surprise and dismay, the health-boat had no sooner reached alongside, than we found ourselves convicted of gross ignorance, and received important information on a topic, which we had neglected enquiring into before leaving England. This was, that cholera existed in Glasgow, and therefore the sanitary magnates, considering that our transit across twelve hundred miles of the Atlantic had been too rapid to allow us to have got rid of the foul infection, considerately forbade our leaving the ship, and placed us in quarantine. Vain were remonstrances, protests, entreaties; the authorities had the latest and most accurate intelligence, and, moreover, they had all the power on their side. Consequently, the one passenger for Funchal was transferred, under a strict guard, to the miserable Lazarretto, and the ship was surrounded by boats bearing villanous yellow flags. Coal-barges came alongside, and commenced discharging their cargo; boats with articles for sale crowded around, and speedily a brisk traffic sprung up. Bunches of cherries were speedily bought up at sixpence each; and baskets, mats, and straw hats were in great demand. Our steward speculated largely in these latter, for which he gave a shilling a-piece, intending to sell them down the coast at half-a-crown, or more if possible. In making purchases when in quarantine, buyers can only examine an article by sight, as no sooner do they touch it, than whether they like it or not, they must keep it,—ay, and pay well for it too. It is a singular example of the foresight of the original framers of quarantine law, that money can always be easily passed from the affected to the non-affected party. Thus, while individuals and property of all descriptions must undergo long detention, and purifications by fumigations, steaming baths, &c., the contagious property of coin is held to be immediately destroyed by simply passing it through water; and so when a purchase has been effected, the seller concludes by holding up a small cup or other vessel, containing water, into which the money is allowed to drop; and this custom prevails irrespective of country, whether the port be Portuguese, Spanish, Italian, Greek, or Turkish. But more seriously speaking, these quarantine absurdities are made extremely vexatious, as well as expensive to those who suffer from them.

In the present instance, not to mention merely the inconvenience, the owners of the packet had to pay for the keep of the coal-heavers for some eight or ten days after our departure,—an outlay which would not be grumbled at were there even a shadow of a reason alleged, but most annoying and unjust when enforced in this arbitrary and needless manner. Considering how much Madeira depends for its prosperity on English trade, the Portuguese, one would suppose, ought to be rather more considerate. Leaving Madeira about sunset, we sighted Teneriffe next afternoon, and about eleven at night anchored off Santa Cruz. The little bay was at this time lighted up by fishing-boats, which at night make use of large flaming torches, to attract the fish. The water here being very deep, we had to anchor not far from the shore, and although we were in quarantine, a mare belonging to a relation of the governor's was admitted to pratique, by being made to swim ashore, while the harness was landed without any ceremony. Teneriffe, after Madeira, looks barren and arid; the ravines and the sides of the mountains being comparatively unclad with vegetation, and the whole country around having a more sun-dried appearance. Santa Cruz itself stands on level ground along the shore; and, from the anchorage, seems a compact and regular town, the most conspicuous building being the cathedral, the Iglesia de la Concepcion. Along the sides of the steep acclivities around, stone parapets have been raised, and the spaces between these and the face of the mountain being filled with soil, level patches have been formed, fitted for cultivation, while it gives to the hills the general appearance of a succession of terraces. Here we looked in vain for the celebrated Peak, but could distinguish nothing amidst the mists and clouds which then enveloped it. But a few hours afterwards we were more fortunate, as, when some fifteen or sixteen miles from the land, the sky cleared up and afforded us a magnificent prospect. We were far enough off to have a good outline view of the entire island, and along its steep hills the lights and shadows were beautifully apparent through the mellow atmosphere of a fine afternoon, while, towering high towards the heavens, the Peak raised its lofty head, the summit showing in clear relief against the blue sky, and halfway down a solitary stratum of cloud, partially encircling the mountain, gave additional effect to the scene.

After leaving Teneriffe we ran towards the coast of Africa, with the N.E. trades, carrying with us delightful weather. Shoals of flying-fishes surrounded us, amusing us with their glittering flights. Rising in various numbers, from half-a-dozen to fifty or sixty at a time, they pursued courses of different lengths, but seldom exceeding eighty or a hundred yards. Many flew on board of us, where they were of course speedily captured, and finally transferred to the cook; one, in its heedless course, struck a lady passenger, who was walking on the poop, with such force as nearly to throw her down. These fish generally rise from the surface with the wind either a-head or a-beam, but once up they can turn in different directions, though not at a sharp angle. Petrels, too, now began to follow in our wake, skimming along the surface, or, more rarely, resting for a moment on the crest of a wave; active little creatures, busily engaged in picking up small objects. So incessantly are they thus occupied that it cannot be merely on matters dropt overboard that they thus luxuriate; but most probably their bill of fare includes also various minute oceanic existences. The species seemed to be that known as the Fork-tailed Petrel,* which is common in the North Atlantic. Early in the morning hardly any are to be seen, but after sunrise they may be observed coming up, either singly or in small parties, and they attain their maximum number shortly before sunset, after which time they begin gradually

---

* Thalassidroma Leachii.

and mysteriously to disappear. After entering the trades the weather, which between Madeira and the Canaries had been close and rather oppressive, became much cooler, and a heavy dew fell at night. On the fourth day after leaving Santa Cruz we got our first peep at the African continent, Cape de Verde appearing in sight. What this celebrated headland may have been in the days of its early Portuguese explorers I know not, but to us, now-a-days, it seemed to have been named on the *lucus à non lucendo* principle, viz., because not a vestige of green could be seen about it. About five o'clock in the afternoon we anchored off Goree, and having got two hours' leave, most of the passengers visited the shore. Goree is a little barren island, only a few miles from the mainland, from which it derives most of its supplies. Towards the sea, where it rises some thirty or forty feet, is placed a fort, not overstrong, but sufficiently so to keep the neighbouring tribes in awe, and to act as a military depôt. On requesting permission to visit this fortress we were most politely received, and a French officer kindly volunteered to conduct us over the place. On returning we walked through the market-place, where we first met with a negro population, here principally composed of Wólofs,* a race to which I shall afterwards more particularly allude.

Next morning, while off the mouth of the Gambia, we encountered a slight tornado, the first one of the

---

* Often incorrectly named Jolofs, which is merely the name of one portion of the Wólof territory.—Vide Koelle's "Polyglotta Africana," p. 16.

season, as we afterwards learnt, marking the commencement of the rains. This delayed us somewhat in threading our way through the intricate entrance to the river; but by nine o'clock we were at anchor off Bathurst. The weather had by this time cleared up, and was succeeded by most scorching heat, which over the low, sandy vicinity of the town was most oppressively felt. Bathurst, though a thriving settlement and the seat of a considerable trade, is by no means a desirable residence. Placed on the flat, alluvial deposit at the mouth of the Gambia, it has nothing to relieve the eye or to beautify the scene, and in the rainy season is partially flooded. The barracks and the military hospital are placed near the shore, so as to catch every vestige of the sea-breeze, which is here invaluable. Further along are low extensive mangrove swamps, indicative of everything except health and dry soil. Bathurst is a military station, several companies of one of the West India regiments being always kept there; and about 140 miles up the river is another smaller depôt, on Macarthy's Island.* A few days afterwards, when off Sierra Leone, I had a good opportunity of watching the advance and progress of one of the tornadoes, which, along this part of the coast, always blow off shore. It made its appearance in the shape of a dense black cloud between us and the land, and

---

* The native population of Bathurst consists chiefly of Wólofs and of Mandéngas; the latter, with the exception of the Púlo tribes, by far the most advanced of the Central African races.

extended about one-sixth along the horizon. At first it seemed to be crossing our course, and to be passing a-head of us, but suddenly its direction altered, and it spread upwards towards the zenith. Presently the cloud arched beneath, leaving visible a little bit of gray sky, after which the dark mass rapidly approached. A white line of foam preceded, and just before this reached us, everything was, for an instant, still as death. Soon, however, the scene completely changed, the storm had burst upon us, and the fierce gale was accompanied by tremendous rain, the drops of which, like hail, caused the face and hands to smart. Thunder and lightning were absent, but the fury of the tempest lasted for upwards of an hour, during which time the violence of the rain beat down the waves, but as soon as this began to abate, an angry, cross sea sprung up. We had been, early in the morning, going from nine to ten knots; but the force of the gale speedily reduced our rate to three. These tornadoes, fortunately, always give good warning, and consequently seldom do much mischief. I afterwards encountered many, much more severe, and also more grand and terrific, but none ever left the same impression as this, the first one I ever witnessed.

Our arrival at Sierra Leone was at night, so that it was not until the following day that I could form any idea of this notable spot. When, however, next morning, at sunrise, I got a good view, I could not help being struck with the extreme beauty of the situation; nor could I fancy that such a lovely place could have proved so fatal to European life. Freetown is built on sloping ground running down to the river-side, and covers an extensive area. The houses are clean-looking and well built, and the streets are laid out with much regularity. Close to the river are various large piles of buildings, chiefly store-houses; nearly in the centre St. George's Cathedral towers over the surrounding edifices; crowning a considerable eminence behind, are situated the barracks; stretching along to the right are Kru-town, and various settlements of civilised Africans; while on the extreme left, at Fourah Bay, stands the Church Missionary College. I experienced much hospitality from the merchant residents, in particular from Mr. Oldfield, one of the pioneers of Niger discovery, and Mr. C. Heddle, than whom few have done more towards developing the resources of Western Africa. Mr. Oldfield had selected well-qualified interpreters for the expedition, adapted for the different languages we were most likely to meet with, viz., I'gbo, Yóruba, Háussa, Núpe, and Bornuese or Kanúri. Sierra Leone is an exceedingly busy, bustling place. The anchorage is usually well stocked with trading-vessels of all sizes and of various nations, shipping or discharging valuable cargoes: numerous boats and canoes are constantly plying to and fro; along the shore are groups of boatmen, porters, and other labourers: hurrying along the principal streets may be seen substantial coloured traders, often with a train of followers: the shops are filled with eager purchasers, the market-place in the earlier part of the day is thronged; while out by Kissy pours from morning till night, backwards and forwards, an incessant stream of people. Not a tribe exists from Bornú or Adamáwa to Timbuktú or Senegambia, which is not here represented; not a race, from the coast of Guinea to Barbary, which does not contribute its quota to the multitude. As various, too, are the numerous costumes, from the ample turban and flowing tobe of the Mandénga or Púlo Moslem, to the more tight-fitting, European garments worn by the liberated African, or from the scanty clothing of some remote aboriginal, to the semi-nautical style of the sea-faring Krúman. But it is on Sunday that the stranger will be chiefly surprised. Then labour is entirely suspended, the places of worship are numerously attended, and the entire population appears clad in its best and most showy attire, free vent being given to the passion for bright colours and fine dress. In Krútown alone, where the inhabitants retain their Pagan practices, is anything else to be witnessed, as there, Sunday evening is devoted to amusement, and dancing to rude music winds up their holiday.

On the morning of the 13th of June, a small steamer made her appearance, and on her anchoring near us, we discovered her to be the "Pleiad" from Madeira, which had called in to coal, and to ship some native seamen. We left the same afternoon, and the "Pleiad" was to be ready by the next day; and we calculated that as we should have numerous detentions, while her only stoppage would be on the Krú coast, to procure a supply of Krúmen, we should both reach Fernando Po about the same time.

Our next place of call was at Monrovia, the capital of the Liberian republic; but here, as our stay did not exceed a few hours, and there was a very heavy sea on the bar, I did not land. I was not a little astonished at seeing a native jump out of his canoe several times, and swim about unharmed, though three or four large sharks were visible in the immediate neighbourhood. The English consul, Mr. Newnham, who was just convalescing from an attack of remittent fever, joined us here, to try to improve his health by a cruise round the Bights. By this time we were so far south, that the northern constellations were gradually sinking from our view, and the Pole Star itself became lost in the mist above the horizon. These were replaced by various brilliant representatives, among which, shining as brightly and as benignly as when first devoutly gazed on by its pious namers, the Southern Cross held brilliant position in the tropical sky.

The rainy season had now well set in, and we had frequent heavy showers, and occasional squalls. On the morning of Sunday the 18th of June, we arrived at Cape Coast Castle, where one of our lady passengers left us, and by eleven o'clock the same forenoon she was married to one of the officers of the Fort, for which purpose she had courageously undertaken this trying voyage. I landed here through the surf, and after having had a look at the place, dined with Mr. Hutton, representative of a firm which had for many years carried on along the coast a most extensive trade, and whose magnificent and most comfortable residence both surprised and gratified me.

During dinner we were waited on by five or six nice clean-looking children, whose history is rather singular. One fine morning Mr. Hutton received as a present from the King of Ashánti seventeen children, a right regal donation truly. What could be done? To have returned them would have been against etiquette, and have shown a want of appreciation of his Majesty's condescension. Mr. Hutton, therefore, having first freed them, acted towards them according to the dictates of his own kindly disposition; he clothed them, fed them, and protected them, and it was some of those children who attended on us. How strangely this must read to persons only accustomed English manners and ideas! What would be the feelings of most people at such a sudden and large increase to their family circle : it would, doubtless, considerably interfere with domestic arrangements. About sunset, just as we were preparing to go on board, a violent tornado, with heavy thunder, set in, and detained us, not altogether unwillingly, as it was not easy for us to tear ourselves away from his hospitable mansion. Still, as the "Forerunner" was to be off by ten o'clock, we had no particular wish to run the risk of losing our passage. It was long after eight before we could venture out, and on reaching the beach we found all the canoemen either drunk or else unwilling to take us off. At length the master of an American vessel persuaded, or almost forced, some natives in his employ to make the attempt. We were accordingly seated in a small canoe, and five men, waiting for a favourable moment, launched us through the surf and paddled off. Our vessel was about two miles off, and we had to go against a head sea; but at length, at the expense of a sound ducking, got alongside, just as they were beginning to despair of seeing us. Half-an-hour afterwards we were under steam for Akrá, at which place we anchored next morning, and where we first heard the sad tidings of the death of Mr. Beecroft, which melancholy event had taken place about ten days previously. Mr. Beecroft's health since his nomination as leader of the expedition had been very indifferent, and had latterly failed so rapidly and to such an extent, that he determined at once to proceed to England. The packet was at Fernando Po; his berth was secured, and all other preparations made, but unfortunately it was too late; his once iron frame sunk under the combined inroads of climate and of disease, and he yielded up the vital spark in the land of his adoption.

With a favourable current and a fair wind we soon

reached Lagos, off which we lay rolling for twenty-four hours. Along the west coast of Africa a heavy swell continues throughout the year, but during the rainy season it is particularly tumultuous. This it is which, breaking on the shores, constitutes the dreadful surf, and which also renders the bars of the rivers so dangerous. In no place is this perpetual roll more felt than in the Bight of Benin, and off Badagry and Lagos apparently reaches its climax. At Lagos too the bar is a shifting one, and is unusually dangerous, so that accidents often occur, and from the immense numbers of sharks constantly present, those who escape the fury of the waves only meet with a more dreadful end. Shortly before my return visit to this place, a canoe with sixteen men was upset, not one of whom, although all were practised swimmers, ever reached the shore. Curiously enough about the same time a boat belonging to H. M. S. " Crane " was also upset. The crew were fortunate enough to get on the bottom of the boat, and the officer in charge took it into his head to swim ashore, a most fool-hardy attempt, yet strange to relate, he was allowed to land in safety. Shipping or discharging cargoes is here a most tedious business. The Fantís, who from Cape Coast Castle to Lagos are always employed as the canoemen, cannot venture to bring off at one time more than two puncheons of palm oil, which is the staple commodity. Arrived alongside, a suitable moment must be watched for slinging the cask, when the canoe is on the top of a roller, and then it must be hoisted away on board at once, and similar or even more precaution must be used in lowering cargo into the canoe. For the information of those who have never seen canoes, I may mention that in them positions are completely the reverse of what they are in boats. The crew sit with their faces forward, and passengers are placed in the bow. Hence in going against a sea, or in crossing a bar, they are the principal recipients of donations of spray or of tops of waves, or other such moist delicacies. Occasionally canoes are fitted up for passengers, by being covered in forwards, but as a general rule every person either landing or embarking along this coast must make up his mind for a sound wetting, and further calculate on an upset every tenth or twelfth time. Landing through a surf is to a novice rather unpleasant. On approaching the shore, the canoe is kept stationary at the back of the breakers, until a favourable opportunity presents itself. The steersman, who is in charge, stands watching with practised eye roller after roller, until a kind of lull appears to be setting in, while the crew, anxiously regarding their chief, no sooner hear his wild cry, than dashing their paddles into the water, with a few strokes they reach the shore. The moment the bottom of the canoe touches the ground, they all leap overboard, and seizing her sides, instantly drag her safely high and dry, and so expert are they that accidents but rarely occur. On board the "Forerunner," ever since we left Plymouth, a solitary rat had been an eyesore to the captain's dog, which had an inveterate prejudice against the whole race of vermin: day after day had this unfortunate been persecuted, followed from shelter to shelter, and forced to resort to new hiding-places. In an evil hour for itself this wretched rat left the comparatively secure abyss of the hold, and appeared on deck. Its determined enemy, ever on the watch, soon discovered this movement, and made a desperate run at it. The only place of retreat near was a scupper-hole, into which the rat speedily bolted, but with such impetus, that it soon popped out at the other end and dropped overboard. It swam bravely, but a strong current carried it astern, where its struggles were quickly ended by the appearance on the stage of a large shark, which composedly swallowed it; seemingly as a mere whet to the appetite. At Lagos we were joined by the Rev. Mr. Crowther, who had come from Abbeokúta to join the expedition. Mr. Crowther was up the Kwóra in H. M. S. "Soudan," in 1841, and since that time has been one of the principal means of introducing into the Yóruba territory, his native land, a successful missionary establishment; one which has already been most fruitful in good results, and which promises to play a very important part in christianising this portion of Africa.

From Lagos the usual route for the mail steamers is to cross directly to Fernando Po, but on this occasion, to give the "Pleiad" more time to reach that island, Captain Barnwell determined first to visit Bonny, and the other rivers in the Bight of Biafra.

We, therefore, after rounding Cape Formoso, steered along shore, and steaming through the discoloured water, which, especially off the Nun, extends several miles out to sea, passed in succession the Nun, the St. John's or Brass, the San Nicholas, the Santa Barbara, the San Bartolomeo, and the Sombreiro, all mouths of the Kwóra, and by sunset were off the New Kalabar. As there was not time to reach the anchorage at Bonny before dark, we pushed on for Old Kalabar, and crossing the bar early next morning reached Duke Town by midday. Our stay here was very short, but I got on shore, and visited the Presbyterian Mission House, prettily situated on a rising ground to the southward of the town, where I made the acquaintance of the Rev. W. Anderson. From this spot there is a fine view of the neighbouring region. Immediately below is Duke Town, with the shipping lying off it. A little farther up is Old Town; while across the river, and at a distance of six or seven miles, is Creek Town, the residence of the principal native traders. On our departure, we were accompanied by the Rev. W. C. Thomson,* who was leaving for England. Those only who have themselves experienced the enervating influence of such a spot as Old Kalabar, can at all appreciate the sensation of pleasure with which he hailed the approach of the refreshing sea-breeze, the first time

---

* I have especially to thank this gentleman for a kind donation of entomological specimens from Old Kalabar, which, besides their intrinsic value, will prove of great assistance when I come to examine my own collection of insects.

he had felt it for three years. It must indeed be a high sense of duty which can induce men to remain so long in such a depressing climate, and the sickly atmosphere of the swampy creeks of a tropical river. The distance from the sea to Duke Town has been variously estimated at from forty-five to sixty miles; the latter being that calculated from the latitude given in Beecroft and King's Chart of the Cross River. It is surprising that, although this distance is annually traversed by vessels of large burden, and with most valuable cargoes, no detailed survey of this river has been made, nor is there at present a reliable chart. Yet the channel is tortuous, sand-banks are numerous, and there is a dangerous bar at the mouth. As an instance of the value of British property at stake, I saw in the river a vessel of nearly 2500 tons' burden. When filled with palm oil, her cargo alone would be worth upwards of £100,000; which must run no little risk while being carried along this unexamined river. The only guide of any worth is a little book of directions, printed at the Missionary Press, and compiled by Captain Lewis, who knows the pilotage better than any man living. This, which to any one who has been once there, is most serviceable, from the want of a chart, is comparatively valueless to a person visiting the place for the first time.

The following morning we had a fine view of the high land of Fernando Po, and also, as the day progressed, of the lofty Camaroons mountain. This, supposed to have been the *Currus Deorum* of Hanno, raises its volcanic head to more than 13,000 feet above the sea; whence it descends abruptly to the very edge of the water. Near its base, on the one side, the Rio del Rey and a smaller nameless stream enter the sea, whilst on its other are the outlets of the great Camaroons river. The next day while steaming down this river under the mountain, we were overtaken by a violent tornado. The rain descended in torrents, while the thunder reverberated in awful solemnity from the rugged chasms and frightful precipices above us. About four in the afternoon we reached Fernando Po, and rounding Point William were soon snugly at anchor in Clarence Cove. To our great disappointment, however, the "Pleiad" had not arrived, nor were there any tidings of her. H.M.S. "Crane," which was cruizing off the island, followed us in, and her commanding officer, Captain Thomas Miller, then senior naval officer in the "Bights," desirous of being able to transmit home tidings of the expedition, sent a requisition to the Admiralty agent in charge of the mails to detain the packet until Wednesday, hoping that by that time the lost "Pleiad" might turn up.

The passage from Plymouth to Fernando Po, including calls at Old Kalabar and the Camaroons, was thus easily accomplished in thirty-two days. The "Forerunner," though not a very comfortable vessel, was very quick; and, under the able management of Captain Barnwell, could do almost anything. It was quite a pleasure to witness the neat way in which he handled her, especially in the intricate passages at the mouths of the rivers, up which too he was his own pilot.

At Clarence I found that the sad news of Mr. Beecroft's death, to which I have already alluded, was too true. From our anchorage we could see his lonely grave under a wide-spreading silk-cotton tree, on Point William; and, throughout the town, many a heart was still grieving over the loss of their kind-hearted protector and friend. On examining the Admiralty instructions, I found that no actual provision had been made in the event of the decease of Mr. Beecroft, but being next to him in seniority, I resolved to continue the expedition, as I considered that, the preparations being so far advanced, and results of no little importance being expected, it would be wrong not to make the attempt. In this I was confirmed by the opinions of Captain Miller and of the acting Governor and British Consul, Mr. Lynslager, who both took a similar view of the case. I quite understood the responsibility I was undertaking, and felt fully that the expedition would start under very different auspices under the direction of such a junior officer as myself, new, moreover, to the climate and the country, from what it would have done if guided by the experienced judgment of the late governor. My anxiety on these points was greatly lessened by the volunteer offer of Mr. D. J. May, second master of the "Crane," who was most desirous of accompanying me. The consent of Captain Miller was cheerfully given, and in Mr. May I had, from that day, a most willing and able coadjutor. His name will frequently occur in the following pages, and I take this opportunity of publicly thanking him for the great assistance he rendered to the expedition. On the evening of Tuesday, the 27th of June, while sitting in Governor Lynslager's, a report was brought that a vessel in the offing was making signals. We all rushed out, and speedily saw her rockets and blue-lights, which were immediately answered, and a bright light was hoisted to guide her to the proper anchorage. By our night-glasses we could see that she was a steamer, and in another hour found, to our great delight, that it was the "Pleiad," a delay on the Krú coast having thus detained her. This news we were enabled to send home next day by the "Fore-runner," which also carried away the sailing-master, who had navigated the ship from England, and those of the crew who were only engaged for the passage out. I also felt it my duty to invalid and send home Dr. William Bleek, who had been appointed ethnologist to the expedition, his health being evidently unsuited for a tropical African climate, especially as it had already considerably suffered. This gentleman was, as might have been expected, much disappointed, and left us with great reluctance, though on calm consideration motives of prudence prevailed.

The next business was to prepare the "Pleiad," and to ship stores and coals, with which duties I had nothing directly to do, they being under the management of the proper officers of the "Pleiad." It will save future explanation if I here mention that, even at this early period, I could see that the sailing-master, Mr. T. C. Taylor, was not adapted for the work. Whatever his capabilities in other spheres might have been, he appeared to be greatly deficient in the energy, decision, and administrative qualities requisite for the position he occupied. Things went on in an irregular manner, stores were confusedly hurried about, and nothing seemed to progress. Seeing this, and being desirous to advance our preparations as much as possible, Captain Miller remained at anchor, and daily sent a party from the "Crane" to assist us. Had it not been for his kindness, matters would have become very complicated, and would have been still more protracted. One gentleman, who had intended to accompany the "Pleiad," as a supercargo, being unable to agree with Mr. Taylor, left us at Clarence, intending to return to England.

Our preparations at last drew to a close; coals had been shipped, and two large iron trade canoes had been put together and brought alongside. The government party now consisted of myself and Mr. May, my assistant, and a black servant, and also Mr. Richards, whom I had engaged as interpreter, he having accompanied Mr. Beecroft in this capacity on several occasions, and Simon Jonas, an Igbo, who had been with the expedition in 1841; there were also Mr. Crowther and his servant, and the ship's complement comprised a sailing-master, three mates, a surgeon, three engineers, one supercargo, a steward, three black firemen, three interpreters, a cooper, a carpenter, four coloured seamen and two boys, and thirty-three Krúmen; in all, twelve Europeans, and fifty-three persons of colour.

CHAPTER III.

THE LAUNCH OF THE EXPEDITION.

THE "Crane" sailed on the 7th of July, and the next afternoon we also made ready for a start, and finally took our departure from Clarence about eight o'clock in the evening. Although there appeared to be a good sea running, the sailing-master persisted in keeping both of the iron canoes deeply laden with coal. But no sooner had we got a little beyond Cape Bullen, than we found such a sea running that the canoes were nearly swamped, and we had immediately to lighten them, which was accomplished with some trouble. We towed them at first, one on each quarter, but finding that they steered very badly, passed them both astern. The next day a very nasty cross sea ran, and we rolled very uneasily, and shipped one or two heavy seas. Sails would now have been a great boon, as they would have steadied us much; but they had been carefully stowed away in some storehouse at Clarence. About noon something went wrong with one of the safety-valves, which obliged us to draw the fires, and this caused us to lose about four hours, during which time we were

July 8.

drifting bodily to leeward; and this, added to the strong current, drove us so far to the eastward, that the first land we made was near the Andoney river. All Monday and Tuesday we kept going slowly along shore, progressing at the rate of about two knots. About sunset on the latter day we were off the river Brass, and here the master anchored all night, for fear, as he said, of missing the Nun; consequently, it was not until nine or ten o'clock on the 12th, that we were off the bar. The weather was rather gloomy, and as we rolled about with the heavy swell, the only visible indication of the river was a long break in the dark green mangroves, which here universally line the coast. Mr. Richards undertook to pilot us in, for which purpose he stationed himself right in the bows, watching with practised eye for the proper channel. The time selected was about a quarter flood, and everything being ready, he took us across by a line a little to the westward of that indicated in Captain Denham's chart. The sea, which was very heavy, was right aft, but, though very deep, we hardly shipped a drop of water. The roughest part of the bar is about three miles from the land, and here our soundings shoaled to two-and-a-quarter fathoms. When in the very middle of the breakers, the tow-rope of the sternmost canoe gave way, and there she was left at the mercy of the waves. To turn was for us nearly impossible; so nothing was left but to trust to her being carried in by the sea and the tide.

Many an anxious eye was turned towards her; but she seemed buoyant and easy, while the Kru-boys on board of her plied vigorously at their paddles. A few minutes more brought her into smooth water, and then all fears for her safety vanished. We passed Palm Point about half-past two, July 12. and shortly afterwards anchored in six fathom water, under Alburkah Island, in a spot fully exposed to the influences of the sea-breeze, which at that season blows night and day.

The engine requiring some repairs, it was determined to effect them here before proceeding further. Mr. May and I went in the gig to examine the channel to the westward of Alburkah Island, and found deep water—from five to six fathoms—close along the west shore. This occupied us until dark, after which we re-examined our instruments, got the barometers freely suspended, compared them, and saw everything in readiness for future operations. The ship swung to the ebb at half-past eight, and in another hour the current was running past like a mill-sluice, being at the rate of five knots and a half. Next day Mr. May and I landed at Baracoon Point to get some bearings. Some natives appeared at a distance, but were very timid, and on our approaching towards them went and hid in the bush. I collected a few botanical and zoological specimens; among the latter a fine bat, a species of *Epomophorus*. We had intended visiting Akássa, from which we were distant about four miles, but were prevented by

D

heavy rain, which drove us on board. In the afternoon we pulled further up the western channel, carrying deep water all along close to the shore. We returned by Alburkah Island, or rather the Alburkah Islands, as this appears to be a group of swampy islets, intersected with creeks. Seeing a little village, we landed, but the inhabitants, alarmed, had completely evacuated the place, leaving it quite at our mercy. My boat's crew of Krúmen were rather desirous of exercising the privileges of conquerors, and of picking up some plunder, but this we at once checked. There was not much left for them, except some large heaps of palm-nuts, which lay in heaps, all in readiness for boiling for the oil. From a heap of bones which was looked on as dju-dju or sacred, I selected the skull of a *Manatus*,* in fair condition. Being now fairly in the river, we commenced giving, morning and evening, to all the Europeans on board, two-thirds of a glass of quinine wine, which contained about five grains of quinine, believing that this would act as a prophylactic or preventive, while exposed—as every one must be while in the Delta—to the influence of malaria. The following morning a canoe came alongside, in which were two Abó men. They did not give us much information, but told us that the inhabitants in this neighbourhood were afraid of us, as they thought we had come with warlike intentions. About nine o'clock Mr. May and I started off to

* Most probably *Manatus Senegalensis*.

continue our examination of the western channel. Deep water, sometimes as much as from six to eight fathoms, was constantly found. We kept as nearly as possible in the course of the main stream, but branches and junctions were so frequent, as greatly to perplex us. The breadth of the creeks varied from 100 to 300 or 400 yards; and the direction was from N.W. to E.N.E. by compass.

Nothing could be more gloomy than these dreary streams, enclosed between dense lines of sombre mangroves, forty, fifty, or even sixty feet in height. The only thing left to our sight was a narrow strip of sky overhead. No dry land was visible, not a canoe nor a native was encountered, and the only sign of life was when here and there a solitary king-fisher, startled by such an unwonted appearance, fled lazily from its retreat, but ere a gun could be even pointed at it, again disappeared amid the dark-green foliage. We at length found ourselves in a creek running west and south-west, which we conjectured to be connected with the Sengána branch; but as the afternoon was far advanced, we were obliged to turn. One place so resembled another, that we had some difficulty in retracing our steps, but coming upon an opening leading due south, we entered it, believing that it would prove a shorter route. Its turnings and windings were innumerable, so that our boat's crew became first dissatisfied, and at last timid; but we persisted, though there was a fair prospect of our having to spend the night in these mosquito preserves. We came to one very shallow spot, across which we had to wade and drag the boat; but after this we began to recognise some objects, and by dark we reached the ship, having been in the boat nine hours, and pulled over some five-and-twenty miles. We found to our great satisfaction that the repairs of the engine were completed, so preparations were made for an early start in the morning.

We were under steam by daylight, but at the entrance of Louis's Creek grounded, and there not being water enough here to allow us to enter, Mr. Richards went in the gig to look for another passage, and after a little trouble found one, by which he took us. This we named after him, " Richards's Creek;" it is rather longer and narrower than Louis's Creek, with which it is parallel. This passed, we were soon in the main river, and under Mr. Richards's pilotage, and with the leads constantly going, got on very fairly. In an ascent of this kind the pilot sits right in the bows, directing the man at the helm by his hand. One leadsman was stationed in the forechains, and another, the most important one, in the dingy, which was slung under the bowsprit. Mangroves were becoming scarce, palms increasing in number and in size, and though no huts were seen, still in recent clearances along the banks were little plantations of bananas and plantains. Every one was in high spirits at our progress, little dreaming that a sudden check was in store for us. About eleven o'clock a small islet appeared in mid-channel, right ahead of us. The pilot wished to pass to the westward, but before the master could make up his mind which course to follow, the "Pleiad" was allowed to run right stem on. The mate ran to get a kedge carried out at once, but was ordered not to hurry himself, although we were still within the influence of the tides, and it was just about the top of high water. Some feeble and badly planned efforts were made to get off during the early part of the afternoon, but, as might have been anticipated, they were ineffectual. Mr. May and I went in the gig and measured by triangulation the breadth of the river, which does not exceed 200 yards. Next morning I expected that by daylight at the furthest, fresh exertions would be made to float, but the master did not make his appearance on deck till after seven. I asked him what he intended doing, and on being answered that he did not approve of working on Sunday, or, as he called it, Sabbath, remonstrated with him in strong terms. This roused him a little, and he gave some fresh orders. About ten o'clock, almost entirely by the energy and skill of the chief mate, we were once more afloat, but by the master's direction we dropped a little way down and anchored close to the bush, and in this unhealthy spot we remained until next morning. The islet $_{\text{July 17.}}$ on which we stuck, was, we found, "Sunday Island;" very appropriately named. Immediately above it on the western side is a small creek, by which canoes come from Wári.

This place once passed the river began gradually to grow wider, and regular banks to appear. Isolated huts of a more substantial appearance than the rude shelters near the mouth indicated that we were now entering the domains of human beings, and Mr. Crowther remarked the great difference between the present occasion and his visit in 1841. Then the banks were densely wooded to the very water's edge, but now there were strips of land along the margins cleared and planted; while small villages and other signs of life showed themselves where all formerly was desolate and uninhabited, and the very people seemed less timid and better clad. As we passed along, numbers of anxious spectators from time to time showed themselves. Among one group we saw a woman suckling her child, who was large enough to be standing beside her. Occasionally we saw natives of a bright copper colour, and I remarked some children with artificial white marks down the forehead, branching off along each cheek. In all these small villages was abundance of fowls and of dogs, and in the neighbourhood were cultivated rice, bananas, plantains, cocos, and sugar-cane. We passed some trading canoes laden with palm-oil, each of which carried a carronade in their bows. Occasionally one or two canoes would come alongside, offering fowls for sale, which we readily purchased for empty bottles or trinkets. Seeing a rather large village on the right bank, I stopped and tried to induce the people to come off to us, but they seemed afraid, and we had not time to spare to go ashore to them. Some large canoes were there, flying showy flags, on some of which were the letters K.B., probably for King Burrow, one of the lower Delta potentates. About noon we passed the Bassa Creek, and about two o'clock reached a very extensive village on the left bank, off which we delayed for a little. Plenty of canoes came off, by which means we learnt that it was Angiáma, being the place where poor Lander received his mortal wound. Among others the chief came alongside, to whom I gave a looking-glass and a red worsted nightcap, which greatly pleased him. I explained to him that we were desirous of hurrying on now, but hoped to pay him a longer visit on our return, when, if they had any articles for trade, we should be happy to deal with them. Diverging branches were numerous, and we passed also one converging one; namely, the O'gubori Channel, examined by Captain W. Allen in 1841. Towards dark we passed another large village on the left bank, and shortly afterwards anchored nearly in mid-channel, having made a very satisfactory day's work.

Morning showed that we were at anchor under a pretty island covered with luxuriant vegetation, which was fantastically styled "Tuesday Island." The weather was unpropitious, the sky being lowering and dark with frequent showers. During the forenoon we reached a creek, coming from the N.N.E., up which the master insisted on going, saying it was the main stream, although the natives on the banks

July 18.

pointed in the other direction. No current was perceptible, and the surface of the water was green with floating aquatic plants. Notwithstanding we went up nearly a mile, until it became so narrow that the " Pleiad " could scarcely turn, and in doing so got partly entangled among overhanging branches. This place was accordingly named after its explorer, " Taylor's Creek." As time pressed, we held only temporary communication with the more important villages. Just above Truro Island, by foolishly keeping too close under a point, we grounded and remained firmly fixed for nearly twenty-four hours, when the ship was at length started by the combined action of a kedge laid out right astern, and a Sampson-post over our bow. On a large sandbank near I found foot-prints resembling those of a hippopotamus; these I traced to some thick bush, where the animal had probably been feeding.

From the mouth of the river up to this point, the country on either side is named Orú. The people are of the same tribe as those who inhabit the tract of country up to the Rio Formoso, where however they are called Ejó or Ojó, by which name also they are known at Abó, at Brass, and even at Bonny. By English palm-oil traders they are often termed Jo-men. Throughout all this district but one language is spoken, with but very little dialectal difference. There is no one king or chief, but every village has its own headman. The people are a wild, rude, and treacherous race, savage, and often unprepossessing in look. Both male and female are much tattooed over the chest and arms, while the particular mark of the tribe is a thick, straight cut down the centre of the forehead and nose, and generally also three lines extending diagonally across the cheek from the inner angle of the eye. The one down the forehead, which is very prominent, and gives a peculiar and unpleasant expression to the countenance, is performed in childhood by making a deep incision with a razor, and then rubbing in palm oil, and the resulting cicatrix is hard, projecting, and blue-coloured. Almost all wear clothes of European manufacture, striped and coloured calicoes being principally in vogue. Among the men, glazed hats, Guernsey frocks, and even monkey jackets are occasionally to be seen. Along the Kwóra they exact a tribute from all canoes, belonging to other tribes, passing either up or down, which is a very fertile source of disputes, and even of bloodshed. Their principal trade is now in palm oil, which they dispose of either to Rio Formoso or to Brass traders.

Across the mouth of the Wári branch, a large island seems to be gradually forming. In Allen's original chart there is here marked a bank covered with water; subsequently, in 1841, vegetation was seen over the spot,* and now it is an island several feet above the water, and covered with tall grass. This is the branch which was examined by Mr. Beecroft, in the "Æthiope," in 1840, and by which I'gbo traders communicate with those of Wári and

* Allen and Thomson's Narrative, vol. i. p. 198.

of Bíni, and with the Rio Formoso; it appears also to be on that side of the river the line of separation between the Orú and the I'gbo countries.

From this point up to Abó nothing remarkable occurred; the weather kept gloomy and wet, until we anchored off the latter place on the afternoon of the 21st of July. Some canoes came and took a look at us; but, though they paddled close to us, we could not prevail on the people to come on board. At length a large canoe appeared, which brought two messengers to welcome us, and to ascertain our intentions, as it subsequently appeared that an idea was entertained that our visit was in some way connected with Mr. Carr's mysterious disappearance. One of the messengers recognised Mr. Richards as an old acquaintance, which inspired them with more confidence. This man, whose name was Alihéli, a Haúsa by birth, was given by King Obí to Lander in 1832, and accompanied him to Fernando Po. He could speak a little English, and as he joined our ship and made himself exceedingly useful, his name will frequently recur. They commenced the "palaver" by drinking a glass of wine with us, a few drops of which they, before tasting it, poured on the deck as dju-dju, or sacred. From them we learnt that King Obí had been dead for nearly nine years, and that since that time there had been no regular king. At Abó, the chief power is elective, and after the death of Obí two parties sprung up, one of which supported the claims of his son, while the other advanced as their candidate an influential person named Orísa. The two sections were respectively entitled the king's people and the Oshiodápara party. Obí's friends were unanimous in their selection of Obí's second son, named Ajé, an active, intelligent, young man; and this was acquiesced in by his less energetic and more peaceful brother Okúrobi or Tshúkuma. The factions had never come to blows, and of late there had been a very general feeling in favour of Ajé; but before he could be finally elected, he was expected to pay several rather heavy sums, which he was now gradually settling. In the mean time, although he took the lead in all foreign or warlike affairs, law and justice were dispensed by a neutral individual not immediately connected with either side. At this moment Ajé was absent, having gone to settle some dispute at Igára; but Tshúkuma, as his deputy, had sent Alihéli to receive us. We promised to come on shore the next morning and pay our respects. I accordingly made an early start, and, accompanied by Mr. May, Mr. Crowther, and Dr. Hutchinson, proceeded in the gig and pinnace, the crews of which were dressed in flaming red caps and shirts. Abó is situated nearly a mile up a creek, the mouth of which is almost invisible from even a very short distance. On entering it we found it, at first, so extremely narrow, that we had to lay in our oars and to use paddles; but, after a time, it opened into a wide expanse, the surface of which was covered with canoes of various sizes. Numbers of inhabitants were to be seen gazing at us, and altogether there was more bustle and activity, and more signs of a trading people than anything we had previously witnessed. Having reached the landing-place we marched in a kind of procession, headed by a Krú-man, carrying the English ensign, and accompanied by a royal messenger bearing a gaudy flag. We had some little difficulty in keeping good order through the narrow lanes, densely crowded as they were by the populace; as natives, both men and women, were constantly coming towards us, and insisting on shaking hands with us, which ceremony is here performed by the two parties taking loose hold of the fingers of each other's right hands, and then slipping them, making, at the same instant, a snapping noise with the aid of the thumb. We were not sorry to reach Tshúkuma's palace, a low dwelling of mud and loose thatch, with a small court, some twenty feet square, in the centre. This was surrounded by a kind of verandah, in which we were placed, a chair being brought for me, and mats for the remainder of the company. Near us was a fetish, composed of some old bones and a few trinkets, and close to this, under a canopy of white calico, was a large mat for his Royal Highness. Presently he entered, accompanied by several of his wives, and other female relatives, who all sat on his left. He seemed a little oldish-looking man of easy disposition, and not much intellect. He was attired in a woollen nightcap, a white shirt, and in home-built pantaloons of native cloth, shaped after an extreme Dutch design.

THE LAUNCH OF THE EXPEDITION.

The court was by this time completely filled with crowds of natives, whose incessant noise and chattering prevented us from commencing, and at last I had to request him to enforce silence. This he attempted to do, in vain, until at last, assisted by the more energetic of his spouses, and in particular by a strong-minded sister, whose shrill tones, heard high above the din, finally beat down all opposition, and produced a temporary calm. I seized the moment, and, by our interpreter, told Tshúkuma, that we had come to make his acquaintance and his friendship, and to ascertain if the people were willing to trade with us.

I expressed our sorrow at hearing of the death of Obí, who had been the white man's friend, also our regret at the absence of his brother. I said that we were desirous of fulfilling the promises made by the officers in the former expedition, and that we should try to do good to his country. He replied by declaring his satisfaction at seeing white men here once more, thanking us for our compliments, and offering, if we could wait a few days, to send a special canoe for his brother. I told him that we had a long distance to go, and that we must proceed while there was plenty of water in the river, but that on our return we should again call. He then proceeded to say, that King Obí being dead, the former treaty expired with him; but that before his decease his father had particularly enjoined on his sons always to be friends with white men; and that he and his people would gladly attend to that bequest. He added, however, that whenever he saw us coming regularly to trade, he would then, but not till then, believe us, as Captain Trotter had faithfully promised again to visit them, but had not done so. I explained to him that this was owing chiefly to the great sickness which had then occurred; and partly, also, that when Mr. Carr was returning, he had been murdered by some bad people. I said that we were anxious to open up the trade of this great river for the benefit of every one, and asked him if ever a boat with a few white men in it passed along, he would order Abó canoes not to molest them? to which he replied, that should there be but one white man in it he would take care of him. During this discussion the women were extremely enthusiastic in their good wishes, which I considered a favourable sign. Dr. Hutchinson had then some special conversation on commercial topics, after which Mr. Crowther asked Tshúkuma whether he would like to have teachers placed among them, to teach their children to "read book," and to instruct them in what was good and useful, to which the answer was a universal shout of assent. He then proceeded to describe to them what had taken place in Yóruba, his native land, in which but a few years ago was nothing but warfare and bloodshed, while now they were cultivating peaceful arts. Tshúkuma replied that he only wished to see the day when this would take place in Abó, but that he much feared it would never come to pass. Nevertheless, if teachers came, ground would be specially set part for them to have a house built upon. Our interview was concluded by my inviting Tshúkuma to pay us a visit on board, after which we walked through the town, followed by admiring crowds, and visited Ajé's palace, which is more extensive than his brother's, and in better condition, and then we returned on board. Yams, bananas, sweet potatoes, coco-nuts, fowls, goats, and fish were freely brought off for sale, and were readily bartered for bottles, brass snuff-boxes, and handkerchiefs. As specimens of the manufacture of the place, I purchased some substantial nets, some thread, grass mats, and brass ornaments. About noon we had a visit from Tshúkuma, who brought with him his head-wife named Ajéibo, his half-sister Adém, and one of Ajé's wives, named O'nna. After showing him round the ship, we asked him and his party below to lunch with us. A large meat-pie was on the table, which I divided among all present, tasting, according to custom, a little bit from each of the plates before offering them to our guests.* I then gave Tshúkuma, as a *dash* or present, a sabre in a brass scabbard, some red baize, and some pieces of showily-coloured calicoes; and gratified the ladies by presenting each with a looking-glass and some needles. After their departure, Mr. May and I crossed the river to the opposite shore for the

---

* This has been rendered customary by attempts at poisoning having been extremely frequent. A slave always tastes a cup before presenting it to his master.

purpose of getting a set of sights; but no sooner had we landed, and begun to arrange our instruments, than a band of natives, variously armed with muskets, spears, and swords, came upon us in a half-threatening, half-alarmed manner. Mr. May and myself, laying down everything, advanced towards them, making signs of peace and friendship; but on seeing us come near them they retreated, still keeping their muskets pointed at us. At last we induced them to stand, and, with a little more persuasion, to shake hands, which ceremony being effected, both parties had a hearty laugh. They watched us adjusting the sextant and artificial horizon with much surprise, and were greatly amazed at hearing the ticking of a pocket chronometer. I collected some plants and insects; among the latter a showy *Cicindela*, with very sharp mandibles, and some homopterous specimens. Next morning Mr. May and I landed at the mouth of the creek, and were successful in getting a good set of sights. About mid-day, after church, some canoes were seen approaching, in one of which a drum was heard constantly beating. This we discovered to contain Tshúkuma, with a large retinue, come in grand state to pay his regular return visit. To-day he was dressed in an engineer's scarlet uniform coat, a pair of duck trousers, and a purple beaver hat; he held in his hand the sword I had presented to him, and round his neck were suspended two small medals given him by Captain Trotter. He brought for us as a present, a bullock, a goat, and 200 yams. Our visitors, who remained on board nearly three hours, were on the whole very orderly. One custom peculiar to this district is, that all women who can afford it, wear ponderous ivory anklets, made from the thickest parts of large tusks. These are so very weighty as to give a strange character to the gait, and a peculiar dragging motion to the leg. They must be put on at first with great pain and difficulty, and when once adopted, are never parted with—not even at death—so that their owners are buried with them. This creates a great demand in the place for ivory, and causes extravagant sums to be demanded for these cumbrous ornaments. I had intended purchasing some, but declined doing so when I found the market value of a pair to be equal to the price of three slaves. Mr. Crowther and myself being desirous of leaving Simon Jonas here until our return, that he might better learn the temper and habits of the people, we mentioned our wish to Tshúkuma, who at once undertook to look after him. In the afternoon Mr. May and I crossed to the place where we had landed the day previously, and meeting some of the people who had then been so alarmed, went with them to their little village, which is named Odágbe, where they received us in a very friendly way, presenting us with Gura * nuts. During our walk I found several insects,

* Gura or Kola nuts, the fruit of the *Cola (Sterculia) acuminata; vide* "Flora Nigritiana," p. 233. These are in great demand throughout Central Africa, and are presented to strangers as a mark of esteem and of friendship.

myriapods, and shells, one of the latter being a species of *Achatina*, which I discovered on the leaves and stems of yams.

Abó, the Eboe or Ibu of Lander and of Allen, is the name of a town and also of a district extending along both sides of the river, from the Orú country towards Igára. It forms one of the sections of the Great I'gbo (Ibo) territory; and though by no means the largest, is, from its position along the Kwóra, one of the most important. The sovereignty, since the death of Obí, having, as I have mentioned, been partly in abeyance, many towns which were under his rule have ceased to pay tribute, and have become independent. The dialect spoken along this tract is called also Abó, and it is readily understood over the whole of I'gbo; but to this I shall afterwards refer in speaking of the peculiar customs and rites of this region.

CHAPTER IV.

ÍGBO AND IGÁRA.

WE left Abó on the 24th of July, encountering just after we had started a number of large canoes returning from some of the markets in the upper part of the river. Although the current ran strong, and there was plenty of water, the "Pleiad" was kept all day at very reduced speed, and consequently made very little progress. Crowded villages were numerous on both sides, indicating an extensive population. In the afternoon we grounded on a sandbank, but easily got off; after which Mr. Richards started to examine the eastern, and Mr. May and I the western passage along Bullock Island. The former was the preferable one, and by it we ascended next day, passing on the left bank a very extensive town, named Ossamaré or Oshimaré, which means "town on the great water;" most probably altered from Oshímini or Osímini, the Abó name for the Kwóra, and which signifies "great water." Among a group of islands opposite A'kra-Atáni, we first saw a small herd of hippopotami, which, however, not liking our looks, soon made themselves scarce. Heavy showers were of frequent occurrence, and the river was slowly rising; but we were informed by the natives that it was still very low. The country now became more open, more cultivation was visible, and high land appeared to the northward along both sides of the river. The banks had been hitherto entirely alluvial, but above A′kra-Atáni, we first saw, partially embedded in clay on the eastern side, some semi-volcanic blocks. On the left bank we passed Onitshá, an important market town, on the beach below which were congregated some five or six hundred people,— and shortly afterwards on the opposite shore, Asabá, the Kíri market of Allen's Charts, also a busy trading place. Along an island named by Mr. Beecroft, on account of the beautiful foliage, "Green Island," we went by the western channel, but almost immediately afterwards the "Pleiad" struck heavily on a sandbank, and remained hard and fast until next morning, when she was, under the direction of the chief mate, again got off.

Close by Ada-mugú, the Damuggoo of Oldfield's Narrative, we saw for the first time circular huts; all those previously met with having been square or oblong, which shape prevails also throughout the the Yóruba countries, and along the main branch of the Kwóra, while to the eastward, and throughout the Haúsa country, the round form is all but universal. A little above this place the vessel was again most awkwardly run aground; this time on the weather or upper side of a sandbank, where we remained for about thirty hours, and before she could be floated, the water had to be blown off the boilers, the deck-cargo placed in the canoes, and then by Mr. Harcus's management the ship had to be dragged nearly twice her own length over the bank. On the 31st of July the cliffs at Iddá were in sight, but the steamer being in want of fuel, I ordered her to be anchored off a wooding place on the western bank, about three miles from the town. To hurry matters I despatched Alihéli to announce our arrival, and our intended visit to the Attá. I went ashore for an hour or two before dark with the wooding party, and collected specimens for a little time. Beside a little pool, shut from the light of heaven by the thick forest of branches, I found a species of *Cicindela*, coloured in unison with its sombre habitation, while from under some dead leaves, I picked up a pretty little flattened myriapod of very peculiar appearance.

We left the ship in the gig and pinnace about seven in the morning, and after an hour's pull, reached the landing-place at Iddá. Here we inquired after our messenger, who had not returned to us, but could learn nothing of him. Presently, however, Mr. Richards recognised an old acquaintance, one of the Attá's eunuchs, who offered to conduct us. After a ten minutes' walk, we arrived at a collection of huts, at the door of one of which we were requested to remain for a few minutes, but presently were asked to enter. Here we found Alihéli, who told us that owing to some party quarrels our message had not

Aug. 1.

been forwarded to the Attá, but that now we should meet one of the head-men. Passing through several outer rooms, we came to a court, where we saw, seated on a window-sill, an elderly man, who was, we were informed, brother to the late A'boko, so often mentioned in "Laird and Oldfield's Narrative," as the great friend of white men, and who had first introduced them into this country. He received us very civilly, shaking hands with us, and ordered mats to be spread for us. He regretted that he could not forward our message without first consulting the other heads of his party, named after their late chief, "A'boko's party," which, however, he had sent to do, and was now awaiting the result. In the meantime, while partaking of some palm-wine and gura nuts, we found ourselves plunged into the midst of Igára politics, and Iddá state intrigue. An Igára chief, named Agabídoko, whose mother was an I'gbo, and who was now residing at a place named Egdokányi, near Ada-mugú, had quarrelled with some of A'boko's people at Asabá market, and had killed several of them. They in retaliation had seized one of Agabídoko's head women, and carried her to Iddá, on which her friends followed and claimed her, but not succeeding, carried off as a trophy three or four canoes. Consequently A'boko's people were closely watching against another surprise, and last night our messenger, who came just as it was dusk, was nearly fired at, being mistaken for an emissary of the enemy. A considerable body was encamped on English island, under the command of Okéyin, one of A'boko's sons, to whom notice of our visit had been sent. A'boko's party claimed, and had been allowed the privilege of introducing all white strangers to the court of Iddá, and therefore it was only politic to comply with the established custom. We assured our host, whose name was Ehimodína, that this was the first time we had heard of this "war palaver," but that it ought not to interfere with our seeing the Attá, as our wish was to be friendly with all parties. He replied that he was delighted to have seen "white men" once more, that he knew we should do good, and perhaps effect peace, but that he could not act without the consent of his colleagues. Fortunately just at this moment his messenger arrived, and we were told we must go to the island and see A'boko's son. I at once said that we were willing and ready, on which Ehimodína offered to accompany us to the shore, and send a guide with us. He had been hitherto dressed in a voluminous loose robe, formed of a large piece of cloth, but he now prepared for his jaunt by donning first a larger, then a smaller tobe, a pair of bag-trousers, a red cap, and yellow leather boots. Being a Mussulman, he had his string of charms round his neck; then taking a whip in his hand, he went out to mount his steed, a genuine Rosinante, but fairly caparisoned. The stirrups were made of pieces of sheet brass, shaped and curved to fit the entire foot. Numerous armed attendants preceded and followed him; and as he went along, the people bent before him lowly to the ground. He left us at the river's edge, while we embarked, and after a pull of upwards of a mile, landed on the western side of English Island. Here we found an extensive temporary settlement, or rather a military encampment, the huts much smaller than ordinary bell-tents, being made of long reeds and bamboos, covered with dried grass. Into one of these we were ushered, where we found Okéyin, an unintellectual, heavy-looking man, but withal with a mild expression. Mats were brought, visitors poured in, and presently fourteen people were crowded into a most uncomfortably confined space, with hardly a breath of fresh air.

After the usual salutations, I told him how pleased we were to see a son of A'boko, who had so befriended former white visitors, and added that we were desirous of at once waiting on the Attá. Okéyin said he hoped we would stay, and that we should see the king to-morrow, but I told him that could not be, as we had a long voyage before us, and could not delay. He and his friends winced a little at this; but, as I remained firm, they consented, asking, however, to see the presents we designed for the Attá. This I at once refused, saying, "It was not Englishman's "fashion; but, if they wished to know, anyone might "accompany us and see." After some demur, this was agreed to, and one of the head men of the party named U'ti, a fine-looking, intelligent, and pleasing person, was sent to conduct us. Having partaken of the usual refreshment of palm-wine and gura nuts, we embarked, pulled back to Iddá, and marched up the hill, two of our Krú-boys preceding us, carrying our ensigns. The day, which at first was cloudy, had since turned out fine and warm, and the sun, shining directly upon us, was rather oppressive. Presently, we were met by a native band, comprising two drummers and a fifer, who played some rude, but lively and not unpleasant airs, on hearing which, our friend U'ti, in his enthusiasm, stepped towards them, and performed a "pas seul au militaire," by no means ungracefully. In this manner we proceeded, numbers of the inhabitants following us, many insisting on shaking hands with us, and now and then presenting us with eggs and fruit. Our first stoppage was at the residence of one of the king's head-women, who, having inspected and approved of us, forwarded us to the hut of one of the head-men, who, in his turn, passed us to another, by whom we were finally led to the royal abode, our route from the river having been at least two miles. We were requested to remain in a kind of open yard, partially surrounded by huts, until the Attá could be informed of our approach. Mats were here spread for us, so we sat down, surrounded by a large crowd of curious but very friendly beholders. Pitchers of palm-wine were brought, and served to us in calabashes, until, at length, becoming impatient, I sent to try and hurry our reception. Several of us amused ourselves by smoking cigars, the natives expressing the utmost astonishment at our Vesta matches and fusees, for instantaneous light.

After a delay of an hour and a half we were graciously informed that the Attá would now receive us; so advancing, or rather creeping, through several very low entrances, walking along dark passages, and taking sundry sharp turns, we were finally ushered into a spacious square court, at the upper end of which, seated on a mud throne, and surrounded by slaves and courtiers, we beheld his Majesty the Attá of Igára. Our reception much resembled that given to the late Mr. Beecroft, in 1840, as described in his MS. journal. As soon as we had all entered, I advanced towards the Attá, on which a number of those around him jumped up, uttered a wild scream, and hid him from our view with their dresses. After a few seconds they retired, and we were told we might now shake hands, which I did, and, having introduced my party, we all sat down on mats spread before the throne. The screaming and hiding ceremony was now repeated, and again after we had placed our interpreter in front. We spoke to Alihéli in English, who translated it into Háusa, which was again rendered to the king in Igára, by an intelligent-looking young man, who, coming forward and making a lowly obeisance, remained kneeling during our interview. His Majesty's state dress consisted of a large figured purple-velvet tobe, reaching from his neck to his feet; his head-piece was a cap covered with white beads, and having, at the sides and in the front, tufts of fine feathers, the latter projecting over his face, so as to prevent a full view of his countenance. Pendant from each ear hung a thin, circular, piece of wood, perforated with various devices, round his neck were innumerable strings of beads, white, blue, and yellow, and against his breast was a large brass plate, closely resembling the sign of an insurance office. In his left hand, which peeped from under his ample sleeve, was a hollow brass tube, attached to which were numerous little bells. A similar article rested in his lap, while, on a small mat before him, was placed a dilapidated stone-ware "Souter Johnny." His Majesty was seated on a bench covered with native-made cushions and clothes, and had, standing close about him, five slaves with large fans, which were employed incessantly, either to cool his cheeks, or, for the more important office of concealing the royal countenance when he laughed, or when he had condescendingly delivered himself of some oracular dogma. When used for either of the two latter purposes the attendant courtiers invariably uttered the wild shriek which greeted our ears on our first entry. The various initial ceremonies being happily concluded, we commenced by desiring the interpreter to convey to his sable Majesty our sincere respects, and the great happiness we experienced in being enabled to wait on him. This having been graciously received, and responded to by an approving nod and a courtly scream, we further made humble enquiries regarding the state of the royal health, expressing our hopes that it remained in a satisfactory condition. We then proceeded to inform him that we had come also to enquire into the state of the country, to know whether peace prevailed, and whether he was willing to trade with us, as we were desirous of redeeming the promises made by the former expedition. We also mentioned the great sickness in 1841, as the cause of the long interval between the visits. The Attá replied that he thanked God for bringing white men again to see him, that he had in his heart all "Captain Trotter's Book," * that he would make good trade and bring plenty of ivory, and that he trusted white men would again settle in his land. He added that the Confluence was too far from him, as he would like to have his friends nearer to him, so that he might send every morning to enquire after them. He then regretted that he had not a suitable *dash* for us, hinting, however, that if we had one for him he would be happy to ease our minds by receiving it at once. Disregarding this for the present, we proceeded to let him know that we intended leaving the next day, on which his Majesty said that was impossible, "it was not good," the ship must come to Iddá and remain for five days. I explained the reason of our hurry, and at last, to quiet him, I promised that the "Pleiad" should be off the town early next morning, and should remain there until noon, when we must positively leave. Mr. Crowther

* This means the treaty made with the Commissioners in 1841: *book* or its equivalent in African languages meaning any document whether printed or written.

now questioned him as to his willingness to receive teachers, who would instruct his subjects in good ways, and also to "read book" and "write book." The Attá declared his entire satisfaction at this proposal, and, after some further conversation about trade, our interview ended by my presenting him with a looking-glass, a razor, a sabre and brass scabbard, a double-barrelled gun, and eight pieces of cloth of different patterns. At the sight of these the King's face brightened, and he appeared in a great hurry to end the conference and to examine the articles, which he commenced doing before we left him, a piece of native cloth having been given to our interpreter for his services. The Attá is said to be about fifty years old; his skin is very dark and he has a heavy, sensual look. Though an absolute monarch he does not seem to possess much real authority, nothing of importance being transacted without the consent of A'boko's party. By this time it was nearly dark, so we walked quickly to our boats, and reached the ship by seven o'clock, having completed a good day's work, and broken through the old custom of not seeing the Attá the same day that the announcement is made to him.

By seven next morning we were at anchor close off Iddá, upon which numerous canoes came off bringing ivory and other articles for sale. I prepared presents for Ehimodína and Okéyin, as also for our friend U'ti, and for various of the king's family and attendants. Our musical band of the day previous

Aug. 2.

came off, and the performers each received a small *dash* in return for which they played at a most astonishing rate, until, incited by their stirring strains, three of our visitors treated us to a native dance on our quarter-deck. Mr. Crowther and I went and paid another visit to Okéyin on English Island, by whom we were presented with a goat and some yams. Under the guardianship of U'ti, two of the king's daughters, named A'ku and U'fo, came on board. I cut two pieces of scarlet cloth scarf-fashion, and put them across their shoulders, telling them that was "white woman's" fashion. We steamed from Iddá about one o'clock, but for the remainder of that day did not make much progress.

The situation of Iddá is very pleasing; and to our eyes, accustomed as they then were to the low grounds and swampy flats of the lower parts of the stream, was especially reviving. Placed on an eminence overlooking the river, the huts interspersed with lofty trees with finely-tinted foliage, and with high land for the back ground, the view was as charming as it was novel and romantic. After inhaling the pestilential miasmata of the Delta, denied the free enjoyment of the air of heaven by lofty frowning mangroves, and being unable to gaze on any objects but the sky above, the river beneath, and an unbroken line of trees along the banks, all thoughts of sickness or of weariness at once vanished on treading these commanding heights, glancing at the rocky cliffs beneath, and freely breathing the invigorating atmosphere. Here, for the first time, we met with the gigantic Baobab or Monkey Bread-fruit Tree (*Adansonia digitata*), with its massive trunk, its spreading branches, and its oblong, pendulous, elongated fruit.

Igára, sometimes, though incorrectly, called Igála, extends along the left bank of the Kwóra, from below Ada-mugú, where it borders on I'gbo, up to the Confluence. Under its original name of A'kpoto it extends inland and along the lower Bínue for a considerable distance. The western part only is known as Igára, so named from a Yóruban chief who conquered the district. Iddá is the capital; formerly a place of great importance, but of late years on the decline. The Attá was at one time a ruler of the first consequence, many countries paying tribute to him, as Kakánda, I'gbira, and Dóma; but his authority even in his own proper dominions is now very feeble. "Attá" is his peculiar title; it signifies father, the Igára for king being "Onú;" by the former he is invariably known to the surrounding nations, but the latter is frequently employed in speaking of him in Igára. The language of Igára is peculiar, but has its affinities chiefly with the Yóruban family,* so much so, that Mr. Crowther could recognise many words. Iddá is the first place where rocks of any magnitude occur. They are chiefly of ferruginous sandstone, the strata being

---

* Koelle, from his philological researches at Sierra Leone, arrives at a similar conclusion, and has formed a class of "Akú-Igala" languages.

nearly horizontal. The cliff on which the town is built, and which presents a perpendicular face towards the river, is said to be 185 feet high by barometric measurement, though to the eye it does not seem so much. Mr. May intended to have ascertained it trigonometrically, but was unfortunately prevented from so doing.*

The tract of country opposite to Iddá, on the western bank, is said to be tributary to Bíni (Benin), and is known as Edó. I made many inquiries after the town of Wáppa mentioned in Allen and Thomson's narrative, but could learn nothing of it. However, during my voyage to England, I met at Sierra Leone with a man from this very district, from whom I found that the town is correctly named Wífa, and that the inhabitants speak a dialect akin to that of Bíni. The name Edó, or, as pronounced by the Abó people, "Edú" or "Idú," is derived from *Ado*, generally contracted *do*, the usual form of salutation, in the same way as Yórubans are, for a similar reason, styled Akú.

While passing a small village on the left bank, inhabited by some of A'boko's party, a canoe came off bringing ivory for sale, from which Dr. Hutchinson purchased, besides several scrivelloes, a fine tooth weighing forty-two pounds. Up to this point the river was bounded by sandstone cliffs and sloping

* This has been variously estimated by different visitors from 140 to 300 feet. *Vide* Laird and Oldfield's Narrative, vol. i. p. 124; Mc William's Medical History, pp. 70 and 285; and Allen and Thomson's Narrative, vol. i. p. 318; also Allen's Chart of the Quorra.

banks, behind which were table-lands, and gently rising hills. But now a change became evident; the rocks seemed altered in character, and huge pieces, more or less modified by volcanic agency, were from time to time visible. Bird-rock, so named by Lander, is a large, white-topped, quartz block, situated nearly in mid-stream; and the mountains, which here line the eastern side are steep, rugged, and conical. We passed the island on which during the dry season a celebrated market is held every ten days, and which is attended by traders from Kakánda to Abó. This meeting, which during the rains takes place on the eastern shore of the river, is called Ikíri or Okíri,* meaning either the "distant market" or the "market between the hills," either of which explanations is suitable. The hills are finely covered with vegetation, between the patches of which the dark extremities of broken strata present themselves, while down the sides extending often to the water's edge, are deep ravines, which, after heavy rains, must be mountain-torrents. We anchored off a little creek, rather beyond the north end of Maconochy's Island, where Mr. May and I landed, and by the light of a beautiful moon proceeded to explore the locality; a little village was found, named Iróko, the inhabitants of which, though at first rather alarmed, soon became friendly; we also stumbled across a bivouacking party, composed of the crews of two

* The name "Bocqua" given by Lander is not known to the natives.

small canoes on their way to some market. Mr. May got a good meridian altitude of the moon, while I examined a large projecting mass of rock on the beach, closely resembling at a distance, the "Bird-rock." This I found to be composed of mica slate, partly altered by the action of fire, the top covered with scales of mica, reflecting beautifully the rays of light, causing a shining, silvery appearance. While seated on the summit, some fifteen or sixteen feet above the ground, gazing at the clear evening sky, and the softly tinted scenery around, I was roused by a splash in the lagoon immediately beneath, and on looking for the cause, saw that a crocodile had landed on the sand, and was taking a rapid survey of me, with which he seemed soon to be satisfied, as he speedily disappeared. About ten o'clock we again landed to try to get a lunar observation; but while in the act of pulling ashore, clouds began to form in the zenith very rapidly; and in less than ten minutes the whole face of the heavens was completely obscured.

Aug. 4.
Next morning showed that we were advancing still further into elevated regions. To the westward were mounts Jervis and Erskine, while rather more to the northward the gigantic Sorácte, with abrupt sides and a rounded summit, rises suddenly from the plain to the height of 1200 or 1300 feet; and further inland "Saddleback" sternly faces the north, but gently slopes in the opposite direction. On the southern extremity of "Beaufort Island," is a prettily

shaped hill, about 180 to 200 feet in height, which I named "Mount Francis." Opposite to this, on the eastern side, is a chain of conical mountains, three of which, close to the river, are very remarkable; the central one, which has an altitude of from 400 to 500 feet, has been named Mount Franklin, and is connected to its immediate neighbours by sharp, rocky elevations. The most northern, which had not previously received any designation, was by Mr. May named "Mount Crozier." We observed nearly in the centre of the river a large schistose rock, with a smooth rounded top, to which a very singular look was given by two veins of bright quartz running through it. Near the "Quorra Bank," the "Pleiad" grounded, but got off without much trouble. Seeing on the left bank huts and numbers of inhabitants, Mr. Crowther and I determined to land, and accordingly, accompanied by Mr. May and Mr. Richards, set off in the gig.

The people received us with the utmost cordiality, and invited us to see A'ma-A'boko their chief, who was, we learnt, eldest son of Old A'boko, of Iddá. We were accordingly conducted first to the abode of the headman of the town, by whom we were introduced to the King, who gave us a hearty welcome, saying he was delighted at this return of white men, his father's friends. I asked him to come on board next day at the Confluence, which he promised to do, as he told us that none of his people would open trade with us until he had himself personally commenced it. He told us that the town of Pánda * had been recently sacked by a body of Fulátas, who were still lingering in that neighbourhood. A'ma-A'boko is about fifty years old, with strongly marked features, and a somewhat furrowed face. His expression is one of firmness and decision, but without any trace of cruelty or evil passion; and he is said to resemble his father more than any of his brothers do. He has ruled near the Confluence for a long period, and now possesses much influence around, being actually, though not nominally, independent of the Attá, and in reality, a more powerful chief. His town, which is named Igbégbe, is finely situated for trade, being nearly opposite the site of the once famous market town of Odokódo.† The huts, which are all circular, were better constructed and more substantial than any we had seen, and the walls of part of the chief's residence were coloured red and blue with camwood, and indigo. The population is numerous but mixed, and consists chiefly of Igára and I'gbira people, the language being that of the latter. During our interview to-day, I spoke to Mr. Crowther in English, who translated my words into Yóruba; they were retranslated to another man in Núpe, who finally addressed the King in I'gbira. This system of treble or quadruple rendering, is not

---

* This is the Fundah or Fandah of former writers, F being a common Haúsa corruption for P.

† Often though incorrectly written Adda Kudu; it is derived from the Yóruba words *odó*, river, and *kò*, to meet. Odó-kò-odó, i.e. odokódo, river meeting river, from its situation at the confluence of the two streams.

only very tedious, but often quite alters the original meaning of a sentence. It is, however, very common at interviews with African chiefs, as it is looked on as etiquette, particularly at a first meeting, for the grandee, whoever he may be, not to understand any language but his own. The Haúsa tongue is the French of Central Africa, being very generally understood, and being the medium by which traders from different countries transact business in common. It was the language which was of most service to us, and by its means the greater part of our intercourse was carried on. We have often been surprised, when paying a private visit to some chief, to find that the individual who perhaps only the day previous, could understand nothing but the dialect of his own district, obliging us to address him by a double translation, could now not merely comprehend Haúsa, but also speak it fluently. African traders are in general good and ready linguists, speaking not unfrequently three or four different tongues; the speed, also, with which they translate a sentence, without almost a moment's consideration, is really surprising. We made inquiries about the Bínue or Tsádda, but except the lower parts, they seemed at Igbégbe to know little about it. They recognised, however, the name Adamáwa, and said that was the country which yielded ivory. A'ma-A'boko told me he would try to send some persons with us to point out the different places, and tell us their names, for which kind offer I thanked him. In returning towards the boat, we met an old lady, a connection of the chief's, who, recognising Mr. Richards and Alihéli, bestowed on each a hearty embrace. During our run ashore, the "Pleiad" had found the channel, and was steaming slowly up towards the Confluence; but before rejoining, we pulled along the eastern bank, rounded Point Tsádda, and dipped our oars in the "dark waters." Being in want of wood, I ordered a convenient spot to be selected along the shores of the "Model Farm," and one being found, we anchored nearly abreast of "Sacrifice-rock." A wooding party was at once sent on shore and set to work; after which I visited Duck Island, and got some specimens of birds and of insects. About seven o'clock, Mr. May and I landed on "Sacrifice-rock," where we got a meridian altitude of the moon, and a set of lunar distances with Jupiter.

Aug. 5. Being very anxious to obtain a good view of the surrounding country, Mr. May, Mr. Crowther, and myself left before daylight, and went in the gig a little way up the main stream of the Kwóra, and with some difficulty finding a landing-place, walked towards the foot of Mount Pátte. We followed a winding narrow pathway, by which, after half an hour's climbing, we reached an elevation of upwards of 400 feet, where on a small plateau we discovered a little village, inhabited by a few Kakánda people, who lived upon this height for security, having been driven from their native homes by Dásaba, King of Núpe, who had, however, been very recently deposed for his cruelty, and forced to fly for refuge to Ilọ́rin, in the

Yóruba country. They received us very kindly, giving us some country beer, the only thing, poor people, they had to offer us. Our intention had been to ascend to the top of the mountain, and visit the villages which we had heard were situated on its table summit, but we now ascertained that these had ceased to exist, while the foot-track having become overgrown, was no longer visible. Not having time to cut a path for ourselves, we were forced to forego this part of our plan, which, however, we regretted the less, on account of the magnificent prospect opened to us from this little encampment. The sun, now well above the horizon, had succeeded in dispersing the mists of the early morning, its rays, still greatly inclined, were brilliantly reflected from the sides of the mountains, and light and shade, strongly contrasted, were well defined in the clear tropical atmosphere. Beneath us was the pretty green-topped Mount Stirling, sadly reminding us of the misfortunes of its last European visitors. On our left was a deep ravine, separating us from another flat-crowned hill, Mount Victoria, while on the other hand was the undulating wooded country, purchased in 1841 for the model farm, and stretching far away to the southward until there arrested by rugged rocky ground and abrupt mountains. Pursuing a somewhat meandering route, the Narrow Kwóra flowing from the northward wound along the base of the western highlands, while full before us came pouring from the eastward the broad, the straight-coursed Bínue, the commingling waters of the two mighty streams forming the expansive, lake-like Confluence, its surface dotted with islets and banks, or rippled by contending currents, while in the distance the united rivers impetuously rushed towards the sea, through the deep defile by which we had so lately ascended. The extensive ruins of the once busy Odokódo, the centre of trade in this place before its destruction by a ruthless Fuláta band, were hid from view by the thick brushwood; but the crowded huts of its important commercial successor were plainly discerned on the opposite shore. Along the banks numerous villages could be detected, while frequently, more inland, a curling wreath of smoke would betray the existence of some sequestered hamlet, half-hidden beneath lofty trees. Far as the eye could reach, over miles and miles, the ground teemed with exuberant vegetation; seeming often in the fantastic appearance of its wild growth to revel in its exemption from culture. Such a fruitful soil in other climes, and with a happier population, would yield support and employment to countless thousands, and long ere this have proved the source of untold wealth. To complete our panorama, quietly at anchor, and now surrounded by canoes, there lay the little "Pleiad," the *avant-courière* of European energy and influence; and I trust, the forerunner of civilization and its attendant blessings, and of better days to these richly-endowed but hitherto unfortunate regions.

Between the two rivers is a long swampy piece of land, formed by alluvial deposits, intersected by channels and streamlets, constituting, indeed, a miniature delta. Its immediate vicinity must be very unhealthy, and its proximity to the model-farm possession is much too near to be pleasant, as during the dry season there must be an immense malaria-yielding surface. Mr. May having completed his sketch and got a set of bearings, we descended by the rugged pathway, and, embarking, soon left the creeks for the open river. I found the temperature of the Kwóra, at this point, to exceed that of the water of the Confluence by, from a degree to a degree and a-half of Fahrenheit. The natives fancy there is a difference in the colour of the two streams, hence, in Haúsa, the Kwóra is styled "Fári n'rúa," or the "white water," while the Bínue is known as "Báki n'rúa," the "black water;" the Igára synonyms of these being "Ujímini fúfu," and "Ujímini dúdu,"* the former word evidently connected with the Abó Oshímini. We reached the "Pleiad" about ten o'clock, and found on board A'ma-A'boko, who had come to pay us a visit, and had brought us, as a present, a goat, some yams, and some jars of beer. I asked him to come below, and had a long talk with him on trade and other matters. He was evidently inclined to be most friendly, and relished much the idea of opening up commercial intercourse with us. I presented him, to his evident satisfaction, with a musket and bayonet, a number of flints, a sabre

* According to Captain W. Allen, the Núpe names are respectively Fúrodo and Fúroji.

and scabbard, a showy ring, and some pieces of cloth. I gave also to the two persons next in authority under him, proportionate gifts, and to two female relatives, who accompanied him, rings and scarfs. One of these latter had two names, Ojéma-ólogu, and Asebí; this habit, which is extremely common, arises, I am informed by Mr. Crowther, from the practice of a different name being given to an infant by every person present at its birth, and to strangers this often causes great confusion, the same individual being spoken of under distinct appellations.

We had been desirous of trying to send letters to England, across the Yóruba country, by way of Abbeokúta and Lagos, and now consulted A′ma-A′boko about the practicability of so doing; but he told us that, in consequence of the late deposition of Dásaba, the country about E′gga was so disturbed that he could not undertake to get them transmitted. This was our second disappointment, for while at Abó we had calculated on sending despatches to Bonny, which was frustrated by intercourse between these two places having been suspended.

Trade was now going briskly on. Some fine tusks were offered, but at very high prices; fowls, eggs, goats, and yams were in abundance, and fair tobacco was purchased at the rate of eleven pounds weight for 1000 cowries. A little boy, in stepping from one canoe to another, fell overboard, and being unable to swim, speedily disappeared. Another boy dived after him, and with some trouble brought him to the surface, and, though carried astern by the strong current, contrived to support him until picked up. On being brought to the ship, I gave the boy a piece of cloth as a present, telling him it was for saving the life of his companion, on which all the natives around shouted and clapped their hands. In the afternoon, Mr. Crowther and I paid another visit to Igbégbe, and the surrounding country. The town is situated close to the river, on gently sloping ground, at the base of a range of hills, and is from twenty to fifty or sixty feet above the highest level of the water. The market was now nearly over, and we only found in it some yams and other vegetables, with a little tobacco, cotton, and a pink-coloured silky-looking material, upon which they set considerable value. Behind are large fields of maize, among which I found many unshapely erupted granitic-looking blocks, some curiously piled on each other. The number of Baobab-trees here is very great, their thick oak-like trunks and spreading foliage being very striking. On returning to our boat we found, seated on a mat, on a rocky eminence near the landing-place, sheltered by a kind of tent and attended by slaves, an old man, one of the eunuchs of the late Attá, who had come to this place to trade. He sent to invite us to speak to him, and receiving us very politely, asked us to sit beside him. He was attired in an ornamented Haúsa tobe, and had on his head a cap of green satin, ornamented with purple plush. After a good deal of conversation he mentioned that he had an article which he wished to have matched, and accordingly gave some directions to a slave, who, disappearing, speedily returned, carrying, with some ceremony, a large calabash, with which he knelt before me. In this was a common japanned earthenware jug, upon which O'gbe, for that was his name, gazed with intense admiration, asking me to give him another like it. I had to regret that it was not in my power to oblige him; but promised, if ever I came up the river again, as I hoped I should do, that I would remember his commission. Next day, after church time, I landed and walked over a portion of the model-farm territory. The shore is lined by a thick belt of trees, beyond which is tall grass, so thick as greatly to impede progression. Great part of this land is low and swampy, and in the more elevated spots are projecting pieces of rock, which would materially interfere with culture. There is, however, ample choice of locality, dry or wet soil being easily found. I saw numerous tracks of wild animals, chiefly of oxen and deer, and in one spot came upon the quite recent footprints of an elephant. I was much struck with some white ants' nests, which, in structure and in size, surpassed any I had ever previously seen. There were about twenty distinct edifices, none less than six feet high, while one in particular was nearly fourteen feet, and turreted like an Elizabethan mansion. During the afternoon, two canoes, with some small horses on board, arrived from Múye, a town some distance up the Kwóra, with a mixed population of Kakánda and Núpe people.

The people of Igára employ no distinctive marks, and are very rarely seen at all tattooed. The inhabitants of Abó are always at once recognised by the men having three short, perpendicular lines, between the eye and the ear, and three shorter horizontal ones on the upper part of the nose, just between the eyebrows, while the women have the same mark on the nose, but have six of the perpendicular lines. In other parts of I′gbo different devices are employed, of which I shall speak hereafter.

On leaving the Confluence, some needless delays took place; and the wood we had on board being of inferior quality, did not burn well; so much so, that five or six times during the day, we had to anchor to get up steam, our entire progress not exceeding six or seven miles. Canoes accompanied us all day, and some petty trading was carried on. Mr. May and I landed at night on the north side, and got a meridian altitude of Vega. In the clearest night, when not a fragment of a cloud is visible, and the stars overhead shining with a resplendent brilliancy quite unknown in more northern latitudes, there is almost invariably a haze along the horizon extending upwards from ten to sixteen or eighteen degrees, and quite obscuring any heavenly bodies within its boundary. This is more remarkable, and of greater intensity in the north and south than in the east and west, but especially in the north; so much

Aug. 7.

so, that since our arrival in the river we had never got a single glimpse of the Polar star. We found that we were close to a little village, the entire population of which turned out; and after a few preliminaries, Mr. May and I had to shake hands with every one present, to the number of forty or fifty, after which the headman gave me a fine fowl. Not having anything to offer him in return, I asked him to come on board and see me early in the morning, which he promised to do. The wood the next day burnt as feebly as before; and after struggling against the stream for about a mile, we had again to anchor. Seeing there was no prospect of advancing at this rate, and that the master was either unwilling or too lazy to find a remedy, I had to desire him to send a wooding party ashore, while Mr. Crowther and I proceeded to a village a little way off, to see what could be effected. We there found abundance of excellent wood, ready cut and dry, which the inhabitants were willing to sell, on which I sent for one of the large iron canoes, which was soon deeply laden at the expense of a few hundred needles, and some little zinc-cased looking-glasses. The village was named A'tipo, and was inhabited by I'gbira people, who are a busy, industrious set. Of this we had a good example, as no sooner did we inquire after wood, than every available man, woman, and child in the place immediately set to collecting and carrying, so that a very animating scene was presented. The late Mr. Beecroft during his ascents of the river, used to purchase firewood very easily and cheaply for salt; but unfortunately our supply of this article, which is always in great demand, was left behind at Fernando Po. A few drops of rain fell at this time, being the first we had seen for ten days. The river had not risen at all for nearly a fortnight, but the natives told us they were in daily expectation of its increase. They said that the previous season had been a very dry one, but that much rain was expected this year. The current ran here from three-and-a-half to four knots, being much stronger than the average. Among other articles brought on board for sale, was trona, or impure carbonate of soda, sometimes in little bags, but occasionally in cakes. This article is in constant requisition in all the markets, and is said to be supplied here from the upper parts of the Bínue. In the evening a canoe reached us, bringing five men and a boy, who had been sent by A'ma-A'boko in fulfilment of his promise, which I had thought he had forgotten or neglected. I accordingly sent back to thank him, and promised to take great care of his messengers, and to bring them back in safety. There were two parties, one being the chief's own man, named Máma, with two followers, who were called Máka and Bámi, the other being headed by a very intelligent man entitled Zúri, who had frequently traded up the river, and who had with him his son Músa, a precious young imp, and a slave named O'robo. I was much pleased at their arrival, as not only would our intercourse with the natives be greatly facilitated, but we could more easily and more exactly ascertain the names of the places we passed.

<small>Aug. 9.</small> Our new wood burnt well, and the supply of steam was easily kept up. As a fine breeze was blow- ing nearly right aft, we fitted one of our canoe-sails on a small spar, and set it on the foremast, the other we hoisted in one of the canoes, which was lashed alongside, and as the wind was fresh, this eased the engines considerably. Every day after we quitted the delta, we had always experienced a fine breeze, more or less strong, blowing, except during squalls, invariably *up* the river. Had we had our sails on board, much fuel would have been saved, and much greater progress been made; but as already mentioned, the master had chosen to leave them behind at Clarence. The channel about this part of the river is very tortuous, requiring frequent crossing over from one side to the other, and very careful sounding. On the south side we saw a little village named "Bofú;" and shortly afterwards, nearly abreast of Harriet Island, picturesquely situated on the edge of a cliff nearly eighty feet high, stands Ogbá. We did not stay at this place, but anchored for the night some three miles further on, under the pretty hill named "Lander's Seat." Early next morning the chief sent to inquire, why we passed him, to which I replied that we were obliged to press on, being desirous of going a long journey, but that we should

visit him on our return. Before getting under steam Mr. May and I landed for sights on Little Harriet Island, which is simply a large sandbank covered with high rank grass. The banks of the river are usually thickly and luxuriantly wooded down to the very water's edge, except in spots cleared for cultivation around the villages. A little inland on both sides are fine ranges of hills, those to the northward being lower and more rounded, while those to the southward are higher, more abrupt, and with numerous peaked eminences. Among these we had some difficulty in recognising Mount Vidal, but at last fixed on what seemed the loftiest and most remarkable, having an elevation of 900 to 1000 feet. The range itself I named after one of the former explorers of the lower Bínue, the "Oldfield Range." Islets of various shapes and sizes became more numerous, among which one particularly attracted our notice, from being covered with huts. We anchored close to the spot, which was just abreast of a large town on the right bank, named Yimahá. On landing, we found that the entire population had left this town from dread of a Fuláta invasion, and had taken up their temporary abode on this little islet, on which they had been residing for three months. The encampment bore every mark of having been constructed in great haste, the huts being composed of dry sticks and reeds, yet these industrious people were weaving, picking cotton, and busily pursuing their various occupations. I paid a visit to their

Aug. 10.

G

chief, a feeble, decrepit, very aged man, named Ozinekú. I regretted much the cause of their exile, and said we were willing to purchase anything they had to sell, particularly ivory, provisions, and firewood. This little place was most fearfully infested with flies, so as forcibly to remind one of the Plagues of Egypt. During our hurried interview we obtained a partial exemption from their annoyance by hard smoking; but even in that short space of time, these little pests seemed to become reconciled to the smell of our tobacco, or even to enjoy it, and darting through the clouds with which we enveloped ourselves, buzzingly mocked at us. Mosquitoes—I need not remind those who have sadly experienced them—are insect nuisances of the first degree of intensity; the sleepless nights caused by their incessant tiny though ominous humming, and the irritating wounds, the results of their blood-thirsty voracity, are too much in the nightly experience of tropical travellers. Sand-flies are, perhaps, still more troublesome pests; minute in the extreme, they almost defy detection, and pass exultingly through the finest gauze; yet, confiding in their number, which is Legion, they prove a most pitiless and most unwearying foe. But of all entomological curses, I do not know one which equals a swarm of ordinary flies. Commencing with early dawn, they pursue, surround, and torment you in the most indefatigable manner. They fly into your ears, they crawl over your face, creep up your nose; and if you happen to yawn, you discover that even your mouth is not sacred. They seem, too, to be omnivorous, and to have the good taste to try whatever is selected as food for man. Hot or cold, raw or cooked, solid or fluid, sweet or sour, are equally the same, and in the excess of their sociality, they often insist upon sharing the very mouthful you are engaged on, or drinking from the glass already at your lips. In the whole range of the insect world Moses could not have called forth a species more calculated to worry, to tease, to torment, or really to plague, than that ubiquitous form which we met with in Refuge Island.

We afterwards landed at Yimahá, where we were received by a solitary individual, who welcomed us with a melancholy smile, telling us that only the day before four Fuláta horsemen had visited them and had inspected the place, and he pointed out, close to where we were, the marks of their horses' hoofs. These restless invaders had found the place deserted, and not having canoes could not attack the refugees on their insular abode; but, as the river would soon be rising, and the place be overflowed, these unfortunates were living in daily, almost hourly, expectation of again being obliged to seek for another shelter. These Fulátas formed part of the band which had so lately sacked Pánda and killed the King Oyigú, and who, not content with the extent of their raid, were seeking for more plunder ere they returned home. Our informant was by trade a dyer, and had come over with two companions to see if their works had been left untouched. He conducted us through this abode of desolation, the numerous substantial-looking huts being forlorn-looking and empty, and the pathways choked up with grass and weeds. We visited the King's residence, and were pointed out the chamber in which, twenty-one years before, "white men" had been received, namely, during Mr. Laird's visit in 1833, which our friend remembered very well. During our short stay here Dr. Hutchinson purchased upwards of 200lbs. of ivory at a moderate rate. In the evening we anchored off the mouth of the O'kwa, a little stream leading to Potínkia, the port of Pánda. Polaris was visible for the first time, but unfortunately no landing-place was near. I watched for a long time for meteors, this being one of their regular epochs, but I did not observe more than half-a-dozen, all very high up, to the northward of the zenith, and describing very short courses.

The morning of the 11th August was the first on which a heavy dew was noted, and a thick mist hung along the bases of the hills until sunrise. Mr. May and I went in the gig to search for a landing-place, and at last were successful in getting to a small sandbank, where we got a good set of sights and an azimuth, after which we pulled to the "Pleiad," already under steam, and coming towards us. Early in the forenoon the master, most unaccountably, and against the advice of Mr. Richards, who was with him, ran up a narrow, shallow-looking channel, and, as might have been expected, got the vessel a-ground.

While attempting to back off, a valve in the after part of the boiler gave way, but the mate succeeded, after some time, in getting afloat by the use of a Sampson post, and shifting the deck cargo. Our chronometer rates had not been very satisfactorily ascertained previously, and as it was supposed that they might have changed since leaving the sea, my intention had been to remain for some days at Dágbo for that purpose, as it was of much consequence to determine these as accurately as possible before entering on new ground. But the engineer's report now made me alter my plan, as he said the repairing of the engine would occupy at least two days. I therefore resolved to delay where we were, as, being not very far from the sandbank on which we landed in the morning, we could make it the scene of operation, and then the set of sights already taken could be reckoned for our purpose. Nearly opposite to our anchorage, on the left bank, stood a small village; from which, after a time, canoes began to come to us. We asked for firewood, which was speedily brought in abundance, and of good quality. In the afternoon Mr. Crowther and I paid the people a visit, and were invited by the headman, who is named Obereku and Abája, to his hut, where he gave us some beer. The place is named Kénde, and was founded about three years ago; but what rendered it peculiarly interesting to us, was, that we found most of the inhabitants to be refugees from Pánda, who had fled after the recent capture of their town, and from them we learnt authentic particulars of this sad affair. The enemy, they said, did not come on openly; but for several days many of them had been arriving at Pánda in small bands, apparently for trade, when suddenly one morning they arose and assaulted the place, so unexpectedly that but little resistance was made. Few were killed, but numbers were made captives, the King being among the former. The city was then burnt, after which most of the Fulátas retired towards the town of Tóto, about which spot they were supposed to be still lingering. Among these exiles thus rudely driven from their houses, was the son of the headman of Potínkia, near Pánda.

Two of the persons who were conversing with us remembered Mr. Laird's visit to Yimahá, and as I appeared well acquainted with his trip, and mentioned the names of various places around, they declared that I must have accompanied him, on which an old man, looking hard at me, affirmed that he recollected my face well, and was extremely sceptical when I assured him that at that time I was a very small boy indeed, hardly so high as his knee. This little village gives a good idea of a recent settlement. Its site was close to the river, the huts not yet continuous, but in little groups separated from each other by yet uncut shrubs and brushwood, and here and there were narrow footpaths leading to small cleared spots, sown with Indian and Dawa corn; on the outskirts lay prostrate huge trees, laboriously felled by their rude axes, but which they had not yet had time to cut up and remove; while a few hundred yards behind was the still impenetrable forest, protecting and bounding them in the rear as the river did in front.

Next morning, Mr. May and I landed on the sandbank, and, having brought a supply of instruments, prepared for a little work. We got a double altitude of the sun, and I took a set of magnetic observations with Barrow's instrument, by which the dip of the needle was approximately determined to be 6° 6′ 58″. The thermometer in the sun ranged from 102° to 114° F. during the six hours we spent in these occupations. The coldest period throughout the twenty-four hours seemed to be about three A.M., the lowest temperature on board having been 69° ·5 F. We again visited the village, when Mr. Crowther and I distributed a few thousand cowries among the poor people, who seemed extremely thankful, and what with the presents we gave them, and their earnings by selling yams, fowls, and firewood, I think it will be long before they forget the visit of the "white man's ship." We had now been a month in the river, and the health of all on board was perfect, and being quite clear of the swamps of the Delta, we were in great hopes that this unlooked-for exemption from disease might continue.

Aug. 12.

On Sunday morning Mr. May and I were again at our station, when a set of lunar distances with the sun was taken, and at three o'clock next morning we once more landed to get a meridian altitude of Achemar, but were prevented by the cloudiness of the sky; the moon shortly afterwards crossed the meridian, but at too great a height to be measured by the sextant in the artificial horizon. We were more fortunate a few hours afterwards in getting another set of lunars, and good sights, which completed our labours, and permitted the chronometers to be re-rated.

The district along the north side of the Bínue, as far as we had come, was known by the name of I'gbira, its extent being, from the confluence eastward, about fifty miles. The chief town was Pánda, now destroyed, and to distinguish the country and its people from another tribe which I shall hereafter allude to, it is often styled I'gbira-Pánda, I'gbira-Ihí, or I'gbira-Egú. The country has been represented, but wrongly, as being called Pánda, which is properly confined to the town.* The people are highly civilised, friendly, civil, and most industrious, and with whom it is of much importance to keep on good terms, as a great deal of trade is carried on by their means. A few Muhammadans are to be found among them, but the great majority are Pagans, but with fewer barbarous rites than any other heathen tribe we encountered. Tattooing is not practised, nor have they any distinctive mark. In person they are rather tall, and well-made, with a sub-typical negro countenance, and they generally keep the body well covered with clothes.

* Thus Koelle in his Polyglotta Africana, p. 9, speaks of E'gbīra the capital of Opánda; whereas it should be the reverse. Opánda also is incorrect, the o being merely an occasional prefix.

They use a peculiar language, differing from the Igára, and having mixed affinities, chiefly with Núpe and Yóruba. There are also many I'gbira towns and settlements along the south bank of the Bínue, although the country there is A'kpoto, subject to, and in reality part of, Igára. During the palmy days of the Attás of Iddá, I'gbira was tributary to them, but at present it is independent of them, and likely to remain so.

The scenery daily increased in beauty as we advanced up this noble stream. Numerous villages were discernible on both banks, the names of many of which we obtained from our Igbégbe party. One of large size, situated at the eastern side of the base of Mount Pleasant, was named Amarán, a little beyond which, opposite the "Bay Islands," was one of our anchorages. Just abreast of this on the north shore is the limit of the I'gbira country, its next neighbour being named Bássa,* a little village, which we could see among the trees, called Abatú, belonging to that district. Mr. May and I landed in the morning on one of the Bay Islands for sights, after which, having an hour to spare, we circumnavigated and explored them. During our return to the ship, we got near a herd of hippopotami, amusing themselves in shallow water, and being not more than a hundred yards from them we had a good opportunity of watching them,

* This appears to be a common African name, for besides the one now mentioned, there is another to the westward of the Confluence, and a third in the Delta in Orú; there is also a Bássa to the northward of the Krú coast.

and if we had had a gun with us, could have had a famous shot. They became alarmed and made off, but one swam towards us apparently to reconnoitre, after which he rejoined his comrades, with, I suppose, important intelligence. A little beyond this we anchored for a short time off a town named A'batsho, the last of the I'gbira settlements on the south side. The chief "I'robo," and his brother "Itshigbása," refugees from Pánda, and sons of one of the former kings of that city, came off to see us, and we were also visited by one of our Kénde acquaintances, Allagabá, late headman of Potínkia. Poor people, they were all in sad tatters, and bore with them ample evidence of their poverty and their privations. They were accompanied by a drummer, to whom I gave a figured handkerchief, on which he testified his excessive delight by making a prodigious rattling on his instrument. At night Mr. May and I had to land for our observations on a small sandbank, on which a crocodile also attempted to gain a footing, but was scared by the light of our bull's-eye lantern; unpleasant as its company would have been, it could not have proved more annoying, nor could he have left so many marks behind him, as did the myriads of sandflies, which at last drove us, bleeding and nearly vanquished, away.

Just above A'batsho the river presents a noble appearance, in breadth far exceeding any part we had seen. Its banks are clothed with tall graceful palms, and other magnificent trees, while numerous islands covered with verdure, which everywhere start into view, pleasantly diversify the scene, and the eye is enlivened by the frequent occurrence of green hills, in bright relief against the dark undulating mountains in the back ground. On the forenoon of the 16th August, the ship was once more run aground, and having been got off again after the usual delays, was allowed to remain at anchor. Since entering the river the master had never once been out of the ship, but this afternoon he announced his intention of going himself to sound. Accordingly, but not until after dinner, he started in the gig, which was well stored with great coats, cigars, and interpreters, and after an absence of an hour-and-a-half he returned, shaking his head ominously, and remarking that we were awkwardly placed, and that he had anticipated this for several days, but said he should examine the channel again next day. I, however, ascertained that four fathoms could always be found, but that he had endeavoured to search for shallow rather than for deep water. Our observations next morning were taken on a little isolated patch of sand, so soft that it would hardly bear the weight of the artificial horizon, and as we were returning we met Mr. Taylor, who had by this time finished his breakfast, setting out on his voyage of discovery. He reached the ship again about sunset, and after due refreshment requested an interview with me, when he stated that he considered it *impossible* for the ship to advance any further. Having made him repeat this opinion in the hearing of Mr. May, I told him that I completely differed from him, and should therefore relieve him from charge of the vessel, and try to take her up myself. Not anticipating such a reply, he tried to modify his opinion, but this I would not permit, so he asked Mr. May and myself to come below and talk the matter over with his chief officers. From them, with the exception of a junior supercargo, he received no encouragement, and as I continued firm in my determination, he made up his mind to get out of his scrape with the best grace he could, announcing that for peace sake he would yield the point, and dropping some hints, meant to be awfully significant, about mutiny and piracy, retired to his beloved couch and cigar.

A record of squabbles of this kind is by no means pleasant, and certainly cannot be entertaining, but I have felt it necessary to record the reasons which obliged me to take such strong steps. We had been thirty-six days in the river, and had not reached Dágbo, the point attained by Allen and Oldfield under trying circumstances twenty-one years before. Numerous, most unjustifiable delays had taken place, and were daily recurring. Disputes between the master and his officers were constantly taking place, so as to render everyone uncomfortable. The season was rapidly advancing, and if some decisive measures had not been at once adopted, the expedition would certainly have proved a failure, and there then would have been no inducement to repeat the experiment. All these obstructions and impediments were most distinctly attributable to Mr. Taylor, who had repeatedly exhibited a most lamentable amount of apathy and indecision, besides displaying great lack of judgment, and an unpardonable want of interest in our success. Nor were the direct interests of his employer, Mr. Laird, better attended to; he never went ashore, nor made any commercial inquiries, all the purchases made having been exclusively effected by Dr. Hutchinson. I was tired of ordering, of stimulating, and of complaining, all attempts to rouse the man even to ordinary exertion having been failures. It was useless to desire him to perform what in his opinion was *impossible*, besides which he had expressed it as his belief that we had now reached the end of the river, which hereabouts expanded into a large lake. On all these considerations, I looked on myself as absolutely obliged to have recourse to the means I have mentioned, and fully justified in assuming the entire responsibility and direction. I therefore told Mr. Harcus, the chief mate, a most praiseworthy and skilful officer, that I should consider him for the future as sailing-master, that his duties should be to look after the ship, and attend to the navigation of the river, a post for which he was admirably qualified. Other arrangements being completed, I ordered steam to be ready for a start by seven in the morning.

CHAPTER V.

THE NEW ADMINISTRATION.

Aug. 18.

By daylight I despatched Mr. Richards in the gig to sound, and by seven o'clock the "Pleiad" was under steam, threading her way along very circuitous channels. When off Erúko a canoe came alongside, bringing me a goat from the King of Bássa, to whom I sent a present in return, promising a visit when we came down the river. We touched the ground several times, but easily got off, and by half-past eleven anchored off Dágbo, certainly by a rather troublesome and winding passage, but which had been only the day before pronounced by Mr. Taylor, after several examinations, as impracticable. A wooding party was immediately sent ashore, and as there was abundant depth of water, the steamer was hauled in close to the bank, which greatly facilitated the shipment of the fuel. Wood was purchased easily and cheaply, and was pronounced by Mr. Guthrie to be of excellent quality. Mr. Crowther and I walked through this little village, now much reduced, and observed numerous plantations of rice, Indian corn, cotton, and tobacco. Dágbo is the first town in the territory of

Dóma, which we were now entering upon, and was the farthest point reached by the "Alburkah" in 1833. At night when Mr. May and I landed, we found mosquitoes so numerous and so active, that we had to set the Krúmen to collect straw and sticks for a fire, and under the protection of the smoke obtained the wished-for observations. Next morning Mr. Richards again went a-head to sound, after which we proceeded with gradually decreasing waters, until at last it did not exceed a fathom and a half. Still as this had been carefully examined we passed on at half speed, and soon reached a better channel. Stretching from below Erúko to beyond Dágbo is an extensive group of large wooded islands, some of them inhabited, to which I gave the name of the "Admiralty Archipelago." Numerous shoals and sandbanks rendered our navigation somewhat intricate; one moment we might be proceeding nearly at full speed along one side, carrying four fathoms, and a few minutes afterwards slowly groping our way along the opposite shore, the leadsman heaving incessantly, and singing out "quarter less two," or "half one." We were gradually approaching the Dóma hills, which, though not high, are prettily rounded, and clothed, not hid, by fine foliage; the centre peak, which is about the highest, I named after the officer who first delineated the range, "Mount Allen." About four o'clock, though we could see no indications of any town, our guide told us that we were off A'kpoko. We accordingly anchored, and getting into the gig under his pilotage, speedily discovered an opening, quite concealed from the river, leading into a fine creek, up which we pulled some two hundred yards, and then landing found ourselves close to the town. To enter we had to cross a ditch, some six feet deep, by three small trunks of trees thrown loosely over. On the further side was a narrow gateway closed up after dark by cross-stakes. The people, especially the younger portion, seemed rather alarmed, but were at length satisfied by the assurances of our guide, who as a trader had been here before, and had numerous acquaintances. We went at once to the house of the headman, who, coming to meet us, asked us into a kind of reception court, where mats were spread for us. When all the spectators had paid their humble respects, Zuri came forward, bending lowly on his knees, throwing dust on his head, and repeating ten or a dozen times a short formal salutation, which elicited from the chief a corresponding number of acknowledgments. He then delivered a message from A'ma-A'boko concerning us, which was well received, after which I paid him the usual compliments, and told him the purport of our visit. I gave him a present of red cloth and calicoes, and received from him a fine goat. Seeing people gathering around us with various articles for sale, I said that if they came off at once with us, we would deal with them, to which all present consented. As had been our custom ever since leaving the Confluence, I made inquiries after two white travellers, but could hear tidings of none. The chief, whose name is Mágaji, is about forty years old, and is an intelligent, good-tempered looking man. We ascertained that no person in A'kpoko had ever seen white men previously, which accounted for the alarm our presence had at first caused. A'kpoko is situated at the foot of one of the Dóma hills, and was by far the cleanest and driest town we had visited. On returning on board we were followed by numerous canoes, bringing ivory, fowls, eggs, and limes; Shea-butter is said to be plentiful, but none was produced. With these people a brisk trade was carried on for long after dark, and many purchases were made.

Hitherto we had invariably kept quite stationary on the Sundays, but, considering the rapid advance of the season, and the vast amount of work in store for us, I felt that I would not be justified in remaining at rest; I therefore determined to proceed during at least part of the day, and accordingly got under steam by six o'clock. A long island, nearly two miles in extent, on which we had landed the night previous for observations, was named after the oldest of British Admirals, "Sir Charles Ogle's Island." Beyond this the river took a northerly bend, and we found a channel with from four to five fathoms. A group of three islands, which we passed in this reach, I named after a celebrated traveller, though in far other climes, Sir John Richardson. About nine o'clock the water shoaled very suddenly in three casts of the lead from seven fathoms to two, and before the engine could be well stopped we were aground, but getting

Aug. 20.

off without difficulty we anchored, and giving the men time to clean themselves, rigged the church for service. In the afternoon the Krúmen having had three or four hours' rest, we again weighed anchor and steamed along a troublesome channel until dark. We passed several villages, chiefly on the right bank, but none of any size. We got the names of Otía, Ayáti, and Zúwo, on the north side, and Aghadúmo on the south. The following morning we had a very heavy dew and a thick mist, lasting until sunrise, after which we had to proceed cautiously, keeping the gig a-head sounding for a considerable distance. Two finely wooded islands, which we passed, were named respectively, "Isabella Island," and "Darwin's Island." We were aground several times, and on one occasion had to shift the deck cargo, and use a kedge. By the carelessness of one of the men a warp got entangled in the fan, which obliged us to anchor, rig sheers, and hoist the fan out of the water, after which it was too late to do much more work. The afternoon had been lowering, and just before dark a line of dark, muddy water was seen coming down the river, being the first indication of the approaching rise. This was attended with a slight squall, and as there were signs of a tornado, all requisite precautions were taken. We escaped, however, very well, merely experiencing a heavy thunder shower shortly after midnight.

Aug. 21.

Our fuel was becoming exhausted, and as we could see no wooding spot near, I became anxious about the means of replenishing our stock. A town named O'jogo was said to be not far distant, where good wood was reported to be abundant, for which we therefore pushed on as rapidly as the very troublesome navigation permitted. For nearly two days it was one incessant scene of getting aground, laying out anchors and kedges, shifting cargo, emptying and refilling the boilers, and sounding in the boats; but finally, by dint of considerable exertion, and of much labour on the part of the Krú-boys, we got into a deeper channel, and shortly afterwards anchored off O'jogo, a pretty little town situated on the eastern extremity of a rather extensive island. Mr. Richards, who had been a-head in the gig, returned on board with the intelligence that two white men were reported to have been very lately in a neighbouring town, on hearing which I immediately went ashore to see the chief. The village was at first rather empty and deserted, but we found that this was owing to a number of the inhabitants having been alarmed at the unprecedented, and to them inexplicable, appearance of a steamer in their waters, and having taken refuge in the adjoining woods. On arriving at the chief's residence, mats were spread for us under a widespreading tree, and presently the chief himself made his appearance; a fine-looking, rather tall, elderly man, carrying in his hand a long stick, from which was suspended a small brass bell, which he rang whenever he heard anything that pleased him. He expressed his thankfulness that white men had

Aug. 23.

reached his town, and hoped that we should prove his friends. I then asked him if it was the case that some strangers were near O'jogo, on which he said it was quite true, some white men had been at Keána, and that he believed they were still there. I informed him that one of our objects in coming up the river was to enquire after two travellers, and that as these might possibly prove to be the persons whom we sought, I should like either to go or to send a messenger to this place. The chief said he would despatch a messenger of his own, and, if I liked, one might go from me at the same time. Both Mr. May and myself were very anxious to visit Keána, believing that we could get our business much more quickly settled personally than by any deputy, besides being able to see a good deal of the country; but the chief advised us not to go, because there would be much detention, as we should have to stop at all the towns and villages we passed, to visit the chiefs, and to be looked at. I therefore thought of our Igbégbe party, and the two headmen expressing their willingness to proceed, I selected them for the purpose. The chief, whose names are O'robo and Amíshi, and also as king of the district, O'jogo, said that as soon as we had gone away he would call a council of his headmen, and make the necessary arrangements; so, not to cause any delay, we at once left, having as usual exchanged presents. A Keána-man walked to the beach with us, telling us that he had very lately returned from that town, where he had himself seen the two

THE NEW ADMINISTRATION.

strangers, who were living in tents, and he described the one as a broad-faced man with a beard, and the other as younger and more lightly made. I asked him on board, and getting Petermann's large atlas of the "Expedition to Central Africa," showed him the frontispiece, on which he at once selected the engraving of Dr. Barth, saying that was one of the faces, only the beard was wanting, and he then hesitated between the portraits of Drs. Overweg and Vogel, but at last selected the latter. This appeared so satisfactory, that I determined to remain until at least I could hear from Keána, and I gave my informant, Osábo, a present for the good news he had brought. Early the next morning Mr. Crowther and I visited O'robo to try to hurry movements, no easy task, and at length, by dint of urging, persuading, and bribing, got matters into a fair train. I then gave Zúri a letter for the "white men," a present for the King of Keána, and 8000 cowries for the subsistence of his party while travelling. At their own urgent request I gave them also a couple of muskets, to fire a salute on arriving at Keána, on which they promised that, although the regular journey was four days, they would perform it in three. This business being settled I got the chief to pay us a visit on board, and was rather surprised that, although he had never seen Europeans before, one of his first requests was for something to drink. As there was very little firewood in the village, we looked out for good wooding spots, and having found one set all hands to work. We then proceeded to make a further inspection of O'jogo, which is of very limited extent, washed by the river on the one side, and surrounded by dense forests, among which were numerous magnificent oil palms, of which the inhabitants make no use. Numbers of monkeys were seen gambolling among the trees, some displaying most wonderful feats of agility. I observed one in particular glide suddenly along a slender branch, and spring from the end of it to another tree, and this at the height of at least thirty feet from the ground.

Just opposite to O'jogo, on the southern side of the Bínue, lived a strange tribe named "Mítshi," of whom we had heard once or twice further down the river, as Mísi or Míshi, and who were described as a lawless set of cannibals. During one of our visits to O'jogo we met several of them, who had come across by canoe, and whose appearance certainly partially justified the accounts which had reached our ears. Wild in look, and ruder in dress, greatly tattooed, and carrying constantly with them their bows and arrows, these men seemed perfect impersonifications of savages. Yet, when spoken to, though at first rather shy, they entered freely into conversation with us; but they were unwilling to tell us much about themselves. At O'jogo they have not a very good character, being considered quarrelsome and treacherous, and we were accordingly warned against them, which, however, we fancied was done out of jealousy, as there had been a rather serious dispute between the two parties, only a few months previously, when several men had been killed on both sides. Wishing, therefore, to see more of this singular race, we selected a morning when a market was to be held at one of their villages, about a mile from our anchorage. As interpreter we had engaged a woman named Onúse, from O'jogo, who was the chief's sister, and occupied the important office of President of the Board of Trade, being supposed to attend to all commercial affairs, regulate prices, and watch the markets; but, when she came on board, she became afraid, and declined going, saying the Mítshis would not like to see so many white men. But on our visit we resolved to go without her, and accordingly Mr. Crowther, Dr. Hutchinson, and myself started in the gig, and pulled towards the town. The moment was inopportune, for, as we approached the place, we heard cries and lamentations, and saw numerous canoes shoving off in a very hurried manner, from one of the occupants of which we learnt that the Mítshis had, on some trifling pretext, plundered the market and driven off the O'jogo people. The landing-place was at the foot of a steep bank, of some eight or ten feet high, on the top of which was a number of natives, variously armed, in an extremely excited state. Thinking, possibly, that we had come to assist our O'jogo friends, they forbade our approach, and, as we drew closer in, bent their bows and drew their swords. I attempted to speak to them, and showed them some presents I had with me for them; but to no purpose. Their numbers momentarily increased, and their actions became more menacing. I had no arms with me, and even if I had it would have been most impolitic to employ them, my resolve being never to take to them on any pretext, except in absolute self-defence; besides which, a quarrel at such a time might have been fruitful in bad results in years to come, and would most certainly have left an unfavourable impression. The boat's crew now got alarmed, seeing the arrows and spears aimed at them, not more than ten or a dozen yards off, and, in their confusion, could scarcely use their oars. The interpreter too got frightened, which increased our difficulties, as we had now no means of parleying with our opponents. Seeing that it was of no use to delay longer, and that a further attempt at landing would only end in a scuffle, I resolved to forego our visit, trusting to some future opportunity. On enquiring afterwards at O'jogo for some explanation of this strange scene, I learnt that such conduct was by no means unfrequent. O'robo told me that the Mítshis were originally a set of slaves, who had rebelled, and, settling in part of A'kpoto, had greatly increased in numbers, had become independent, were spread over an extensive territory, and were very troublesome neighbours. Their language was quite peculiar, and did not resemble any of the surrounding dialects.*

* Koelle gives specimens of it under the name of Tíwi; others are printed in the appendix to Crowther's Journal.

THE NEW ADMINISTRATION.

The village at which we had tried to land was called "Akpáma," and a little further up was another called "Wantíli;" but each one is independent of the other. From this latter village we met, the same afternoon, several men, who appeared very friendly; and, not more than three days afterwards, we fell in with, in O'jogo, the very chief who had so opposed our landing at Akpáma. When questioned as to his reasons for his behaviour, he said that then he did not know much about us, but fancied we might be coming to take part against them, and further, that at that moment he could not have answered for the conduct of his people. I explained to him our wishes in going to visit him, and asked him to come on board and see us, which he promised to do, saying everything now was settled and understood, and he would tell his countrymen to trade with us. I believe that this unfortunate tribe, being against everyone, and everyone being against it, has rendered it extremely suspicious of any visitors, their rude minds not being able to comprehend anything beyond war and rapine, except trade, which they hold to mean every man enriching himself, when possible, at the expense of his neighbour. The Mítshis, as far as we could judge, are all wilder and less intelligent than any of the other African races with whom we have had intercourse, except the Báibai Djúkus. Their skins are usually, but not invariably dark, and the negro profile is well marked. Over each eyebrow is a series of short perpendicular cuts, and on each cheek they have usually a curved incision, thus ⁓◯ ; some are also marked on the arms and the sides, with various devices. Their clothing is but scanty, and the head is kept uncovered. Their arms are spears, short broad-pointed swords, and bows and arrows; the scabbards, made of light-coloured goatskin, are often prettily ornamented with indigo and camwood.

A great commotion was caused in O'jogo, one afternoon, by Mr. May's measuring a base line along the shore, for taking the breadth of the river by triangulation. The chief, with the heads of the war department, and several privy councillors, came down in great tribulation, supposing this was some preparatory step on our part to taking possession of his dominions. It took a long time to satisfy his doubts and anxieties, the explanation being rendered the more difficult from trigonometry and surveying not having formed a part of his early studies, but we gave him to understand that we were only measuring the river to know where to find deep water the next time we paid him a visit. The very same evening, our movements again excited alarm, as we were ashore for observations, having with us, as was our custom, our lantern. It was then very hard to persuade these exalted personages that we were not practising the black art, for what other reason could be assigned for our gazing at the stars, and bowing our heads towards the earth? We quieted their apprehensions for the time, but so strong was the impression, that next morning the old chief sent off a deputation to confer with us concerning these mysterious rites. To prevent all further disquietude I immediately went and called upon O'robo, and by Mr. Crowther's kind assistance, managed to explain our proceedings in a manner intelligible to the royal comprehension. This important business being finally settled, the chief introduced us to two embassies, from towns along the river, sent to O'jogo to make enquiries about the strange ship which had been reported to have made its appearance in the river. One of these, headed by two chiefs, named Akándo and Akpáke, was from Jefúlla, the King of A'kpa, while the other envoy, Gabídoku, came on behalf of Mohámma, King of Kóndoku. Being about to go on board, I invited these people to come with us and inspect our vessel, so that they might judge for themselves. We became great friends with O'robo, who sent us, as presents, on different occasions, large messes of food prepared according to the rules of Dóma cookery. One of these closely resembled what is known to Europeans along the coast as fúfu, and the other what is there also called palaver sauce. The first is made properly of yams, which ought to be cut into small pieces, dried, pounded, and boiled, and then made up into small rounded masses; but where yams are scarce or not to be had, it is prepared from Indian or dáwa (dower) corn treated much in the same way, but which does not eat so nicely. The sauce is a dark-coloured, oily stew, made from fish, fowl, meat, or all together, with palm oil, seasoned with capsicum, and often coloured green with the dried leaves of the baobab tree. Its appearance is rather against it, but when carefully prepared is far from unpalatable, and by the natives is reckoned a most savoury compound. The orthodox method of partaking of these delicacies is to have the fúfu in one calabash, and the sauce in another; then taking a piece of the yam in the fingers, dip it into the sauce, and transfer the whole to the mouth. In some of the more refined places, as at Igbégbe, little pellets of rice, strongly peppered, are served up in the palaver sauce, and render the dish more piquant.

One forenoon Mr. May and Mr. Harcus, while pulling about in the gig, being near Akpáma, landed, and having been very well received, succeeded in inducing the old chief whom I had invited to accompany them on board, and though a little shy at first, he soon gathered confidence, but no sooner was this visit known at O'jogo than another warning about the Mítshi character was sent to us. As another market was to be held next day, I wished to attend to see the articles for sale, and to endeavour to purchase a bullock, which we had been told was procurable on that side of the river. Alihéli, our interpreter, tried to persuade me not to go myself, and at last came and seizing hold of my hand, said, " You must not go, it no be good ;" so finding from this that there was still some prejudice against white men, and believing that my presence would only defeat our object, I gave up the idea. Alihéli went, but before he would start, insisted on having a pistol with him. He returned in the afternoon, having only been able to buy a dozen very inferior yams, and he reported that the people had behaved badly to him, and tried in the most open manner to steal some handkerchiefs from him. I examined the stock in trade of a woman who was going to the market, and found it to consist of a little antimony, some Indian and dáwa corn, and some small bags of salt. These latter contained in each about a small breakfast-cupful, the selling price of which was from 250 to 300 cowries. It was dark-gray coloured, and was said to be obtained from the neighbourhood of a small lake near Keána.

Day after day passed away, and still no tidings from our messengers. Rumours of arrivals from Keána frequently reached our ears, but, on enquiry, were found to have no foundation, and were raised, I have no doubt, to induce us to prolong our stay. I began to get restless and impatient, and at length, after eight days' delay, resolved, as my health was better adapted for the journey than that of any of the other Europeans, to go to Keána myself. I accordingly went to the chief to make arrangements for a guide, and had settled to start next morning, when my plans were suddenly altered. Osábo, the man who had originally given us the intelligence about the white travellers, visited us again this forenoon, and for the twentieth time, we made him repeat his story, and having it rendered word after word, discovered that a most important mistake had been made in the translation. Instead of his having reached O'jogo six days before our arrival, we now found that he had been there for six weeks, and it was previous to that date that he had seen the mysterious strangers; a view of the case which totally upset all our prior calculations. Supposing the travellers to have been Drs. Barth or Vogel, it was unlikely that they would have remained nearly two months in one town, where no effort had been made to detain them; moreover, if they were really the personages, the report of our stay at O'jogo must have long ere now reached them. Further delay would seriously have affected the ulterior results of our voyage, so I came to the determination to allow two more days, and finally to depart at daylight on the Monday morning following. Heavy rain had been falling, and the river was decidedly rising, a difference of upwards of five feet having been measured since the day we anchored. Our wooding party had been hard at work, and had been successful in getting excellent fuel, but the quantity cut was not great, owing to the hardness of the wood, and the imperfect tools they had to use. The only wood-cutting implements which the master had supplied, were small hand-hatchets, of poor material, the edges and handles of which were constantly breaking, and the labour of cutting with them was immense. Often have I watched a tall muscular Krúman, who, after hitting away with all his might, and perspiring at every pore, could only succeed in getting through a small branch, which would have been readily severed by two or three blows from a good American axe. We had not a single cross-cut saw, but one sledge-hammer, which was borrowed from the engine-room, and the only wedges were such as Mr. Guthrie managed to manufacture from spare soft-iron fire-bars, and which seldom, if ever, exceeded an inch-and-a-half in thickness. The wonder is, that, with such exceedingly faulty and imperfect tools, we ever managed to cut the quantity of wood we did. Visitors from towns further up the river continued to pour in upon us, and among others a man who had lost one foot and part of his leg by the bite of a crocodile, for whom Mr. Guthrie undertook to construct a serviceable wooden leg.

Our detention at O'jogo was not lost to us. Mr. May, with Mr. Guthrie's assistance, had constructed, out of a spare brass engine-cock with a double joint, a sextant-stand, which greatly facilitated him in the use of that instrument. Repeated observations of various kinds enabled our position to be fixed astronomically with considerable accuracy: the chronometers were carefully re-rated; the river was measured and surveyed, and the dip of the needle ascertained. Mr. Crowther got a vocabulary prepared of the Dóma, or as it is also termed the Arago language, and also secured a few Mítshi words; and, lastly, it enabled us to become well acquainted with the habits and disposition of the people, and to ascertain the resources of the country. Dóma, formerly powerful, has become of late a declining state, and has lost its independence. The principal provinces are Agatú, the westernmost district along the river, in which Dágbo and A'kpoko are situated; Dóma proper, in the centre and more inland; and Keána to the eastward of these. Dóma and Agatú have been subject to the Fulátas of Zaría for ten years, while Keána pays tribute to Báutshi. O'jogo, formerly in Dóma proper, has been for some years tributary to Keána, which was brought about as follows. A man named E'gu, son of a King of Dóma, was killed while residing at O'jogo. His mother was a Keána woman, so his father applied to the king of Keána to help him to avenge his death, and the matter was finally ended by O'jogo being seized by, or ceded to, Keána. Dóma at one time paid an annual contribution to Igára, and Keána was formerly to some extent tributary to Wukári. The language of this district is peculiar, and has affinities principally with the Núpe. The men are usually above the average height, many being six feet or upwards in stature. In person they are generally spare, their skins are usually very dark, the facial angle is considerable, and they are very intelligent. Among them I observed a peculiar shape of skull very frequently, namely elongated and greatly compressed. Many elderly persons of both sexes are to be seen, indicative of health and longevity. The hair of the men is usually kept wholly or partially close cut or shaved; the beard seldom makes any show until

CHAP. V.] THE NEW ADMINISTRATION. 113

about the age of thirty, and seldom ever exceeds two or three inches in length. Many of the women stain the eyelids with antimony, and a few colour the whole skin with camwood. The dress consists of a simple hip cloth, over which is another piece of cloth fastened round the waist, and reaching variously from just above the knee to half-way down the leg, and in cold weather a thin piece is thrown loosely over the shoulders, or by those who can afford them, Háusa tobes are worn. Children use no covering at all until about six or seven years of age, and they usually have round the neck, the wrists, and the hips, strings of beads or cowries, as amulets. Women wear a large piece of cloth from the waist to the knees, leaving the breast generally uncovered. The principal ornaments in fashion are armlets or wristlets, either fine brass ones bought at the Confluence, or smaller ones from the Háusa markets or from Wukári; but sometimes they are made by loosely twisting round the arm thick brass wire rods. Rings are mostly of brass or copper, more rarely of ivory; anklets are seldom worn; necklaces of beads or of pebbles, or charms of cowries, are in constant use. The ear-ornaments are usually small bits of pebble thrust through the lobe. The men generally carry, as arms, swords from twelve to twenty inches in length, slung over the shoulder; a sharp-pointed knife, with a hollow handle, through which the hand is thrust; and also long-handled spears with pointed heads. Less frequently bows and arrows appear, these being reserved for warfare or hunting. I saw one man with a rough leather sheath, made of bullock's-hide, extending from the wrist nearly to the elbow, to prevent the skin being chafed by the bow-strings, while on the right forefinger was worn a short iron thimble for the same purpose. The form of salutation, when an inferior presents himself, is by kneeling down, bending the head towards the ground, throwing dust against the forehead and on the head, and repeating some words of greeting, which ceremony, if the comer be of sufficient consequence, is repeated by the other party. But if two friends meet on the road they merely shake hands or embrace each other. There is no general national mark in Dóma, but many of the inhabitants are seen with ten or a dozen curved lines along each cheek; and among people from Keána, especially women, I have noticed, under the left eye, two rows of very short perpendicular lines, thus, ⁂ Polygamy is here, as elsewhere, customary, but is not carried to any very great extent. One singular custom prevails, at least near O'jogo. The sisters of the chief never marry, but are allowed to select any man they choose, and to give him up when they get tired of him. We saw one woman who had a family of eleven children, most of whom had different fathers. A very curious currency exists in Dóma, and is known as far as Katshína. It is of iron made in the form of a small hoe, with a long spike at one end, thus,

These are tied up in bundles of a dozen, or thereabouts, and thirty-six are said to be the ordinary price of a slave. This strange money is in Dóma and in Korórofa called Akíka, by the Mítshi I'bia, and in Háusa Ageléma.* With this, as with most other African tribes, the early part of the evening is the time when most of the food is prepared. It is then that their corn is ground, the bread baked, the fish or meat cooked, and their beer brewed; all these operations being exclusively in the hands of the female part of the population. To grind their corn a trunk of a small tree is hollowed out, into which the grain is put, while two, or sometimes three women, standing around, with long heavy sticks beat it and pound it, delivering their blows in excellent time; it is then roughly sifted and reduced to meal, by rubbing it between two stones. I observed a curious game played by boys at O'jogo. A little conical pit, some three or four inches deep, is dug in the sand, at the bottom of which is placed on its base a shell, prepared by removing the body whorl and mouth of a species of *Limacolarius*, and leaving the conical spire. A number of boys sit round, all holding in their hands a number of similar shells, and each in his turn spins one of these into the pit; most of which, when they cease turning, fall resting on the side. At length one falling settles on its base, apex upwards, the fortunate possessor of which wins all the shells which happen to be at the moment in the hole.

* *Vide* Appendix B.

Crocodiles are very abundant in the vicinity of O'jogo, and are frequently killed by the natives. Another allied and very singular inhabitant of the river is a False-Gavial (*Mecistops*), of which my assistant purchased a skull for me, the only one we saw or heard of during our voyage. I got some specimens of a fine vulture (*Gypohierax Angolensis*), well distinguished by its clearly-marked, showy plumage.

About noon on the Saturday before we left this place, Mr. Taylor said to me he had been thinking of having one of the trade canoes sent to the Confluence to trade until our return. To this I made, of course, no objection, only wondering how such a plan had not been sooner thought of, and not left to the very last moment. The canoe was at some distance wooding, so I at once recalled it, had it cleaned out and made ready, and a cargo having been got ready by great exertion on the part of Dr. Hutchinson, it was almost all shipped by night. The next morning I selected eight Krúmen and three others, an ample crew, and besides quite as many as could be spared, though more were urgently asked for. At Mr. Taylor's request, I allowed the second engineer to accompany the canoe, Mr. Guthrie finding that he could be well spared. Mr. Crawford, the junior supercargo, was selected to have charge of the trading concerns, so the party consisted of thirteen in all, with an easy run down before them with the stream. While getting ready their provisions, a cask of sugar was found to be missing, which caused a great commotion, so much so, that the canoe did not leave us until some miles above O'jogo, in the hopes of the lost commodity turning up. As soon as I heard the report, finding that only six pounds of sugar were in the ship, I immediately ordered it to be put aside in case of sickness, and until our return to Fernando Po we were entirely without this luxury; there the missing cask was discovered in a warehouse, having been left behind in the confusion of starting.

Above O'jogo the current ran nearly three knots, the river being for a short distance confined between banks, behind which was finely wooded rising land, where also oil-palms were noted for the last time. Along the river edge, generally partially embedded in the banks, were large unshapely looking blocks of rock, bearing evident marks of igneous action. A village on the right bank, named Ajáma, is the first stage on the road to Keána. About noon we anchored off a considerable town on the same side, where we landed and visited the chief. The town is called Rógan-Kóto, and though in Dóma, is an I'gbira settlement, whence its name; Kóto being the Háusa synonyme of I'gbira, and Rógan meaning huts or sheds. By the inhabitants it is known as Ajéwon-I'gbira, but the former is its more usual designation. It was first built about twenty-eight years ago, and though nominally independent, yet pays tribute, a kind of black-mail, to Keána. It is surrounded by a wall, with numerous loop-holes for firing arrows

Sept. 4.

through. The year previous to our visit this town had suffered severely from an attack by a party from Láfia Beribéri, whose return was greatly dreaded. Rógan-Kóto is by the Djúku inhabitants of Korórofa called "Pumávo," and by the Mítshis "Djáshi-A'gbira," which latter means "I go to I'gbira." Jáda, the chief, regretted much that we could not make any stay, but promised to trade with us on our return. We here met the man for whom Mr. Guthrie had made a wooden leg, so we asked him on board to have it fitted on, which was done, much to his delight. The hour and a-half that we remained at anchor off this place was not wasted by its pushing inhabitants, many of whom came off in haste, bringing with them any articles they had to dispose of. In Rógan-Kóto I observed some sandstone rock, the strata being nearly horizontal, and the only instance in the Bínue, where secondary rocks were visible near the river. On the south side was still the Mítshi country and nearly opposite Rógan-Kóto is one of their towns, Abágwa, from which people frequently come over for trading purposes. On a large island immediately to the eastward are two towns, named Kóndoko and A'kpa, being those parts from which messengers had been sent to inquire about the "Pleiad." They are inhabited by people from Korórofa, and being the first place along the river where Djúku tribes are met, they are known in I'gbira, Igára, and Núpe, as A'kpa. About three o'clock we had to anchor to get up steam, so Mr. May and I took advantage of the short delay to get a set of sights, and accordingly landed on a sandy beach. While Mr. May was arranging the artificial horizon a band of natives, with spears and bows and arrows, from A'kpa, who had been for some time watching us, rushed towards us, but when within some half a dozen yards of us they suddenly stopped, on which I went towards them, holding out my hand, and showing that I was quite unarmed. Seeing this they laid down their spears, and on our making signs to them to keep quiet while we made our observations, they all knelt down, regarding us with great astonishment. We had nothing to give them but a few bright glass buttons, which, however, pleased them much. Further on in the afternoon we passed another large, walled town, inhabited partly by Djúku, partly by I'gbira people. This, which is named Abítshi, is said to have been founded about forty-five years ago, by a band of slaves from Iddá; it forms the easternmost limit of the range of canoes from the Confluence, and with Rógan-Kóto, is the principal place where the commodities of the upper and lower Bínue are exchanged. It is situated on the west side of an extensive island, which I have named "Clarendon Island." During the greater part of this day we had seen in the distance the peaks of two hills on the Dóma side of the river, and as the day advanced their outline became more and more distinct. They are not very elevated, the highest not exceeding from 450 to 500 feet, and the other being from seventy to eighty feet less, but from the country to the westward of them being flat, they are visible from a considerable distance, and form good leading marks. The one I named "Mount Beecroft," after the lamented gentleman who had been expected to head our expedition, and the other "Mount Æthiope," so called from the steamer in which many of his African explorations were performed. Towards sunset we reached another long, extended island, nearly in the middle of the river, and proceeding along its south shore, anchored abreast of it. From some villagers whom Mr. May and I fell in with, while looking for a landing-place, we learnt that the eastern boundary of the Mítshi country is somewhere opposite to this island, which we named after Captain Washington, the present distinguished hydrographer of the Admiralty.

The following morning we continued our onward course, passing numerous islets, scattered in various directions, and seeing several villages on both sides of the river. A fine range of hills ran nearly parallel with the river on the north side, one extremity touching the water. This I entitled the "Ellesmere Range," while the central peak, some 600 feet in height, was called "Mount Egerton," and two others of the hills were denominated "Mounts Latham and Christison." Judging from the character of the débris, and from the appearance in some breaks on their sides, they are composed of unstratified rocks. Among them is one pretty, little round-topped hill, covered with a beautiful green sward, which received the title of "Mount Jessy." During a temporary

Sept. 4.

stoppage, a canoe with a single man ventured alongside, from whom we learnt that we were now in Korórofa, and that the river is by its inhabitants designated Nú, but is also known as the Bínue. The inhabitants and language of this extensive territory, which is strictly confined to the south side of the river, are known as Djúku. Just beyond the "Ellesmere range" the current runs very strongly, averaging four knots, and the river takes a northerly bend. The banks on the south side are very high, and along the top, picturesquely placed nearly at the foot of a table-mountain, we could see a village, which we afterwards found to be A'nyishi. The hill which rises directly from the water side, attaining an altitude of some 400 feet, was called "Mount Herbert." Behind, and partially isolated from the "Ellesmere range," we discovered another prettily shaped hill, which I named, after the naturalist of the voyage of the "Samarang," "Mount Adams." In this beautiful locality, favoured as it seemingly is in situation and in soil, secured by its elevation from the rising of the river, free from swamps, and abounding in healthy situations, not a trace of a human habitation could be seen, nor was there visible the smallest attempt at cultivation. Many hills near this place have a very peculiar aspect, some being quite isolated, and rising with steep sides almost suddenly from flat land near the river. To one such, on the south side, with a long table-top, I gave the name of "Mount Trénabie," while another, on the opposite shore, abrupt towards the south-west, but sloping to the eastward, I called "Mount Traill," after a former esteemed preceptor, now at an age when most others would be seeking repose from the cares and toils of literature and science, the learned and indefatigable editor of an eighth edition of the "Encyclopædia Britannica." Fresh breezes blowing daily up the stream, we got a spare forecastle awning fitted as a temporary foresail, which sensibly affected our progress. Our speed, too, was increased, by having only one of the iron canoes in tow, the two of them being a great drag. Though no towns or villages could be seen to enliven the prospect, yet everything around us wore a smiling aspect. The river, still upwards of a mile in breadth, preserved its noble appearance, the neighbouring soil teemed with a diversified vegetation, and the frequent recurrence of hill and dale pleased and gratified the eye. Nor was animal life wanting, for from out mast-head we enjoyed the novel sight of a large herd of elephants, upwards of a hundred in number, crossing a little streamlet, not much more than a mile from us. Two large islands were again passed, one of which, of a peculiar, somewhat triangular shape, was named after Admiral Smyth, deeply interested in all African discovery, while the other, nearly one entire forest, received the title of "Hooker Island," after the no less amiable than distinguished botanist of Kew.

We had all day been anxiously looking out for signs of man, and in the afternoon were highly pleased by discovering a large walled town on

Sept. 6.

the south side, off which we accordingly anchored, and though it was rather late, I immediately landed. Previous to our arrival numbers of people had been observed along the banks, but on the approach of the gig they all disappeared, and when we reached the shore the only person left to receive us, was a solitary individual, who between fear and excitement could hardly utter a single word. I walked up to him, extending my hand, which he surveyed most suspiciously, and at length touched with as much reluctance as he would a piece of red-hot iron, but finding that it did not burn him, and that we were quite friendly, he threw down his spear, and danced and shouted for joy, exclaiming that he would lead us to the town, which was at some little distance. Having to pass some marshy ground, he insisted on carrying me across some streamlets, shouting all the time at the top of his voice in Háusa, "White men, white men! the Nazarenes have come; white men good, white men rich, white men kings; white men, white men!" Presently his shouts were responded to, and we saw a large band, fully armed, rush along a narrow path, vociferating wildly. Their approach had certainly something threatening in its look, so much so that our boat's crew, getting alarmed, scampered back to the boat, leaving Mr. May, Mr. Crowther, Dr. Hutchinson, and myself, with Mr. Richards, and my assistant, to face the strangers. Even our valiant little interpreter, Aliheli, felt insecure, as seizing my arm he whispered hurriedly "We must go back to ship."

We, however, continued to advance, and presently encountered the rude-looking throng. On hearing that we were friends, the leading man first threw himself wildly into the arms of our conductor, and then flying headlong against me, grasped my hand and shook it vehemently. Each one of our party had his own body of admirers, and in particular Mr. May was quickly cut off and surrounded, and became a distinct centre of attraction. Of the remainder of the crowd, some ran rapidly towards us, presenting the butt-ends of their spears; others drew their bow-strings without arrows in them; many threw themselves on the ground and went through an extemporaneous course of gymnastics, and all shouted aloud. Every one appeared in an ecstacy of delight, while our guide continued to exert his lungs in such an extraordinary manner, that we were afraid he would rupture a blood-vessel, and I am quite certain he got off cheaply if he had nothing beyond a simple sore-throat. After this wild welcome had subsided into some semblance of a merely enthusiastic greeting, I told the most consequential-looking man that we wished to visit his king, to whom he at once conducted us. We went along a narrow pathway, only sufficient for single file, enclosed between tall dáwa corn, the stalks of which waved high over our heads. Presently we arrived at the gate of the town, strongly palisaded, and crossed the ditch which surrounded the walls. Numbers of astonished natives, of all ages and sexes, lined the way, all the men carrying spears,

THE NEW ADMINISTRATION.

swords, knives, and bows and arrows. We soon reached the king, who, in the centre of a large crowd, attended by the head men in the place, stood to receive us under the shade of a wide-spreading tree. I approached and saluted him, and introduced my party, with all whom he shook hands, and then looking upwards said, he thanked God that white men had come to his country. I rapidly explained to him our wishes and our objects, adding, that as it was nearly dark, we should pay him a longer visit next day. Numbers now pressed forwards to shake hands with us, and about us there could not have been fewer than from 400 to 500 people, mostly armed. On our return to our boat we were numerously escorted, and previous to our embarking I gave our stentorian friend a handkerchief, and a small snuff-box, which seemed nearly to overpower him. During the evening a present of some jars of beer from the king arrived, and from the messengers we were able to obtain some particulars about the place. Its name is Gándiko, and, though in Korórofa, is a Púlo* settlement. It originated in the mission of a Púlo force, chiefly composed of slaves, to attack Wukári, in which they failed; but afterwards, instead of returning, they preferred founding towns for themselves. They intermarried with the Djúku, and have since become very numerous. The district is named Zhibú, and a few

---

* Púlo is the correct name for the people often styled Fuláta, being their own designation. In Háusa they are called Fúlo and Fuláni; Fuláta is their Bornuese title.

miles further up the river is a town of the same name, the principal one of these settlements. Close to Gándiko are two other towns, Gankéra and I'bi. The languages spoken are principally Púlo and Djúku, but Háusa is also understood by many. About one-half of the people are nominal Muhammadans, the remainder being Pagans.

Early next day messengers again came off from the king to wish us "good morning," and to ask us when we would be ashore. Heavy rain considerably retarded our movements, but about half-past nine, having first sent off a wooding party, we started for Gándiko. According to custom we first called on the Geladima, or prime minister, who, on being informed *officially* of our object, conducted us to the king's abode. There we were received in the usual manner, and having interchanged compliments were about to discourse on other matters, when the arrival of the king of Gankéra was announced. There seemed to be some doubts on the minds of the Gándiko magnates whether the royal visitor should be admitted, but we requested them not to regard our presence, but to act according to the customs and etiquette of the place. They were accordingly introduced, after which I told them we had come from the white man's country to view this land, to make friends with the chiefs and the people, and to talk of trade and of improvement. All present having plainly expressed their approbation, the king said he was convinced that without intercourse with white strangers his country would never flourish. I then gave A'ma and his Geladima presents, and requested the king of Gankéra to send on board, on which a similar present would be ready for him. A'ma then requested my acceptance of a fine sheep and of a large pitcher of beer, after which we left. Gankéra not being far off, we went towards it, and after a ten minutes' walk through corn-fields reached it. We found it much to resemble Gándiko, only that it was larger, and better laid out. In these towns the huts are less crowded, and have about them little plots of ground planted with vegetables, being the first signs of horticulture we had met with. On the sides and roofs of the huts were trained pumpkins, gourds, and other cucurbitaceous species, while in their gardens were numerous plants of ochro (*Hybiscus*), and graceful papaws (*Carica papaya*) with still unripe fruit. In a little market we found women bartering beer for bundles of corn of different kinds. Hearing that there were horses we asked to see them, and were accordingly shown several fine Arabs, nicely groomed and cared for, and in fine condition. In each stable hung oval-shaped shields, made of elephants' hides, large enough to cover and protect both rider and steed. The possession of horses is one of the distinguishing marks of the Púlo tribes, one too which adds greatly to their power and to the terror of their name. Most of the inhabitants were clad in native-made clothes, but some appeared in garments made of goat-skins, while a few wore still more scanty coverings of green leaves. During our walk we again met the old chief, Garíke, who made me a present of a mat. Annual excursions for the purpose of collecting slaves are made from these towns chiefly against the Mítshis, which may account for the suspicions they entertained of us, especially as many of the Púlo people are light-coloured. It was in Gándiko and Gankéra that we first met with any of this noted race, well distinguished from all other Africans in feature and in figure. Here, from admixture with Djúku blood, their skins were darker, and more of the Negro countenance prevailed than in their own true domains; and the two chiefs, A'ma and Garíke, had marked Ethiopic faces. The ship was all day crowded with visitors, and some trade was done, upwards of a hundred pounds of ivory having been purchased, chiefly for light calicoes. A Mallam, one of our guests, gave me secretly, and as an invaluable present, a small paper with quotations in Arabic from the Kurân. While on shore, seeing a fruit which was new to me,* I went to gather some specimens, but succeeded at the expense of being badly stung by a multitude of little red ants, diminutive pests capable of inflicting wounds quite out of proportion to their magnitude. A Krúman, who assisted me, was so covered with them that to get rid of them he flung himself headlong into the river.

We weighed anchor early next morning, and by the aid of a good breeze went up rapidly. About noon we anchored off a large town, which we

Sept. 8.

* A species of *Kigelia.*

believed to be Zhibú, and some natives being visible on the banks, Mr. Crowther and I landed to speak to them. They were at first rather shy, but on my mentioning that we were desirous of waiting on the king, one man said he would go and announce us and return as soon as he could. We therefore pulled on board, and in about half an-hour three special messengers arrived to welcome us, and to conduct us when ready. We therefore started at once, and found on the shore a large armed escort waiting for us. The town is situated nearly a mile from the river, on a rising ground, the country around being well cleared to allow of an extensive view and to prevent surprise by an enemy. On our road we encountered a fine specimen of African travelling. Right across the path, extending some twenty or thirty yards in all directions, was a deep, muddy pool. Double it we could not, as at either end was a marshy ditch, so we had to cross it mounted on the shoulders of our Krúmen, who, although mostly tall men, were immersed above the hips. This little obstruction passed, we proceeded along a field planted with ground-nuts (*Arachis hypogea*), and reaching the gates entered into the city. The circular huts, with thickly thatched roofs, are disposed with some degree of order and regularity, so as to form streets, or rather lanes. On approaching the palace we were requested to halt in a large open space, fronting a substantial looking building with a dome-like top, surmounted by a long spire crowned with an ostrich-egg. Presently an officer approached,

K

who from his *distingué* look and elegant carriage must have been Lord Chamberlain, or at least Master of Ceremonies, accompanied by an individual bearing gracefully in his hand a long white wand, who probably held the office of Usher of the White Rod. These evidently important personages advanced on tip-toe and whispered a communication to the officer who had conducted us, who, in his turn, waving his arm desired us to follow him. This we did, and entering the palace precincts passed through an entry chamber, and proceeding along a winding-passage reached the reception hall, where we found ourselves in the august presence of Bohári, alias Zúmbade, monarch of Zhibú. I advanced and saluting him in Háusa, shook his hand, which being done by the rest of the party we seated ourselves on mats. Our interview was much in the usual style, the king expressing his satisfaction at our arrival, and saying that neither he nor any of his people had ever seen a white man before. After talking of trade, we were asked how long we were going to remain; to which I replied that we should stay all next day, but that afterwards we must try to get farther up the river. The king said that we should not be able to proceed, as there were numerous rocks and banks; but I told him that nevertheless we should make the attempt. I then gave him a sword and brass scabbard, a red cloak, some white calico, and a looking glass, in return for which he offered a fine sheep and a calabash with butter. He then retired, and calling on our interpreter asked if we would purchase slaves. I replied "certainly not;" adding that white men did not buy other men, as they considered that to be wrong and sinful. Bohári had evidently some idea of this from his not asking the question openly, but doing it in a secret manner. He then sent an attendant for a Háusa tobe, which on his return the man put on Dr. Hutchinson, he being the tallest and stoutest of our party, qualifications which in Africa are held in great admiration. The king is only a half Púlo, if so much, and has a sensual disagreeable look. His Geladima again was a most intelligent, civil man, and extremely friendly with us. We walked through the town, which is very clean, and thickly populated, and is enclosed by strong palisading. The inhabitants are mostly Moslemin, but have no mosques, their devotions being performed in the open air. Numbers of visitors presenting themselves, as there were no canoes, I kept one of the ship's boats running to and fro all the afternoon. The country opposite to us on the north side of the river, was Báutshi, and we were told that Koróorfa is often, from its capital, named Wukári. One man who had been up the river and knew the Fáro or Páro, said that a canoe could go from Zhibú to Hamarúwa in from thirteen to sixteen days. I inquired for the name Zánfira, given to the river in Petermann's Atlas, but no one recognised it. The Koróorfa name is, as I have already mentioned, Nú, but the term in more general use is Bínue.

K 2

Early next morning I went ashore to get a set of magnetic observations, but was much interrupted by crowds of curious spectators. A more serious inconvenience was, that as every one carried with them steel in some shape or another, the needle vibrated so much as quite to prevent any reading off, and being alone I could not by any means manage to keep the people at a sufficient distance. About eight o'clock the king rode down, on which I asked him to come on board, which he declined doing. About an hour afterwards, as he still remained on the banks, I sent Mr. Richards to give him another invitation, which this time he accepted, provided that all the natives already on board were sent ashore. This was done, and I then found that his majesty felt annoyed because some of his subjects had dared to commence trading before he had returned our visit. As soon as he reached the ship a salute of three guns was fired, after which he was led round the ship. He set his affection on a tumbler and a wine-glass, which were given him, and he then asked for a bottle of medicine, which was made up for him. On his return to terra-firma he was surrounded by courtiers, some of whom kissed his hands, others his feet, while the people around clapped their hands. The royal visit over, business had to be attended to. The steward went ashore and opened a small market under a tree, and was most successful in procuring a good stock of fresh provisions, in the shape of sheep, goats, fowls and ducks, the latter a large and very delicious bird, closely allied to the Muscovy duck. Boats were sent to bring off traders and visitors, and in a short time the decks were crowded. Some Háusa merchants happened to be passing through Zhibú at the time of our arrival, who had been purchasing ivory in Korórofa, and they, of course, preferred selling it at once to taking it to a distant market. Dr. Hutchinson, at the close of a busy day, found that he had purchased 620 pounds of ivory, including many fine teeth of hippopotami. The goods most in demand were white calico and handkerchief pieces; cowries were not understood, and were taken only by the Háusa men. I bought many ornaments as specimens, chiefly wristlets, rings, hair-pins, &c., of brass and copper. Corn-fields are numerous and extensive around Zhibú, the principal kinds being maize and dawa corn. Gero, which is also cultivated, is abundant along the river, but is not to be found to the westward of the Kwóra, except in a few places in Dahómi. The value of these grains to the African can hardly be properly estimated: they supply a large portion of his daily food: ground fine and baked they form his bread; in moist cakes they are known as túo or fúfu; fermented they yield him beer; the refuse helps to feed his poultry and his goats; and in war the commissariat contains principally heads of maize, previously roasted and mixed with pepper and salt. Strange to say yams are not grown here, nor are they to be obtained in any quantity beyond Rógan-Kóto, from which it may be inferred that their cultivation is either neglected by or unknown to the tribes near the river, except those of the I'gbira race, who, wherever found, either in their own country or settled in other districts, have always a keen eye towards the useful, whether in commerce, in the arts, or in agriculture.

CHAPTER VI.

THE UPPER BÍNUE.

WE left our anchorage off Zhibú on the morning of Sunday the 10th of September, and shortly afterwards discovered, to the northward, at a distance inland of from fifteen to twenty miles, a range of mountains, among which were three distinct peaks, the highest of which I named Mount Humboldt, and on the south side we saw, afar off, a curious isolated conical hill, which was called "Mount Daubeny." During our stay at Zhibú, Mr. Harcus had fitted a spare quarter-deck awning as a square-sail, and on being tried it was found to answer capitally. About ten o'clock we anchored for church, and did not again proceed until the afternoon. The course of the river was more winding than usual, and trended well to the northward; the banks were mostly marshy, and no traces of villages could be detected. In the evening we had considerable difficulty in finding a spot to land on for observations; but, after pulling about, got to a grassy islet, with a bank some four or five feet above the water. We jumped up, and making our Krúmen trample down a clear

Sept. 10.

space, planted a stand and fixed the artificial horizon; but scarcely had Mr. May taken his sextant in his hand, when a loud grunt, in most unpleasant proximity, announced that we were not the only possessors of the soil. On looking about, we found we were right in a hippopotamus track, that the animal was alarmed and wished to get away, and might at any moment be expected to rush along, upsetting us and our instruments. Pleasant enough certainly, but we were even then ignorant of how highly we had been favoured, as presently a similar sound of disapproval reached our ears from the opposite side, and we now discovered that, about three yards from where we stood, the little path diverged in two directions, and that each position was occupied by the enemy. What was to be done? If we retreated ignominiously, all chance of ascertaining our latitude was gone, as the planet was close to the meridian, and clouds were forming. A hasty plan of a campaign was sketched out, in which it was provided that, should our opponents charge in too great force, each of us should seize a part of our gear, dive into the boat, and try to escape in the darkness. In the meantime, while Mr. May attended to the scientific and engineering departments, I was stationed as an advanced corps, to keep the foe in check, which I effected by means of our invaluable bull's-eye lantern, the light from which I directed first along the one path, then along the other. The minutes certainly seemed unusually prolonged, but at length Jupiter was benignant, and condescended to shine into the mercury from the other side of the meridian. The angle was read off and noted, our traps were secured, and we hastily embarked and shoved off; but we had not got many yards away, when a loud splash behind us announced the triumphant descent of the river-horse. Our anchorage was near the shore, which, during the night, exposed us to the blood-thirsty attacks of unusually voracious mosquitoes.

The following day was wet and cloudy, and we wended our tortuous course among innumerable sand-banks and islets. Sometimes the banks were clad with an elegant fan-palm, not previously seen, but which became extremely abundant as we advanced. Another isolated sugar-loaf hill, rising to the northward to the height of some 400 feet, I named after the amiable and highly gifted Professor Edward Forbes, little then dreaming that, among the first European intelligence I afterwards received, would be the sad news of his premature, his irreparable loss.

Sept. 11.

The landscape now was greatly varied; instead of, as formerly, our view being bounded by tree-tops on both sides, our range of vision was vastly extended. Nor was it even restricted by the low hills which, along either side, confined the valley of the river, for, far beyond, the eye could detect lofty eminences and mountain peaks. One group, higher by far than any we had already encountered, was visible along the horizon in the extreme south, and from which we must have been distant from thirty to forty miles. This Mr. May entitled the Albemarle range, while two singular-looking peaks were denominated "Mount Keppel," and "Mount St. Jean d'Acre." At the western extremity two other high and remarkable mountains were named Mounts "Herschel" and "Biot." On the 12th we passed the first affluent which we had observed since we left the little O'kwa, below Pánda. It is of inconsiderable size and flows from the southward, but forms at its junction a small fluviatile delta. We made enquiries afterwards about it, but could never accurately learn the name. Some told us that it was called Bankúndi, and that a few miles up it was a small village called Akám, while others again reversed this, naming the river Akám, and the town Bankúndi. Immediately above this the main river suddenly contracted, until not more than 200 to 250 yards across, along which the current ran like a sluice, being from five to six knots. Although this narrow rapid was not above half a mile in length, it took us fully three quarters of an hour to get beyond it, nor could we have managed it had there not been a little breeze to fill our sails, as, when under steam alone, when the wind fell, we just stemmed the current, without advancing an inch. Further up, the river again widened into a large stream, and we made more headway. Fuel was beginning to become scarce, and we began to look out anxiously for a place to get a supply. No good wooding spot could be seen from the mast-head; so, about noon, we anchored opposite to a place where were some small trees, and hauling alongside the bank, sent all hands on shore. In spite of several heavy showers a good deal was cut before night; but it was green and small, and we were obliged to remain all next day to chop it up fit for the fires, now a very laborious operation, as the hatchets were much impaired by continual use. Our anchorage was at a very peculiar spot, as just ahead a double stream poured upon us; one, the smaller of the two, came nearly directly from the east, while the other ran from the northward, doubling a long projecting cape, which was named Point Lynslager. We subsequently ascertained that some miles further up the river diverged into two branches, enclosing a wide, irregular island. On this point, where some observations were taken, we found some very recent human footsteps, probably of natives who had landed from a canoe. Some specimens were here shot of a Skimmer, the *Rhynchops orientalis* of Rüppell, with its singular projecting lower mandible. The green wood burning badly, little steam could be kept up, and our advance was slow, and we were further retarded by two tornadoes, each of which obliged us to anchor for a time. One law attending these heavy squalls is, that near a river they almost invariably follow its course and blow down it, and thus their direction is, locally, very varied. We encountered a good many during our stay, and did not observe a single exception to this. Their general origin is from the eastward, but when they approach a stream they deviate either to the northward or to the southward, according to its direction. A large dry tree was discovered near the bank on the south side, which looked as if it had been seared with lightning, and which, in the impoverished condition of our fuel-bunkers, could not be quietly passed by. The water being deep we anchored close in, and warped alongside the shore, and speedily every available hand was busy wooding. Boughs within reach were quickly detached, and a rope having been thrown over a larger branch, some Krúmen climbed up, and by dint of hard cutting and chopping, in due time little was left remaining but the parent trunk, which was of too great dimensions to admit of its being attacked with our playthings. It was, indeed, a hard enough task to reduce what was already on the ground to a portable condition, and it was almost painful to watch our fine, muscular fellows labouring and toiling to so little purpose, and aiming at a miserable stick blows which, with proper instruments, would have felled a bullock. Off some of the neighbouring trees, and from damp ground around, I collected some very interesting lichens and fungi, and, imbedded in a species of the latter, I found specimens of a beautifully marked fungus-eating beetle. In breaking up an old hollow branch, I came upon a nest of mice with very long tails, and managed to secure the old one and four young ones.

Sept. 14.

THE UPPER BI'NUE.

The morning of the second day we spent at this place two canoes were seen going down the river along the opposite bank. A bright-coloured flag was hoisted to attract the crews, and after a cautious approach and long parley, they drew near and came on board. Two of the people were very intelligent, and gave us much information, none of which pleased us more than hearing that we had quitted Korórofa and were now entering the province of Hamarúwa. The opposite bank was still, however, Báutshi, but some hills which were visible along the horizon towards the east were in Adamáwa, and were named the "Fumbína Mountains." They told us that they were going up the little river which we had passed a few days before, to a town named Wúnobo or Wúrobo, and that they had left Tshómo, a village beyond Hamarúwa, only two days previously. This news was very cheering, as it inspired us with fresh hope, seeing, moreover, that the waters were still gradually rising. In the evening while Mr. May and Mr. Harcus were on the bank taking observations, a growl was heard not very far from them, and presently one of the crew, who was ashore casting clear a rope, rushed towards them giving the alarm of a leopard. Being very intent on their occupation, they paid little heed either to the warning or to the growling, until suddenly the latter was repeated in a most threatening and unmistakable manner close to their elbow. The interruption was most ill-timed, as very few minutes more would have brought Vega to her meridian height, but as an appeal to the beast's generosity or respect for science would probably have been treated with contempt, nothing remained but to shut up the apparatus and to make a hasty retreat. The alarm being given, lights and rifles were speedily in requisition, but nothing could be seen of the intruder, which had most likely been attracted by the smell of a goat killed at sunset. Our shore work being finished the warp was let go, and the "Pleiad" swung to her anchor in the stream, carrying as passengers legions of mosquitoes, destined to revel for the first time in their lives on white men's blood.

By the first peep of light we were once more screwing ahead, our eyes fixed on the Fumbína Mountains; but the day was unpropitious to us, as we were several times aground, besides being delayed by a sharp tornado, so that we did not make above a dozen miles. During the following day, which was Sunday, I was obliged to keep all the Krúmen busily at work for several hours splitting wood, as our stock of small timber was already burnt. I felt considerably indisposed, and was not able to attend to matters, so that I was not sorry to be able to have a little rest. Next forenoon we anchored off a village on the left bank, named Zhirú, and I landed with Mr. Crowther to speak to some natives. They were friendly and asked us to the town, which was a little distance from us; but feeling very unwell I had to return on board, after which Mr. May, Mr. Crowther, and Dr. Hutchinson visited the town. The principal personage they

Sept. 20.

met with was the Hamarúwa governor, named Imóru, the rest of the inhabitants being Aborigines, speaking a dialect of Djúku. From the advance of the river the neighbourhood of the village was a perfect swamp, and looked very unhealthy. Before we started next morning, the steward went on shore to try to get some provisions to buy, but was unsuccessful. The governor came off to see me, a sharp, but civil and intelligent man, with true Púlo cast of countenance. The current ran strong, but with the aid of a fresh breeze we advanced slowly. All the smaller branches of wood having been consumed, nothing remained on board but large blocks of timber, which with our poor wedges and want of hammers were most difficult to reduce to manageable pieces. At length we hit upon the plan of blasting, using, of course, a very small charge of powder. Mr. May was now taken ill, showing decided symptoms of remittent fever, so I had to take him in hand. We were overtaken by a canoe in which was the governor of Zhirú, who brought us as a present, the hind quarter and leg of a buffalo, which had been killed by the hunters that morning. The meat not looking very tempting, I gave it to the Krúmen, who had a grand feast on it, but the bones I preserved for comparison with those of other species.

Another day had to be spent labouring away at the huge lumps of wood, which still lumbered our decks, and which unfortunately, after being cut up, burnt only indifferently. Frequently branches and portions of trees floated past, and whenever they came near enough we attempted to secure them, but from the strong tide this was no easy matter. A boat was usually sent to intercept them, but if after the seizure the vessel was missed, the only course left was to make for the shore, and there cut up the prize, as it was impossible to tow even a small piece against the current. Frequently in capturing a piece of wood, not large enough to burn for ten minutes, the boat would be carried down upwards of a mile. A small dry tree having been discovered along the shore, the Krúmen were despatched with their hatchets to demolish it, but from the rise of the river and the bank being flooded, they had to stand up to their waists in water to accomplish it. Evidently a sudden rise had lately taken place. Large masses of grass, almost forming small floating islands, were continually passing us, and great quantities got athwart our hawser, or foul of the boat alongside. Happening to look a little attentively at one of these heaps it was discovered to teem with animal life, whereupon they were all closely examined, and yielded a most abundant zoological harvest. Lizards, snakes, frogs, and insects, formed the staple, but other occasional denizens from time to time turned up; even mammals were not unrepresented, for I captured a curious shrew mouse, evidently out of its element. Beetles, locusts, and grasshoppers boarded us in vast numbers, but were quickly made prisoners and transferred to my collection; two fine chameleons were detected in the very act of creeping in through a hause-hole, seized, tried, and condemned; and a large toad which had contrived to perch itself, puffing and panting, on the top of the fan, only escaped my fatal grasp by diving headlong into the rushing tide. So substantial was this grassy drift across the bows of our iron canoe, that I could stand on it, though up to my ankles in water, bottle in hand, consigning such living things as had escaped the deluge to the world of spirits. Among other captures were some specimens of an animal known at Sierra Leone as the "ground-pig;" it is a large rodent, a species of *Aulacodus*, and when fresh is very good eating. These were too far gone to allow even their skins to be preserved, but their skeletons are now among my African gatherings.

About two o'clock some canoes were seen approaching, which, on reaching us, we found to contain a messenger from the Sultan of Hamarúwa, who had heard of us, and now sent to welcome us. This man, whose name was Ibrahim, was a very important personage, combining in himself the highly onerous and responsible offices of Chancellor of the Exchequer and President of the Board of Trade, from the latter of which positions he was usually designated Sáriki'n Háusa, as most commercial transactions were in the hands of Háusa people. When this party came on board we were at anchor getting up steam, and when shortly afterwards the screw began to turn, some of the natives, in great alarm, jumped overboard and got into the canoes. During this forenoon we

Sept. 21.

were steaming so close to the right bank, that outspreading branches frequently stretched right across the ship; and, on one occasion, to save letting go the anchor, a warp was passed round a large tree, by which we swung for half-an-hour. All our small fuel being at length expended, we had to drop anchor for the night, when the messenger left us, promising to visit us betimes.

In the morning, in the midst of heavy rain, a boat's crew was despatched to cut up and secure some dry branches, which hung along the bank, and by the help of this supply we got the fires lighted. About eight o'clock Sáriki'n Háusa returned to us, announcing his intention of starting forthwith for Hamarúwa, and asking what message he should convey from me to the Sultan. I said I should send a special messenger with him, and selected Mr. Richards for the purpose, desiring him formally to announce our arrival, to thank the king for his courtesy, and to mention my intention of visiting him as soon as the ship should reach the next town. Hoping to expedite matters, and to be able to obtain useful information, Mr. Crowther very kindly volunteered to accompany him; so the gig having been manned, these two gentlemen departed, attended by Sáriki'n Háusa and Alihéli, and taking with them a small present for the Sultan. As the distance was said not to be very great, we were in hopes that they might be able to return to the ship by dark. After upwards of two hours struggling against a strong current, sometimes

Sept. 22.

barely holding our own, and then, when a little steam could be raised, vigorously screwing ahead, we at length anchored off the little town of Gúrowa. Having been aware of our approach, natives soon came off to us, in very rickety canoes, one of which was upset alongside, and as the people were unable to swim against the impetuous stream, I had to send a boat to pick them up. In the afternoon Dr. Hutchinson and I landed, and saw the governor, who was a Púlo. The inhabitants are of the same race as those of Zhirú, but with a greater Fuláta admixture. The huts are all circular, but neat, well kept, and each surrounded by a bit of garden-ground, growing ochro and pumpkins. The town itself is surrounded by dense bush and forest, so thick as almost to defy penetration, and obliging all communication with other places to be by water. I saw two large Baobab-trees, covered with pendulous fruit, and made an attempt to reach them, which was unsuccessful on account of the closeness of the intervening brushwood. Mr. May was now so much better, that he was able to resume his usual duties, so speedy was his recovery from his attack under the modern rational treatment.

From what we learnt at Gúrowa, we did not expect Mr. Crowther and Mr. Richards back at night, nor did we feel much surprise at their not making their appearance next morning, as we found that to go to Hamarúwa, they had to proceed by canoe along a creek, and afterwards had a long walk before them.

Many people came on board to visit us, and to see the ship, and from some of them I got abundant information about neighbouring countries. All were familiar with the Páro or Fáro, the confluence of which was said to be from six to seven days' journey by canoe; and as a day's journey *up* the river seldom exceeds from twelve to fifteen miles, the extreme distance of this river from Gúrowa must be from seventy to a hundred miles; most probably between eighty and ninety miles. On asking them if they knew of a place of the name of Taepe, as mentioned in Petermann's Atlas, none knew anything of it, but they spoke of a town called Bundú,* near the meeting of the two rivers. I inquired also about the town laid down as Juggum, and the Kóana tribe, but could learn nothing of either; the latter I believe, however, to be properly named Kwóna, as a few days' later, I heard of a race of this name living to the southward.

High ranges of mountains run along the course of the river on either side, approaching to within a few miles of the banks, the intervening ground being a flat alluvial soil. Those to the northward are named the Múri Mountains, from an Aboriginal race who either still inhabit the neighbouring districts, or at all events have been but lately driven from them. The mountains are very continuous, the sides often precipitous, and the summits sharp and irregular. We obtained native names for two peaks, viz. Wurkóni and Tángale, which latter is the most remark-

---

* Probably the "Bundang" of Petermann's Atlas.

able, and perhaps the highest, being about 3000 feet. The southern heights I have already mentioned as the Fumbína mountains, in general altitude from 2000 to 3000 feet, although occasionally a more lofty summit presents itself to view, among which one of the nearest to our position was Bak'n dútshi. Mount Tshébtshi * was too far off to allow of an estimate, but its height must be considerable. The town near its base bears the same name, and not that of Tshebtshóma (Chebchóma). Gúrowa itself does not support much trade. A few scrivelloes were brought off and purchased, and we got some provisions. I went to have a look after fire-wood, but could find but very little. The river continued to rise, and the current alongside, upwards of four knots, was constantly causing canoes to upset; indeed Mr. May and myself coming on board after dark with an inexperienced boat's crew, very nearly ourselves got a ducking. Several of our visitors were nearly drowned, and I was surprised that, with the number of crocodiles which abound, no more serious accident occurred. As our party had not returned by the evening, we began to be a little uneasy about them; but hoping they might even after dark be on their way towards us, a masthead-light was hoisted as a guide.

My principal informant had been more than once at Yóla, and had travelled also as far as Loggéne or Loggóne. From him I gathered the following information. Hamarúwa is an extensive and powerful

---

* Sometimes pronounced "Shébshi."

Púlo province, tributary to the Sultan at Sókoto, and considered but little inferior to Adamáwa. The present Sultan is the third who has occupied the throne since its conquest by its present rulers, his predecessors having been his brother and his father. It comprises a considerable extent of country, on both sides of the river, extending from Korórofa and Báutshi or Báushi to Adamáwa. Prior to its occupation by the Fulátas, this country was occupied by various independent races, the Múri being on the north, and several races speaking dialects of Djúku on the south. Different tribes still remain in a state of semi-independence on the confines of Adamáwa, and to the eastward along the river; they are all heathens, and are considered very barbarous. Several countries pay annual tribute to Hamarúwa, among which are Wukári, as having been conquered by the brother or uncle of the present Sultan, and Zhibú, as a Púlo dependency. The tribute consists chiefly of slaves, and the amount varies according to the success met with in their annual predatory excursions. In what they look on as a productive year, Wukári sends from thirty-five to forty slaves, carried off mostly from the Mítshis, or from the barbarous nations living beyond Korórofa. Adamáwa, again, is principally situated to the southward of the river, though it also claims territory to the northward, in the direction of Mándara. It is likewise a Púlo province, tributary to Sókoto, and is very productive in ivory, elephants being extremely numerous. Adamáwa is not synonymous with the name Fumbína, but merely, I apprehend, applies to that portion of it which has been conquered by the Púlbe (i.e. Fulátas). I am inclined to think that formerly along the south side of the Bínue, from the confluence of the Kwóra to the Fáro, there were three extensive territories, namely A'kpoto, Koró-rofa, and Fumbína, and that all the other tribes are of more recent origin. Thus the Mítshi tribe has encroached partly on A'kpoto, and partly on Korórofa; a portion of the latter again is now comprised under Hamarúwa; while a large division of Fumbína is absorbed in Adamáwa, and some smaller outlying districts are included in Hamarúwa. The name Adamáwa is derived from Adáma, the Púlo who first invaded Fumbína, *wa* being a common suffix. I could not learn the origin of Hamarúwa, but believe it to be altered from Hamadúwa, from some chief, Hámadu or Muhámadu being a common Púlo name. *Wa* is a very frequent termination to names of towns and of countries, as Adamáwa, Hamarúwa, Gúrowa, also Kukáwa, the capital of Bornu; Yákuba, the chief town of Báutshi is probably euphoniously altered from Yákubwa, its founder having been called Yákub, i. e. Jacob.

On Sunday morning I began to consider about sending off a searching party to inquire after our friends, when fortunately about seven o'clock, the gig was made out, and soon got alongside. Mr. Crowther and Mr. Richards, tired and footsore,

Sept. 24.

were immediately beset by numerous questioners, all being anxious to hear of their adventures. The road to Hamarúwa they considered to be fully a dozen miles; and from its very bad nature, especially after the then recent heavy rains, it was not until sunset that they reached the town. They were well and comfortably lodged, and in the morning the Sultan, in his anxiety to see them, granted them an early audience, contrary to the long established custom of the country, which requires messengers to wait for thirty days before being heard. He received them most favourably, gave them presents, and had a long conversation with them. Mr. Crowther asked him among other matters, if he would object to our sending teachers to instruct the barbarous people who inhabited many of his villages. The Sultan, shrugging his shoulders, replied certainly not; but they were such Kéferi,* such savages, that he doubted much whether anything could be made of them. He then gave Mr. Crowther a large piece of native cloth to take to me, and also sent by him a letter in Arabic, of which the following translation I owe to the kindness of Edwin Norris, Esq.

"In the name of God! Praise be to God, the sufficient One! Salutation to Mohammed!

"The Emir Mohammed to you. He bids you

---

* This word has a very extensive use among the tribes on the Kwóra and Bínue, and is applied by them to designate any people more savage than themselves. Its derivation is from the Arabic, and in the Yóruba it means "an unbeliever, a heathen, a pagan." *Vide* Crowther's Yóruba Vocabulary, p. 178; also Appendix D.

have patience, and to stay in this place until he sends to the north countries, to the Emir Bawsh,* and to the first Emir.† Whoever wishes to buy of you the things which you have, let him buy what he likes. This is the Emir's command to you until tidings of you reach these countries. Every one may get what he wants through you, for all the shopkeepers of the place run to you to get what you have with you.

"Health!"

The composition of this elaborate state document, which occupied several hours, detained Messrs. Crowther and Richards so late, that it was dark long before they reached Wúzu, the place where the boat had been left, so that they had to sleep at this little village all night. All had a jaded, worn-out appearance; even the stout Krúmen who accompanied them were stiff and wearied. Sáriki'n Háusa also came with them to get an answer to the Sultan's letter, and to make some trading arrangements. I resolved myself to go and see the Sultan; and although Mr. Crowther tried to persuade me to wait until horses could be procured, thinking that no time ought to be lost, I determined to set out at once. Dr. Hutchinson and Mr. Guthrie also, not alarmed by the dreadful accounts of the roads, made up their minds to go with me. A fresh boat's crew was selected; a few necessary preparations made, and along with Sáriki'n Háusa, and Alihéli our interpreter, we shoved off about half-past eleven. We

* The Sultan of Báutshi. † The Sultan at Sókoto.

had to pull against the stream for a few hundred yards, when we reached a little opening, by which the rise of the water enabled us to take a short cut, though for part of the way, instead of using oars or paddles, we moved along by seizing hold of the long reeds and grass which surrounded us. Presently we got to a fine creek from 200 to 250 yards wide, flowing in a south-westerly direction with a current of two knots. We proceeded along this for about three miles, until we reached Wúzu, a village on its banks, where we disembarked, landed our effects, hauled up the gig and secured her, and gave the oars, tiller, crutches, and other small gear belonging to her, to the care of the headman until our return. We then marshalled ourselves under the shade of a gigantic Baobab, and found our force to consist of three Europeans, viz., Dr. Hutchinson, Mr. Guthrie, and myself, Alihéli the interpreter, my black servant, five Krúmen, and Sáriki'n Háusa, with two attendants—a rather imposing array. A horse was talked off, so one of the Sultan's men was left to bring it after us, while we marched a-head, our crew shouldering our baggage. For a few hundred yards the path was dry, but then large pools began to appear in quick succession, and the road became more and more muddy, until at last it was completely under water. We picked our steps rather carefully at first, until finding all our efforts insufficient to keep ourselves clean or dry-shod, we dashed headlong through it, and sometimes the inundated portions were so deep, that we had to cross them, mounted on the shoulders of the Krú-boys. At length the steed, a sorry-looking animal, overtook us, and we—that is, the white men—bestrode it by turns. The pathway, usually so narrow as only to admit of single file, was for the greater part of the way bounded on either side by tall grass or by low trees. Sometimes it led through cornfields, the stalks of which were so long as quite to protect the foot-passengers from the sun, and even at times actually waved over the heads of the horsemen. We passed two small villages, and several farms as they were called, not exactly coming up to our idea of the broad acres and beautiful regularity of English agriculture; but being patches of cultivation bearing different varieties of corn, close to which dwelt some of the servants or slaves of the proprietors. We toiled for many a dreary mile across this level plain, now almost an entire swamp, the road seeming much longer from the difficulty of progression, and being shut out from any extended view. The sun began to verge towards the western horizon, and many an inquiry was made as to when the city should be seen. By sunset we reached the foot of some rising ground, along the ridge of which we could just discern columns of blue smoke in faint relief against the evening sky, and there, Ibrahim called to us, lay the promised city. We climbed along an irregular and rather rocky path, for some distance; and when within half-a-mile of the walls, were met by crowds of curious inhabitants. The wells from which their water is procured were close to our route; and as we passed, the last pitchers were being filled and carried off on the shoulders and heads of, I cannot say *fair*, damsels. More horses were brought, on which we were mounted, and as the shades of evening were rapidly falling, we rode in, the first Europeans who had ever visited Hamarúwa. We were conducted to the opposite side of the town, a considerable distance, and at length arrived at the abode of Sáriki'n Háusa, where we were informed we were to be quartered for the night. Here an ample hut and a large yard were set apart for us, in which we deposited our traps, and we then sat down to rest ourselves, after a journey from Wúzu, according to my pedometer, of fourteen miles and a half.

It being by this time quite dark, we lighted our lanterns, but before we had well been able to arrange ourselves, a message of congratulation came from the Sultan, and scarce had it been delivered before crowds of the inhabitants came to welcome us. For nearly half-an-hour the only business transacted was an incessant shaking of hands, which pretty well wearied us, after which we began to look after some supper, and set the Krúmen to boil their rice. A very pleasant mess was made for us, prepared by adding to milk and water some Indian-corn-meal mixed with a little red pepper. Our repast was hardly finished when a royal present was brought us, consisting of several calabashes filled with meal fúfu, known by the

Púlbe as túo, and a green-coloured sauce, made chiefly with butter. This, with the addition of a little salt, was by no means unpalatable, except that the meal, having been ground on a soft stone, was sandy and gritty. By nine o'clock we were very glad to be able to stretch ourselves for the night, we selecting the yard, while the Krúmen preferred the hut. A heavy dew fell, but neither did this, nor numbers of most lively mosquitoes prevent us from enjoying a good sound sleep. The Krú-boys, again, were terribly bitten in the hut, and were glad to come to the open air to escape from their tiny persecutors.

By daylight we were all astir, and having hung up our damp clothes to dry, and made prepara- tions for breakfast, we went to look around us. Sept. 25. The ridge on which the town is situated runs along the base of the Múri Mountains, one of which, nearly enveloped in dark clouds, now looked frowningly down upon us. Altogether the position of the town is good, being on a tolerably dry soil, quite above the marshy plain below, and commanding an extended view. Its dimensions are considerable; the breadth I measured, being a mile and a quarter, while the length must be fully two miles. The number of inhabitants could not, according to our computation, be under eight thousand. About half-past six heavy rain set in, and continued with occasional intermis- sions for nearly two hours. This drove us to seek the shelter of the despised hut, where, however, to protect ourselves from insects, we had to kindle a

fire and to light our cigars, so that with rain without
and smoke within, our position was not an enviable
one. We afterwards found that in the river at this
very time a heavy tornado came down, which nearly
cleared everything off the deck of the " Pleiad," while
here, only sixteen miles off, and almost in the mountains, we had rain without a breath of wind; so very
local, it would thus appear, are the effects of these
dreadful hurricanes. Early in the morning Sáriki 'n
Háusa had gone to the Sultan to request an early
audience for us, and we had since despatched another
messenger, but by nine o'clock the only answer which
had reached us, was the arrival of another large
consignment of túo, similar to that sent us for
supper.

As the rain began to clear off, numbers of the
inhabitants came to see us, and we soon got on very
friendly terms with them. We amused ourselves
by purchasing mats, rings, ear-rings, wristlets, hair-
pins, and other ornaments, made of lead, copper,
or brass, for which we gave trinkets, and handkerchief pieces. Razors were here, as in all Muhammadan
places, in great demand, and much prized. A young
woman asked me to buy a couple of rings from her,
for which I proposed to give in exchange some red-
printed calico. Wishing to possess a larger piece,
she took off another ring and added it to the former
ones, on which I increased my quantity. Still she
was not satisfied, but taking off rings, ear-rings, and
hairpins, one by one, she gradually divested herself of

every ornament, until she managed to get several yards of the tempting material. Her last hairpin she held in her hand for some time, looking alternately at it and at the coveted article; but at last, as though thinking that copper rings and brass pins could at any time be got at Hamarúwa, she gave it up, and marched off in triumph with the showy dress, resolving to become for the time the envy of all her acquaintance. I met with but one interruption, from a wild-looking, overgrown fellow who suddenly came to the door of our hut, and rudely dragged away a woman with whom I was bargaining for some mats, declaring that she was underselling them. I said little at first, but on the man's becoming further insolent, I ordered him off, saying I would speak of his behaviour to the Sultan, and finally I ordered one of our crew to turn him out of the yard. None of the natives took his part, but were rather pleased at seeing the bully silenced, and after a time, he came back in a cringing manner, wishing me to buy his sword, which, however, I declined doing.

As this was the first occasion on which we met with Fulátas in great numbers, I shall enter into some little detail concerning them. In Hamarúwa, as in other Púlo towns, although the inhabitants are all Muhammadans, yet the women are permitted to go about unattended; their faces are not considered sacred from the unhallowed gaze of the Giaour, neither do they exhibit the extreme strictness nor the bigotry of the Moslemin of the East. Among

them are to be constantly seen numerous Mállams—
or learned men—with white turbans, and usually a
piece of cloth over the mouth and lower part of the
face. In appearance they are far removed from the
Negro, and the profile is frequently nearly European,
and their skins, never black, are at times very pale-
coloured. They have not a muscular look, nor are
they of full flesh. Their stature is rather above the
average; and their long, spare-made limbs seem
well adapted for activity and endurance of fatigue.
Their foreheads are high, and at times expansive;
the features long, and the chin pointed; the nose is
straight, or at times almost aquiline; the usually
blue expressive eye, has a wandering, restless cast;
while the lips, which are inclined to be thick, exhibit
the only marked Ethiopic affinity. They occupy a
high place in the scale of intelligence and quickness,
and in commercial concerns they are keen and active.
Their manners appeared to us, after meeting with so
many rude tribes, cultivated and pleasing, and their
persons were kept tolerably clean. Most of the men
wear tobes, almost all have turbans, straw hats, or
some kind of head-dress, and many sport loose
trowsers. Being Muhammadans, the head is commonly kept shaved, but the hair is allowed to grow
on the chin. Most of them carry with them charms
enclosed in little leathern cases, hung round the neck,
and generally consisting of scraps of Arabic writing,
or of verses from the Kurân. The women were certainly by far the best-looking whom we saw, and

were dressed with some degree of taste. The fashionable ornaments consisted of ear-rings of lead or brass, massive, and often tastefully ornamented brass pins in the hair, and generally armlets or wristlets of the same metal. Their dress chiefly comprised a long piece of native cloth, wound several times round the body, and reaching from beneath the armpits to below the knees, the end of which is, when the weather is cold or wet, thrown loosely over the head. Under this are one or two other similar folds, only not quite so large, and reaching from the waist. A few of the younger ladies of the place, probably the belles, wore round their heads narrow wreaths or circlets of neatly plaited dyed straw, or reeds, which had a very graceful effect. The custom prevails here of dyeing the edges of the eyelids with antimony, and it certainly gives softness to the expression; the finger-nails, too, are stained with henna, which plant is extensively cultivated in the gardens. The ordinary language is the Púlo, but Háusa is also nearly universally understood. Our host Ibrahim was a fine example of his race, of prepossessing look, with much quickness, intelligence, and information; he was, moreover, what there might be called a man of education, being able to speak and to write Arabic.

I showed to some people about me my pocket compass, trying to explain to them, that one end of the needle invariably pointed in the same direction, and that by it I could always find my way. One man, who had apparently heard of this instrument before, began to ask the position of different places around, and as I usually looked at the needle before answering, the spectators thought it gave me information in some mysterious manner. I was put through a strict geographical examination, and was asked in rapid succession to point in the direction of the Fáro, of Yóla, Zhirú, Nak, Zhibú, Wukári, Yákuba, Sókoto, Káno, Katshína, Tumbuktú, Bornú, Loggóne, Wádai, &c., and having a tolerable acquaintance, both with the map, and with the situations of these localities, the crowd were much amazed at the correctness of the stranger. One travelled Hadji, hoping to puzzle me, demanded that I should indicate the situations of Mékka and of Stamboul, on which a woman requested me to stop, as she was afraid that the child, of which she was then pregnant, would be marked with a compass, or be born white. A Mallam, being desirous of seeing me write with a black lead pencil on paper, I tore off a little bit, and, writing the words "Hamarúwa, 25th of September, 1855," gave it to him, on seeing which all around became eager to possess similar scraps. I wrote accordingly, until I had expended all my spare paper, when I discovered that these were looked on as charms, the men considering that the possession of one would insure success in hunting, or in war, while the female part of the community believed that they would prove preservatives against sickness, and would render the marriage-bed fruitful.

Being anxious to reach Gúrowa by night, we

determined, as it was nearly noon, and as no messenger had yet returned, to walk towards the king's, but fortunately met on the way our friend Sariki'n Háusa, who was then coming to conduct us. While approaching the palace we fired, at his urgent request, several blank shots, to the mingled terror and delight of the beholders. At the outer-gate, where we were detained for two or three minutes, we saw lying outside a large heap of sandals, as all entrants were obliged there to uncover their feet, and likewise to leave their spears or other offensive weapons. We were presently requested to proceed, and passing through a court-yard, where many persons were seated on the ground crosslegged, were ushered into a large, substantial hut, the door of which was shaded by a curtain. On entering, Sariki'n Háusa desired me to sit right before the Sultan, and placing Dr. Hutchinson and Mr. Guthrie on either side of me, he ranged our retinue behind. He then himself knelt down in front of us, signing to Alihéli to come close to him and do likewise. We were seated on good Turkey rugs, and about were carelessly strewn cushions of bright-coloured European cloths and satins, red and yellow being the predominant shades. Across the capacious hut, immediately before us, hung a curtain of striped pink and white silk, which concealed his majesty from our view. As soon as we were seated the spectators shouted and clapped their hands; the Sultan, through his interpreter, then welcomed us, saying how glad he was to see us, and how pleased he felt that white men should first visit Hamarúwa during his reign, as such an event had never occurred during the rule of any of his predecessors. He then gave an order to Sariki'n Háusa, who, taking from under the screen three fine Háusa tobes, put one on me, and one on each of my companions. He presented me also with three poisoned spears with the heads covered, with one unpoisoned spear, and also with a basket of fine gúra or kóla nuts, the latter esteemed as a mark of great favour and friendship. Having returned thanks for these, I inquired of Sariki'n Háusa whether the curtain was to be raised or not, but was told that, according to custom, the Sultan would remain unseen during our conference. I therefore proceeded to say that we had come from a powerful country named England, far away on the great sea; that the Queen of our country, who was a very powerful Queen, was desirous of being at peace and on terms of amity with all monarchs, that she wished to aid in promoting the welfare of all places however distant, and was therefore anxious that her subjects should cultivate trade and commerce wherever it was possible to do so. That it was for this purpose that we had now come to Hamarúwa, and while feeling highly gratified with our reception, we hoped that the Sultan would always deal kindly and justly towards white men, and that we trusted that they again would invariably behave properly towards him. We then mentioned the articles which we were desirous of purchasing, enumerating in general terms the nature of our goods. To this the Sultan replied in very friendly tones, saying he felt honoured by receiving the subjects of so great and so good a Queen, and assuring us that he would use his utmost endeavour to promote our views, to assist our designs, and to further trade. I then told the Sultan that on our return down the river it was my intention to visit Wukári, which was, I understood, one of his dependencies, and would, therefore, feel much obliged by his sending a message or a letter by us, stating that we were his friends, to which he replied, " most certainly, he would gladly do so." I then gave him his present, consisting of several pieces of white and coloured calico, two velvet tobes, a sabre and brass scabbard, and a double barrelled gun with spare flints and powder. Dr. Hutchinson gave him specimens of the various kinds of goods we had on board, and Mr. Guthrie offered him a supply of writing materials and a map on which was pointed out the position of Hamarúwa, with all of which the king seemed well pleased. The silk screen not being very thick, and as the king sat between me and an open door, I could see his figure and actions, though I could not distinguish his features. He wore a fine scarlet robe, and when the gifts were laid before him, he examined them with much interest, especially the sabre and the writing materials. He then said h was the slave of the Sultan at Sókoto, and must send a special messenger to inform him of our visit, and asked me if I would give him a present to send to his master, which I promised to do. I was next informed that two bullocks had been ordered to be secured for us, for which I expressed our thanks, and then requested the Sultan to let us have horses to take us back to Wúzu. We were much pressed to extend our stay until the succeeding day, but I excused myself on account of having much to attend to; adding also, that no trade would be commenced until Dr. Hutchinson got to the ship. We therefore said farewell, and on leaving the royal presence * the ceremony of clapping the hands and shouting was repeated. Sariki'n Háusa now took me to see the bullocks, but on reaching the enclosure we found that only one had been caught, a fine black bull,† which, on Mr. Guthrie's getting rather too close to him, was desirous of taking somewhat unpleasant liberties with him. I engaged some people to bring these animals to Wúzu, after which we returned to make ready for our journey. We all wore our tobes, which seemed to inspire the inhabitants with intense respect for us, our attire being ample evidence that we were persons whom their Sultan delighted to honour. Immediately outside of the town are fine waving fields of corn, beyond which, on the sides of the mountains, is abundant rich pasturage for their goats and cattle. In the gardens are grown numerous herbs and vegetables, and about each hut are several papaw trees. On the outskirts, on the side next to the river, are many

---

* In October, 1854, the Sultan met Dr. Barth at Káno, and gave him an account of our visit.

† The skin of this beast, which is the *Bos Dante* of Link, marked with a small hump on the withers, is now in the British Museum.

Baobabs, at that time covered with fruit. I measured one of them, by no means the largest, and found its circumference, at three feet above its base, to be thirty feet, while close to the ground it must have been forty feet. The trunks, though thus of great diameter, are seldom tall, but, at a height of from twelve to sixteen or eighteen feet, begin to throw off, all around, widely spreading branches. The trunks, too, are nearly circular, and seldom or never show any disposition to form the laminar buttresses so common in the allied *Bombaces* or silk-cotton trees. I have observed these *Adansoniæ* only in the neighbourhood of towns and villages, which, Mr. Crowther informs me, corresponds with his knowledge of their localities in the Yóruba country; I fancied, too, that the fruit, though less numerous, grows to a far greater size near the river, and in moist situations, while in hilly regions and in dry soil it is smaller and more abundant.

I managed to start our Krúboys with the baggage by half-past one, and then as only one horse was brought, Mr. Guthrie, as the oldest of the party, was mounted, while Dr. Hutchinson and I agreed to walk on in the hopes of the others being brought after us. When, however, we had got about a mile on our way, seeing no sign of the steeds, Dr. Hutchinson declared that he would return and inquire about them, while I resolved to proceed, telling him that he might overtake me. I accordingly went on my way, picking up a few plants, and examining the rocks and the soil. Having got to the bottom of the hill, and finding the road as before very wet, I pulled off my shoes and stockings and went barefooted, that being by far the easiest mode of progression along a path of this description. In this way I had walked alone for from seven to eight miles, when I lost almost all trace of the path. Having ascertained by my compass the position of the river, I endeavoured to work my way in that direction, but soon got more entangled than ever. I climbed up several trees to look around, but could not discover a single guiding mark. I was completely in the bush, the grass and brushwood being so long, thick, and close, that every step I took was a severe exertion. It was now past sunset, and getting rapidly dark, and as it was only too evident that I had lost my way without any chance of bettering myself, the next question came to be how I should pass the night. The most comfortable and the safest spot seemed to be up a tree, so I tried one, and got as high as I could, but did not much relish my quarters. All the others near me were too small, but I recollected having observed some time before a tall Baobab, which I determined again to search after. I took a good mark, so that, if unsuccessful in my cruise, I still might have something to fall back upon, and starting with a good run to clear the grass, was fortunate enough in a few minutes to get a glimpse of the wished-for harbour of refuge. Luckily for me it had a double trunk, with a distance between of about two feet; so tying my shoes together, and casting them over my shoulder, I placed my back against the one trunk, and my feet against the other, and so managed to climb until I got hold of a branch by which I swung myself further up, and finally got into a spot about twelve or fifteen feet from the ground. Here I placed myself on a branch, about a foot in diameter, projecting at nearly right angles, and by leaning against the main trunk, and stretching out my legs before me, I found I had a tolerably comfortable seat, whence I might peer into the surrounding obscure. The night, fortunately, was not very dark, the stars gleamed overhead, while vivid flashes of lightning over the neighbouring hills enabled me, from time to time, to cast a momentary glance around me. I got on my shoes and stockings as a protection against insects, then passed a piece of cord loosely round the branch, so that I could pass my arm through it and steady myself, and finally made preparations for repose by kicking two places in the bark of the tree for my heels to rest in. About eight o'clock I distinctly heard in the distance the hum of human voices, and shouted to try and attract attention, but to no avail; believing, however, that there were some huts near, I marked the direction by a large tree. Feeling rather tired, I lay down on my face along the branch, throwing my handkerchief over my head, and passing each of my hands into the opposite sleeve, to prevent them from being bitten, I was soon in a state of oblivion. I must have slept upwards of four hours, when I awoke rather stiff, from my constrained position, and had to try a change of attitude. To pass the time I lit a cigar, and, as I had but one, I only smoked half of it, carefully putting back the remainder to serve for my breakfast. A dew was now falling, crickets and frogs innumerable were celebrating nocturnal orgies; huge mosquitoes, making a noise as loud as bees, were assaulting me on all sides, and some large birds were roosting in the tree over my head. I tried in vain to doze away the hours, but I had had my usual allowance of sleep, and not being a bigoted partizan of the drowsy god, even when I really required his aid, he refused to attend to my invocations. I watched with most painful interest the rising and setting of various constellations, and was at length delighted with the appearance of Venus, showing that morning was now not far off. A fresh novelty next presented itself, in the form of sundry denizens of the forest, crowding to pay homage to their visitor. Howls of various degrees of intensity continually reached my ears, some resembling more the high notes of the hyæna with occasional variations, and others, very close to me, being unquestionably in the deep bass of the leopard. I once fancied that I saw a figure moving not far from me, but could not be positive. As light began to suffuse itself over the eastern sky, my nocturnal companions gradually retired, until at last I was left alone, yet not solitary, for that I could not be, as long as the incessant buzzing in my ears told me that my Lilliputian winged antagonists were yet unwearied in their attacks, and still unsatiated with blood. At length, as gray dawn was being supplanted by brighter daylight, I ventured to descend from my roosting-place, where I had spent, not altogether without comfort, upwards of eleven hours.

My first endeavour was to find a foot-path, and, after a little search, I stumbled over a little track, which, however, as it led in a wrong direction, I had to abandon. A more prolonged investigation discovered another, very narrow, and almost hidden by long grass, which, after the heavy rain, was lying right over it. To prevent my again straying, I was obliged to bend forward and walk, almost creep, along a kind of tunnel, pulling up a few stalks and letting them fall, as a guide in case I should have to return. Though in my elevated quarters the dew had been slight, on the ground it had been very heavy, and in a few minutes I was completely drenched. When I emerged at the other extremity of this path, which was about half-a-mile long, and was again enabled to look round, I saw a little circling smoke, towards which I immediately made, and found a few huts. Some Aborigines appeared, and, after their surprise had subsided, I managed to explain, by means of a few broken Háusa words, that I had lost my way, had spent the night in a tree, and now wished to get to Wúzu. They pointed out the way to me; but, as it was not very evident to my European senses, I induced one to come with me as a guide, and we accordingly trudged along through

Sept. 26.

mud and water, by a route which, to any but a thorough-bred native, would have been impossible to keep to. After walking, or rather wading, in this manner for two or three miles, we fell in with my black servant and a couple of men armed to the teeth, going in search of me. They could hardly believe it to be me, especially when I told them how I had passed the night, for they had already consigned me to the jaws of the wild beasts which abound in this neighbourhood. I accordingly dismissed my guide, a happy man with my pocket-handkerchief, which was all I had to give him, and continued my walk to Wúzu, at which place I arrived about nine o'clock, after a morning's jaunt of nine or ten miles. The natives, who were there in numbers, were astonished at my appearance and my story, and were no less surprised when they saw me devouring, with great gusto, my breakfast, which the steward had very considerately provided for me, and which was the first food I had tasted for twenty hours.

Many traders from Hamarúwa were at Wúzu, with ivory and other articles for sale, so in going to the ship we took with us, in the boat, Sariki'n Háusa, and as many of these persons with their goods as we could manage to pack away. Our pull up the creek was a long one, being against the current; but we got on board about noon, and a scene of activity at once commenced. Dr. Hutchinson purchased, at reasonable rates, all the ivory we brought off, being about 360 pounds, and of good quality. Canoes being very scarce, not one fourth part of the traders could get on board, and I had to land many in our boats. I bought several brass ornaments, among which was a pair of finely-wrought brass anklets, weighing together five pounds, made by a Káno workman resident in Hamarúwa. I also got two small silver rings, but could not ascertain whence the metal was obtained; but believe it to have been brought by caravans across the desert, from the markets at Ghadames, or, as they term it, Gadamáwa. Another purchase was a handsome sword and scabbard, with a sash and tassel attached, of red woollen material, which is much valued. This was made at Káno, which seems to be both the Birmingham and the Manchester of Central Africa, its Háusa traders spreading themselves and their goods and wares far and wide. Intelligence came off during the afternoon of the safe arrival of the bullocks at Wúzu; but, as I thought they would not, after their journey, be in a fit state to be killed, I ordered them to be tied up until the morning, especially as I wished to have the skin of the one and the skeleton of the other for specimens. The chief of Gúrowa sent to say that he wished to go to Hamarúwa in the morning, but had no canoe, on which I let him know that a boat was to be sent to Wúzu, in which he could have a passage.

Sariki'n Háusa being about to return to Hamarúwa the next day, to bring for sale some of the Sultan's ivory, I gave him a present to be sent to Sókoto, of the same value as had been given to the king. For his own very friendly offices I offered him a small gift for himself, intending to give him a better one on our departure, and, as the afternoon looked dark and lowering, I asked him to remain on board all night, which he did. Mr. Crowther and I had a long conversation with him, and obtained much information, especially about the Púlo provinces. He told us the names of all the Muhammadan States of Central Africa, and the titles of their various rulers, also the different routes to Yóla and Yákuba as performed by himself, all of which will appear in the Appendix. He gave us, too, many Púlo words and expressions, which made us regret much that we had not a grammar of that language with us, as we might have tested its correctness, and probably added to it.* On asking him if he knew the original seat of the Púlbe, he said that he had been always told that the country they came from was near Tumbuktú, and was named Mále, probably meaning the district of Mélli south-west from that city. This differs a little from the story given by Mr. Koelle's informant at Sierra Leone, who traced his race from Fúta Tóro, to the northward of the Gambia; but, after all, the difference is trifling, as the Mélli of Arab geographers includes "Fúta Tóro." From these regions they migrated eastward, as a pastoral race,

* On our return to Fernando Po, I found waiting for me copies of a Púlo grammar, edited from Macbrair's MS. by Edwin Norris, Esq., and was sorry that they had not reached us sooner. This grammar applies more especially to the language of the Western or Red Púlbe, which differs only dialectically from that of the Eastern tribes.

and where now stands the city of Sókoto, the vision appeared to the priest Fódio, which inspired him to action and to deeds which ended in the subjugation of the fairest provinces of Central Africa. At this moment there are two great divisions of the Púlo race—the one the Western or Senegambia Púlbe, and the other the Eastern Púlbe, to whom the name Fuláta, as given by the Bornuese, more particularly applies. In appearance the people of these two branches closely resemble each other; those whom I met up the Bínue being the same in feature and in manner with the Púlbe of Tímbo and of the towns near Sierra Leone. I do not, however, consider that their primitive seat was in the countries between the Gambia and the Senegal, but am inclined rather to think that their easterly progress was a secondary migration. The word "Púlo" signifies "yellow," or "brown," from the light complexion of the people; and among many other nations they are known by terms expressive of this feature; thus in Koróroſa they are called "Abáte," or white people. In listening to Púlbe talking, especially if from a little distance, I have often been struck with a resemblance in sound between their language and Arabic; it is however less harsh and guttural, the likeness consisting merely in the general impression conveyed to the ear. I have also fancied that there is an analogy both in dress, in make, and in habits, between many of the Fulátas and the Beduins. They possess in common the same wandering turn, the same spare limbs, and they both keep the lower part of the face muffled, though this latter probably depends on their both spending much of their time in sandy deserts. The Fulátas, however, are more pleasing in features and in their address; nor do they exhibit the Beduin dislike to cities or fixed abodes. I do not mean to attempt to trace any direct connection between these two singular races, but only to note the ideas suggested by hasty glances at each.

No recent intelligence of any white travellers could be obtained, though it was known that one had some years previously visited Yóla. Both the Sultan and Sariki'n Háusa, however, said that about a year previously they had heard that a stranger was residing in Sókoto. They likewise confirmed the report which had reached us of the decease of Sultan Béllo, and they informed us that his successor was named Alihú, who was now the supreme ruler of all the Púlbe.

In the afternoon, about half-past four o'clock, a curious phenomenon was witnessed. During a heavy shower a brilliant complete rainbow was seen in the south-east, and immediately afterwards a supplementary bow, also entire, showed itself at a distance of nine or ten degrees from the primary one, the two extending from horizon to horizon, forming a gorgeous spectacle, contrasting most strongly with the intense darkness of the surrounding clouds. While gazing on these, I was equally astonished and pleased by the appearance of a portion of a third *eccentric* bow, extending from the western extremity of the primary one, and seeming as a tangent to it. Its colours were in the same order as those of the primary, and it did not extend sufficiently far to intersect the secondary one. It remained visible for nearly ten minutes, but faded before either of the great arches.

For nearly a week before we reached Hamarúwa sickness had been showing itself among our Krúmen in rather a peculiar form. They complained of general debility, with swelling of the lower limbs, and on Dr. Hutchinson's first drawing my attention to it, we had some difficulty in assigning a reason for these affections. On watching, however, attentively the symptoms for a day or two, no doubt was left that the disease was scurvy, the peculiar stiffness of the joints and the softness of the gums being unequivocal. This led to an inquiry as to the amount of food given to the Krúmen, which had been arranged by Mr. Taylor. The Krúmen were fed entirely on rice, and although going through immense exertion daily, had been kept on a ration not exceeding a pint and three quarters, a quantity which Dr. Hutchinson had already increased on his own responsibility. The disease prevailed chiefly among the younger Krúboys, who had never anything at all but rice, while the older hands, who had occasionally come in for various little pickings, preserved their health longer and better. The Sierra Leone men also, who had been allowed a scanty portion of meat, escaped better. From Gúrowa and Hamarúwa no fresh vegetables were to be obtained, and not much fresh meat, but I now directed the flesh of one of the bullocks given me by the Sultan to be handed over for the sole use of the Krúmen, and Dr. Hutchinson gave them from his private stores wine and arrowroot. There were no spirits on board, and though I am no advocate for their indiscriminate employment or regular issue, still I think most decidedly that no vessel going on any such service as ours should be entirely without them. Often I have regretted that, after the very severe labour which our men had frequently to undergo, it was out of my power to order them something of the kind, as I am convinced that it would have been beneficial. This omission was quite contrary to the wishes of Mr. Laird, who had no idea that the "Pleiad" had not had some rum included among her stores, and who had given a *carte blanche* to the sailing-master to order everything requisite for the cruise.

The above cause very much interfered with the amount of work done daily, and it was the more annoying as it was one which could have been avoided by the most ordinary amount of foresight. Another difficulty which now weighed heavily upon us, was the scarcity of fuel, not that suitable trees were entirely wanting, but they were very few, and at a considerable distance from the ship, so that with a debilitated crew, and still more debilitated instruments, it was impossible to cut the amount of wood requisite for steaming against a strong stream. I was therefore obliged to relinquish the idea of a further ascent in the steamer, a very disagreeable alternative, as there was abundance of water, and the river had not yet ceased to rise. My wish had been to persevere as long as there was sufficient depth for the "Pleiad," until we observed symptoms of the falling of the river, as with the powerful current we could accomplish our descent very rapidly. Mr. May and myself, notwithstanding, resolved to make a short boat voyage and to attempt in this manner to reach the Fáro. I had the less compunction in leaving the steamer off Gúrowa, as the anchorage was perfectly healthy, and there appeared every evidence of a good and profitable trade lasting for some time. Our first plan was that Mr. May should ascend the river by boat, and that I should try to reach Yóla by the shortest overland route, but from this I was strongly dissuaded by Mr. Crowther, whose experience of African travelling added much weight to his opinion, and subsequent events made me feel satisfied that I had not undertaken this journey. The gig was accordingly got ready, five Krúboys selected, and we took a Sierra Leone man who spoke Háusa as our interpreter and our cook. We shipped a small bag of rice, a few pounds of salt pork, some biscuit and cocoa, enough for three or four days' consumption, and took also for our private use some Quinine wine, which on such excursions should be considered as indispensable. We ought to have started immediately after my return from Hamarúwa, but a slight accident happening to the gig, we were detained until the following morning, by which we escaped a violent thunder-storm, during which the mainmast of the "Pleiad" was struck by lightning, but fortunately the electric fluid escaped by the conductors, without doing us any harm.

In the morning everyone was up before dawn. The pinnace was sent to Wúzu, with the steward and a party to kill the bullocks. Sariki'n Háusa also took a passage in the boat, *en route* to Hamarúwa, intending to return in a couple of days with a further supply of ivory, as I had told him we should remain at anchor for at least that time. I left the vessel under the charge of Mr. Harcus, the chief mate, in whom every confidence could be placed, ordering him if no sudden or unusual danger occurred in the height of the water, to stay at Gúrowa until our return, which would be in from three to four days. If he felt obliged to start, he was to leave a message for us at Gúrowa, and he was not, if possible, to proceed beyond Zhibú, and in the meantime I desired every exertion to be made to secure sufficient firewood to carry the "Pleiad" to that town. Lastly, having learnt that some wild animals had been killed the previous night, I desired my assistant, Mr. Dalton, to go ashore and endeavour to make some purchases for specimens. These matters having been finally arranged, Mr. May and I embarked, a little after six o'clock, our only passenger being a little pet dog, my constant companion.

After the tornado of the night the morning was dark and gloomy and raw, and, to avoid the strong current, we had to pull near in shore, crossing the river from time to time, following closely the line of slack water. In about two hours we entered a narrow creek on the northern side, and presently discovered a village, surrounded, and almost intersected by water. Here Mr. May and I landed, and desiring our boat's crew to shove off and to get their breakfast, we asked for the headman. To our astonishment we were shewn quite a youth, whom we recognized as a late visitor on board, and whom we found to be the Púlo governor of the village, which is named Tshómo.* We sat down on the beach on a mat, and presently an old man was pointed out to us as the native chief, though there was nothing in the least *distingué* in his manners or his appearance. Old, dirty, and savage-looking, his *tout ensemble* was the reverse of prepossessing, as he sat, or rather rolled in the dust alongside of us, scantily clad, and smoking a greasy pipe. The proper opening of the creek by which we went to Wúzu is situated here, the opening by which I formerly crossed into it, being merely one rendered practicable by the great height of the water. The Aborigines here are of the same race as those of Zhirú and Gúrowa, and call themselves Báibai, being one of the Djúku tribes of Koróroſa. They have the Negro features more strongly marked than any people we had met since leaving the Delta. The skin is very

---

* Also at times Tsómo or Shómo.

dark, almost black, the nose is broad and flat, the cheek-bones rather square; the eyebrows overhanging and very bushy, the ears large, with pendulous fleshy lobes. They are not a muscular race, but they are large-boned. The expression is heavy, deficient in intelligence, and frequently savage. Withal, however, the profile is not very prognathous, the chin and mouth not projecting much. They wore very little clothing, that of the men being composed of scanty pieces of cloth or of skins, and that of the women of leaves. They are not traders, but live mainly by hunting and fishing. I saw a quantity of flesh of a hippopotamus which had been killed the day before, cut into long, thin stripes, and hung in the sun, the smell being now anything but fragrant. In the centre of the village, I found a pile of skulls and heads of hippopotami, buffaloes, deer, leopards, and crocodiles, this part being considered sacred, and dedicated to the God of Hunting. I wished to purchase some as specimens, and after some debate, was allowed to offer terms. Not having the means with me, either of buying them or of stowing them away, I gave a man a note to take to my assistant at Gúrowa, which he said he would do. At Zhirú, where a similar heap was seen, the people obstinately refused to sell any of their spoil. The only information I obtained was the names of the towns we should pass, namely, Láu on the left bank, and Bándawa and Djín on the right bank, all more or less subject to Hamarúwa, beyond which was Dámpsa inhabited by a race so wild, as to be considered, even by our savage acquaintances, as *Keferi*, and who were said to amuse themselves by cutting the throats of unwary travellers. On leaving Tshómo, we managed to push our way through some long grass, and rejoin the river by a short cut.

For some days previous to our leaving the ship a fresh breeze had blown up the river, on which we had reckoned greatly for assistance during our cruise; but now, when we most needed it, it was not to be obtained. We had, therefore, to trust almost entirely to our oars, and consequently did not progress rapidly: as the sun became very powerful, we spread our awning, which was a great protection to us. During the whole of our sojourn in the Kwóra and in the Bínue, the regular daily breeze was from the sea *up* the river; and this we found to be the rule to the furthest extent of our explorations; but I frequently observed that when the usual order of things had been upset by the occurrence of a tornado, or other violent atmospheric action, the sea-breeze for a day or two following, was not nearly so strongly felt as usual, and at times did not exist; and this was now our case, as the thunderstorm of the preceding night had been succeeded by a close, sultry day, with scarcely a breath of wind. About mid-day we made fast to some long grass at the river side, and allowed ourselves half-an-hour for dinner, after which we again pushed on, and just afterwards, on rounding a point, surprised a young elephant, which was standing quietly half immersed, but which no sooner observed us, than it speedily dashed a-shore, and disappeared in the bush. We saw another one during the afternoon, on the opposite side of the river from us, a fine old male, with a magnificent pair of tusks; he came down quietly, entered the river, by means of his long trunk enjoyed a refreshing shower-bath, and then deliberately again mounted the bank. This was the only opportunity I enjoyed of watching the African elephant, and though so far off that I had to observe the animal with the glass, I was particularly struck with the large size of the ears and the rounded forehead. In Central Africa, where it exists in enormous numbers, it is not, during life, applied to any useful purpose, and in intelligence it is believed to be inferior to its Indian congener.*

The banks of the river appeared to be nearly flooded, and except in one small spot we did not observe a single place where we could have landed. No villages were passed, and the only thing indicative of life during the day, was hearing at a little distance from us the sound of a hunting party pursuing a buffalo. I listened to the cry of this animal, which is very peculiar and differs greatly from the low of domestic cattle, closely resembling a low, prolonged blast, from a shrill hunting-horn. A

---

* The characters of the African elephant are so peculiar and constant, that it has by Frederick Cuvier been properly constituted into a distinct genus, named "*Loxodonta*," from the structure of the teeth. Though now only sought after by hunters, it was in former ages trained for warlike purposes by the Carthaginians and other nations, and this was the species, too, most frequently exhibited at Rome.

thunder-cloud at one time threatened us, but fortunately passed off to the south-west. After a long pull, our men were much revived by seeing in the afternoon a village on the left bank, towards which we made. Some canoes paddled off as if to reconnoitre, and then speedily returned to report their observations. The sun was fast verging towards the horizon, and its setting rays were brightly reflected from the huts, and from a pretty green hill behind, while immediately to the westward a grove of tall trees, looking down in sombre grandeur on a wondering group of natives who stood gazing at the sudden apparition of the strange canoe, added picturesqueness to the scene. The village which was Láu, seemed to be in two parts; so landing at the one nearest, we advanced, and shaking hands with the persons next to us, asked where the king resided. They informed us that he was to be found in the other division, so, as no time was to be lost, we again shoved off, and a few strokes of our oars brought us to the spot. Again we jumped on shore, and on repeating our inquiries, were conducted among some huts to a small open space, where we were asked to sit down on a large log. After a little delay, a tall, elderly, paralytic man came forward, who was, we were informed, the native chief, the Hamarúwa governor being absent. The people, who were all Báibai, were very civil, and seemed glad to see us. They gave us information confirming what we had heard at Tshómo, but said that beyond Djín, on the same side, was an independent place named Bátshama, although nominally it was within the Hamarúwa territory. We asked numerous questions about localities near the Páro, and found that many of our names were recognized, among others, the town of Bundú, and Mount Bágale, but no one knew anything of Taepe. To the confluence by canoe, from Láu, was, they said, reckoned five good days' voyage. The village of Wurabéli, at the foot of the mountains behind Láu, which is the first stage on the short route to Yóla, was, we were told, entirely inhabited by Púlbe. Among those standing around, one man was pointed out to us, as the son of the King of Kwóna, whose town was situated inland about two days' journey. This Kwóna must, I consider, be the Kóana of Dr. Barth, concerning which I have made many fruitless inquiries. The people at Láu seemed very poor, and had nothing to barter; their huts appeared to be tolerably neat, but in their persons they were quite as dirty as those of Tshómo or Zhirú. A few Púlbe who were among the residents, were our chief informants, and seemed completely to look down upon the native *Kéferi*. As it was quite dark we shoved off, and anchored about 100 yards from the bank, and prepared our supper. About eight o'clock a canoe approached and hailed us, telling us that one of our recent acquaintances wished to come off to us and have a little conversation, probably hoping to get a present; but we excused ourselves, saying it was too late, and that we were tired. A heavy dew was falling, so we quickly made our night preparations, the awning being in readiness in case of rain. Not having much spare room, some of the crew stowed themselves away in the bottom of the boat, while the others laid the oars together and slept on them, Mr. May and myself, with our instruments, occupying the stern sheets.

Before sunrise we were again under way, leaving behind us Láu and its inhabitants. The green hill we had observed the previous evening shewing so resplendently at sunset, looked, if possible, now still more beautiful, the rays of the early sun sparkling brilliantly among the dew drops, and brightening the delicate tints of the verdure. We called it Mount Laird, that we might leave on record thus far up the Bínue, the name of our excellent friend, who had so largely contributed towards the present expedition. A little wind springing up, we set our sail, which enabled us more successfully to contend against the powerful current, and in this manner we proceeded along an island, situated in the middle of the river, which we named after our ship " Pleiad Island." On rounding its eastern extremity we observed on the right bank, elevated some fifteen or twenty feet above the water, the village of Bándawa, the position of which had been pointed out to us at Láu. The breeze now freshening permitted us to lay in our oars, and to have our breakfast, without losing any time. Towards noon we saw ahead upwards of a dozen canoes, which we soon overtook, and found to contain from seventy to eighty people, returning from a hunting expedition, the odour of some of their spoil being unpleasantly evident to our sense of smell. A wild, savage-looking set they were, many being entirely unclad; but when we came close to them, they got alarmed, and paddled in among the long grass out of sight. None of them could speak Háusa, and we could only make out that Djín was still beyond us. While engaged upon our dinner we came rather suddenly on a herd of ten or a dozen hippopotami, which were amusing themselves in shallow water, but did not appear much to mind our intrusion, merely expressing their disapprobation by loud snorting. Shortly afterwards, while passing between two islets, another popped its head above water, so close to our quarter that we could have almost touched it with an oar, but, alarmed by our unlooked-for proximity, it quickly disappeared. River-horses, as far as I have been able to observe them, seldom venture into deep water except when crossing from one spot to another, and, though gregarious, I have rarely seen them together in large numbers. During the day their favourite haunt is in still water over some shallow, or on sandbanks connected with an island. In such places they are to be seen tranquilly basking in the sun, frequently with the head only above the water. If at all alarmed they immediately disappear below, occasionally coming to the surface to breathe and to look around. They can remain under water for a long period, but I never had a good opportunity of ascertaining their extreme limits of endurance. When more sportively inclined they may be observed splashing clumsily about, opening their enormous jaws, displaying their tusks, and tossing their huge heads in anything but a graceful manner. When reposing on sandbanks they usually form one extended line, at which times nothing is visible but a profile view of a long row of faces, just above the water, the small eyes and the swollen muzzle then constituting the most remarkable features. It is from sunset to sunrise that they usually visit the shore for feeding, &c., and near marshy spots or grassy islets their peculiar noise, something between a grunt and a snort, may be heard throughout the night. Their flesh is greatly prized, for which they are much sought after by the natives, the hunters employing in the chase chiefly poisoned arrows : their tusks form excellent ivory, and bring a much higher price in the markets than that yielded by the elephant.

The wind again failed us, and our crew, somewhat fatigued, laboured hard at the oars ; the way, too, was sensibly prolonged by our having so frequently to cross the river, to take advantage of the eddies, and to avoid the full force of the current. Not having passed a single human habitation since morning, we were not a little overjoyed and cheered by observing a few straggling huts on the north bank, towards which we made, and about four o'clock landed to try to procure some information. The few inhabitants whom we found did not seem much alarmed, and one old man, after clapping his hands and welcoming us, gave us to understand that Djín was close by, and offered to conduct us to it. Having shipped him as our pilot, we accordingly pulled about a hundred yards further up the river, and entering by a narrow mouth, proceeded along a very winding creek, where we had to push our way through long grass and reeds, or to pass under overhanging branches; and, surrounding its upper portion, we discovered an extensive town with a dense population. On landing, a large crowd had already assembled to meet us, while numbers of natives were wading and swimming across an arm of the creek, eager to get a peep at the pale-faced strangers. We told them we wished to see their king, on which we were asked up into the village, and requested to wait beneath the shade of a huge tree. Mr. May and I, having asked for a mat, seated ourselves in this spot, and presently were surrounded by not fewer than from five to six hundred natives, who formed a large ring around us. No one could speak Háusa, so that we could hold no direct communication with them, until three Fulátas and two Bornuese, who were temporary residents, pushing forwards, placed themselves beside us, and from them we learnt, that the inhabitants were still Báibai, speaking Djúku; that the Páro was fully four days' voyage by canoe, that Bátshama was more than a day's journey from Djín, and that Dámpsa was nearly the same distance beyond it, and that half way to Bátshama was a village named Dúlti. We could hear of no trade, nor of any article of commerce, hunting and fishing being the chief supports of the inhabitants.

In external appearance the people of Djín closely resembled those of Gúrowa, of Tshómo, and of Láu, with the same irregular markings on the upper arm; we had, however, during our progress, marked a gradual increase in savage aspect and manners as we got further eastward, the natives of Láu, and of Tshómo, being less civilized than those of Gúrowa; while, in their turn, they were surpassed by the uncouth crowd which now encompassed us. The men all carried spears and short swords, and both sexes were exceedingly scantily clad, some even being entirely destitute of any garment. Such a continual din and shouting was carried on, that it was with much difficulty we could distinguish our own voices, and many were our vain endeavours to procure a temporary respite. As neither king nor head-man made his appearance, we asked repeatedly why this was, but received only evasive, unsatisfactory replies. The sun was now down, and we were anxious to escape from the mosquitoes and other plagues and pestilences of the swamp, we therefore told our friends that as we were tired, we should now go on board our boat and sleep, an announcement which seemed to cause some dissatisfaction; but we shook hands with those around and walked on. One of the Fulátas then asked us to his hut, where he showed us mats, on which he said we might spend the night; but we thanked him, and declining his offer went towards the boat. No sooner, however, had we got on board than a crowd of persons seized the gig, declaring that we should not leave, but should remain at Djín. We remonstrated quietly with them, and at last they said that if we were really fatigued, we might sleep in the boat, but it should be where we then were—a most delightful and repose-inviting spot. Our acquaintances seemed inclined to become troublesome, or at least to wish to press their polite attentions to an unpleasant extent, while we were equally desirous of getting rid of them. Our Krúmen, who were not a little alarmed, were ordered to stand by all ready at an instant's notice. Mr. May seized the tiller, while I took one or two trifling articles, such as small mirrors and clasp-knives, which I distributed to the most influential looking individuals within my reach, and particularly to one who appeared to be our "special retainer." The *ruse* took, the glittering trinkets were eagerly examined, while we, seizing the moment that they let go our bow, shoved off, and vigorously paddled down the creek, watching closely with the last glimpse of twilight to observe the turns and curves by which we entered, and to avoid breaking our heads against the jutting branches. Before the astonished multitude, who had thus let their prize elude their grasp, could make up their minds what course to pursue, we had regained the river, and dropping a little way down landed at the huts where we had formerly been, and where Mr. May got an observation for latitude. Our old friend the pilot joined us, and presented us with a fowl, on which I delighted his heart by giving him a gay coloured handkerchief. We again pushed off, and anchoring in three fathoms water, got ready our evening meal, and made all snug for the night. About eight o'clock some people came to the beach opposite to us, and hailing us, tried to induce us to go ashore, telling us their king would now receive us, and that there was ivory for sale; but as we had not been over-civilly treated by daylight, we had no desire to pay an evening visit to Djín. Our Krúmen, who had hardly yet recovered from their fright, told us that during our absence ashore a band of natives had made two or three attempts to drag the boat high and dry, and to commence pilfering. Throughout the night numerous river-horses were busily engaged on an extensive marsh not far from us, and their discordant sounds might, probably, have disturbed the repose of less practised sleepers; we, however, when waking from time to time to look around, merely listened to them as a rude lullaby, and again slumbered: the night, though dark, was fine and clear, and we could occasionally distinguish the dim outline of their bulky figures, as they plunged from the bank into the river.

By early dawn we were again at work, and pulling along the northern shore soon passed Djín, below which we observed two large herds of cattle feeding, all of which were white or light-coloured, with small humps on the withers, evidently a breed similar to those of Hamarúwa, from which they only differed in not having among them any dark-skinned individuals. A canoe followed us, containing some of our quondam friends, who used their utmost powers of persuasion to make us return with them; but their logic and their rhetoric proving alike ineffectual, they soon gave up the trial. About a mile and a half further we saw a small village, of which in passing we demanded the name. The reply was not altogether distinct, but we understood it to be "Abíti." Near all these villages, along the banks, were numerous small fishing-stations, which are arranged as follows:—Through a kind of pulley at the upper extremity of an upright pole planted at the water's edge, a rope passes, which is attached to the further side of the wooden rim of a large bag-net, the opposite side of the rim working in a kind of hinge at the foot of the pole. When the rope is let go, the net sinks until the mouth is below the surface, and in this way it is allowed to remain until fish are supposed to have got entangled in the meshes, or to be within the bag, when by hauling on the line the net is hoisted out of the water and its contents secured.

To our great delight a fresh breeze blew, and we made rapid progress. The river was still rising, the banks everywhere were overflowed, and the water was pouring over them into the adjacent country. The mountain ranges on either hand still continued, and the Múri chain appeared some miles ahead of us to come close to the river. We were now under Tángale, and could well remark its fantastic rocky summit, and its sides barely covered with trees, and furrowed by precipitous torrent courses. Between the mountains and the river we saw some high sloping ground, presenting an abrupt face towards the river. The Múri range probably extends to some distance towards the north, as we could make out several successive peaks behind each other. Tángale appears to be the greatest elevation, and towards the east the heights gradually diminish. Among the opposite or Fumbína mountains, the hills were more sloping and the peaks less acute, and among them were several curious table-tops. The general altitude was in this direction much inferior to Bak'n Dútshi, Kwóna, and other eminences at the western extremity; but these altogether compose a large group rather than a chain, and what are seen from the river are merely the northern boundaries of a mountainous region. Considerably beyond us, standing close to the river, and quite apart from the regular range, we distinguished a peculiar conical hill, estimated at about 500 feet in height, to which we gave the title of "Mount Gabriel."

About half-past ten we entered a creek on the north side, running nearly parallel with the river, and shortly afterwards sighted a village, at which we soon arrived. To our astonishment the first thing which brought us up was our running the bow of the gig against a hut, and on looking around we found the whole place to be flooded. We advanced right into the middle of the village, and found no resting place; right and left, before and behind, all was water. People came out of the huts to gaze at the apparition, and standing at the doors of their abodes were, without the smallest exaggeration, immersed nearly to their knees, and one child I particularly observed up to its waist. How the interiors of the huts of these amphibious creatures were constructed I cannot conjecture, but we saw dwellings from which, if inhabited, the natives must have dived like beavers to get outside. We pulled in speechless amazement through this city of waters, wondering greatly that human beings could exist under such conditions. We had heard of wild tribes living in caverns and among rocks, we had read of races in Hindustán roosting in trees, of whole families in China spending their lives on rafts and in boats in their rivers and their canals; we knew, too, of Tuáriks and Shânbah roaming over vast sandy deserts, and of Eskimo burrowing in snow retreats, but never had we witnessed or even dreamt of such a spectacle as that of creatures endowed like ourselves, living by choice like a colony of beavers, or after the fashion of the hippopotami and crocodiles of the neighbouring swamps.

A little distance from us we espied a large tree, round the foot of which was a patch of dry land, towards which we pulled, but grounding before reaching quite to it, Mr. May and I waded to it, instruments in hand, to take observations. We were barely allowed to conclude, when nearly the entire population of the place, half-wading, half-swimming across a small creek, came upon us, and stared at us in wild astonishment. A hurried set of sights being taken, we carried our things back into the boat, and as we wished to get another set about three quarters of an hour after noon, we tried to amuse ourselves and to spend the intervening time as we best could. We were now able to look a little more attentively at our new friends, who in large numbers crowded round, and who, male and female, were nearly all equally destitute of a vestige of clothing. One young man understood a few words of Háusa, and by his means we learnt that this was the Dúlti of which we had heard at Djín, and that the inhabitants were of the same stock as at the other villages; but they were by far more rude, more savage, and more naked than any of the other Baíbai whom we had encountered. A canoe came near us, lying in the bottom of which was a curious large fish, of which I had just time to make a rough eye sketch, when I had to retreat to the boat, and Mr. May, who had been exploring in another direction, also returned. The behaviour of these wild people now attracted our notice; the men began to draw closer around us, to exhibit their arms, and to send away the women and children. Their attentions became momentarily more and more familiar, and they plainly evidenced a desire to seize and plunder our boat. A sour-looking old gentleman, who was squatting on the branch of a tree, was mentioned as their king; but if so, he made no endeavours to restrain the cupidity of his *sans-culottes*. Part of a red-shirt belonging to one of our Krúmen was seen peeping out from below a bag, and some advanced to lay hold of it, when suddenly my little dog, who had been lying quietly in the stern sheets, raised her head to see what was causing such a commotion. Her sudden appearance startled the Dúlti warriors, who had never seen such an animal before, so they drew back to take counsel together, making signs to me to know if she could bite, to which I replied in the affirmative. Matters were beginning to look serious; our crew, as usual, were timid, and Mr. May and I had only ourselves to depend upon in the midst of three or four hundred armed savages, who were now preparing to make a rush at us. There was no help for it; we had to abandon all hopes of our remaining observations, and of so fixing an exact geographical position. As at Djín, I seized a few trinkets, and handing them hastily to those nearest to us, we shoved off while the people were examining these wondrous treasures.

Still anxious, if possible, to get some further observations not far removed from the spot where the former ones were taken, we pulled about among trees and bushes, but without any success. At length we shoved in among some long grass, hoping to find dry land, but after having proceeded until completely stopped by the thickness of the growth, we still found upwards of a fathom of water. At this moment Mr. May's ear caught a voice not far behind us; so we shoved quietly back, and found a couple of canoes trying to cut off our retreat. Seeing this we paddled vigorously back, there not being room for using our oars, and the canoes did not venture to molest us. We were quickly paddling across the flooded plain, when suddenly a train of canoes in eager pursuit issued out upon us. There were ten canoes, each containing seven or eight men, and they were sufficiently close to us to allow us to see their stores of arms. Our Krúboys worked most energetically, and we went ahead at such a rate that our pursuers had complete occupation found them in paddling, and could not use their weapons. At this moment we were about a couple of hundred yards from the river, towards which we made as straight a course as possible. Not knowing how matters might terminate, we thought it advisable to prepare for defence, so I took our revolver to load it, but now, when it was needed, the ramrod was stiff and quite immoveable. Mr. May got a little pocket-pistol ready, and we had if required a cutlass, and a ship's musket, which the Krúmen, by this time in a desperate fright, wished to see prepared, as they kept calling out to us, "Load de big gun, load de big gun." Could an unconcerned spectator have witnessed the scene, he would have been struck with the amount of the ludicrous it contained. There were our Krúboys, all as pale as black men could be, the perspiration starting from every pore, exerting to the utmost their powerful muscles, while Mr. May and I were trying to look as unconcerned as possible, and, to lessen the indignity of our retreat, were smiling and bowing to the Dúlti people, and beckoning to them to follow us. Their light canoes were very narrow, and the people were obliged to stand upright. The blades of their paddles, instead of being of the usual lozenge shape, were oblong and rectangular, and all curved in the direction of the propelling stroke. It was almost a regatta, our gig taking and keeping the lead. Ahead we saw an opening in the bush, by which we hoped to make our final retreat, but we were prepared, should the boat take the ground, to jump out at once and shove her into deep water. Fortune favoured us, we reached the doubtful spot, and with a single stroke of our paddles shot into the open river. Here we knew we were comparatively safe, as if the natives tried to molest us in the clear water, all we had to do was to give their canoes the stem and so upset them; our only fear had been that of being surrounded by them while entangled among the bushes. Our pursuers apparently guessed that we had now got the advantage, as they declined following us into the river, but turning paddled back to their watery abodes, and so ended the grand Dúlti chase.

CHAPTER VII.

THE RETURN.

WE were certainly not sorry that our affair at Dúlti had ended without our coming to any open rupture, which it was our policy as well as our desire by all means to avoid, as we did not wish to have it recorded that the first visit of Europeans to these wild regions had been marked by quarrelling or by bloodshed, as such an event would have tended to convince these savages that our advent was not that of friends, as we called ourselves, but of foes. Much may be said in excuse for the behaviour of these poor wretches. Accustomed to visits from none but enemies, there arrived unannounced at their village a party of strangers, whose complexions were fair and resembled those of the Púlbe whom they so dreaded. Actuated by no sense of honour, nor restrained by any high moral or religious sentiment, they merely saw in us a weak handful whom they thought they could crush, and in our clothes and instruments, inviting objects which they, as the stronger party, ought to appropriate. That was the only chain of reasoning followed by their

Sept. 29.

savage minds; they were powerful, we seemed to be weak; the temptation was too strong for them, they made the attempt, and, fortunately for us, they failed. Our determination had previously been to advance as far as we could until the noon of this day, and then to return; so, in accordance with our resolution, we had now, although most reluctantly, to head down the river. We could not have been at Dúlti, more than fifty or sixty miles from the Páro, and had the wind blown as freshly during the first two days of our excursion as it did upon the third, I have little doubt but that we might have been able to attain the wished-for confluence. As it was, we had added about thirty miles to our chart, and had visited several villages, and met with strange people and stranger scenes. All the natives we had encountered during our cruize were Baíbai, but those at Djín and Dúlti used a distinct dialect from the Djúku inhabitants further west. Our interpreter, who understood a little Djúku, could make out many words at Tshómo and at Láu, but afterwards he was completely puzzled. From this I am inclined to believe that there are several distinct dialects of the Djúku language; and that the one spoken in Koró-rofa differs considerably from that used by the more eastern Baíbai: and this accords well with what I have since learnt from Dr. Barth, who informs me that his specimens of Djúku, obtained near the Páro, do not at all correspond with those given in Koelle's

"Polyglotta Africana," which latter again we have ascertained to agree with the spoken dialect of Wukári.

Although Mr. May and myself much regretted having so early reached our "ne plus ultra," yet our boat's crew took a very different view of the subject. Ever since we had visited Djín, they had been living in fear and trembling; and one Kruman, not content with assuring us that he was destined never again to see his wives and children, in cannibalic horror, anticipated his fate, and in imagination saw himself slain, cooked, and devoured. During the ascent all hands had been too closely occupied to allow of surveying, so this duty had now to be resumed, the leadsman being stationed in the bows, and Mr. May sketching in the sides of the river with their ever-varying direction, and taking outline views of the mountains. The westerly breeze blew freshly against us, and being opposed to the current caused a considerable ripple; but the stream being the stronger, we went with but little exertion on our part, at the rate of fully three knots an hour. The sun's rays falling nearly directly upon us, through a perfectly cloudless sky, were so powerfully felt, that we were obliged in self-defence to set our awning, although it somewhat retarded our progress. Just before two o'clock we reached Djín, and landing at the scattered huts to the westward of the town, got a set of sights: while thus occupied, many natives came across the swamp, and gathering around, were urgent in their entreaties that we should re-visit their city, which however we respectfully declined. As they increased in numbers they showed a disposition to be again troublesome; so our operations being concluded, we gave a small present to our guide of the day previous, and took our departure. While close to a little grassy islet a few miles below this, we came upon a small herd of river-horses in a sportive humour, apparently playing at bo-peep or some such analogous game. One suddenly popped up its huge head close to us, but amazed at our interruption, lost no time in again disappearing below the surface. Shortly, Mount Laird and the eastern end of Pleiad Island were made out, and passing along the northern shore of the latter, by half-past four o'clock we reached Bándawa, and by five, Láu; off both which villages we were met by numerous canoes. Below Láu we examined on the south bank what had seemed to us, during our ascent, a rocky cliff; but we now found it to consist of a bank of red clay some fifteen feet high, with a layer of vegetable mould on the top. As long as we could make out the river's sides, we continued our progress, but, though now only a few miles from Gúrowa, being unwilling to have a blank in our chart, we anchored for the night, although the weather looked very threatening, and distant lightning in the east presaged a storm. We made, accordingly, every preparation, having our awning ready in case of rain.

The moon set shortly after midnight, and was succeeded by intense darkness, every thing around being unnaturally still; the air was hushed, the wind no longer sighed among the branches, and nothing was heard save the rippling of the ceaseless tide. The sky became completely overcast, one by one the stars disappeared, while numerous indications heralded an approaching tornado. A few minutes were left us to make ready to meet it, which we employed to the best advantage we could. More cable was given, all heavy weights and top-hamper were placed in the bottom of the boat, while Mr. May and I gathered our instruments and our few valuables around us, and covered ourselves as we best could with a scanty waterproof sheet we had with us, merely leaving our heads clear, so as to be able to look around. Our Krúmen stripped themselves, and wrapping their blankets about them, were ready to attempt to swim for it in case of necessity. Even my little dog seemed to comprehend the coming strife of the elements, and nestled closer beside me. The rudder was shipped, and the yoke-lines laid ready to be seized at a moment's notice. By this time the eastern heavens were brightly illumined by flashes of vivid lightning, the electric clouds quickly drawing nearer and nearer to us. These flashes issued from strata higher than the pitchy tornado cloud, which, by their light, showed black as ink and rising rapidly above the horizon. Still in our immediate neighbourhood the unearthly quiet reigned, all noise, all motion being ignored, and the very atmosphere seeming a blank. In this state,

Sept. 30.

however, we were not long permitted to rest; already could we distinguish the hissing of the coming whirlwind, and straining our eyes, we fancied we could discern a white line of foam stretching across the river. Presently it burst on us in full fury; the hurricane, sweeping along, enveloped our tiny craft, and large drops of rain struck fiercely against our faces as we attempted to peer into the obscure. Our only fear had been that the gale might catch us on the broadside, as, our boat being but light, it might have upset us, and left us among the crocodiles and river-horses; but, fortunately for us, it blew right a-head, and we rode easily. The rain, which threatened to be a deluge, ceased after a few minutes, and, still more to our astonishment, the wind greatly moderated, but these were succeeded by the most terrific thunderstorm I ever witnessed. Flash followed flash almost instantaneously, until at last the whole sky was lit up with one incessant glow of the most brilliant light. At last the clouds were right over head, and for upwards of an hour every part of the heavens to which we could look, had its own electric bolt. It was impossible to count such creations of the moment, but there must always have been every instant from ten to a dozen flashes, until at last we were utterly unable to distinguish each single thunder-clap, as all were mingled in one prolonged and continued peal, now for a second more faintly rolling, now again grandly swelling, and echoing in deep reverberations from the rugged sides of the mountains. Everything was plainly visible; the island near us, the banks of the river, and the more distant hills, all were distinctly seen.

Above us, around us, the forked lightning unweariedly still pursued its jagged, angular course, while one huge bolt, disdaining the tortuous path followed by its fellows, passed straight towards the earth, piercing the ground opposite to which we lay at anchor. Among the hills the storm raged still more furiously, the lightning playing unceasingly around each mountain summit, while ever and anon a bright spark would suddenly descend into some of the ravines below. Sometimes the passage of the lightning was from cloud to cloud, even at considerable distances; and then the stream of fire would spread, furcate, and divaricate, like the branch of some huge tree. These currents were of a purpler tint, and of smaller diameter, while those which descended were of a brighter red, and showed a much larger body of light. These aerial bolts were quite distinct from the ordinary discharge of two opposite clouds, and were not the mere passage of electricity from one to the other. During the occurrence of a few unusually near and vivid flashes, Mr. May and I were distinctly sensible of a feeling of warmth in our faces. At length there was a kind of lull, and the storm seemed to be decreasing, when a small whitish cloud was observed in the far east. It was a true cumulo-cirro-stratus, and must have been tremendously charged with electricity; for as it passed slowly along, we plainly saw constant powerful discharges. For some miles it continued to scatter around incessant forked bolts; but at length these became gradually fewer, and died away, while the cloud altered its shape to cirro-cumulus. A fresh breeze sprung up from the westward, and for a little time we were apprehensive of a squall up the river, which would not have been so pleasant; but fortunately this did not occur. By a little after three o'clock this magnificent storm had quite ceased, leaving no trace behind, save a distant thunder-peal, or an occasional flash of lightning among the mountains. Intense darkness prevailed; and now that the war of the elements was ended, we could hear about us the snorting of numerous hippopotami, which during the tempest had in fear been cowering among the reeds. Anxiously we waited for the morning; but it was not until half-past five that we could distinguish the river-banks; but these again visible, we weighed anchor, and resumed our voyage and our survey.

Nothing could have been more fortunate for us than our anchorage of the previous night. On either hand were lofty mountain ranges, and as the tornado approached, the clouds divided into two parts, each attaching itself to one of these chains, along which the storm raged in its greatest intensity, leaving the intervening space, where we were, comparatively free; and it was to this circumstance that our exemption from the wind and rain is to be ascribed. A few miles below us we could see the clouds again uniting, and pursuing their devastating course along the river; and to their further effects I shall have again shortly to refer.

We commenced the morning's exploits by rudely interrupting the early repast of a young river-horse, which was comfortably browsing on a grassy islet, but which, annoyed at the proximity of the impertinent strangers, plunged headlong into the river, and from the direction it took, probably passed right under the boat, but we saw the creature no more. Thick mist hung over the land, the horizon was cloudy and indistinct, and the air felt damp and chill, very different from the intensely hot atmosphere and clear sky which we had experienced when we ascended this part of the river. A little after seven we were abreast of Tshómo, immediately above which town two pretty green hills standing side by side, close to the water's edge, were named Mounts Katherine and Eleanor. We were now within sight of Gúrowa, the position of which we recognized by means of two peculiar, very tall trees, and we immediately began to look, but to look in vain for the "Pleiad." What could have become of her, or where could she have gone? The river was still rising, so that could not account for her disappearance. Many were our conjectures, but at length we concluded that she had gone to Zhirú to look for wood. By eight we were at Gúrowa, where we landed to call on our acquaintances, but found the place now nearly a deserted

P

village. The various distinguished visitors, and other persons of rank and quality, who had been attracted thither by the appearance of our steamer, had now returned to their own seats or to the gaieties of the metropolis, leaving behind them none but the government officials and the aboriginal natives. Still we were kindly welcomed, and these uncouth, unlettered beings seemed a highly civilized race after the pilfering savages we had met with during our cruise. We could merely learn that the vessel had left the morning after we did, certainly a hurried-looking proceeding; but at length our curiosity, or perhaps our anxiety, was gratified by two despatches being produced for me, one from my assistant, the other from Dr. Hutchinson. The latter being semi-official, I shall quote its information. From it we learned, to our surprise, that the water had fallen twenty-four inches, and therefore it had been judged expedient to proceed downwards. This we could not well explain, as the top of a sandbank, near the landing-place, which four days previously had been distinctly visible, was now quite covered. We further found that 10,000 cowries and some cloth were to be left for our use to purchase provisions with, so we made enquiries after this treasure, but could hear nothing of it; on appealing, however, again to the document, we discovered a postscript previously overlooked, which mentioned that after due consideration the cowries were not to be left, as there was some doubt of trusting the people. This error in judgment we did not approve of, as it might have been a question between our starving and the loss of a paltry sum, but fortunately we were quite independent. None of us were great gourmands, so our stock of provisions yet looked well up, our bag of rice being nearly half full, and having a little cocoa remaining. With the last of our stock of trinkets, we made a few presents, and purchased a fowl; then having gathered some sticks for firewood, we bade farewell to our friends, and went on in search of the "Pleiad." The letter mentioned that she would probably remain at Zhibú, a distance from Gúrowa, by the river, of about 100 miles.

This unlooked-for departure of the steamer considerably disarranged our plans. Careful sights had been taken before we left in the gig, and it was intended that, on our return, the chronometers should be re-rated, so as to insure accuracy during our voyage down. I had also anticipated finding that the trading gentlemen had reaped an abundant harvest, as ivory had promised to be abundant and cheap, and Ibrahim had gone to Hamarúwa to procure a larger quantity for sale. But I feared that such an abrupt departure would not be understood by the Sultan, especially after all our fine speeches to him, and as his people could not report that the river was actually falling. I had hoped, too, that Mr. Crowther would have been enabled to learn a little of the habits and of the history of the Báibai, and to pick up further information concerning these little-known regions.

I regretted particularly not again seeing our friend Saraki'n Háusa, to whom we had been so much indebted, and to whom I had promised a present on my return, which I was now utterly unable to do, and had no means either of explaining to him the cause. I had certainly left orders that, in the event of any emergency or any sudden fall of the water, the "Pleiad" should not be kept at Gúrowa for us; but here, without any such reason, we were left behind, many miles from our ship, which, had we been in need of help, could not have yielded it; and indeed had any mishap befallen us in the upper regions, we and our boat's crew must either have fallen among the barbarous tribes, or else made a desperate effort to fight our way to Hamarúwa, while, from the distance and the want of communication, our friends on board could have known nothing of our fate.

Silently, and with somewhat heavy hearts, we shoved off, disappointed at finding all our plans thus frustrated, and fearing that the sudden and inexplicable departure of our party might sadly embarrass any future visitors, and injure their chance of success by impairing the *prestige* which we had been all along endeavouring to establish for white men. The sun, however, hitherto concealed under the thick mists of the morning, now bursting through his cloudy prison, began to shine brilliantly in true tropical style, and the brightness of surrounding objects soon served to dispel our gloom. No longer searching for eddies, or creeping along in-shore, we now sought midstream, and aided by a powerful current, we progressed very rapidly. Before noon we had passed Zhirú, where the line of the river and the soundings being connected with what had been done formerly, we were able to lay in our lead-line, and clap on an additional hand to the oars. We recognized many objects well remembered during our slow ascent, and noted the mouth of the creek leading from Tshómo and Wúzu, and passing Bománda. This end, employed by canoes *en route* from Zhirú to Hamarúwa, is not nearly so eligible as that near Gúrowa, as it is further from the capital, and there being a strong tide to contend against. Two hours afterwards we were opposite Nák, and here we pulled close along the northern side to look for the opening of a small river from near Yákuba, said to join the Bínue near this spot, but were not successful in our search. We had now reached that portion of the river where we had observed the banks lined with a beautiful fan-palm, and which now again gladdened our sight. Shortly after four o'clock we passed the spot where a fortnight before we had wooded in the "Pleiad;" but the huge tree which we had then partially cut down, and which was at that time fifty or sixty yards from the river, was now surrounded by water, and we pulled close past it. A little way further on, the bank had given way, and the river was pouring in over the country with terrific violence. Grass and bushes had been swept clean away, and nothing had been able to resist the force of the flood, save some tall palms, the strong round trunks of which were the only visible signs that the vast sheet of water before us was but of moderate depth. Just before sunset we reached a place where the river divided into two branches, surrounding an irregular island, and meeting at Point Lynslager. We had ascended in the steamer by the western branch, but now we determined on returning by the other, which we fancied might be shorter, and besides by this route we should be going over new ground. A little way down, this branch again divided, and we selected, without much consideration, the more eastern channel. The current, as before, was with us, but soon began to slacken. We nevertheless pulled on for a couple of hours, but without reaching Point Lynslager. Our course was tortuous, but the general direction being correct, we continued our voyage. The creek which had been gradually narrowing, now began to spread out, and at length the vast expanse of water which we saw by the moonlight, plainly indicated that we were cruising about over submerged country. Our men were tired; but being timid, they said they wished to pull till they reached the "big water;" but signs of exhaustion being evident, and not being well able to pilot ourselves among the tree-tops, we anchored in a convenient spot in two and a half fathoms, after a pull of about eighty miles. We were nearly free from mosquitoes, and the only sounds heard throughout the night were the grunts of hippopotami, revelling, no doubt, in such a congenial situation.

Morning shone out fine and clear, and with the first peep of dawn our anchor was weighed. Mr. May got to the mast-head, but made no discovery; but as it got a little more light, we made out to our delight, though at a great distance, the conical top of Mount Forbes, which formed an excellent leading-mark, and which also showed us that we were more to the southward than we had reckoned. We also distinguished in the north-west some high land, for which, as we thought it might be near the river, we accordingly steered. The depth of water varied from two to four fathoms, the average being about two and a half, and a slight current, of about one knot, still remained in our favour. As far as we could observe, all around, for many miles, was one vast extended lake, the tops of clumps of trees showing here and there like little scattered islets. Everything wore marks of a deluge. A savoury odour borne down by the breeze called our attention to the decomposing carcase of a buffalo, surprised in the low lands by the flood, while still nearer to us floated the dead body of a lioness, which, though at any other time I would have looked on it as an invaluable prize, was now, in our hurry and difficulty, allowed to pass unmolested. The trees and the tops of the bushes were covered with locusts eagerly seeking refuge from the world of waters, or else swarmed with other innumerable forms of insect

Oct. 1.

life, enough to have gladdened the eyes and rejoiced the heart of any entomologist, but from which I was obliged to content myself with picking, *en passant*, a few stray specimens. We observed also, afterwards, a canoe paddled by two natives; but not being able to see any habitation, or any dry ground towards which they might direct their frail bark, we began to speculate whether the Aborigines of these localities might not be amphibious animals. We continued to sail in a south-west direction, believing that ultimately we must thus reach the main river; and at length, about nine o'clock, could hardly believe our eyesight, when right before us coursed a rapid stream. Into this we quickly pushed, and found ourselves, to the especial satisfaction of the Krúmen, once more in the Bínue, having pulled for nearly seven hours, and over fully twenty miles of flooded country, and having found ample reasons why these regions remain uninhabited.

The spot where we rejoined the Bínue was several miles below the junction of the Akám or Bankúndi river, and we regretted that we had missed seeing the narrow portion of the river just above that place, as we had been curious to note the state and force of the current at full flood, as we remembered well the rapidity with which it ran during our ascent, when it had nearly baffled our utmost efforts. Our men now pulled with redoubled vigour, and, taking good heed not again to try dubious channels, we went cheerily along, hoping to reach Zhibú by the evening.

However, about half-past eleven, one of our men, quick and sharp-sighted as Krúmen ever are, suddenly exclaimed " Dere de ship," and sure enough, some miles a-head of us, we could make out her mast-heads, her hull being concealed from us by an intervening point. Knowing that there was no town in that neighbourhood, we were much puzzled to fancy what she could be doing; but, on getting nearer, finding that she was broadside to the stream, and evidently not at anchor, the real cause was too apparent. It was not, therefore, with the most comfortable feelings that we got alongside, and stepped on board, to find the "Pleiad" aground in a very awkward position.

We were soon put in possession of the movements of the steamer. Mr. Harcus, careful and zealous as he invariably was, found on going ashore that the water had drained off some low grounds, where it had accumulated after heavy rain. Anxious about the safety of the ship, and desirous of fulfilling my orders, he made numerous inquiries about the state of the river, and received conflicting replies. Mr. Crowther and Mr. Richards, both acquainted with African seasons, assured him that there was no danger in remaining; but others on board, some of whom had for some time previously been alarmed at our long stay, and who had been frequently asking me when I intended to retrace our steps, thinking that since I was absent the chief obstacle against turning back was removed, exerted all their persuasions and arguments now to accomplish this feat, and succeeded in inducing Mr. Harcus to believe that an actual fall of water had taken place. Accordingly, the "Pleiad" left, and having but a small stock of firewood on board, the fuel was soon exhausted, and the only remaining plan of descent was by allowing her to drop down with the stream, which, Mr. Harcus, having a thorough acquaintance with river navigation, managed beautifully. At length, on the second day, that was on the 29th, he was desirous of passing by a narrow channel, which offered the greatest depth of water. To prepare against any contingency, a hand was stationed by the anchor in order that it might be let go at a moment's notice. Unfortunately, just at the mouth of this place, the man at the helm either paid no attention or did not understand the orders; the ship's head was paying off in the wrong direction, so Mr. Harcus sung out to let go the anchor, a command which was obeyed after the lapse of about a minute. This delay, short as it was, was fatal; before she could be brought up, the vessel struck on the weather end of a long bank, and remained fast, with a powerful current playing on her broadside and driving her further on. The tornado of Friday night had been experienced in full force, the wind blowing with terrific violence, and sweeping the decks. Such was the history of this unfortunate voyage; the ship had now been nearly forty-eight hours in this position, and every day the river was expected to fall, and if so, she would very soon be left high and dry.

Mr. Harcus appeared worn out with anxiety and hard work, but no one, except Mr. Guthrie, seemed to be at all zealous in their assistance. Having received his report, and ascertained the various particulars, fresh efforts were commenced, but, from the rapidity of the stream, much difficulty was experienced in laying out the anchors in good positions. By night all hands were well exhausted, and labour was suspended until the following morning, when the attempts were again renewed, and, in the course of the forenoon, were crowned with success, as we managed to get the afterpart of the vessel hove off until the current caught her on the opposite quarter, when she speedily swung round to an anchor previously laid out a-head. The remainder of the day was spent in repairing damages, and preparing for another start; but we were all rejoiced at being once more afloat, and freed from the difficulties which had so seriously threatened us.

During the forenoon a canoe was observed coming up the river, and on being hailed came alongside. It contained a Báutshi trader returning with two slaves and some ivory; the practice being to buy both of these *commodities* at one time, and during any land travelling to oblige the slaves to carry the ivory. The latter being of good quality was speedily purchased, but with the other we could have no concern; and on the man's departure Mr. Crowther besought him to be kind and considerate towards the poor captives, which he promised to be. The slaves, two young men, were secured by irons in the bottom of the canoe, and looked sullen and savage. They were Báibai, and had been purchased at Gómkoi, the chief town of a large district in Korórofa. This town is situated on the side and top of a hill, and is about five days from the river. During the journey travellers must sleep mostly in the bush, there being few, if any, villages on the way. The inhabitants are all Báibai, are pagans, and speak Djúku; they are all clothed, though scantily, some of the women wearing a covering made of leaves. He had with him several spare pairs of slave-irons, one of which I purchased, and was glad to find it was of native manufacture, and had not been procured from any people calling themselves civilized. He had also with him several bundles of pieces of iron, pointed towards the extremities, but thicker in the middle. Similar pieces we had seen at Gúrowa, but had not ascertained their use, and were now surprised to find they were money, and therefore analogous to the hoe-shaped pieces formerly seen at O'jogo. One hundred of these, which were named "Kántai," our friend informed us formed the average price of a male slave from Hamarúwa to Wukári, so much more were these bits of metal esteemed than human creatures. He likewise told us that horses were sent from Báutshi to Gómkoi, and that for one horse five slaves could be procured. He confirmed the intelligence we had formerly gleaned about the small confluent branch which we had seen, which was, he said, named Bankúndi, Akám and Wúrobo being villages on its banks. This trader was bound for Dáli, a town on the right bank, about a mile above where we were; thence he intended to proceed inland to Dámpara, to Wázai, and to Yákuba. The inhabitants of Báutshi were, he stated, nearly all, if not all, Muhammadans, and the languages spoken were Háusa and Púlo, but principally the former.

Everything being ready, we commenced our voyage about nine o'clock, and under Mr. Harcus's management dropped down beautifully. We once got into shallow water for a short time, but the depth was mostly very great, often from ten to twelve fathoms. Nearly all along the banks were flooded, and the country inundated. Once the current swept us alongside the bank, and we got entangled among the bushes, but by the use of our sweeps and a kedge we got off easily. By seven o'clock we were off Zhibú, and accordingly fired a gun and dropped anchor.

Oct. 3.

By this time a good many of the Krúmen were in the sick list, affected, as before mentioned, with swelling of the feet and legs, and with great debility. Their daily allowance of rice had been increased by Dr. Hutchinson to two pints, but proved an inadequate quantity. We had, hitherto, been rather unsuccessful in our inquiries after suitable provisions, so that I had now to order more vigorous steps to be taken to endeavour to procure fresh meat and vegetables for their use, and our small remaining stock of wine was laid aside entirely for the sick. The firemen who had immense fatigue to undergo, in an atmosphere often of from 120° to 130° F., had been originally allowed a quarter of a pound of salt meat daily, which I had previously doubled, but now I ordered fresh meat to be issued also to them whenever practicable. I am obliged again to allude to these matters, that any subsequent expedition may avoid making similar blunders, and so escape the amount of sickness which we encountered, and which was solely to be ascribed to deficient and improper nutriment. Though completely opposed, as I have stated, to the regular employment of spirits, an occasional glass of grog would have been of immense service to our crew, and I should make a point of being well stocked with rum before again undertaking a similar voyage. The late Mr. Consul Beecroft used always to allow his Krúmen fresh meat and a small quantity of spirits every day, by which means he not only kept them in good health, but got from them a much larger amount of labour than they could have executed under the falsely economical system. I regret much thus to be compelled to admit that we suffered from such a complaint as scurvy, a disease the causes leading to which are now so thoroughly understood, that under the most ordinary management it is never seen, and which bids fair to be soon remembered with things which have been, but in the victualling arrangements made at Fernando Po, common sense as well as physiological principles were entirely overlooked.

CHAPTER VIII.

FURTHER DISAPPOINTMENTS.

In the morning we dropped into our former position, and passing a hawser ashore, hauled close in. During our previous visit the bank had been six or seven feet above the river, but now it was completely covered, and the whole country was under water to within 120 yards of the walls of Zhibú. This being a good wooding station, our first care was to send the Krúmen ashore with their hatchets to procure a supply. Having lost the opportunity of getting fresh rates for the chronometers at Gúrowa, I determined to remain here for five days, to enable Mr. May to obtain them satisfactorily; and accordingly a set of sights was taken this morning. Being slightly indisposed, I did not go on shore, but requested Mr. Crowther to visit the king for me, and to give him a red velvet tobe, which I had kept for him. Several visitors came on board, from some of whom I obtained information about the river. One man had been at the confluence of the Páro, and mentioned among other places, which he had visited, Tshámba, Bundú, and Kwóntsha, possibly the Bundang and Kontsha of Petermann's Atlas. They all knew Gómkoi, and said that halfway to it was a town named Súntai, while about three days' journey beyond it was another Djúku town, Alúnge. A town which we had seen above Zhibú, we learnt, was named Sháro or Tsháro, and its chief Belál, and another town, two days' journey towards the east, was called E'rima. Opposite Tsháro, on the Báutshi side, is a village Básoi. I found, too, that Wukári was not above a long day's journey from Zhibú, and that the route was much frequented. Mr. Crowther, on his return, told me he had visited the King, whom he found surly and uncivil, hardly thanking him for his present. The Galadima, again, or Prime Minister, had behaved to him with much kindness and cordiality. The King said that the sword he had received formerly was broken, and that he therefore wanted another one; but on being asked to exhibit the broken blade, he made various frivolous excuses. Mr. Crowther ascertained that a messenger from the King of Wukári was now in the town, waiting for us, and, if possible, ready to be our guide to that place.

Being very desirous of visiting this important town, we went on shore next morning, and calling on the Galadima, asked him to accompany us to the King, which he readily did. On seeing his majesty, I told him the purport of our errand, and asked him for a guide and horses, saying, I was ready to pay him any reasonable price. His manner from the very commencement plainly indicated that he was not over-anxious that we should perform this journey, probably from a feeling of jealousy, and being unwilling that his rival should derive any knowledge of us, except through him. I asked to see the Wukári messenger, but on his being produced he could give us no information, being awed by the presence of the King. Bohári then said, there were only two horses in Zhibú,—a statement which we knew to be positively false; and he added, that these horses could only take us as far as Zú, an open place about halfway to Wukári, where traders from the two towns meet; that at this place we should have to sleep all night, and send to Wukári for fresh horses, and for his assistance in the matter he demanded 3 long sabres and 30,000 cowries,—a most exorbitant charge. Mr. Crowther mentioned to him the inhospitality of wishing to make strangers sleep in the bush, when, if he liked, he could easily otherwise arrange it, and I told him that I would consent to give him one sabre and 16,000 cowries, which was ample allowance. Seeing he could not deter us from trying, he drew back from the bargain, on which I got up, telling him that he was breaking faith with us, and that I would no longer treat with him. He now asked me again to be seated, and after some further conversation, it was agreed that horses should be ready for us next morning at sunrise, on which we took our leave. He spoke, however, with such reluctance, that I fully anticipated finding fresh obstacles put in our way.

We found extensive preparations being made for enlarging the town. Numbers of long stakes had been cut, and laid at regular intervals, so as to make the walls include a space of about 100 yards beyond their present site. Outside the gates were fields planted with ground nuts (*Arachis*), of which there were two kinds; one, the commoner one, with obovate leaves and a yellow flower, yielding the ordinary nut; the other, not yet in flower, but with elongate, acuminate leaves, and said to produce a round nut. The steward had been tolerably successful in his pursuit of fresh meat and vegetables, as several sheep and goats had been purchased, besides a good supply of pumpkins —a most valuable acquisition in the state we were in.

Shortly after daylight Mr. Crowther, Dr. Hutchinson, Mr. Richards, and I went ashore, and proceeding to the King, found, as we had fully expected, no horses. On demanding the reason of this, we were told that we had not paid for them, a statement which confirmed our ideas of the King's secret intentions, as the day before, when I offered to pay one half before starting, and the remainder on our return, I was told not to mind. Rather indignantly, I asked Bohári if he thought we were going to cheat him, or whether he thought the bargain was not fully as advantageous for him as for ourselves. Dr. Hutchinson offered to go on board and fetch the sabre and cowries, which he did, and they were displayed to the King, who then said, that he did not want cowries, and that they did not suit him. We then asked for the messengers, and said we should perform the journey on foot under their guidance; but the King said, that could not be, as they were not ready, having yet to prepare food for themselves. I said, that was no matter, as we should supply them with abundance, on which, at a sign from the King, they disappeared, and could not again be found. Finding all our endeavours to be thus frustrated, and having no means of finding the way ourselves, I rose and told the King that he had grossly deceived us, and that I should not again believe him, and that should I again return to the Bínue, as I hoped I should, I should take care to inform the Sultan of Hamarúwa, his master and our friend, of his bad behaviour. He winced under this, and I could see, from the ominous silence around, that he met with no support from his followers. I then refused to shake hands with him, but went directly on board with my party. We had hardly got outside the gates when a messenger came running after us, asking us to return; but I replied that if the King had any communication to make, he should send it properly on board, more particularly as now the sun was high up, and it was much too late to start.

Shortly after our return on board, one of the Galadíma's people came off, and told us, from his master, that, after our departure, the Galadíma and several others had spoken strongly to the King about his conduct, and that it was trusted no quarrel would ensue; on which I asked him to thank the Galadíma for his good offices, and to assure him that I had no dispute with anyone but Bohári. Not long afterwards the Galadíma himself arrived, and said that in consequence of the urgent remonstrances made by himself and other head-men, he hoped yet to arrange matters and to be able to procure guides and horses for us for next day; and he therefore requested that I would again see the King, whose behaviour he extremely regretted. I replied by thanking him for his good wishes and kind endeavours, but said, that, as the King had wilfully and openly broken faith with us, I could not again trust him. I added, that as I looked on him (the Galadíma) as our sincere friend, I would, entirely out of deference to his feelings, send messengers to the King this evening, and that, as I had not the remotest wish that the people should suffer for the fault of their ruler, I hoped trading would go on as usual. With this he expressed himself satisfied and took his leave. In the afternoon I sent Mr. Richards to the Galadíma and the King, and Mr. Crowther volunteered to accompany him. On their return they gave such an account of their interview that I immediately determined to decline having any further communication with the King, and sent to intimate this resolution, thanking at the same time all those who had assisted us. A kind of festival was held at Zhibú this afternoon at the installation of a new Saraki'n Dọki, or Master of the Horse, of which Mr. Crowther has given a description in his journal.*

* Pages 134, 135.

Bohári is a Báibai by birth, and completely destitute of the Púlo polish. It is easy at a glance to distinguish between those who have Fuláta blood and the true Báibai. The former have mostly skins of a lighter colour, in person they are taller and more slender, and their general appearance is more civilized; they have the head shaved, wear head-dresses and Háusa tobes; their expression is less rude, and their manners are milder. The Báibai, again, are darker-skinned, shorter, and more robust; their features are more strongly marked, their behaviour is more rude, and their looks more savage. They seldom or never shave the head, which is kept uncovered, but have, occasionally, the hair on either side done in two slender plaits. The ear-lobes are large and pendulous, and pierced with large holes, through which are passed ponderous ear-rings. The shape of the head is usually circular, and the forehead retreats greatly. The upper arm, however, is not marked as among the Báibai further up the river.

The sick-list continued to increase, being recruited almost entirely from among the Krúboys, the symptoms in all being of a similar description.

Whether from fear, or whether from an order from the King, I do not know, but no trade was carried on, and very few natives came off to us. Some Wukári men were anxious to know why we did not visit their city, on which we told them the reason, which they said they would make known on their return. Mr. Crowther got some specimens of Djúku words, which were found, on comparison, to agree almost exactly with those of Koelle. A slave-hunting expedition was said to be preparing, and a man came off to Mr. Crowther to ask for a charm to insure success.

The water first showed decided signs of falling about the 3rd of October, and by the 5th the decrease was very perceptible. On the evening of that day, having completed our wooding, we let go our warp, and swung further out into the stream, which relieved us greatly from the attacks of mosquitoes, and besides removed us from the immediate proximity of what was now commencing to be marshy land. On Sunday afternoon I sent Mr. Richards to say farewell to the Galadíma, to thank him for his friendly behaviour, and to offer him a present.

Oct. 9.

Monday morning, being the fifth from the date of our arrival, turned out fine and clear, so that there was no difficulty in getting sights, and finishing the chronometer business; so, having laid in a good stock of fresh provisions, we weighed anchor, and turned our head down the river. Just before we started, some fish were brought on board, amongst which I was delighted at finding a *Polypterus*, probably either *P. Senegalensis*, or else a new species, as it differs from the one found in the Nile. Some miles below Zhibú we passed a long island, which was named "Crowther Island," after our excellent and much-esteemed friend. A little before one we anchored off Gándiko, and found the banks still so flooded, that when we went ashore the boat took us very nearly into the town. As a matter of course we paid a visit to the King, and renewed our former acquaintance. We saw some very fine sheep here, the largest we had met with. They all stood high, having long legs, and had black and white fleeces. Sheep in this country seldom or never get fat, their fleeces are more hairy than woolly, and never grow long or thick. The King having heard me inquire about corn, sent me off some bundles of the different kinds grown in the vicinity. There was very little trade, some hippopotami teeth and lead-ore being the only articles offered for sale.

The kinds of corn grown along the Bínue are four; namely, maize, or Indian corn,[*] two kinds known along the coast as Guinea or Dáwa (often, though incorrectly, *Dower*) corns, and Géro. The first is universally cultivated; the stalks grow to a height of from six to eight feet, and it is known in Háusa as Másara. It is used mostly whole, being roasted and eaten either alone or with a little pepper and salt, in both of which ways it is very palatable; it is more seldom ground. The ripe grain is yellow, but is also found white, purple, or red. The Guinea corns are also widely spread, especially one kind, known as Dáwa or Dáwa-Másara; the other, called Dawúra, being more rare. They are species of *Holcus*, and the stalks grow to a height of from eight to ten feet, or even upwards. The fruit is

---

[*] *Zea Mays.*

arranged in loose panicles, and the grains, when ripe, are pale-red, though white and dark-coloured varieties also occur. This grain is used, when ground, for making bread and other articles of food, the sweetest and most pleasant native beer is prepared from it, and a red dye is said to be obtained from the ripe stalks. The fourth kind, named Géro, is very abundant along the Bínue, but to the westward of the Kwóra is said not to be so plentiful, though I have been told that it is cultivated on the upper parts of the Gambia. It is a species of *Penicillaria*, and its small, rounded, greenish-yellow seeds are nearly sessile, on a long cylindrical spike. It is in daily household use, and most of their beer is prepared from it, though it is not so palatable as the beer from the Dáwa.

Before leaving Gándiko, Mr. May got a good observation for latitude, and also measured by triangulation the breadth of the river, which he had also done at Zhibú. I had a short visit from the old chief of the neighbouring town, Gankéra, after which, about eight o'clock, we got under steam and passed rapidly downwards. In the vicinity of Gándiko are numerous trees of a species of *Kigelia* (p. 128), bearing a very peculiar fruit. The trees are of considerable size, with (digitate) leaves; and I have generally noticed them as growing very near the river,—often, during the floods, actually in the water, so much so, that I have gathered the fruit from the boat. The fruit is pendulous from the extremity of a long slender stalk, and bears some resemblance to a large, compressed cucumber. It varies in length from eight or ten inches to a couple of feet, and is filled with a somewhat hard, white pulp. The fruit is not used by the natives, but is said to be eaten by monkeys and by elephants, and also by some birds. The first spot where we met with this tree was near O'jogo; it was more abundant further up the river, and the last place where I saw it, was between Tshómo and Láu.

Below Gándiko the country in its then deluged condition was rather uninteresting; but we soon came to the region of hills, those pretty green ones near the river, which we had named during our asscent. We passed in succession, Mount Traill, Mounts Trenabie and Adams, and finally reaching Mount Herbert, anchored just beyond it, in seven fathoms. An unfortunate accident befel us here. By the neglect of the man acting as boatswain the cable was not properly bitted, and as we had a five-knot current carrying us astern, and our steam being exhausted, the chain spun out rapidly. The break was worn by constant use, and of no service; and it appeared that the cable would run out to the clinch, when all of a sudden the end appeared on deck, and before it could be jammed in the hawse-hole, or anything else done, it had disappeared overboard. The other anchor was immediately let go, and brought us up.

Some canoes tried to come off to us, but owing to the immense strength of the current were nearly upset alongside, and one only managed to get properly to us. It brought a message from the chief of the village situated on the height above us, named An'yishi, to welcome us, and ask us to come ashore; so I sent to say we would go and visit him. We accordingly went; and finding with some difficulty the landing-place—which was quite concealed by tall trees—prepared to ascend by a winding path a cliff composed of volcanic blocks. I measured its height above the water by the aneroid barometer, and found it to be seventy-six feet. The first sound we heard on arriving at the top was, " Salaam Aleikum;" to which we replied, " Aleikum Salaam." This is a form of salutation we very rarely met with, the more frequent one along the Bínue being the " Háusa sanú" or " láfia," the answer to which is " Birká," or thanks. The word " Marhába " is employed to welcome a person from a distance, or who has been long absent. Fulátas often use " Wal-ejáma," meaning, " How d'ye do?"

An'yishi is a small village situated rather picturesquely at the top of the cliff, and nearly at the foot of Mount Herbert. It was first built about two years ago, and is inhabited entirely by Djúkus of Korórofa, being directly subject to Wukári. The place was surrounded by numerous cultivated patches bearing maize and Dáwa corn, and among the huts were many Papaw trees and Croton bushes. These latter I have noticed in great abundance near many of the towns, and they grow, I have been informed, in equal plenty near the coast. Those which we noticed were covered with fruit, the oil from which might be easily prepared, and form a very valuable product; the seeds are employed medicinally by the natives. We went to see the chief, who received us in a most friendly manner in the open air, just outside of his hut. Mats, and buffalo and leopard skins were spread for us to sit upon, and we commenced our interview through the usual chain of interpreters; but one of them making some mistake, the chief laid aside etiquette, and addressed us directly in Háusa. When we told him of our wishes and the objects of our mission, he raised his hands in utter amazement, and it was some time before he could find words to express his gratitude. Poor man! brought up as he had been in the midst of war and rapine, driven from place to place by rude oppressors, obliged day and night to keep a vigilant watch for the stealthy approach of the foe, and never daring to perform a journey but with sword girt and spear in hand, such an idea as that of simple philanthropy was quite ignored in his system of philosophy, nor could he imagine people coming from a far-distant land to endeavour to assist or do good to utter strangers. He told us that only two years previously he and his people had been driven from their former seat, Sundúbe, by Bcribéri from Láfia, who frequently during the dry season ford the river. Wukári was described as a very large town, about twice the size of Zhibú, and thickly populated. The king, Anjú, is much liked, being himself a Djúku; he speaks Háusa with ease. From An'yishi to Wukári is three good days' journey; the first stage to Akwóna occupies about ten hours, thence to Arúfu or Afiái, two towns not far from each other, twelve hours; and finally to Wukári also twelve hours. He said he had sent to some neighbouring villages to ask the head-men to come and meet us, and that the following day they would all be present. A man was pointed out to us who had lately been taken captive near Gándiko, but who had managed to effect his escape. Gándiko, Gankéra, and I'bi, or their inhabitants, they call Katshára or Katshála, but from what cause we could not learn. The territory on the other side of the river, opposite to An'yishi, belongs to the Keána district of Dóma; the distance from An'yishi to Keána is a day and a half, the night being spent at Mágidi. The bearing of Keána from An'yishi is about west north-west, and that of Mágidi about north-west. They confirmed the name "Nú," as being the correct Koróroſa designation for the river, but said it was quite as well known as the Bínue.

From what we learnt, the journey to and from Wukári would occupy from six to seven days, and we also were told that the King would be offended if we did not remain with him for five or six days, so that under any circumstances it could not be performed in fewer than ten days. This was an amount of time, which with a rapidly falling river, a sickly crew, and many things on board requiring constant looking after, I could not consider myself justified in so occupying, and had, therefore, to give up the last chance of visiting Wukári. I resolved, however, to send a message to the King, telling how our endeavours had been opposed and frustrated, and hoping that we should be more successful another time. The cloth worn by the inhabitants of An'yishi is chiefly of Wukári manufacture, but some of a finer texture, and occasionally with a red thread through it, is from the Dóma markets. The usual pattern of Wukári cloth is an alternate blue and white stripe, but the blue is scarcely of so dark a shade as what I saw in other places. The cloth is rather coarse, and is thick and strongly made.

The following morning we again went ashore, and getting under a large tree, soon established a market. Dr. Hutchinson looked principally after ivory, the steward sought after provisions, while Mr. Crowther and I inquired after manufactures and ornaments, &c. Some balls of camwood were brought to us, but they had been got from other markets. We purchased several large lumps of lead-ore, got near Arúfo,* where it is said to be in abundance, and to be found near the surface. It can be bought cheaply, as the people do not place much value on it. Among the spectators we were

Oct. 11.

---

* Since our return, specimens of this have been analysed in London, and yield the following results :—"Galena or lead ore, sixteen hundred weight of lead (equal to 80 per cent.) and three ounces of fine silver to the ton of twenty hundred weight."—See Hutchinson's Narrative, p. 146.

much pleased at recognising some Mítshis, and soon got into conversation with the head man of the party, a most intelligent person, named Njóro, who spoke Mítshi, Djúku, and Háusa. He called himself Mútshi, which was, he said, the same as the word Mítshi used further down. He said we were not far from the confines of the Mítshi territory, and that his own village, named Wúm, or Iwúm was not far distant. He was anxious that we should go home with him, and said he hoped on our return we would visit his countrymen. He told us that the people of Korórofa and of Mítshi are friendly, and that along the frontiers their towns are much mixed, as he expressed it to Mr. Crowther by inserting the fingers of the one hand among those of the other. He then gave Mr. Crowther the Mítshi numerals, and some other words of that language. He asked us the name of our monarch, which we repeated to him several times, until he himself said slowly, Vic-to-ria, which he remarked sounded well, and like the name of a great Queen. Being obliged to go on board, I asked Mr. Crowther, who was going to walk with Dr. Hutchinson to Anúfo, a town on the other side of Mount Herbert where they would meet several chiefs, to deliver a message for the King of Wukári. This he did to Abíki, the chief, who said that his Galadíma was shortly about to proceed to Wukári, where he should deliver it in person. Njóro, being anxious to see the ship, went on board with me, and was greatly delighted with everything he saw, but was especially struck with a large mirror in the saloon, and with the clock, the use of which was explained to him. Among other little bits of information which he gave me, was that the name of the King of Keána was Adúso. He told me also of two Korórofa towns, one named Kwóto, about two days' journey from An'yishi, and another called A'kate, very near the Mítshi boundary. He and his followers were all tatooed, just like the Mítshis we had met at O'jogo, and though with similar features, were less savage-like, and wonderfully more intelligent and less suspicious. Nothing could have exceeded the frank manner in which Njóro made our acquaintance, or the open way in which he answered our questions, or passed remarks to us. Several of the females of his party were stained with camwood, and one boy had on a necklace of English trade beads. Yams are said to be cultivated about Wukári; a few specimens were seen at An'yishi, but of a very indifferent nature. We were told that the name of the Púlo who first made war on Wukári was Súfa.

The river ran with such velocity that our light gig, pulling five oars, and manned by as many muscular, stalwart Krúmen, was unable to make any headway, so it was impossible to attempt to drag for our lost anchor in the boat. We therefore cut up all the wood we had on board, and getting up good steam, got our grapnels overboard from the steamer, and worked for nearly three hours, until we had only sufficient fuel left to carry us to the nearest wooding place. We had, therefore, after an unsuccessful hunt, to turn the ship's head downwards, and to commence our descent in the midst of heavy rain, the atmosphere being so thick as almost to prevent our seeing the shore on either side, and quite to spoil our parting view of the pretty hills of the Ellesmere range. Of several villages seen during our ascent, the only evidences now visible were the tops of some huts, showing just above the surface of the water. We passed along the north side of Washington Island, and my intention had been to stop at Abítshi, but on nearing this place we could hardly recognize it, so completely was its appearance altered by the greater part being under water. We therefore went on, and at a little before three o'clock anchored off Rógan-Kóto. Our friend Onúse came off to welcome us, and she informed us that our messenger, Zúri, was waiting for us at O'jogo; she did not know the particulars of his trip, but no white man had returned with him. Scarcely was our visit to the chief Jáda over, when numbers of canoes came off, bringing with them for sale corn, pepper, rice, yams, fowls, goats, as well as cloths, mats, &c., showing, in their eagerness for trade, and their anxiety to make the most of their time, their I'gbira blood. The inhabitants all told us that they were delighted to see us once more, as they had heard a rumour of our having had a fight with Fulátas up the river, which we assured them was certainly not the case. Being in need of a supply of fuel, I thought it advisable, as our tools were nearly worn out, and the strength of the crew impaired, to purchase wood instead of cutting, as it could be got of excellent quality, well dried, and at a very cheap rate; besides which, we should save two or three days in time. Dr. Hutchinson, therefore, went ashore with Alihéli, well stocked with handkerchief-pieces, romals, and also needles and zinc mirrors, and bought capital well-seasoned wood from the people, as fast or faster than six or eight men could carry it forty yards to the boat, and so by night we had a good stock on board. Among other articles brought off by the people was a kind of starch, resembling cassada; some ivory also was offered, but at very high prices. Mr. May was successful here, as he had been at An'yishi, in getting sights for longitude, as well as observations for latitude. We met some more Mítshi men here from the opposite town of Abágwa, from whom Mr. Crowther obtained a few more words. The people of Kóndoko, or Akóndoko, who were formerly living on an island in the centre of the river, having been driven from their abodes by the rising of the waters, were at this time residing a little way beyond Rógan-Kóto, where they had erected temporary huts.

From a man in Rógan-Kóto I learnt that the proper I'gbira name for the river is Irihú, or Ilihú, often contracted Lihú; also that I'gbira and Igára call Háusa Abákpa, while Háusa calls I'gbira "Kóto." A woman to-day mentioned a people living near Zaría, whom she called Gbándawa, but she could tell little more about them than that they spoke a peculiar dialect. The journey from Rógan-Kóto to Keána occupies a day and a half, the night being spent at a village called Tufíye. Having now a stock of wood sufficient to carry us to the Confluence, and all trading being finished, we left Rógan-Kóto, and reaching the high wooded country near it, about half-past eight were off Ajáma, and passing the narrow part of the river below, where we now found nine fathoms' water, at nine o'clock anchored off O'jogo, and immediately landed. The town was reduced by the rise of the water to very narrow limits, and when we stepped out of our boat we found ourselves in the middle of the huts. Mr. May got a set of sights, after which we called on the chief, and sent for our messengers. Máma and his two men were all ready, but Zúri and his followers were not to be found. I gave them, therefore, half an hour, after which I said I should leave, whether they were on board or not. I was glad to have Máma, on A'ma-A'boko's account, but as for Zúri I did not so much care, as his conduct had on several occasions displeased me. As no trade was to be done, I went to say "Good-bye" to old O'robo, and to thank him for taking care of the messengers, and I delighted his heart by giving a green merino cloak and 10,000 cowries to defray his expenses. We now embarked, and I found Zúri in a canoe alongside grumbling very much about going, and making various excuses. He said some trading women had come from Keána with rice to sell to us, on which I told him I would give them a small present to prevent any disappointment. Finding nothing could induce me to remain, he said he would not go, when I replied that it was a matter of perfect indifference to me, and as the anchor was now at the bow, I went forward for a few minutes. On my return aft I was a little astonished at finding that Zúri had bundled all his goods on board, and was now sitting in a sulky mood in the iron-canoe alongside, the Keána women having returned to O'jogo. Subsequent events induced us to believe that Zúri intended to play these poor women false, by persuading them to follow him down the river, when he would have endeavoured to seize them for slaves. Zúri brought with him his domestic slave O'robo, his son Músa, and a still younger son, named Bowálla, whom he had picked up during his cruise. Zúri was a fine-looking man, and had a great reputation for gallantry. According to the custom of his country he had many wives, but instead of keeping them all in one harem, he followed the example of English sailors, who are accused of having a wife in every port; and accordingly he had his spouses distributed among the various towns which, in his peregrinations, he was likely to visit. When we first reached O'jogo we were introduced to the wife who was stationed there, a rather good-looking young woman. Since that time, however, they had quarrelled and separated, and Zúri having undertaken the charge of her child, was now bringing him along with himself. But another boy accompanied him, very different in appearance from the others, entirely unclad, and evidently not cared for or looked after. Suspecting him to be a slave, Mr. Crowther examined Zúri very closely, and though he seemed uneasy when spoken to about him, yet he assured us that this boy was a domestic slave, whom he was taking with him as a companion to his youngest son, as he had belonged to his mother. He was told that as a domestic slave we had no desire to interfere, but that he must recollect that no English ship could be for a moment permitted to hold a slave intended for sale, and thus it was passed over, but our suspicions having been aroused we determined to watch narrowly.

The difference in the level of the water since we last passed along this part of the river, not only greatly increased the facility of our navigation, but had also completely altered the aspect of all around. Nowhere could now be seen the little islets on which we used formerly to land and take our evening observations, while we quietly steamed over the sandbanks which had so puzzled and distressed us. On our way we passed by a Yímahá canoe, which was returning from Abítshi, which place I believe to be, as I have already mentioned, the most eastern town visited by canoes from the lower part of the Bínue. By three o'clock we were at anchor off A'kpoko, and immediately went on shore, landing almost at the very gate of the town. As soon as Mr. May had got his observations, we crossed the moat, which was now full of water, by the old, primitive bridge, and found the city-gate all decorated with bones and other articles, as dju-djus, forcibly reminding us that we had left Muhammadan countries, and were now among Pagan tribes. On reaching the King's house we were speedily met by our old acquaintance, who gave us a very warm reception, one, too, which was really genuine. I told him our stay would be short, and asked him to tell his people that, if they wished to trade, they must come off directly, and I invited his majesty to come on board and visit us. Canoes followed us off, with a little ivory, goats, fowls, eggs, limes, &c., for which cowries were freely taken. About five o'clock Mágaji arrived, and having looked over the ship, was extremely pleased with all he saw. I gave presents to him and to his attendants, on which he offered me a goat, and a white cock, without a a single dark feather, the latter being considered in this place a mark of great friendship. He said this year had been a happy one for him, as he had seen and made friends with white men, whom he hoped, would often, often revisit his country.

Early the next morning we had a sharp tornado, which left the atmosphere very cool. We got under steam a little after six, and in two hours were off Dágbo, where we anchored, and as it was Sunday had the decks cleared, and remained quiet for the rest of the day. When here formerly there were banks eight or ten feet high, but now the whole country looked like an immense swamp. It had been entirely overflown, but with the subsidence of the river part had drained off, leaving here and there extensive pools, from which and the surrounding moist ground there must have been copious exhalations. The spot was not one which we would have selected from choice, but necessity had left us no other alternative, we required wood and had to get it where we best could. Our stay, would not, however, be long, and our anchorage was not near the bank. After church service, Mr. May and I landed, and with some difficulty found a spot sufficiently firm to enable us to stand upon. The inhabitants had all left their huts, and were now encamped on higher ground at some miles' distance. Much of their corn was stacked on high stages, on which it had been placed to keep it clear of the water. Some Agatú people came alongside during the afternoon, from whom I got a little information, which will be given presently.

This evening I had a conversation with Zúrí, and got from him the particulars of his visit to Keána. He and his party reached Keána towards nightfall, and, according to custom, fired a salute. Next morning they waited on the King, offered him his present, and delivered the message. They were informed that two light-coloured travellers, with two black attendants had been in Keána, but had left it forty-seven days previously for Dóma, and Zúri had since learnt, that, after a residence of three days in Dóma, they had departed thence for Tóto and A'bashi in the I'gbira country. This part of his narrative I am inclined fully to believe, especially as it was corroborated by Máma, who had no reason for trying to deceive us. That there had been some strangers in Keána I have no doubt whatever; besides Zúri's account, our informant at O'jogo repeated the story again and again without any variation, and further the information was originally volunteered by him, before he ever saw Zúri. Who these individuals were is a very different question. I suspected, for various reasons, that they could not be Drs. Barth and Vogel; an idea since proved to have been correct. Possibly they were Fulátas, who, from the lightness of their complexion, are often in Central Africa styled "white men." About the rest of Zúri's tale I am rather sceptical; he said that the King of Keána was not kind to him and his party, that he prevented them from leaving for several days, and that finally they had to make their exit by night. This is not at all likely, the King had no reason for ill-treating them, they came to him well-provided with the best travelling credentials for that country, namely presents, and they passed to him from a friendly town. If any such occurrence really took place it must have been owing to misconduct on the part of Mr. Zúri, as he has about him a considerable spice of the rogue, and no doubt united business with pleasure and traded on his own account to some advantage.

Zúri told me that the country marked on the maps as Zegzeg, is by its own inhabitants, as well as by

I'gbira and Dóma, always called Zúzu or Zózo, or Zaría from its chief town. In other parts of Háusa it is named Zigizígi, whence Zegzeg. Certainly the only names I heard for it were either Zaría or Zózo, which latter, I heard a man one day pronounce Zéze. Dágbo at one time paid tribute to Wukári, and afterwards, prior to its conquest by the Púlbe of Zaría, to Bássa, from which country it had often suffered much. Near it stood formerly an A'kpoto settlement, named Abógbi, the Abóhi of Allen and Oldfield, but some years ago its inhabitants had again to return to the south side of the river. It was situated to the eastward, and not to the westward of Dágbo. Dágbo is placed at a considerable distance from the Dóma hills, and not at the base of them as represented in the sketch in the admiralty chart.

After a close, disagreeable night, during which all hands suffered much from the predatory attacks of legions of bloodthirsty mosquitoes, we were well pleased to see the first peep of morning, though it brought with it no cool refreshing breeze. We passed a warp ashore, hauled closer in, and sent the Kruboys to cut wood. The headman of Dágbo sent me a goat, for which I had to give a return present. Not a breath of wind all the forenoon, and at noon the thermometer on board stood at 96·5° F., in the shade, so that I ordered the wooding party to knock off work and come on board. About two o'clock we weighed anchor and dropped down the river towards Erúko, off which place we anchored about four.

CHAP. VIII.]   FURTHER DISAPPOINTMENTS.   249

Shortly afterwards some of us landed, and paid a visit to Itshibíza, headman of the place, and one of the sons of the King of Bássa. Notwithstanding their late disasters we found the inhabitants active and bustling, engaged in various pursuits. This is the furthest place up the Bínue where palm-oil is made, for although the oil-palm grows abundantly for many miles above this, it is not applied to any use. I saw the manufacture of the fine oil prepared from the kernel, going on, which was done by breaking the nut with a stone, bruising the kernel, and boiling it with water, when the oil is skimmed off the top. This, which is of a pale yellow colour, and more fluid than the ordinary oil obtained from the sarcocarp, is used principally for purposes of cooking, and is sent in small quantities from Erúko in various directions. Erúko is surrounded by a double palisade of tall trees, leaving a space of from ten to twelve feet between the rows. The trees grow so closely together that even a boy could hardly squeeze himself in. Beyond the present town stand the ruins of a former Erúko, burnt several years ago. We examined the remains of some of the huts, which exhibited a higher order of architecture than we found at any other spot. The walls were more substantial, better put together, and often smoothly covered outside with a kind of mortar. The plans were more regular, windows had been formed, and small recesses left in the walls to act as cupboards. There had been faint attempts in some to architectural ornament, and rude figures were still to be traced on the walls. The huts had been coloured, too, both outside and inside, with a faint degree of regularity, that is to say, not in rude daubs, but with red, white, and a bluish-black, laid on evenly, and equally tinted all over. Near these ruins new huts are already beginning to appear, and a fresh population to spring up. I saw large plantations of a fabaceous, pinnate-leafed plant, but not in flower, used for poisoning fish. After sunset I collected numerous specimens of a handsome, showy beetle, allied to *Mylabris*, they were caught chiefly on stalks of grass, or on leaves of Dáwa corn. Around Erúko is much cultivated ground, including numerous fields of corn, near one of which I saw the only flock of Guinea fowl (*Numida*) I encountered anywhere. I bought some fine showy pipes, made, some of clay, some of copper, with bowls deep enough for a German, said to be manufactured at E'kpe, on the borders of I'gbira. These are always fitted with a long wooden stem, and in smoking them they are frequently passed from one to another round a large circle. I observed several women with fancy, or, as they are there considered, *beauty* marks, not indelible, done on their faces and breasts with a blue colouring-matter. I saw several others also, with the Kakánda and Ishábe marks on their cheeks. Alihéli, who, when a boy, had visited this place with Lander, upwards of twenty years ago, was, this afternoon, recognized by two persons, one an elderly woman, and the other a man of about his own age, who was, during their former acquaintanceship, as Alihéli expressed it to me, "too much sauce boy," meaning that he had been an impudent young rascal. The Bássa people have very dark skins, and strongly marked features, and are more typically negro than the inhabitants of either I'gbira or Dóma. They had formerly, and even now partly retain, a rather bad character, as being turbulent, wild, and dangerous to travellers. During Oldfield and Lander's visit, an I'gbira canoe, passing to market, was seized and plundered, and was only rescued by Lander's prompt interference; one of the actors in this piece of violence, now an elderly man, was pointed out to me. Now they seem improved, tempered perhaps by their recent misfortunes, and their behaviour towards us was extremely correct. Owing to the inroads of the Fuláni, many people from Bássa had sought refuge on the south bank of the river, when some were still residing at a place named Agowowóro. Now, however, as the invaders had all left the country, most of the refugees were returning. I had some difficulty in obtaining the correct name of Erúko. Mr. Crowther and I made a number of persons pronounce the word, and we found it to vary thus—Orúko, Olúko, Erúko, Elúko, such is the uncertainty of a merely spoken language. We took Erúko as having the majority of voices; but the same individual, if repeating the name several times, would generally introduce a variation before finishing, especially substituting, as is often done in Africa, the liquids *l* and *r* for each other.

We got many particulars of the attack of the Púlbe on Bássa, which, with what we had learnt before, enabled us to form a tolerably correct idea of the whole affair. It commenced by the refusal of the people of A'fo, named also U'sha and E'kpe, living on the borders of Bássa, to pay their usual tribute. Adáma, King of Bássa, not feeling himself sufficiently powerful to coerce them, requested assistance from the Fuláni, and accordingly A'ma Dógo, or more correctly Mukáma Dógo, meaning "tall man," a Púlo chief of Zózo, came with an armed band for that purpose. A'fo being subdued, a quarrel arose between A'ma Dógo and Sénani, brother of the King of Bássa, and chief of A'kpata, which led to a general attack on the whole country. Ikéreku, the capital, about fifteen miles from Erúko, was sacked and rendered desolate, and many of the people were slain or made captive, and thus the cupidity of the King led to the desolation of his territories. Bássa people are said to have come originally from a town near Zaría, named Gábi, hence in remembrance of their origin, one of the titles assumed by their king is Agábi. From Ikéreku to Pánda the journey occupies four days, and to Dóma ten days, but during the rainy season there is much difficulty by the way, as most of the roads are under water. The A'fo mentioned above is so named by Dóma and Háusa, but by Ig'bira it is called E'kpe; the language spoken is chiefly I'gbira; it is a great manufacturing town, chiefly for articles of hardware, and iron ore is said to be plentiful in its vicinity. E'kpe is about half a day's journey distant from Pánda, and is, strictly speaking, within the Bássa border, but almost adjoining it, to the westward, is another town named Agwása, which is in I'gbira. A'bashi is a town about a day's journey to the north-west from Pánda, and hence to Toto, a rather important seat of trade, is also a day's journey to the northward and eastward. A'kpata is a day's journey north-north-west from old Ikéreku.

Being desirous of communicating with the King of Bássa, it was arranged that Mr. May should visit him, as he and I could not, as matters went, both be absent from the ship for any length of time. He intended to have started at daylight, but was prevented by a violent tornado, which came on during the night, and was followed by heavy rain, lasting until after six o'clock. About seven he landed, accompanied by Messrs. Crowther and Richards and Dr. Hutchinson, and had a cool pleasant walk. The King was living in a newly-erected village, about two miles and a-half from Erúko, and which has been also called Ikéreku. Everything around him betokened indigence, and he said his people were yet too poor to trade with us. The party returned a little after ten; and as there was nothing to delay us further, steam was got up. Mr. May brought with him the curious long seed-vessel of a shrubby bush,* used by the

Oct. 17.

* Belonging to the natural family *Asclepiadaceæ*.

natives for poisoning their arrows, and I got some good specimens of the grain named Dawúra.

Early in the afternoon we were off A'batsho, where I had resolved to remain until the following day. We landed, and as soon as Mr. May had got a set of sights, set off on a voyage of discovery. Close to the shore there are a few dwellings, chiefly for fishing purposes, which compose, I rather think, the original A'batsho, but now the principal town is placed about a mile inland, having been founded about six months prior to our visit, by refugees from Pánda. Thither we bent our steps, walking over a fine tract of country, which bore little evidence that it had been but recently brought under cultivation; a good footpath had been made, trees had been cleared away, or burnt to arrest farther progress, and fine maize and magnificent Guinea corn were growing all around us. And when we arrived at the village all had a settled look, nothing seemed hasty or temporary. We found Moháma, the chief, suffering much from lumbago, but he arose and welcomed us warmly, telling us how happy he was once more to meet us, as he also had heard the report of a quarrel and a fight between us and some tribe up the river during which several lives were said to have been lost. He entertained us with beer and Kola nuts, and on our departure gave us some fine yams and a goat. I gave him some cloths, a looking-glass, and a knife, and as he seemed to be suffering much, I promised to send him some medicine. We found the industrious inhabitants all hard at work, some picking cotton, some weaving, some spinning, others preparing for to-morrow's market. In the market we observed small balls of camwood, cotton, mats, impure lime prepared from burnt shells, yams, pepper, soap, &c. I bought a pot of honey, not the vegetable syrup which is so named near Hamarúwa, but the genuine produce of the bee. Near A'batsho two or three Shea-butter trees were growing, but I could not learn that they were abundant. On returning to the ship we found alongside canoes with goats, fowls, yams, mats, and firewood, all of which met with a ready purchase. Since we had been able to obtain vegetables, but especially yams, the improvement in the health of the crew was very marked. No fresh cases of scurvy now presented themselves, and those on the sick list were rapidly convalescing, a clear proof, if it was required, of the nature of their complaint.

As I before mentioned, a watchful eye was kept over Zúri and the poor little boy. At length Máma confessed to Alihéli that he really was for sale, on which Zúri was taxed with telling a falsehood, which he admitted he had done. I told him, as formerly, that no slave could live on board our ship, and that I looked upon the boy as practically free; but as I considered that he might have erred in ignorance, I should ransom the boy, paying him the market value at the Confluence, which I ascertained to be nearly 50,000 cowries, equal in real value to from three to four pounds sterling. I therefore from that moment took entire charge of the boy, whose history was related to us as follows :—He was a Mítshi by birth, his father having been a native of that country, and his mother being a Djúku. His father was dead, and during some domestic quarrel he had been seized from a town named Tómbo, nearly opposite to O'jogo, by some of his mother's relatives, and sold as a slave. He was a fine healthy boy, about eight or nine years of age, and remarkably intelligent and quick. His skin was of a copper colour, and not nearly so dark as those of most of his countrymen whom we had seen. He very soon learnt to consider us as his protectors, and became much attached, especially to Mr. Crowther and me, and to my assistant.

We were early under steam, and in a couple of hours were at anchor off Amarán, an I'gbira town, also peopled principally by Pánda refugees, but which we had not visited during our ascent. It was market-day, and hundreds of curious spectators thronged around the landing-place, anxious to get a peep at the "Pleiad" and her crew. Mr. Crowther, Mr. May, and Dr. Hutchinson who all landed, described the scene as remarkably busy and animating. Here we obtained the cheering news that our fellow-voyagers in the canoe at Igbégbe were all alive and well. The king, named A'ba, came on board, and to him and to his headman I gave suitable presents, receiving from them a fine goat. Our purchases here, with the exception of some native manufactures, consisted principally of firewood. An hour's steaming brought us to Okétta, on the right bank, which presented a very ruinous appearance. The water allowed us to come very close to the bank, so much so, that at first the inhabitants seemed alarmed, but they soon recovered their confidence. Here, for the first time, Mr. May got a sun's meridian altitude, the height previously having been too great to be measured by the sextant in the mercurial trough. A short visit was paid to Aikúta, the chief, with whom was residing one of the sisters of Oyigú, late King of Pánda. Our next visit was a flying one to our old friends at Kénde, with all of whom we shook hands, after which we again proceeded, and, aided by the strong current, anchored, a little before three, at Yimahá.

We landed, and presently went to visit Ogára or Moháma, now, by the death of Oyigú, King of I'gbira, and, on account of the destruction of Pánda, resident in this place. He is elder brother of Moháma E'te, the present King of A'batsho, both being sons of Opánaki, who was one of the sons of Malegedú, the first king of Pánda. He was formerly, on account of some quarrel, obliged to leave I'gbira, and, after some wandering, finally settled in Rógan-Kóto. By religion he is a Muhammadan, and he speaks I'gbira and Háusa fluently: in appearance and manner he much resembles his brother, but his travelling has much improved his mind, and we found him highly intelligent, shrewd, and well informed. He told us that the country was still in a very poor state, owing to the recent aggression, and that his people hardly knew yet what to do. As long as the rainy season lasted, and there was plenty of water, bush, and long grass in the way, they were safe; but as soon as the dry season set in, they would be liable to fresh violence. Most of the Fuláni had left Pánda, but were still in the neighbourhood of Tóto. They laid the whole blame on the Bássa people; and alleged, and I believe with truth, that after the destruction of Ikéreku, its inhabitants, jealous of Pánda, directed the attention of A'ma Dógo to that quarter; and a pretext being speedily found, its sack and ruin followed. One old chief, named Mádaki, who was present, showed me the scars of several extensive flesh wounds which he had received during the assault. The King appeared much gratified with our visit, and gave us, on our leaving him, some jars of beer, and a goat. We then walked through Yimahá, which now presented a very different scene from what it did when we passed up the river. Then it was silent and still as the grave; the huts were empty; the market-place deserted: but now a change had come o'er the spirit of their dream. All was activity, bustle, and animation, presenting a scene such as could not be equalled in any part of Africa but in I'gbira. Though the day was well advanced, business still went merrily on; idlers were few, and everybody and everything wore an aspect of importance; the traders still lingered at the place of sale, and the artisans still plied at their respective trades.

In the market I noted, among other commodities, salt, beer, palm oil of both kinds, shea-butter, corn, yams, dried yams for making fúfu, dried fish, the powdered leaves of the Baobab tree used for colouring various dishes, different seeds, mats, bags, cotton-grass and mixed cloths, the bulb of an orchidaceous plant used as food, impure lime, cam-wood, &c. Many extensive dye-works and weaving establishments were around; and we discovered a blacksmith hard at work at his forge, and handling with no little dexterity his rude tools. His blast was caused by a primitive pair of bellows, consisting of a couple of goat-skin bags attached to one end of an iron nozzle close to the fire. Seizing hold of these, one in each hand, he alternately compressed and expanded them, and filling the one while the other was being emptied, kept up a continuous current. Air was admitted to them by a small hole pierced in each, and when filled, this was closed by a slight movement of one of his fingers. Mr. Guthrie was so pleased with this man's ingenuity, that he gave him a hammer and some other articles likely to be of use to him. Mr. Crowther and I went with Alihéli to visit an old lady, a distant connection of his, but she—as soon as we were introduced—smiling, said she was rather in *deshabille*, and producing a little bit of looking-glass and her galena-case, proceeded to stain her eyelids, and to arrange her head-dress.

Yimahá was so named by Ahóko Zinekú, its founder and first chief, from the tents having been originally much scattered, its derivation being from the I'gbira "aimahá," to scatter, or scattered, equivalent to the Háusa word "berekéti." The Háusa pronunciation of the word is Yimashá. Almost adjoining Yimahá, to the eastward, are two villages, which we did not visit, named Bogúlogo and Ohérehu, the chiefs being respectively Ahóko and Ohurihíni.

Among various scraps of information picked up here concerning I'gbira, is the following. The founder and first King of Pánda was named Malegedú, he was a native of Kóto'n Kárifi, and before he commenced building Pánda, resided for some time at Tóto. He lived in the early part of this century, and since his death eight kings have occupied his throne—a list of their names, &c., will be given in the appendix. Kóto'n Kárifi, or as it is often called Kúttum Kárafe, obtained its title from the rocks on which it stands being impregnated with iron. This is its Háusa designation, Kóto meaning I'gbira, and Kárifi being iron; the natives call it Egú, and their language is I'gbira. It formerly was tributary first to Iddá and then to Pánda, but at present is semi-independent.

An exceedingly hot, close afternoon, was succeeded by heavy rain all night, which brought the atmosphere to a more pleasant standard, and at daybreak we saw the mountain range to the southward enveloped in a thick morning mist, through which only the taller of the mountains showed their heads. This was soon dispelled by the rising sun, and as soon as the landscape was clear, Mr. May took outline views

Oct. 19.

of Mount Vidal, and the other more remarkable peaks. Zúri, who had been ashore all night, brought off the intelligence, that on the previous evening a council, comprising all the head men, had been held by the King, to consider a proposal made to them by the Fuláni, namely, to pay an annual tribute of one hundred slaves. It was thought, however, that though one hundred were now asked, another season two hundred might be demanded, and if these were not forthcoming there would be a fresh pretext for assault. As long as the roads were wet and unpassable, they were safe, and they resolved, if again molested, to retire to the south side of the river and settle there. In the meantime, the Fulátas were allowing them to ransom their captives. Mr. Crowther and I went ashore early and paid a private visit to the King, who, throwing aside all his state etiquette, had a long conversation with us. We told him of the wish of many I'gbira people, now residing in Sierra Leone, to return to their native country, which Ogára said he trusted would speedily be the case. He hoped also to see us again ere long, when possibly his people would be in a more prosperous condition, and better able to trade with us. On Mr. Crowther's asking him if he would object to teachers coming to his country, he replied, quite the contrary, he only wished they were now with him. He then spoke of the deplorable condition of his subjects, and mentioned that although they had managed to ransom most of the head men, yet numbers of women and children still remained captives. We expressed our deep sympathy with their misfortunes, telling him also how our country disliked war, more especially when of this unprovoked and predatory nature, and how much we held in abhorrence driving captives into slavery. But as something more substantial than mere words, I said that as soon as I got on board I would send him four bags of cowries (80,000), to be applied by him in the redemption of his people as he considered most advisable, on which all present seemed much moved, and thanked us heartily. We then alluded to the offer from the Fuláni, which the King said he should reject; I was much pleased to hear this, as, had it been accepted, a fresh slave mart must have been established. I therefore applauded his intention, saying, it was preferable to remain as independent as possible, and should, which we trusted would not happen, another attack be made on them, it would be better for them to secure a safe retreat on the A'kpoto shore, where they might in comparative safety and quiet pursue their industrial occupations. On taking our leave I gave him a velvet tobe, which pleased him greatly, as he told us that all the royal robes and dresses were in the hands of the Púlbe. Desirous of getting a good supply of the fruit of the Baobab tree, which was here plentiful and large, I offered a few cowries for any good ones brought on board; in half an hour we were nearly inundated, but I was able to make a very excellent selection, and to purchase forty or fifty good specimens for the value of about a shilling.

There was very little ivory at Yimahá, but in other respects a brisk trade was carried on during our stay. Yimahá is a very busy place, and its inhabitants being of an active disposition and quiet demeanour, it may, if left undisturbed by the Fulátas, again become a flourishing town. Its situation is good, and as the people are orderly and extremely well disposed towards us, it must, if our intercourse ever becomes established, be an important station.

We remained until noon, that Mr. May might obtain a meridian altitude of the sun, after which, getting under steam, we resumed our passage. We anchored for a short time off O'gba, prettily situated along the verge of a steep cliff, rising some 80 or 100 feet above the river. Several of us landed, and scrambling up by a rather precipitous footpath, in a few minutes found ourselves in the heart of the village. It commands a fine prospect, extending to many miles along the river, and also over a fine extent of level ground, stretching far away towards the mountains in the north. The chief, named Kpánaki, was absent, his usual residence being at Okpángana, on the other side of the river, but we were introduced to his deputy, who was his sister, and who acted, as Alihéli briefly explained to us, as "big-man" of the village, meaning thereby the principal official. There being no inducement to remain, we quickly descended, jumping from block to block of igneous rock, until we reached the bottom. A couple of canoes, bringing a few fowls and goats, accompanied us, and presently two others came alongside, one of which had been sent from Okpángana to follow us, and to express the chief's regret at not being able to call on us, as he had just lost one of his wives. I sent him by his brother, who was his messenger, a small present, with the expression of our condolence at his loss. From the other canoe, which was returning from market, a tooth of twenty pounds weight was bought. We again got under steam, passing in rapid succession many small villages, among which were A'tipo, Ohimokógi, and finally Gánde, a little place inhabited by Igára people. It being almost dark, and the navigation rather intricate, we anchored for the night near the Duck Islands. Dr. Hutchinson and Mr. Taylor went in the gig to visit their friends in the canoe, and on their return reported that Mr. Crawford and Mr. Gower were both sick, and that little trade had been done, as it seemed to have been interfered with by the King's order.

CHAPTER IX.

THE CONFLUENCE.

SINCE we had last been here there was a great change in the appearance of all around. Sacrifice Rock, on which we used to land for observations, and which was then high above the water, was now completely hidden, nothing being left to indicate its locality but the top of a tall bush, which had managed to withstand the fury of the flood. The Duck Islands were reduced to very narrow limits, and the confluence of the two rivers seemed to be greatly expanded and enlarged. After daylight we got up steam, and soon were off Igbégbe, where we anchored not far from the landing-place. Oct. 20. Mr. Crawford, on being brought on board, looked very white and thin, but this did not proceed from endemic fever, which again had considerably affected Mr. Gower. The canoe was moored in a very ill chosen locality near the shore, sheltered by tall trees from the refreshing breeze, and, now that the water was falling, close to moist mud. They said they were afraid to anchor further out, why I could not make out, as thirty yards would have made all the difference between a healthy and an unhealthy spot. A warp was passed to the canoe, and she was hauled alongside, and the proceeds of six weeks' trading were taken on board, which only amounted to 278 lbs. of ivory, 192 lbs. of shea-butter, 192 lbs. of tobacco, and some red pepper—a most wretched result; but Mr. Crawford had been so tied down by the orders he received about prices, that he could not give even a fair market value. I discharged and paid the men who had accompanied us up the Bínue, giving them an amount which completely satisfied them. This I did as they had been with us seven weeks, had behaved well, and been often very useful, besides their journey to Keána. Zúri, certainly, had occasionally been troublesome, and I could not approve of many of his proceedings; still, through him I had got much information about names, places, and manners. Moreover, I considered that in rewarding them well I was only paying a slight compliment to A'ma A'boko, who had been so friendly to us. I offered also to settle with Zúri for the boy, but he had not a bag to contain the additional cowries. When the canoe parted from us at O'jogo we had given directions that the Krúmen should employ their spare time in cutting wood for our use. This had been done, but one large pile, which had been stacked too near the river edge, had been swept away; several boat-loads, however, still remained, which we commenced shipping at once, as the place where it was stored was nearly a mile distant from us, on the opposite side of the river.

On landing, I made some inquiries about the person alleged to have been stopping trade, and found that it was the Galadíma, whose name was Dagána, and who, having been charged by the King with the safety of the party, had been consequently very frequently about them, and they probably, from not knowing better, fancied he was interfering with them. I learnt also, however, that in consequence of the grumbling which was caused by the very low prices offered, the King had advised his people to cease trading until the return of the ship. We then went to visit A'ma A'boko, and to thank him for his kindness to our people during our absence. We fancied that the King received us rather coldly, and soon found that our friend Zúri had been before us, and had been telling him various untruths to try and prejudice him against us. He had very much understated the payment he had received, had told that Kings up the Bínue had got far more valuable presents than those offered to A'ma A'boko, and in particular he had dwelt on the cowries given to the King of I'gbira. The King mentioned all these points, asking if we had forgotten him altogether, if any other chief had taken as much trouble concerning us, or had equally cared for our men when we were far away. I said that Zúri had quite deceived him about his remuneration, which was more than treble what he had admitted, and in proof of this I had

Máma called, and examined before all. I pointed out Zúri's wish for mischief in his garbled stories about presents, and finally, as to the cowries at Yimahá, I told the King that he ought to be thankful that he had no relatives who required to be redeemed from slavery. With this explanation he was perfectly satisfied, and we immediately got upon our old terms. We then spoke of the Model Farm territory, and I said that though we had left it unoccupied, yet it was ours by purchase, and that we intended going over to look at it before we left. The King laughed and said that, properly speaking, it was his, as he had never been consulted about it, nor had he received any of the purchase-money, thus indicating a feeling of independence of Iddá. We then took our leave, and walked through the town, where we found everyone extremely civil. We visited several of the numerous dye-works, and in one weaving establishment we found that some of our Turkey reds had been taken to pieces, and the threads, neatly knotted, were now being interwoven with some of their own white and blue. We heard that, owing to continued disturbances at Iddá, all of A'boko's party had left, and had formed a new settlement for themselves; that the Okíri market had been discontinued, and now that two markets were held instead, one at Igbégbe, and the other at A'boko's new town. That at Igbégbe took place every five days, and, as the next day was one, I resolved to remain for two of them, and accordingly intimated this to the trading gentlemen. This delay would also allow Mr. May again to rate the chronometers. Before going on board we measured the apparent fall of the river, which, to this time, amounted to twenty-four inches. A few scrivelloes were brought on board, and also a fine tooth of eighty-seven pounds, which latter was purchased for 37,000 cowries and some red cloth.

I must here make a digression, for the purpose of giving a short account of the people living near the Confluence, and who are to be met with at I'gbégbe. Núpe, the Núfe and Nýffe of previous writers, is a country of ancient date, situated to the eastward of the Kwóra, and bounded on the south by I'gbira. Its inhabitants, now partly Moslemin, and partly Pagans, are a very ingenious and trading race. Among their articles of manufacture are cloths, brass ornaments, and necklaces made of pebbles, which they cut and polish for the purpose. Their language is peculiar, and, as their traders travel over a wide extent, it may be heard spoken in many places. Fully one half of the population employs no national mark, and that used by the remainder consists of a short cut, proceeding from near the inner angle of the eye, in a slightly curved, diagonal direction, about two-thirds across the cheek. Núpe, its people, and its language, are in Haúsa known as Tákpa (Táppa). This country has, unfortunately, been for many years in a very disturbed state, the cause of which I will now endeavour shortly to relate.

A good many years ago, two persons contested for the throne, namely Mamagía (often Mángia and Magía), andEderísa. The former referred his case to the Fuláni, who, as umpires, divided the kingdom between the claimants, but making both pay tribute to a third person called Asúmo, and hence named Asúmo-Sáraki. This person, a Púlo by descent, if not by birth, was son of Mallam Den'do (often also called Mallam Músa), by a Háusa woman, and was a grandson of the Sultan Béllo. Before he was thus placed over the country, he had quarrelled with, and tried to kill, his half-brother, Dásaba, who, however, escaped from him, first across the Kwóra, and finally to Ladé.Ederísa's head-quarters were about E'gga, while Asúmo-Sáraki and Mamagía resided at Rábba. On the death of Mamagía, Asúmo-Sáraki seems to have assumed the entire rule of Núpe, especially asEderísa left no heir. All the feelings of Asúmo-Sáraki being Púlo, the Núpe people supported Dásaba, who, as his mother was a Núpe, might be looked on more as one of themselves. Thus assisted, about 1845 or 1846, he attacked his brother, defeated him, and destroyed Rábba, after which Asúmo-Sáraki took refuge in the Háusa country. Rábba though sacked and burnt, soon began to recover and to be repopulated, but was no longer the seat of government, as Dásaba fixed himself at Ladé. Dásaba, who is also called Mahamásaba, or, by contraction, Músaba, is of a cruel and tyrannical disposition, and was dreaded alike by his subjects and his neighbours.

In the early part of 1854, his people rose against him *en masse*, drove him into exile, and selected in his stead Báziba, son of Mamagía. Dásaba fled to the Yóruba country, and was received and sheltered by the Muhammadans of Ilǫ́rin (the Alyorie of some maps). Of this we had been told in August during our ascent; but since that time another change had taken place, and Dásaba, assisted by Moslemin from Ibádan and Ilǫ́rin, had effected a bloodless revolution, having, by dint of promises of better behaviour for the future, induced his subjects again to receive him. Not feeling, however, very secure at Ladé, he was desirous of forming a settlement on the Model Farm territory, and had made such a proposal to A'ma A'boko, who, on his part, was partly inclined to favour the design, thinking that such a powerful chief as his friend might prove useful. It was on this account, therefore, that Mr. Crowther and I spoke to the King about our claims to the ground.

Just above the Confluence, along the right bank of the Kwóra, live a people who have been long known as Kakánda. But this is not their native name, and I have been unable to ascertain exactly by what other race it was originally applied. I believe that the term Kakánda embraces three distinct tribes, named respectively Bássa, Ishábe, and Bonú, differing from each other in language and in national marks. In Sierra Leone people from all these three places unite and live together. Not having visited their countries, I cannot speak positively, but from what I

have been able to gather, I think Bássa and Isábe are chiefly known as Kakánda, and in Igbíra and Igára, this name is applied mostly to the latter. Bássa is, I believe, nearest to the Confluence, and the mark of the people is two or three broad, unsightly-looking, curved lines, extending from the temple along the cheek nearly to the chin. Their name for the Kwóra is " E′du or E̱′du," and for the Confluence or for the Bínue E′tshi. Their chief towns are E′imafa, half a day's journey from the river, and Tshéberi, four hours further on. I fancy that Bonú is next, which is possibly the " Puna " of Clarke's Vocabulary.*
Its dialect I was told by a Bonú man more resembles Isábe than Bássa, but yet they can contrive to understand each other. Their mark is also two or three broad lines like the Bássa, but crossed by some shorter and finer ones. Their principal town is Owí, and another is named Dónyi, which is beyond Ogú. As to Isábe, the distinctive mark is composed of four lines along each side of the face, and the chief town is Igbído, the Kakánda of some charts, and the Budu † of Captain Trotter's reports, and I believe that Múye, near the river, is another. Two or three miles behind Igbégbe are two villages, named Pátta and Tshewú, inhabited by refugees belonging to these tribes, who had fled thither to escape from the marauding visits of Dásaba.

On the morning following our arrival trade began

* Page 86.
† The Buddu of McWilliam in Allen and Thomson's Narrative, vol. ii. p. 80.

early, and promised to be brisk. Among other visitors was Zúri, who made an attempt to carry off the little Mítshi boy. I spoke very sharply to him, telling him, now that the boy was free, if he dared to lay a finger on him, I would have him thrown overboard. I then ordered him out of the ship, saying I would follow and see the King on the subject. Accordingly, accompanied by Mr. May and Mr. Crowther, I landed and went straightway to A'ma-A'boko, and having had Zúri sent for, I commenced by recapitulating everything connected with the boy, how Zúri had brought him on board without leave; how, when questioned, he had told a falsehood, and had afterwards confessed to a different story; how he had assented to his ransom, and expressed himself perfectly satisfied; and lastly we reminded the King of Zúri's behaviour the day before, and of the stories he had then told. Máma, the King's own man, was then examined in corroboration of my statements, and Zúri, on being asked if all were true, replied "Yes;" but added that he had bought the boy for A'ma-A'boko, on which I said, that in that case I should pay him nothing, but should give the amount to the King. A'ma-A'boko, however, declared that he had no concern in the matter, and had nothing to do with Zúri's getting the boy. I then told the King and those about him the views of England concerning slaves and the slave-trade, and taking Zúri as an example, pictured him living at home in ease and comfort, until another stronger and more powerful than he came, and, carrying him off, sold him into captivity, far away from home, wives, and children, where he had to labour at the will of, perhaps, a harsh master, and content himself with the simplest fare grudgingly bestowed. I concluded by saying that in this case, I was willing to assume that the man had erred in ignorance, and should therefore, whenever properly called upon, pay a fair market-price for the boy, but that we objected to, and totally repudiated slavery, because our God told us it was wicked, and moreover had commanded us to do unto others as we would they should do towards us. The King and those around assented to all I had said, remarking that it was "very good," and the King expressed himself perfectly satisfied, and convinced of Zúri's bad behaviour. We then took our departure, and called on the Galadima, who informed us that our ransoming the boy had given general satisfaction throughout Igbégbe. Being market-day, we walked through the market, where we heard among other tongues I'gbira, Igára, Núpe, Haúsa, Yóruba, Ishábe, Bonú, &c. ; and among articles for sale, we noted palm oil, palm-nut oil, shea-butter, cotton, cloths, mats, bags, calabashes, pepper, cam-wood, magnificent yams, tomatos, papaws, plantains, bananas, corn, beer. We also visited a blacksmith's shop, and inspected a brewery of rather a simple description. The decks of the "Pleiad" were covered with traders and their gear, and active trade went on, the women proving the keenest hands. Ivory was not very abundant this day. I paid to Máma 51,000 cowries for the little boy, and I asked him on going on shore to make it be generally known that the following day being Sunday was with us a day of rest, or, as they better understood it, our "God's day," and that we should not trade. Some canoes alongside were upset, and one poor woman lost all her effects, so that I had to give her a small present to make it up.

The decrease of the water was now very perceptible, and we could daily observe a difference of several inches. I gave the Mítshi boy the name of William Carlin, and determined to take him with me to Sierra Leone, that he might be there educated and looked after, hoping that, if spared, he might one day prove a blessing to his own people, and his own land. Dr. Hutchinson during the day purchased a good deal of ivory, amounting to 467 lbs., all of good quality, and including one tooth of 107 lbs. I bought some specimens of a raw silky-looking material, round some cocoons, which was highly prized, and said to have been brought from the Haúsa country. Our sick men having now abundance of appropriate food, were improving rapidly.

Oct. 23.

Mr. May left at daylight in the gig, and landing near Mount Stirling, ascended Mount Pátte, from the top of which he described the view as being most magnificent. He brought me with him a nice assortment of plants, which he had gathered during his walk, and which proved very interesting. Much palm-nut oil was brought on board, and was offered at a very reasonable rate, less than the common oil, but none was bought, except about a puncheon purchased by the steward. A most unaccountable apathy prevailed in the trading department, and except by Dr. Hutchinson, no steps were ever taken about commerce. Mr. Guthrie requiring oil for his engines, had to go a-shore and buy it for himself, and he got an ample supply in about half-an-hour. We were close to a capital market, abundant opportunity was offered, but instead of being improved, nothing was heard but expressions of alarm all the time the ship was allowed to remain. Yams of fine quality were very cheap; but instead of laying in here a sea-stock, this was delayed till our arrival at Abó, when four times the price was paid for an inferior article. I weighed several of the largest, which I found to vary from twenty to twenty-eight pounds. The yams differ much in shape and appearance at different places. At Igbégbe they were very irregular and bulky, being generally short in proportion to their thickness. I tried to bring some of the largest home, but failed. I received numerous presents from the natives of various kinds, most of which required some sort of acknowledgment. I purchased some specimens of an agricultural implement, made in the shape of a spade, but used as a hoe. They are about ten inches square, and are rather concave superiorly. A short wooden handle is fitted to these, forming an angle of about 50° with the upper surface. These are made at E′kpe and at Tóto, and are much in use throughout I′gbira and the adjacent parts of Dóma.

On the morning of our last day Mr. May and I landed to measure a gigantic Baobab-tree, which we had seen a little way beyond the town. Oct. 25.
At eighteen inches above the ground its circumference was eighty feet; but here the trunk divided into several portions. Most curiously another and a very distinct tree had got intimately mixed up with it, the trunk of which had sprung up among some large branches, and was for some feet above the ground so closely enveloped, that it was almost impossible to distinguish it. Other parts of the Baobab trunk and branches were covered with epiphytes and climbers, the latter being principally *Fabaceæ*. I have observed that lichens are very rarely seen on the trunks of *Adansoniæ*. Preparations were now made for departure. Our final observations were taken; the fall of water during our stay was ascertained to be nearly six feet, and the name of the steamer and the date were conspicuously painted by Mr. Guthrie on a large block of rock. With Mr. Crowther and Mr. May I went to say farewell to A′ma-A′boko, and to thank him for his invariable kindness towards us. We again introduced the subject of the model farm, telling the King that Mr. May had been to see it, but that we felt assured he would look after it, and not allow it to

be occupied until our return; to which he replied "Certainly," nothing but sickness or death would prevent his doing so. Mr. Crowther then questioned him as to his desire to have teachers placed in his town, and to his willingness to receive and protect any I'gbira people who might be desirous of returning to their native country. With this he was much pleased, saying if they came they should all have his warm support, adding, that his people were a trading people, and averse to war. Before taking leave I gave him several presents; amongst others, some bundles of green, red, and yellow cotton thread, which I left with him, hoping that some of his weavers might find use for it in their looms, and so possibly a market might be opened for this stuff for the next vessel. Dagána, the Galadíma, who is a Núpe by birth, is a fine specimen of his country, active, frank, and hospitable; he never met any of us on shore, without insisting on our going to his house, where whatever he thought we might like was produced. He was of the greatest service to us, as he spent much of his time on board, keeping order among the visitors, and furthering the ends of trade. Among the Muhammadans are a few Mallams, who know a little Arabic, and from them I purchased several MSS., which however consisted chiefly of extracts from the Kurán. During one of my wanderings I came upon a school, kept by an old Mallam, where children were being taught to repeat passages from the Kurán. We got into conversation, during the course of which Stamboul happened to be mentioned, on which I said that our Sovereign and the Sultan of Stamboul were friends, and that at that very moment she was assisting him to defend his country against a powerful oppressor. Immediately on hearing this, all about me got up and shook me by the hand; then calling their friends they told them the news, on which they also surrounded me, and insisted on going through the same ceremony. Among the superstitions of the heathen part of the population is the following, similar to one practised in Yóruba:—If there be two entrances to a hut, or two passages to any part of a dwelling, one is kept closed up by a string being put across it, and some djú-dju article hung up over it, and this obstruction is generally allowed to last for about a month, when it is changed to the other opening. Yórubans come to Igbégbe from Ilórin, by way of E'gga or Ladé; one whom we met was highly intelligent, and was our chief informant about Dásaba. One of our sailors was the bearer of a symbolical letter from this place to the I'gbira in Sierra Leone; it was similar in construction and translation to that mentioned in Miss Tucker's "Abbeokuta,"* and consisted of a red parrot's feather attached to one end of a piece of thread, while to the other was fastened a bit of hard wood, burnt at one extremity; and in the middle were secured four cowries, two and two, with their faces towards each other, one pair having

* Page 262.

the small end uppermost, and the other pair with the large rounded end upward. Mr. Crowther thinks the interpretation may be as follows :—The red feather may indicate prosperity on the part of the senders, and that the return of their friends is speedily expected; the hard wood may mean that they were well and strong, and the blackened end that they were mourning for the loss or absence of their countrymen; and the cowries may denote both wealth and well-wishes, those with the small ends up being suggestive of a desire to see their friends face to face, while those inverted may allude to the disordered state of the country.

At two o'clock the whistle sounded shrilly to warn persons out of the ship, and in ten minutes' time we were under steam. Just at starting a curious thing happened: the two swivels in the bows were loaded and primed, and the second mate had gone for a match while I remained standing beside them. Suddenly one, which had been exposed to the sun, went off in a rather unaccountable manner, for though the sun's rays playing on the polished surface, had greatly heated the swivel, still it could hardly be to the extent of igniting gunpowder. I therefore suspect that some object near, but which escaped attention, must have acted as a lens, and that the concentrated rays had been accidentally directed for a moment towards the priming. A fresh head breeze blew cool and pleasant, and steaming in mid-channel, we soon lost sight of Igbégbe, and left behind us that interesting and pleasant spot. If the commencement then made be pursued, Igbégbe must be one of the principal trading depots, and from its excellent situation, and the active habits of the people, must eventually become a place of much importance. We soon reached Mounts Crozier and Franklin, and the granitic Beaufort Island, and steaming past the site of the Okíri market, and the Bird-rock, the latter deeply immersed, by sunset had arrived nearly at Agbedámma; we continued, however, until after dark, when hearing voices ashore, we anchored in five fathoms water.

In the morning Mr. May went to measure the river, while Dr. Hutchinson landed at Agbedámma, and after a short time returned, bringing with him Ehimodína, one of our Iddá friends. He is a fine-looking old man, with a commanding appearance, and is almost reverenced by the whole of A'boko's party. On his coming on board all the natives knelt before him, and he was saluted in a similar manner even by his nephew, Okéyin or Okéyin-A'boko, whom we had formerly met at English Island, and who had now come from their new settlement Ututúru, on the right bank, just opposite our anchorage. I asked him and his uncle to come below to breakfast, when Okéyin made a hearty meal, but Ehimodína, who is a Muhammadan, could not eat before any of his followers, but taking a fancy to some bread, asked for a piece of it, which he carried home with him. They told us that the quarrel with Agabídoko was yet unsettled, and consequently all their party had left Iddá and were settling in this neighbourhood. Thus the Attá was deprived of his best and most influential subjects, who, always keeping together, will probably before long form a new and independent state. The great secret of the spread of power of A'boko's party is that all of its members are on friendly terms, and on public matters think as one man, keeping clear of petty strifes and private quarrels. Among them are no keen factions or political rivals; the different brothers, who are the leaders, are all on the most fraternal relations with each other, and the common weal seems to be the object nearest their hearts. They are a commercial rather than a warlike race, though, when requisite, they show that they are both able and willing to defend themselves. Doubtless, they contain the germ of a future powerful race, they deserve to be independent, and will, I trust, use their power for the promotion of their country's good. Ehimodína is the patriarch of the whole party, and Okéyin the chief of this particular division. A good deal of ivory was brought on board by these people, which was readily sold, and Dr. Hutchinson had by noon bought 555 lbs. Just abreast of where we were, Okéyin pointed out to us, to the westward, a few miles from the river, a valley, which led into the country of I'gbira-Shíma. He and Ehimodína described the inhabitants as being rather a wild set and not tributary to Igára. A little below Agbedámma, on the same side, stands a town named O'ko-Odógbo.

All trade being over, at two o'clock we fired a gun,

and weighed anchor, and just before four reached Iddá, where we got close enough to the landing-place to pass a warp ashore. Mr. May and I landed and got a set of sights, and being joined after dinner by some others of our party, we walked into the town. It bore evident marks of its late desertion, as everywhere were seen empty and ruinous huts. Mr. Crowther and I met with an A'kpoto man, who told us that the inland districts are nominally subject to the Attá, and that the language is mostly Igára, but that well to the eastward it somewhat resembles that of Dóma. One of the largest towns in A'kpoto is A'nkpa, the chief of which is named Omiákpa. He spoke also of an E'lugu town which he had visited, which was called E'nike. A threatening tornado hurried us on board, but fortunately it passed chiefly to the eastward.

Alihéli to-night repeated a singular story to me, one which he had told me before, and which he always affirmed to be correct. I do not know what to think of it, as it seems improbable, but yet I have never found Alihéli telling anything approaching an untruth. It is that when the Expedition of 1841 was at Iddá, Captain Trotter and the other Commissioners did not see the Attá at all, but that he was personated by a headman named O'sata, who is since dead. He says he first heard this shortly after the Expedition left, and has since repeatedly known of its having been freely talked about at Iddá, having himself been told of it when there on trading business. The present Attá, whose name is Amatshédi, an indolent and unpopular man, has been Attá for nearly twenty years. During the early part of his reign he was but little seen at Iddá, and it was usually given out that he was at war with some rebellious subjects in A'kpoto, though more generally believed that he was living in seclusion not far from his capital, enjoying an *otium sine dignitate*. Alihéli stated that he had mentioned this story to Mr. Beecroft when at Iddá in the "Ethiope," in 1845, but that gentleman did not seem to pay much heed to it.

In the morning I sent Alihéli to the Attá, to intimate our arrival to his Majesty, convey our respectful compliments, and also carry what would be far more satisfactory to the Royal mind, a nice present. I did not go myself, having no respect for the character of the Attá, and being unwilling again to go through the hideous ceremony of an audience, by which, moreover, nothing could be gained. Trade was very dull, and no ivory made its appearance. Many visitors came off to us, among others the Galadíma, Onúpia, who had with him as a slave an Albino boy. Alihéli on his return brought with him two of the King's eunuchs as messengers, and two of his daughters, who were desirous of visiting the ship. The messengers brought the Attá's compliments, and an intimation that he had a bullock for us, if we would send for it; on which I said that people would be despatched the same afternoon. I then gave each of the messengers a red shirt, and selected something more

Oct. 27.

feminine for the young ladies, after which they all took their departure. A young Núpe, who was on board, who was lately from Ladé, spoke of I'ssa as *present* King of Núpe; but his meaning could not be well ascertained. Towards sunset eight stout Krúboys were selected, and having been well provided with some pieces of strong rope, were sent after the bullock. Wishing to see the capture, I and several of the officers accompanied them, and after a walk of two miles to the place mentioned, were disappointed by finding no bullock there; and the only explanation offered was, that being possibly tired of waiting for us, it had gone to rejoin the herd in the bush. Vexed at being thus again deceived, I sent a sharp message to the Attá, and returned towards the shore. It was now nearly dark, and a wild festival was being celebrated in honour of a war-chief who had died the day before. Numbers of men, with their bodies coloured, their faces disfigured, and in fantastic dresses, rushed at full speed wildly about, armed with spears and swords, screaming, shouting, and uttering hideous cries. At first it was reported that some unfortunate was about to be sacrificed to the *manes* of this deceased warrior, but on inquiry we found to our joy that this was incorrect, and that the ceremony would be a bloodless one.

Iddá is most decidedly on the decline, and notwithstanding its fine position and its many advantages, it must continue to droop as long as its rulers continue indolent, selfish, and tyrannical. The trade has completely departed with A'boko's party, who, at Ututúru, hold extensive markets, which are attended by people from a great distance. Abó canoes come up to them, as Ajé is on friendly terms with the A'bokos, probably as he finds them to resemble himself in being energetic and practical.

Mr. Crowther and I landed early, and going to the Galadíma, had a long talk with him on various matters. He sent for some palm wine for us, but, just before drinking himself, was about, according to custom, to pour a little on the ground as djú-dju or sacred, when Mr. Crowther stopped him, explaining to him the folly of such offerings—to all of which he lent a willing ear. He gave us a long account of Igára, with many of the traditions handed down, and recounted the names of twenty Attás; but, most unfortunately, both Mr. Crowther and myself were without our pocket note-books, and so we lost the list. The present Attá is the twentieth. The country of Adó, or Edó, opposite Iddá, is believed by the natives to have been peopled from Ifé, which place, according to Yóruban tradition, was also the cradle of their race.* From Adó, it is said, sprang the kings of Igára, of Bíni (Benin), and of Abó, and secondarily from Iddá the kings of Núpe and of Pánda. What is now known as Igára was formerly all A'kpoto. As to the origin of the name Igára,

---

* See Crowther's Yóruba Grammar, second edition, introductory remarks.

occasionally Igála and Igána, there are two accounts: one derives it from a Yóruba warrior, so called, who, having attacked a tribe living on the western side, opposite Agbedámma, drove them first across the river, and then further to the eastward; which event is known in Yóruba tradition as the Igára war. The other is that the three kings just mentioned were brothers, and were sent by their father to found fresh settlements. The King of A'kpoto at that time was named Igára, and when the stranger arrived from Adó he lived as a hunter, and sent most of the fruits of the chase to Igára. But after a time followers from Adó joined him until, growing powerful, he refused to acknowledge Igára, or to give him any share of his spoil; this led to a quarrel, which ended by Igára being driven into the interior, leaving only his name behind him, on which the first Attá ascended the throne. The Galadíma said that the language of the Adó people closely resembled that of Bíni, to which place they were tributary, and he added that boys and men were sent from Adó to Iddá to be made eunuchs of. He told us that in A'kpoto were many large towns, and he spoke of a country bordering on A'kpoto, which he called Ojúgu, probably O'jogo.

At several of the market-towns on the south side of the Bínue, near the Confluence, and at Igbégbe, we had seen a peculiar sort of country cloth, ornamented by perforations, which were done during the weaving, and which, we were told, was made by the

I'gbo people, the *g* here being pronounced hard. We had made many inquiries about this race, but until our conversation with the Galadíma could learn nothing satisfactory about them, but now we found they were the same as the " I'bo," I'gbo being merely the hard pronunciation of this name. These cloths are most probably manufactured in E'lugu, that being the I'gbo district nearest to Igára, and the cloths being found chiefly in the markets near the Confluence.

On our return on board about eight o'clock we found a band, comprising five drums and two fifes, playing on the shore very vigorously, but still not unmusically; to reward their exertions I sent them a few handfuls of cowries, with which they were vastly delighted. When we arrived at Iddá in August we landed on the beach a few tons of patent fuel, to be reserved in case of any emergency. This we now found quite safe, and having shipped it, it was put aside to be used in crossing the bar. At half-past eight we were again under steam, and leaving behind us the fine cliffs of Iddá, turned our head once more downwards. The country passed during this day's voyage was rather uninteresting, flat and wooded near the water, and with slight elevations a little way inland. To the right was Adó, while on the other hand was Igára. The only places of any consequence passed were, to the eastward the village of Abijagá, and to the westward the little river coming from the Adó country. By two o'clock we were at anchor off Ada-mugú, and with Mr. Crowther, Mr. May, and

Dr. Hutchinson, I immediately went ashore. The people, a rude-looking set, at first seemed alarmed, and came in a large body armed with swords and muskets to receive us. The numbers of the latter weapon rather surprised us, used as we had been of late to no missiles but arrows, but we were now approaching the coast. On inquiring for their King, they answered that he was lately dead, and that his son, having committed a murder, had been obliged to flee from the place. After a good deal of talking a headman was pointed out, who appeared very unwilling to acknowledge his responsible situation, but at length, by dint of perseverance, laughing, talking, smoking our cigars, and showing them how completely we felt at our ease, we succeeded in allaying their fears, and in becoming friendly. The first symptom of confidence exhibited was by the headman advancing and offering me as a present thirty cowries and a couple of kóla nuts. His example was followed by the head djú-dju man or high-priest of the village, and some others, so that I was in a fair way of speedily becoming wealthy. But at length their contributions ceased, and though the amount of their donations, about 100 cowries, equal to about three pence sterling, was not exactly a fortune to me, yet it answered its purpose by evidencing their feelings towards us. We quickly struck up a trade in yams and firewood, both of which were abundant and of good quality. The latter was purchased for blue romals and needles, and we kept up the trade until after sunset, when it

U

was too dark to continue. The yams were very different from those of the Confluence, being long, slender, and pointed at either end, but very well flavoured. Fish, beer, and red pepper were also produced, and we obtained a curious box, carved to imitate a tortoise with its head extended. From a canoe returning from a market at A'ra in Adó, I bought some mats, which Mr. Crowther at once recognized as being similar to those made by the Yóruba of Ijebú, and there named A'ba, showing thereby that the customs, &c., of Adó are more connected with countries to the westward than to the eastward, and thus indicating their origin.

During the following day, which was Sunday, we remained quietly at anchor, having told the natives that no business would be transacted. The forenoon set in very hot, and at four o'clock the thermometer on the poop stood at ninety-six degrees. A slave who came on board told us, that he was from a place called Bagári, near Bornú, and that before he left his own country, he could speak Arabic readily. During our stay at Ada-mugú, besides a Meridian altitude of the sun, Mr. May got two sets of lunar observations.

The district around and behind Ada-mugú is named Abáji, and the language is Igára, though I'gbo is also understood. Ada-mugú was founded by A'boko, on the site of a former Abáji village, at a time when he had quarrelled with the Attá; the ground being given to him by the Abáji people.

A'boko used often to act quite independently of the Attá, and at one time made war on Agatú entirely on his own account. The latter part of his life was spent chiefly at Iddá, but his sons are scattered over various towns and districts, wherever their adherents live, or they possess property. A'ma-A'boko, the eldest, succeeded to Igbégbe, as that was his mother's country. Not far from Ada-mugú is a town named Onujá, which was built by the son of a former Attá, who was compelled to leave Iddá, being too fond of thinking and acting for himself. Below Ada-mugú are two towns, one of which, Igbokéyi, is the residence of Agabídoko, and the other, named after its proprietor, "Amidóko," belongs to a chief who lives at Iddá.

Early on the 30th, canoes were alongside with firewood, sheep, fowls, eggs, bananas, coco-nuts, limes, yams, pepper, palm-wine, &c. While steam was getting up, Mr. May went in the gig and measured the breadth of the river, after which we got under way. On the left bank we saw the Igára town Omọdọmọ, and on the right we passed two market towns in Adó, a little way from the river, named A'ra and Utó, both founded by A'boko. In these the principal articles for sale are country cloths, mats, and provisions. Utó was formerly named A'boko's market; and near it, a little more inland, stands Oría, also a market-place, the inhabitants of both of which places speak Igára and Abó, as well as their own language. These markets are chiefly frequented by people from Iddá and from Abáji. A'ra was given by A'boko to Agabídoko, but some interest is now claimed in it by Ossamaré; its inhabitants are termed A'param or A'pram. Between Abó and Utó there fell out, many years ago, a serious quarrel, and ever since, Abó people have ceased to attend its market.

CHAPTER X.

I'GBO.

WE now bade adieu to Igára and Adó, and entered the I'gbo territories. Immediately adjoining Abáji to the southward is Inám, the people of which, though an I'gbo race, formerly paid tribute to the Attá, and afterwards to Obí. A branch here joins the river, known as the Inám river, and the Inám country is nearly a day's canoe-journey up this stream. The people trade chiefly at Asabá and Onitshá, in country cloths, corn, yams, fowls, &c. Next to Inám, but nearer the river, is Nsúgbe or Isúgbe, founded upwards of twenty years ago by a man from Abó, who, having killed one of his wives, had to leave that place. The dialect spoken is Abó, and tribute was formerly paid to Obí; but, since his death, to nobody. Their town, also named Nsúgbe, is on the north side of the Inám river, but the district extends on both sides. The people deal in similar articles to those of Inám, but trade principally at Onitshá. Inám and Nsúgbe are supplied with muskets mostly from Iddá, to which place they are brought from Abó. At the time of our visit the

Oct. 30.

value of an ordinary musket at Iddá was from 10,000 to 12,000 cowries, and at Abó, from 8000 to 9000 cowries; the value of a flint at Abó was 20 cowries. Below Walker Island, on the right bank, stands a small village belonging to Asabá, and named A'param-U'gboru. The language is Abó, and its market is visited by traders from Igára, and from Inám. At half-past eleven we anchored off Asabá, and landing, Mr. May got an observation for latitude, after which we ascended a sloping path leading to the town. The inhabitants, at first rather alarmed, soon became reconciled to our appearance, and we were conducted to their King, followed by a large and gradually increasing crowd. Asabá is finely situated on a rising ground, about 100 feet above the river, and is surrounded by walls, and by palisades of tall trees. The huts are numerous, but widely apart; they are oblong, well-constructed, and many are whitewashed or coloured. The inhabitants, extremely numerous, were disposed to be friendly, but are a wild, rude-looking people, much tatooed. The principal marks are three perpendicular ones along the breast and belly, the centre one being straight, and the side ones curved; another behind, following the curve of the armpit, and going downwards; seven short, perpendicular incisions on the forehead, and a curved row of small lines under each eye. These are to be universally seen, but some extravagant individuals also sport others. The gardens are hedged in with tall coco-palms, plantains, and bananas; yams are abundant, and fowls, fine sheep, and cattle seem plentiful. Altogether we felt surprised that such an unprepossessing race should have a town so rich, so clean, and so well laid out. All the men carry arms, muskets, knives, swords, &c., and many have in their hands a kind of musical, or rather, an acoustic instrument, made of a small elephant's-tusk such as a scrivelloe, polished and neatly ornamented externally, with a small square hole near the apex communicating with the central hollow, and through which, when they blow forcibly, a loud and disagreeable sound is produced. I was anxious to purchase one of these but did not succeed. We were conducted to the King's house, and seated, some on mats, some on carved wooden stools, under a verandah, which sheltered us from the intense heat of the sun. An immense crowd stood around, and their look, their manner, and above all their noise, told us we were among a people differing much from those we had lately been familiar with; in short, that we were once more among the active, though often troublesome, I'gbos. There are a number of petty chiefs in Asabá, who made their appearance in full costume, all clad in a similar manner. Each had round the waist a large piece of white calico, and a belt of leopard's skin. They wore red caps, decorated with white and red feathers, which I found are only borne by warriors, each feather denoting an enemy slain in actual warfare. Some of our entertainers had as many as five or six, and I am told that Ajé at Abó is entitled to display seven. Round the eyes was a white-coloured ring, on the arms were ivory wristlets; strings of cowries and charms hung round their necks, and each carried in his hand a fan. At length the head chief, an old man, named Ezebógo, came forward, habited like the rest, but with more ornaments. After our salutations, I spoke of friendship, of trade, and of education, and particularly enlarged upon the evils of war, and the benefits of peace, all of which was well received. Some most delicious palm-wine was then handed round, of which we all drank deeply, and, refreshed by this delightful beverage, we arose, and, after another look round this extensive place, returned to our ship, accompanied by a messenger, who came for a present for Ezebógo. From some people on the shore my assistant got some nice specimens of fish, and of fresh-water crustaceans. There are very few canoes at Asabá, but for what reason I could not learn. It is excellently adapted for a trading-station, and any European in ordinary health could live here as well as in any similar tropical spot. The district behind Asabá is named Igbúsa, and in it are two towns called Ogbóri and Ogbóbi. A little above Asabá is said to be a village named Asabútshi. Palm-wine is the drink of all the I'gbo towns, and its use extends as far as Iddá, above which beer replaces it. The Muhammadans, though they will not touch beer, yet readily drink palm-wine. The palm-wine which we so admired at Asabá was obtained from the oil-palm, and had been sweetened with honey. Half-an-hour brought us to Onitshá, where on landing we found the market, which is held close to the river, nearly broken up, hardly any traders being left. Among the canoes were several from Abó. The town is situated from two to three miles from the river, and we had not time to visit it; but we met the King's son, who is named Odíri, and by him I sent a message to Akazúa his father. Onitshá is in E'lugu, and the dialects spoken are E'lugu, Isuáma, and Abó. The first king of Onitshá was named Udógu, who was alive about the time of Laird and Lander's voyage. Odíri told us that the fancy cloths about which we had been so often inquiring, were made near Onitshá. He gave us the names of the following E'lugu towns, from which people attended the market held here every five days, namely, Obótshi, Ojá, U'mu, O'bba, Nkpó, Abája-Ezongánran, Abája-O'bba, Uké, Akúku, Obú, Otó, Newú, Ozhi-Owére, Ofú-Abája, Ntéja, Nkuére, Nzhíbe. Different kinds of fancy cloths are distinguished by different names, as Owówo, A'naba-Obíri, and Nwéga. Mr. Crowther spoke to Odíri about sending teachers, and mentioned to him the desire of many E'lugus to come and settle here, on which Odíri said all would be willingly received and welcomed, and would be protected as long as they continued to conduct themselves properly. The country about and behind Onitshá is elevated and dry, and quite as eligible for a settlement as Asabá. Here also, canoes are few and small. By half-past three we were again wending our way down the river, passing on the right bank some villages named O'ko, and on the left, the district of Odégbe, which is close to the river. I was anxious to have visited A'kra-A'tani; but not knowing the exact locality itself, and trusting to Alihéli, he allowed us to pass it before mentioning anything about it. It is said to be opposite a creek named the O'ko creek. Tradition relates that the original inhabitants of Abó were named A'kra, and when driven away by the race who came from Adó, they went and settled in different directions, their towns being distinguished by the prefix of A'kra to the previous name of the spot; thus we have A'kra-A'tani, A'kra-U'gidi, and A'kra-Utéri. About six o'clock we anchored off the mouth of a creek running behind Ossamaré, and down which is said to be a town named Osútshi. Opposite to our anchorage, on the right bank of the river, is a village named Ut'shi.

A sharp squall from the north-north-east brought us a deluge of rain and heavy thunder, lasting till after six o'clock in the morning. The thermometer fell to 74°, which actually felt cold. About seven o'clock we got under steam, and passing by Bullock's Island, which belongs to Ossamaré, at eight o'clock anchored off that town. We were almost immediately surrounded by canoes of all sizes, some so small as to contain only one person, who sat with the legs projecting over the sides of his tiny bark, and when it was desired to alter the direction of the canoe, one foot was dropped into the water, according to the side to which it was wished to steer. The speed with which these little canoes move, and the ease with which they turn, is almost incredible; three or four may be seen hurrying towards one common point, and every second the concerned spectator expects to hear the crash of a collision, and to see the occupants struggling in the tide; but no—just as destruction, to the eye of the stranger, seems inevitable, with a dexterous movement of the foot and a smart stroke of the paddle the catastrophe is avoided. Two persons named Kaiméne and Eyín brought me presents of yams, and I offered them some things in return. The one was satisfied, but the other grumbled, on which I recommended him to take back his yams, which made him alter his tune, as he had only come to see what he could make. At eight o'clock I went ashore to pay a visit to the King, an old man, called Nzedégu. The town is very inferior in situation to either Asabá or Onitshá; it stands close to the river, and now especially, after the heavy rain of the night, was particularly muddy and filthy. To reach the palace we had to cross, by a narrow plank, a deep dirty pool, and this frail bridge bent so much in the middle as to immerse us to the ankles. Our conversation was of the usual nature, and though the King at first made some complaint about our not stopping off his town during our ascent, yet we contrived to give a satisfactory reason, and to establish a perfectly friendly understanding. Mr. Crowther explained to Nzedégu the nature of his visit, and the wishes of the Church Missionary Society to send teachers among them; a statement which was eagerly listened to. After exchanging presents we retired, and presently re-embarked. Ossamaré is in Isuáma, but is closely connected with Abó, to which until the death of Obí it was tributary. A considerable quantity of palm-oil is brought from the interior for shipment, being the principal port of Isuáma. The palm-oil is either sold directly to Abó and Orú traders, or else it is taken to Abó for disposal. A little ivory occasionally reaches it from Iddá, but is generally sold to Isuáma at a high rate. In speaking of Isuáma it is often used in the contracted form of I'su.

On the right bank below Bullock's Island stands Okpái, after which the Abó territory proper commences, the first town in it being A'se. Opposite the south end of Bullock's Island, to the eastward, is the district of Obágwe, with a town of the same name, below which is U'gidi, in which is situated A'kra-U'gidi. To the southward of U'gidi, still near the river is Ógú, and further down the district and town of Egbóma. Rather behind Egbóma stands Ugúta, the inhabitants of which come to the river for fishing and trading. At the mouth of the affluent, commonly marked in charts as the Bonny creek, is Ndóni, inhabited by a trading people, who go as far as Iddá for oil, which they bring to Abó for sale.

They speak the Abó dialect, and are reputed as skilful artisans. Red-coloured varieties of palm-oil bear a higher price in the river markets than the darker-coloured sorts. At A'kra-A'tani, two small jars of red oil cost 2000 cowries. The kernel oil is only manufactured about the Confluence.

About two o'clock we were at our old anchorage off the Abó creek, and shortly afterwards, Mr. Crowther, with Dr. Hutchinson and Mr. Taylor, went on shore, and on their return brought off Simon Jonas, who reported that he had been very well treated and cared for by Ajé. Just after our departure he had a severe attack of illness, but was carefully watched and nursed. He had lately visited Ossamaré, A'kra-A'tani, Onitshá, and Asabá, at all of which places he had been well received, as also at O'ko-A'la, about a day's journey up the Abó creek. Wherever he had shown himself, he had been looked upon as a superior person, such influence do knowledge and civilization confer on their possessors. He had found the people always attentive, desirous of information, and retentive of what was taught them. He told us that there were many Isuáma and Ndóni people resident in Abó at this time; that many canoes had been lately from Brass and Orú, but none from Bonny; and that cowries were of but little value in the Abó market, as he had seen 2000 paid for a single fowl. I had been very desirous of getting a pair of large ivory anklets, such as were worn by the Abó ladies, and had commissioned Simon to procure me a pair, but as he found that their price would have been equal to the cost of four slaves, he wisely declined getting them. He told me also, that the name by which the river is known in the interior of I'gbo is "Anyím." I had told the trading gentlemen, that if they found any trade, I was perfectly ready to make any convenient stay, though one day would complete all that Mr. May and I wanted; after being ashore, however, they stated that they saw little prospect of doing much. Our stock of tea was about exhausted, when, this afternoon, out of curiosity I ordered a chest, which had been kicking about and owned by nobody, to be opened, and it was found to contain eight large cases of tea! Another such box, opened after we had been passing most of the night in entire darkness, not being able to afford lights, proved to be filled with excellent composition candles!

Alihéli related to me a circumstance regarding King Obí, which I heard confirmed at Iddá, and at Igbégbe, and which seems quite to free him from any suspicion of being concerned in Mr. Carr's murder. On hearing of this untoward event, Obí immediately sent to the Attá, to acquaint him of it, saying it was very unfortunate and would injure their prospects of trading with white men, and asking what steps ought to be taken about it. The Attá not feeling himself sufficiently powerful to act, sent to Dásaba, requesting his assistance in punishing the murderers. This the latter readily agreed to, and offered to lead an army to the sea, provided the Attá would furnish canoes when required. Accordingly he marched along the right bank, until opposite A'da-mugú, when getting into swampy ground, he was afraid of losing his men, and therefore retraced his steps, making up for his disappointment by pillaging and destroying all the Kakánda towns and villages in his way. Obí's father was named Ogbóma. Ajé has four large war-canoes, and about 250 slaves, while Tshúkuma has five smaller canoes, and about 50 or 60 slaves.

In the morning I went ashore with Mr. May, and with difficulty finding ground firm enough to support us, we got a set of sights. I sent Simon Jonas in the gig to bring off Ajé and Tshúkuma, whom I had invited on board, and in the meantime I settled with Alihéli, who now returned to his own abode and his two wives. He had proved most faithful and most valuable, and had been the means of procuring much information for us. Should I be so fortunate as again to ascend the Kwóra, I should consider my staff incomplete if he were not included as one of its members.

About half-past eleven, Tshúkuma and his head wife came alongside in the gig, on which I ordered two guns to be fired. He was attired almost exactly as he had been when I last saw him. Presently Ajé was seen to approach in a large canoe with seventeen paddles of a side, and accompanied by several of his wives, and some of his brothers and their wives. Another salute was fired, after which we received our visitors on board, and with some difficulty got them all seated on the poop. Ajé is a tall, rather stout, young-looking man, very superior in appearance to his brother, and is said in manner and countenance greatly to resemble his father. He appeared dressed in home-made scarlet-cloth trousers, a scarlet uniform coat, a pink beaver hat, under which, apparently to make it fit, was a red worsted night-cap, no shoes, beads round the neck, and in his hand a Niger-expedition sword. After talking of general matters, I spoke of his father, of Captain Trotter, of trade, and of our wishes and intentions, on which he replied that he considered that whatever his father wished or promised was binding on him, adding, however, that we seemed very long in carrying out our part of the agreement. I gave him a double-barrelled gun, a large sabre, a scarlet tobe, some cloth and beads, and some scissors, mirrors, and needles for his wives, and also three krus (27,000) of cowries for his kindness to Simon Jonas. This last he said must be shared by his brother, on which I offered Tshúkuma an equal amount, and gave him also other presents. With all Ajé seemed dissatisfied, and asked, why we did not give so much as Captain Trotter did,* on which I mentioned our long voyage, the many presents we had given away, and of our stock being exhausted. Still he asked for things I had not, until I was obliged to speak more plainly, telling him how unreasonable his behaviour was, and how unlike what I expected

---

* The enormous amount of presents given in 1841 proved very embarrassing to us, as we were always expected to bestow an equal quantity.

in a son of Obí. He then laughed, showing that he was merely trying to get as much as he could, a daily Abó practice. He next asked for the traders, who were sent for, and showed them a quantity of firewood, yams, palm-oil, and a bullock he had for sale. He proved a very keen hand, and only parted with his articles at a high price; he looked to everything himself, saw things handed on board, and the cowries counted. He gave me as his *dash* a bullock and 200 yams, which latter were here, though very good, very small and rounded. I took him round the ship, fired a swivel off before him, and showed him the engine. I explained to him that as our provisions were nearly expended, I could offer him but little; on which he said he would merely ask for some biscuit, which I gave him. He was much amused with the shower-bath, which he called all his wives to look at, and was much pleased with a German accordian which I gave him. Some one, rather foolishly, asked him to a dinner of salt pork and yams, with a glass of sour claret, however he sat down with us, and the meal passed over tolerably. The palm-oil was all rejected, as it could not be started on board, and no casks were sent on shore for it. Ajé told Mr. Crowther and me, that if any order had been left in July, he could have had plenty for us. The river was now falling quickly, and the decrease of the water was perceptible daily. Our sick-list was gradually diminishing, and the few who remained were convalescing rapidly under good food. On examining our stock of edibles, we found that we had made our calculations very fairly, as by the time we should reach Fernando Po, we should have nearly consumed everything. There were now on board just four days' fresh provisions for all hands, half a case of biscuit, and flour for eight days for the officers, but there was abundance of rice and of yams on board, so that we could not starve, and I had no desire to leave the river as long as we had any provisions fit to eat.

Mr. May and Mr. Harcus made an early start to sound for a supposed rock, marked in Allen's Chart. They found a shoal patch with three fathoms, while all around it were seven and eight fathoms. As the trading gentlemen intimated that they could do nothing more, I resolved to start in the afternoon. In the meanwhile Dr. Hutchinson went to try and get some firewood, but returned with a very small supply, saying he thought Ajé was interrupting the sale. On this, with Mr. Crowther, I started off to see Ajé, while Dr. Hutchinson went again in the pinnace to look for fuel. We found Ajé at home, when I mentioned that he had not kept his promise to us about firewood, and I told him that Englishmen liked to do business promptly. He apologized and said we should have what we wanted in the morning, but I answered that would not do, as I should leave in another hour. We got, however, very friendly, and had a long chat. Mr. Crowther then spoke to him of a site for teachers if they were sent here, when Ajé told him that any spot he selected would be reserved for that purpose. He gave us some capital palm-wine, and seeing that we relished it, ordered a quantity to be sent on board. Before saying farewell, he asked my name, and ordered two messengers to attend us and see us safely off. He told us finally that he should expect to see us about the beginning of the next rainy season, on which we said we could not promise, but hoped we might then return. On our way down the creek we got wood enough to load both boats, and a man gathered for me a specimen of the Malaghetta-pepper plant. We did not get up steam, but dropped down the river, anchoring for the night off A'kra-Utéri.

As in addition to what I learnt while in the river, I got much information about I'gbo from persons belonging to that country at Fernando Po, and at Sierra Leone, it will be advisable here to embody all the interesting facts connected with it. I'gbo, as I have formerly mentioned, extends east and west, from the Old Kalabár river to the banks of the Kwóra, and possesses also some territory at Abó to the westward of the latter stream. On the north it borders on Igára and A'kpoto, and it is separated from the sea only by petty tribes, all of which trace their origin to this great race. In I'gbo each person hails, as a sailor would say, from the particular district where he was born, but when away from home all are I'gbos. And yet considerable differences exist between different parts of this extensive country, and the dialects spoken also vary greatly. Those of which we heard during our voyage as being well marked are the Abó, E'lugu, Isuáma, and A'ro, of which that of Isuáma is the most widely diffused, the softest, and the best adapted for the lingual standard. E'lugu is in the far north, close to Igára, and near it, to the eastward, are two smaller districts, Isiélu, and Isiágo. Of Abó I have already spoken fully. Isuáma is the most central division, and at the same time the largest. A'ro is more to the south-east, and is, as I shall presently have reason to mention, a very important place. Of other minor districts I may mention the following. About a day's journey up the river from Okúloma (Bonny) is "Ndóki" as it is termed by its own inhabitants, but by the I'gbos of the interior it is styled O'kwa. Near this is "Ngwá" through which it is said, no rivers nor creeks run, so that the people have to dig wells for water. In it are many villages, in which the streets are left very wide. North-west from Ngwá is O'zuzu, where the language differs slightly in dialect, and in which every town has its own chief. The people employ a peculiar mark, viz., three rows of minute lines from the ear to the angle of the eye, the middle row straight, and the two others converging towards the eye; two curved lines of small incisions from the lobe of the ear, curving along the cheek, to the end of the lines at the eye, and two short rows of similar lines under the eyes towards the nose, and a line of incisions of the same kind down the forehead and nose. A similar marking is employed by some of the neighbouring districts. O'zuzu people trade much with New Kalabár, which they know as Bom, but also as Karabári or Kalabári. There is plenty of palm-oil in O'zuzu, and abundance of cocos and yams. To the north or north-north-west of O'zuzu lies "Mbóhia," called at Bonny "Ikpófia." There are few towns here, it being chiefly a bush country. The derivation being from *Mba* country, and *Ohia* bush. There is but little oil made here, and the people are warlike. Close to it is another similar district, and with inhabitants of like propensities. It is named Ogóne, but at Bonny is known as Egáne. The people of Ndóki and Ngwá are reputed cannibals, that is to say, after war they eat the flesh of their enemies, but generally in secret. One of my informants assured me that, when a slave in Ngwá, he was an eye-witness to a repast of this nature. It took place after the death of a lady of property, when some slaves, purchased for the occasion, were slain and feasted on. From two to four days' journey north from Bonny, is a large and important market town, named Ogobéndo, but which at Bonny is always called Bónde. It is a grand dépot for slaves, as well as for palm-oil and provisions, and supplies with the former New Kalabár, Bonny, and Andony, as well as other neighbouring countries. When the foreign slave trade was being actively carried on, this town was in the zenith of its wealth and importance, and even since has declined but little, as it still remains the centre of the home slave mart for the coast, and the south of I'gbo. I inquired particularly after a supposed district or tribe, mentioned by Clarke and some other writers, as I'tshi or Brétshi, but found that this was a misapplication of the term. There is no place of this name, but I'tshi, which means "cut-face," refers to certain individuals who are marked by numerous cuttings on the forehead, which greatly disfigure the countenance. I fell in with one of these I'tshi, who confirmed all this, and told me that this practice prevails chiefly in Isuáma, and that it is confined to the families of the wealthy. As far as I could gather, it is only the males who are thus hideously tatooed, though in I'gbo it is reckoned becoming, and entitles the possessors to respect. The word Brétshi is wrong, Mbrítshi being the correct term, but I'tshi is more frequently employed.

To the northward and eastward of Ndóki is a large district named Abányim, where the I'gbos and people from Old Kalabár meet for trade. Not far from this stands the noted city of A'ro or A'no, where is the celebrated shrine of *Tshúku*, or the deity to which pilgrimages are made, not only from all parts of I'gbo proper, but from Old Kalabár, from the tribes along the coast, and from Orú, and Nímbe or Brass. The city is described as being nearly three times the size of Abó, and as extremely populous. The inhabitants are skilful artisans, and manufacture swords, spears, and metallic ornaments, specimens of all of which I have seen, and can therefore testify to their being very neatly finished. The town is always mentioned with great respect, almost, at times, with a degree of veneration, and the people say " *Tshúku ab yama,*" or " God lives there." The dialect of A'ro is peculiar, but Isuáma and E'lugu are also much spoken, as well as E'fik or Old Kalabár, and numerous other languages are to be heard among the crowds of pilgrim-votaries who throng the shrine. The mark used in A'ro consists of a series of (from ten to twelve) short horizontal lines, just before the ear. Of other places of which I heard, without being able to obtain any remarkable particulars about them, I may mention Abám to the north of Ogobéndo, Isiápo a small district between Ndǫ́ki and Bonny and which may be reached by canoe, Oráta to the eastward of O'zuzu, and finally Omiúnsi, a town in E'lugu, the inhabitants of which are said to be very short, but very stout.

The religion of I'gbo is entirely Pagan, mixed up with numerous rites and ceremonies, neither in general so frightful nor so bloody as those practised in Bíni, in Dahómi, and other more western countries, but still all of a pre-eminently superstitious character. The I'gbos all believe in an Almighty-being, omnipresent and omnipotent, whom they call *Tshúku,* whom they constantly worship, and whom they believe to communicate directly with them through his sacred shrine at A'ro. But they speak also of another and a distinct Deity, who at Abó is known as *Oríssa,* but throughout other parts of I'gbo, as "*Tshúku-Okéke,*" " God the creator, or the supreme God." Abó people believe that after death, those who have been good on earth may either go to Oríssa and abide with him, or they may, if they like, visit any country on earth; and so slaves often, when dying, say that they will go and revisit their native land; if, on the other hand a wicked man dies, it is understood that he is driven to *Okómo*, or hell; derived from *O'ko*, fire, and *mo* spirit. In Abó every man and every woman of any consequence keeps as djú-dju or sacred, the lower jaw of a pig, or, until they can procure this, a piece of wood fashioned like one. This is preserved in their huts, and produced only when worshipped, or when sacrifices are made to it, which are at certain times, at intervals of from ten days to three weeks. The particular days are determined by the djú-dju men or priests, and by them intimated to the people. They sprinkle this djú-dju with palm-wine, and touching it with a kola-nut, speak to it, and ask it to be good and propitious towards them. It is named *A'gba*, meaning pig, or *A'gba-E'zhi*, or pig's-jaw; but when kept as djú-dju, it is also termed *Ofúm*, or "my image," and also *Tshúku*. People also select particular trees near their huts, or, if there are none in the neighbourhood, they transplant one; these they worship and call *Tshúkum*, or "my God." They hang on these bits of white baff (calico,) as signs of a djú-dju tree, and as offerings to the deity. No one ever touches these, and if they rot off they are replaced. Little wooden images are also used, and are styled *O'fo-Tshúku*, or "images of God," and to these they talk and pray. When a man is suspected of falsehood, one of these is placed in his right hand, and he is made to swear by it, and if he does so falsely it is believed that some evil will speedily befal him. Sacrifices, principally of fowls, are made to these latter, as to the former. In Isuáma and in E'lugu there are similar usages, but the pig's-jaw is not employed, and no white baff is hung on the trees. At Abó one large tree is held as djú-dju for the whole district, it is covered with offerings, and there is an annual festival in honour of it, when sacrifices of fowls, sheep, goats, and bullocks are made. When a man goes to A'ro to consult *Tshúku*, he is received by some of the priests outside of the town, near a small stream. Here he makes an offering, after which a fowl is killed, and, if it appears unpropitious, a quantity of a red dye, probably camwood, is spilt into the water, which the priests tell the people is blood, and on this the votary is hurried off by the priests and is seen no more, it being given out that *Tshúku* has been displeased, and has taken him. The result of this preliminary ceremony is determined in general by the amount of the present given to the priests, and those who are reported to have been carried off by *Tshúku* are usually sold as slaves. Formerly they were commonly sent by a canoe, by a little creek, to Old Kalabár, and disposed of there. One of my informants had met upwards of twenty such unfortunates in Cuba, and another had also fallen in with several at Sierra Leone. If, however, the omen be pronounced to be favourable, the pilgrim is permitted to draw near to the shrine, and after various rites have been gone through, the question, whatever it may be, is propounded, of course, through the priests, and by them also the reply is given. A yellow powder is given to the devotee, who rubs it round his eyes, which powder is called in I'gbo, *E'do*. Little wooden images are also issued, as tokens of a person having actually consulted the sacred oracle, and these are known as *O'fo-Tshúku*, and are afterwards kept as djú-dju. A person who has been at A'ro, after returning to his home, is reckoned djú-dju or sacred for seven days, during which period he must stay in his house, and people dread to approach him. The shrine of *Tshúku* is said to be situated nearly in the centre of the town, and the inhabitants of A'ro are often styled *Q'mo-Tshúku*, or God's children.

Mọ ndjó means a bad or evil spirit. The greatest or worst of evil spirits, is named *Kamállo*, possibly equivalent with Satan. His name is frequently bestowed on children, and in some parts of I'gbo, especially in Isuáma, Kamállo is worshipped. No images are made, but a hut is set apart, in which are kept bones, pieces of iron, &c., as sacred. Persons make inquiries of this spirit, if they wish to commit any wicked action, such as murder, when they bring presents of cowries and cloth to propitiate this evil being and render him favourable to their designs. If the individual intended as the victim suspects anything, or gets a hint of his adversary's proceedings, he also comes to worship, bringing with him, if possible, more valuable offerings, to try to avert the impending danger, and this is called *Eríse náo*, or "I cut on both sides." *Kamállo* means "one going about everywhere and in all directions." Another evil spirit is named *Igwikálla; álla*, meaning "ground," and *I'gwik*, "one who lived above before coming down." In Isuáma if a man is sick, the doctor often tells the friends to consult *Igwikálla*, and he is also worshipped by persons wishing to injure others. His supposed abode is generally in a bush, which has been well cleared all round, but occasionally huts are dedicated to him, and priests execute his decrees.

Throughout I'gbo the bodies of the dead are generally interred. In Abó this is invariably done, and the grave is always in the hut of the deceased, but this does not prevent the place remaining inhabited. In Abó slaves used always to be sacrificed on such occasions, and so late as the decease of King Obí, Simon Jonas told me that forty slaves were killed, these being specially purchased for this horrid purpose, domestic slaves never being so treated. As far as I could learn, however, this practice is gradually dying out at Abó, if it is not altogether extinct. Graves, therefore, of chiefs are large pits, into which are first thrown a number of dead slaves, then the body of the departed, and lastly some more slaves. In Isuáma it is only rich persons who are buried in their own houses, the bodies of slaves being simply interred in the bush. In Isuáma a part only of the clothes of the deceased are thrown into the grave, but in Abó almost the entire wardrobe and all the ornaments descend with their late possessors into the tomb; thus women, too, are buried with their rings and anklets, a practice which serves to keep up the enormous price of the latter, which, again, are seldom, if ever, worn in Isuáma.

In E'lugu, Isuáma, Ebáne,	Bullocks are killed and eaten, guns are fired, Dancing and other amusements take place.
In Abó, A'ro, Bóm, Ndóki, Orú,	In addition to these above mentioned, slaves are killed.

In I'gbo time is measured by years; by seasons, as the dry season, the rainy season, &c.; by moons, of course about twenty-eight days; and lastly, by a shorter period, analogous to our week, but consisting only of four days. These are termed as follows:—

  First day, E'ke,   Third day, Nkwó,
  Second day, O'ri, Fourth day, A'fo.

E'ke corresponds to our Sunday, and on it no regular work is done. Some pass this day in idleness, others consult their *O'fo Tshúku* and other images or sacrifice to them. But they are not very strict about its observance. This last division of time shows itself in many ways, thus their markets are held every four days.

 The food of the inhabitants of I'gbo consists of yams, corn, rice, bananas, plantains, coco-nuts, palm-oil, and other esculent vegetable matters, also fowls, sheep, goats, bullocks, or the flesh of any wild animals.

Dogs are occasionally eaten at Abó, as also in Igára and Núpe, but not so regularly as in Bíni, Orú, Nímbe, Ebáne, and New Kalabár. There is a considerable traffic carried on at Abó in dogs, which are purchased at Iddá, and are sold to supply the delta of the river. The price of a large dog is usually one bag of salt, and of a small one, one piece (seven fathoms) of common calico. Cats are procured from Iddá for killing vermin, but are not used as food. Rats are eaten, as far as I could learn, at Nímbe (Brass). Monkeys are prized as food all along the river, except by the Haúsa Muhammadans, who hold this animal in great abhorrence. At Abó a great medium of barter is salt, which is brought up from Nímbe and from Bíni, and is always in demand. Slaves are almost always purchased with salt, the prices varying somewhat according to the condition of the market. The average price of a stout male slave is from ten to twelve bags of salt, or from 60,000 to 70,000 cowries, and for a good-looking young female, eight to ten bags of salt, or from 45,000 to 50,000 cowries.

Throughout I'gbo great wars are now seldom heard of, but petty quarrels often occur. The last time Abó was at war was about 1851, with Dásaba, when one Abó man, and ten or twelve of Dásaba's party were killed. The usual style of disputes generally ends in the capture of a canoe, or the confiscation of a cargo. When King Boy was at Abó, in 1842, about the time of Lieutenant Webb's visit in the "Wilberforce,"

Obí taxed him with having been concerned in Mr. Carr's murder, which, however, Boy would not admit. But his precipitate retreat from Abó was looked on as strong evidence of his guilt, and from that period none of his canoes ever came to Abó until about three years before our visit, at which time several arrived for trading purposes. A quarrel, however, soon took place, which ended in the Abó people seizing the cargoes, and the Nímbe men retreating and carrying off some Abó canoes. Since then friendly relations have been dropped, but a year before the arrival of the "Pleiad," two headmen had been deputed to go to Nímbe to try and settle differences. But various diplomatic difficulties and delays had occurred, and when I heard the story, the Abó envoys were still residing at the court of Nímbe.

Not to lose time in the Delta, we were under steam as soon as we could distinguish our way. Mr. Guthrie told me, from the trials he had made, that shea-butter was not well adapted for the engines, being dirty and too solid, and that it was only fit for lubricating slides. The palm-kernel oil again was excellent, quite as good as the castor-oil of India, and could be employed in any part where the engine was warm, but not for the shaft, where only olive-oil could be used. The character of the vegetation on the river's banks was now changing. *Bombaceæ* were becoming abundant and seemed to replace the *Adansoniæ* of the upper regions. About nine o'clock observing much cut wood near a village, we anchored close off it, and going ashore easily purchased for trinkets a considerable quantity. The village, which is the first one in the Orú country, is named Agbéri, and the chief, called Agbekúm, had been on board as we passed on our ascent. Since that time he had been on a pilgrimage to A'ro, to inquire why his wife had no children, and from this place he had but just returned. Mr. Crowther and I were delighted at such an opportunity presenting itself of getting some direct information about this mysterious place, so as soon as the trading operations were fairly set a-going, we got closeted with this man in his hut. He was still djú-dju, but we did not feel any particular dread in sitting by him, and besides as strangers it was permitted to us to visit him. He went by canoe from Agbéri to a creek nearly opposite Abó, and entering it, proceeded to a place named Igbéma (Egbóma?), whence he finished his journey by land. On arriving at A'ro the priests gave him some yellow powder, which he showed us, and which they said would kill him if his heart were bad: he also exhibited some articles, as guardian images, also obtained from the priests. He was unwilling to speak freely of Tshúku, whom he told us could not be seen, but could only be heard through the priests. He told us there were many people from Old Kalabár living in A'ro, and also some whom he termed "Ibíbi," whom I believe to be from the country known to white traders as "Egboshári," near the Cross river, as the E'fik name for that place is

Ibíbio. We saw here an A'ro slave, when I had an opportunity of examining the distinguishing mark of that place, to which I have already alluded. Some of the people were much interested in seeing Mr. Crowther writing, and were extremely astonished when handing his note-book to me, I read "Agbéri" and "Agbekúm," the names of their town and of their chief. The chief said that if any intimation had been given to his people, they could have collected plenty of palm-oil ready for us to ship now. He told us also, that the nearest district inland from Agbéri was Akpófia (Mbóhia), from the borders of which they were distant about a day's journey, or from fifteen to twenty miles; while we were wooding, Mr. May measured the breadth of the river, and got a meridian altitude of the sun. This latter confirmed a careful observation taken at Abó two days previously, the result of which was altering the latitude of Abó by eight miles.* About half-past twelve we were under steam, proceeding towards the sea, and passing many villages, off none of which we called, being desirous, if possible, of getting as far as Angiáma. During the afternoon we had a very fresh breeze blowing up the river with occasional rain. We continued until nearly seven o'clock, when as it was becoming too dark to see our way clearly, and Mr. May having to

* On mentioning this since our return to Captain Allen, that gentleman said he would have little doubt in preferring Mr. May's observations to his own, as the latter were taken twice, and with an artificial horizon, while his were taken with an imperfect natural horizon, and while he was suffering from indisposition.

revise this part of his chart, we anchored off the lower mouth of the Wilberforce Channel. This channel is in Allen and Thomson's Narrative * called the O'guborìh river, but I see on referring to Vogel's Journal,† that on asking some natives who were at a distance their name for it, they only *fancied* that they gave it as "Oguberri." I should rather think that there is some mistake here, and that this name does not refer to the river at all, as I always found that they had but one designation for the river and its branches, viz., "Osímini," except when they described any creek as leading to a certain place. This was about one of the most unpleasant anchorages which we had during our voyage, the air was close and unhealthy, and we could by the moonlight see large patches of mist hanging about the tops of the trees. Mosquitoes crowded on board, possibly to welcome us on our return, but the pleasure of meeting was not reciprocal, nor could we persuade them to take a quiet hint and retire. I detected one settling in the most cool and impudent manner on the back of my hand, preparing to enjoy an extemporary banquet. I fancied I recognized this savage intruder as being the same which had, during our ascent, committed on me an assault to the effusion of blood, but in the heat of my indignation I sacrificed this sanguinary gnat, without allowing time for mutual recognition, so that this question of identity must remain for ever a doubtful point in history.

* Vol. i. p. 184.   † Page 50.

The morning brought with it no refreshing breeze, and all around us was enveloped in mist. During the night there had been heavy rain, and occasional showers continued until daybreak. As soon as we could see we weighed anchor, and dropping down about two miles were abreast of Angiáma, where, as the water was deep, we hauled alongside the bank. Mr. Crowther and I immediately landed, and found the place intolerably wet and muddy. The moist ground was yielding abundant malarious exhalations, and the sun's rays had not yet succeeded in penetrating through the murky atmosphere. For the first time I was conscious of a disagreeable, sickly smell, and after a short time felt so faint that I had to return on board and get something to revive myself. Before this, however, we had found out the King's house, and telling him we wanted fuel, requested him to desire his people to sell it to us. After we had firmly established commercial relations, I had a second interview with the King, whose name is Ndáwa, to whom I spoke of the folly of his people in trying to obstruct the free navigation of the river, and in attempting to keep all trade in their own hands. I told him we were desirous of being friendly with them, but that if ever the Orú men tried to oppose or injure us, we had the power, and should feel obliged to resort to force; but that instead of driving us to employ such unpleasant means, how much better would it be for all, were enmity laid aside, and quarrelling, which would only lead to bloodshed, entirely foresworn. To all this the King returned most peaceable replies, and ended by giving me a sheep, and some yams and coco-nuts, on which I presented him with a red cloak, which pleased him no less than it delighted the spectators. On walking through the town I fell in with a doctor's shop, a great curiosity, but was unable to see the learned gentleman himself, and to claim him as a professional brother. It was a small room, wonderfully clean, and painted, the sides being striped with blue, black, red, and white, and the back checked with the same colours. Two pots of herbs in steep were placed on a tripod, composed of three branches springing from a common origin. Two divining rods, many long pointed sticks, (one cut like a crocodile's head, another carved to resemble a tortoise, and a third painted rudely to represent a man,) were in different corners, while hanging around the walls were numerous strings of cowries and other charms. Coco-palms were very abundant, and at that time hung all round with fruit. This is the place where Lander was attacked when returning in an open boat to rejoin Oldfield. Since that time the village has been moved about 300 yards further up, but the place opposite which he received his mortal wound is marked by a tall palm-tree. We left Angiáma about a quarter past nine, with the intention of having no more stoppages until we arrived at the mouth of the river; we passed many crowded villages, the inhabitants of which gathered along the banks to observe us. As the water permitted, we generally steamed near the bank, for the purpose of inquiring the names of the towns; but the people usually replied by telling us to come ashore and find out for ourselves, for which we had neither time nor inclination. Palms were gradually increasing in number, and after passing Sunday Island, we came upon our old friends the mangroves. Just above Louis' Creek, the soundings, it being low ebb, decreased greatly; for a short time we had only one fathom; but we cautiously advanced under Mr. Richards's skilful pilotage, and presently at the mouth of the creek, again were able to steam on boldly ahead. A few minutes more and we were gratified by having a distant view of the sea, and of being refreshed by the cool sea-breeze. At a quarter past three, we anchored off Baracoon Point, exactly sixteen weeks from the time we had left it behind us when upward bound, and we felt especially thankful that we had all been spared to return in health and strength after a four months' sojourn up the river Niger.

There appeared to be a heavy sea on the bar, but as that did not concern us, we spent the remaining portion of daylight in clearing out the canoes and getting them ready for towing, and in getting the coals, &c., they contained on deck. The evening was clear and cloudless, and about nine o'clock we had a good opportunity of watching a partial eclipse of the moon.

Early in the morning Mr. May and Mr. Richards went in the gig by the creek to the Brass river, to endeavour to get some news. The hands on board resumed their task of clearing out the canoes. At 6·30 and 6·45 A.M., we heard guns in the distance, and fancying that they might be from some ships in the offing, we replied to them, but we subsequently ascertained that they had been fired by the ships at the mouth of the Brass river, a distance from us of ten miles. Some heavy thunder-clouds with rain passed over us from time to time during the day. At half-past eight work was knocked off, and at ten we had church service, when Mr. Crowther offered up a special thanksgiving for the return of the expedition with the entire crew in safety. In the afternoon we prepared for sea, securing the deck cargo, and passing the canoes astern, as I was anxious to attempt the bar in the morning. I had been desirous to get to the mouth of the river at this time, being just after the top of the spring tides, when the bar could be most easily crossed, and luckily we had been able to hit our time very nicely. About sunset Mr. May and Mr. Richards returned, having had a pleasant cruize, but having been unsuccessful in obtaining any European intelligence later than what we were aware of in July, when we left Fernando Po, so cut off from home news are many of the palm-oil ships. Mr. May ascertained that the town marked as Brass Town in the maps is incorrectly so named, it being called Tuwón, the true Brass Town of white traders, or Nímbe, being thirty-five miles from the sea. As an example of the conduct at times of civilized people, I will here relate what had occurred in the Brass river very shortly before this period. A white trader, then agent for an English house, had, out of a mere freak, ordered a native who came on board his ship one day to be seized and flogged. This lad's father, however, was a man of consequence on shore, and, on hearing of this outrage, he summoned his friends, and in two large canoes attacked and boarded the ship. The white Captain armed his Kruboys with muskets, but they, unwilling to quarrel with the natives, or to fight in a bad cause, gave way; the captain then retreated towards his cabin, but just as he was entering it, he was laid violent hands on, in the scuffle had one of his thumbs nearly cut off, was put into a canoe, taken ashore, and fastened to a tree, where he was left for twelve hours, and the natives said openly they would have killed him, but that they feared a visit from an English man-of-war. This same individual trained his Krúmen to fight with the Krúmen of the other trading ships in the river, and in short, endeavoured to carry on his trading by brute force. Such transactions as these were formerly of daily occurrence, but now fortunately they occur but rarely; but what can be expected of native tribes, who see before them, acted by so-called civilized men, deeds which would disgrace a very savage?

About nine o'clock a canoe from Brass came alongside, bringing two black men, coopers, natives of British Akrá, who begged of me to take them away. From their statement it appeared that they had been in the employ of the supercargo to whom I have above alluded, but had been summarily dismissed by him some eight or nine months previously, without their wages being paid, and since they had been living on shore in a very poor way, chiefly by the kindness of the man who now brought them in his canoe. They had on several occasions tried to get away from Brass, by ships leaving, but their captain had always interfered to prevent this, and the masters of vessels to whom they had applied, unwilling to give offence to the stronger party, or anxious to avoid any misunderstanding, had invariably refused them. I examined the men separately, and got the same story from each, and their tale was confirmed by the native. I had no jurisdiction, nor had I the means of inquiring into the merits of their case; however, it would not do to leave the poor fellows to their fate. I therefore resolved to look on them as distressed British subjects, and determined to carry them to the nearest English consulate, when I could hand them over to the authorities. I paid the native for his kindness in caring for them, that he might know that all white men are not ungrateful brutes. This man told us that the native name for Brass is Nímbe, but that by Abó it is termed Itebú. Nímbe calls Orú, Ejó. The Brass dialect differs but slightly from that of Orú. Akássa is, he said, an Orú village. The Brass name for the Nun is Akássa tọ́rọ, for the Río Bento, Tuwón tọ́rọ, for the San Nicolas, Kóla tọ́rọ, for the New Kalabár river, Kálaba tọ́rọ, for the Bonny,

Okúloba tóro, and for the Old Kalabár, Efíngi tóro, *tóro* being water or a river. The Brass mark consists of six short perpendicular incisions, between the eye and the ear.

Of the measures employed as hygienic most were of a general nature, the only more specific one being the free use of quinine. The amount of sickness was very little, so that, except with the scorbutic cases, Dr. Hutchinson's really medical duties were not onerous. Of the Europeans, the most exposed to climatial influences, were Mr. Harcus, Mr. Guthrie, Mr. May, and myself. Mr. Harcus was chiefly exposed during the day, and suffered only from frequent headaches from the effects of the sun's rays. Mr. Guthrie, besides undergoing daily an immense amount of fatigue, slept regularly on deck, and nevertheless escaped entirely. Mr. May and I were ashore whenever opportunities occurred, and as often by night as by day; we had frequently to land in swamps and other unhealthy spots, yet Mr. May had only one very short and not severe febrile attack. I, in addition, always slept on deck, and was roused regularly at twelve o'clock, and at three in the morning, for the purpose of recording meteorological observations, but while in the river, I had constant health. I mention these circumstances to show, that under proper precautions, Europeans may not only live quietly, but even commit with impunity what, some years ago, would have been considered as terrible indiscretions.

CHAPTER XI.

FERNANDO PO.

MOST of us on board were more or less excited. The white men were anxiously debating on how the bar might turn out for our purpose of crossing it; the Sierra Leone people were rejoiced at leaving the river in safety; and the Krúboys were wild with delight at the speedy prospect of seeing again their homes and their wives. Everyone was early astir, long before daylight, but even then we were, to our great joy, able to satisfy ourselves that a slight land-breeze was in existence. The tide was not yet suitable, the flood running strongly, but at length we weighed anchor for the last time, and steaming slowly down, were off Palm Point at six o'clock, at which time we could barely make out anything half-a-mile from us. But there was no swell, no sound of rushing breakers, and no signs of a south-westerly breeze, all of which augured well. By this time it was about slack water, so we pushed forward at full steam, and at a quarter to seven had crossed the bar, without having encountered a single roller, and never having had less than three fathoms water.

Mr. Richards told me this was his eighth passage, and he had never once before seen the water so smooth. There are three passages across the Nún bar, one to the westward, examined by Mr. Beecroft, which is long and narrow, but deep; one in the middle, which is in every sense intermediate; and an eastern one broader, but with less water, which was the one by which we left the river. For steamers it does not matter much, but as the tide sweeps across them, it is of consequence that sailing vessels should select the one which allows of most room, as often when it is most needed, just in the breakers, the breeze fails. After having come out by the eastern passage, it is necessary to keep along shore, towards Brass, for a couple of miles. A light breeze sprung up from the south-west, which filled our square-sail and helped us along. We observed a sail, which was soon made out to be a schooner at anchor, from which we saw a boat putting off, and shortly afterwards Captain Robertson, of the schooner "Mary," of Fernando Po, came on board of us. He brought us a newspaper, an immense treat to us, though it was some three months' old, and it gave us an account of the early part of the Russian war. This little vessel was bound from Bonny to the Benin river, but had been retarded by light winds, and a strong current running east-south-east two knots. Nothing else occurred during the day; our provisions now consisted of yams and sardines, and, although we had plenty of these, and they were very good, some discontent showed itself, a few of our voyagers fancying themselves on the verge of starvation. On the afternoon of the 7th November we were near Cape Bullen, so decorating ourselves as far as our means would allow, we steered into Clarence Cove, and firing a salute, which was returned by Governor Lynslager's formidable battery, we anchored at twenty minutes to six o'clock. I at once landed, and going up to the Governor's, who was also acting-consul, and Mr. Laird's agent, I reported our arrival, and telling him that as my connection with the "Pleiad" was now at an end, I resigned all further charge over her, and requested him to take the requisite steps for handing her over to Mr. Taylor, or to whomsoever he thought proper, which he at once undertook to do. I also delivered over the two Akrá men, whose case he undertook to investigate, and to forward. The most pleasant portion of our business yet remained, namely, getting our letters, none of us having heard anything from Europe later than the 24th of May. And singularly enough, I believe, throughout the whole batch of correspondence, not one of us received any disagreeable news. The papers told us of the landing of the allied troops in the Crimea, and of the glorious battle of the Alma, so that we had plenty to occupy our thoughts. Having now the means, I gave, on my return on board, all hands a glass of grog, while the Krúboys got the large drum to have a dance, and celebrate, after their own fashion, their happy return.

Next morning I discharged Mr. Richards, Mr.

Scott, and Simon Jonas, whom I had engaged at Clarence. I then got as many of my things ashore as possible, and locking up the remainder, took my final leave of the little "Pleiad," on board of which I had spent four eventful months. Mr. Crowther took up his abode with a friend on shore, while we were much indebted to the kind hospitality of the Governor, and of Mr. Snape, who accommodated in their comfortable houses, Mr. May, my assistant Mr. Dalton, and myself, and where we kept clear from the disputes and disagreements which daily occurred on board of the steamer.

Our time at Clarence was spent in anything but idleness, we had our journals to write up, our instruments and collections to pack for the voyage home, and Mr. May had to make a clean copy of his chart, and to go over many of his calculations. I had expected to find waiting for me further instructions as to my procedure, but as none had arrived, I was left to act according to the best of my judgment.

Among the residents at Clarence at that time was Peppel, ex-King of Bonny, who was living there in a somewhat anomalous condition. By various means he had become very unpopular with his subjects, which involved English traders in the river in such difficulties, that the late Mr. Consul Beecroft had to go to Bonny to endeavour to settle matters. As a precautionary measure, as threats of assassination were openly talked of, he recommended King Peppel to go over to Fernando Po, and with a little persuasion got him on board H.M.S. "Antelope," by which vessel he was, in February, 1854, conveyed to Clarence. He had, however, been kept since, it is said in accordance with orders from England, as a kind of prisoner at large, of which he was well aware, but against which he urgently remonstrated. The very night of Mr. Beecroft's death, he tried to escape by the "Bacchante" steamer, and he had since made another attempt. He came and paid me a visit, which I returned, and we soon became very friendly. He is a tall, intelligent-looking person, but with a rather cunning eye. He speaks English very fairly, and can sustain a long conversation. His remarks were extremely shrewd, and he avoided making any very strong statements. He became King of Bonny on the 9th of April, 1837, since which period his name has become well-known along the coasts of the Bight of Biafra, and his influence extended far into the I'gbo country, reaching to Abó. Of course in the accounts he gave me, he always put the best complexion to all his proceedings, a version of things which I afterwards had occasion greatly to modify. His acquaintance with the English form of government, and his general fund of information much surprised me; he knew the names and offices of all the cabinet ministers, and often referred to Wellington and to Napoleon. Of the latter he was a great admirer, and alluding one day to the fate of that greatest of generals and of politicians, he proceeded, *parva componere magnis,* to sketch a resemblance between his own detention in Fernando Po, and that of the French Emperor at St. Helena. "Why," said he in his peculiar way, and pointing to a print of Buonaparte, "why your gubberment keep me here, I no do bad like he, I be free man, I be King." Whatever my thoughts were I could only reply, that, were he injured, doubtless before long, and as soon as government knew accurately of his case, he would be fully compensated, as the maxim of England was to dispense even-handed justice to all. He exhibited a document from the consul, stating that he had no authority for considering him as a prisoner, and he likewise showed me two letters or certificates, signed by two English trading captains, who testified that, being present when Peppel left Bonny, he did so of his own freewill and accord, and he wound up by observing that our behaviour to him would lessen our influence among the palm-oil tribes.

Peppel usually appears in European boots and trousers, with a loose shirt as an external covering; in his left hand he carries a long silver-headed stick, his right arm being useless, from an attack of hemiplegia or partial paralysis, induced, it is said, by undue indulgence in strong drinks and the pleasures of a Bonny table, and too great devotion to his numerous wives and concubines. By an agreement with his people, they were to allow him while absent at the rate of £300 a-year, and he said nearly two years' arrears were due by our government of the sum stipulated to be paid him by the treaty for abolishing the slave-trade, which latter I understand he has religiously adhered to. He gave me at different times much information about Bonny, and some specimens of the language, which will appear in the Appendix. He said the first King Peppel,* derived his title from selling pepper to European traders, from which the article he dealt in became his own designation, one letter, as is often the case, being substituted for another. The revenue derived of late by Peppel from the increased palm-oil trade, must be little short of, if it does not equal, that made in the palmiest days of the slave-trade. His income from shipping dues and other sources, I have heard reckoned, on sound authority, at from £15,000 to £20,000 a-year. The Bonny people claim an I'gbo descent. Their territory, which is not very extensive, is by them named Ebáne, whence Bonny. By the I'gbos, it is pronounced Obáne, and by New Kalabár Ibáne. The Bonny-town or Grand Bonny-town of the English is correctly Okúloma, by Brass called Okúloba, for which I heard at Bonny the following derivation. When people first came to this place to build a town, they found it a vast swamp, where bred numbers of a bird resembling a curlew, which they called Okúlo. After settlers became numerous these birds deserted the

---

* "And then *Pepprell*, the King's brother, made us a discourse, &c."
"We had again a long discourse with the King, and *Pepprell* his brother, concerning the rates of our goods and his customs. This *Pepprell* being a sharp blade, and a mighty talking *Black*, &c." See Barbot's Voyage to New Calabar, 1699, in Churchill's Voyages and Travels, vol. v. p. 559.

spot, whence they said Okúloma, *i.e.*, the curlews fly away. Peppel said that Abó men often called Bonny Osimíni-ku, but I have myself at Abó heard of Okúloma. New Kalabár is in Bonny named Karabári, but is also known as Bom; the language differs somewhat from the Ebáne, but not so much as to prevent people of the one tribe from understanding those of the other. Orú is known at Bonny as Ejó or Esó. Bonny men talk of Abó as E'be and A'be, but sometimes distinguish between Abó and Okurotúmbi in Orú, styling the one Abo'bá or Great Abó, and the other Abo'ntá or Little Abó, so that Lander was not so far wrong about "Little Eboe" after all. Bonny people do not make their own canoes, but purchase them from the Bássa people in Orú. Much palm-oil is bought by Bonny traders in Ndọki, which place is known to them as Mína. Among places mentioned to me by Peppel as known to himself were Ndéli, U'zuzu, Ikpófia, Egáne, and A'bua, these being written according to his pronunciation. Ndọki, Ngwá, and parts of Isuáma and E'lugu, can, he stated, be reached by canoe. He also said that A'ro, to which his people make pilgrimages as well as the I'gbos, is from four to five days' journey from Bonny-town. In Bonny no national mark is employed, but in New Kalabár some mark along the forehead over the eyes and shave parts of the head. Between Bonny and New Kalabár is a small territory named Okríka, inhabited by a separate tribe, but tributary to Bonny. The people from this place never trade directly with white men, but are obliged to sell their articles either to New Kalabár or Bonny traders; they spend much of their time in canoes, and are great fishermen. Beyond New Kalabár are people living on the river Sombréiro, who speak a dialect nearly approaching to that of New Kalabár, to which place they bring palm-oil. To the eastward of Bonny are the Adóni or Andóni people living on the river Andóni or St. Domingo. About 1848 or 1849, there was a war between Bonny and Adóni, which ended in the subjugation of the latter. The religion of all these places is fetish paganism, the djú-dju or sacred object of Bonny being the Iguana, of Okríka the pigeon, and of New Kalabár the shark. Further along, at Brass or Nímbe the snake is the djú-dju. At Bonny the week of seven days has for some time been adopted, but formerly, king Peppel informed me, the week was one of eight days, of which he gave me the names of five, but he had forgotten the others. At Bonny and in that neighbourhood blue baff or calico is used as mourning, at the Benin river and in that direction white baff is similarly employed, while at Brass both are worn. Old Kalabár is known at Bonny as well as in I'gbo as Efíki, and at A'ro they talk of a people living near or among the E'fik, whom they call Mon or Mong. Old Kalabár is not known at all at Abó. At Bonny yams are not cultivated, for home use a few are got from Okríka, but the greatest supply is from the market at Ogobéndo; the ships again have to send for this valuable tuber to Fernando Po.

z

Chiefly from Mr. Snape, who has spent some years in the Rio Formoso, I got much information about the countries near Bíni (Benin). In many old maps this large and important town is named Oedo, evidently the same word as we met with in the district called Adó or Edó, opposite Igára, and derived from the same source. The present king is a young man, and succeeded to the throne about 1850, at which time several hundred slaves were killed, and the anniversary of his father's death is yet annually observed in the same sanguinary manner. This king is favourable to the English, and does what he can to promote trade; of articles brought from the interior to Bíni, part goes to Lagos, part to the ships in the Rio Formoso. Bíni is a good day's journey distant from the town of Gáto or Agáto, which is situated up a long, narrow creek, communicating with the river. It was lately visited by an English trader, who was kindly received. Agáto is the place where Belzoni breathed his last, and though it is usually said that he died of dysentery, yet the natives who remember him all assert that he was poisoned, and that the person who administered the poison to him is still alive. This person is the head djú-dju man, or high-priest of Bíni; he resides at Agáto, and is a great rogue. He is well-known to the English by the name of Parsons, and it is thought that Belzoni's papers are yet in his possession, as he is not known to have destroyed them—he will not part with them to any of the white traders, but it is said that he would deliver them to any stranger coming especially for them. The people in the country below and near Agáto use a mark, thus •.•, on the temples, opposite each eye. Up the Rio Formoso, towards the Abó territory, live a people speaking a distinct language, who bring palm-oil to the trading ships, and who are called Sóbo, being tributary to Bíni. A district to the westward of the lower part of the river, near its mouth, is called Tshékeri, but which is known in Abó as Iwíne, which name they commonly apply to all traders from the Bíni countries. In Nímbe Tshékeri is called "Senáma." The town of Tshékeri, up a short creek, formerly a place of some importance, is now nearly deserted. The son of one of the chiefs of this place, whose name was Wáko, built a town up another creek, nearer to the sea, and this he called Jákwa. On his death, two of his sons, who were born within a few hours of each other, disputed the succession, Djéri, having the larger party, retained Jákwa, while his brother, Héfia, moved to another creek near the channel leading to Lagos, and there founded another town, which was termed Jakwatía, and which is now nearly as large as Jákwa. The Tshékeri people bring much oil for sale, but very little of it is the produce of their own country. Nearer to the north-west point the inhabitants differ, and are probably connected with Ijebús, and along the coast are many groups of huts of this people. To the east and south-east of the Rio Formoso, is the large district of Wári, inhabited by tribes of the Ejó, or Orú. Their chief town, or Wári, mentioned by older writers as Owarree, was visited by Mr. Beecroft, and is about a day and a half's journey by canoe from the anchorage. A large branch of the river, about three-quarters of a mile broad at its junction, leads to this town. Wári, though semi-independent, yet pays some tribute to Bíni. The late King Té, of Wári, had two sons, born so nearly at the same time, that each contests for priority, and, on the death of their father, contended for the throne. Neither of them are as yet of age, and Té's principal wife, named Dólla, acts as Regent, and the one son resides at Wári, and the other at Batéri, nearer the Rio Formoso. Up the various creeks and branches, the waters are infested by a wild, piratical set, who live almost entirely in their canoes, and who subsist by plundering traders while on their way to markets, often adding murder to their other crimes. They extend their ravages from the Brass river on the one side, as far as the Lagos creek on the other, and in the Rio Formoso they are known to the English as Jo-men, evidently a corruption of Ejó. A few years ago they became so troublesome, and did so much injury by interrupting trade, that the masters and supercargoes in the river, after having applied to the consul for advice and interference, to which no reply was received, fitted out some armed canoes for the purpose of chastising these river pirates, which they managed to effect. Salt from the lagoons, near Tshékeri, is transported in considerable quantity into the interior ; and another commercial article is a kind of wood named "salt wood," which grows on the borders of the salt, swampy creeks; this is annually cut and burnt, and the residue, which forms a semi-vitrified looking mass, is sold as salt.

Being anxious to learn a little of the singular people who inhabit Fernando Po, a little excursion was planned to go to one of their towns, which had not been visited by white men for several years. Accordingly a party, including Mr. Crowther, Mr. Snape, and myself, with Mr. Richards as our interpreter, started one morning by boat from Goderich Bay. We pulled about a couple of miles along shore, and then landing, proceeded on foot. Heavy rain had fallen during the previous night, leaving the ground very soft and muddy. Our way was by a narrow foot-path, with barely room for single file, up a considerable ascent; and as we walked along we sank nearly ankle-deep every step we took, rendering the labour of progression very great. We had always seen the Fernandians coming into Clarence with long sticks in their hands, the use of which we could not make out until to-day, when we found it almost impossible to proceed, or to avoid tumbling, without such sticks. On either side of us was thick forest —palm-trees being very numerous. Many native huts for the manufacture of palm-oil were seen, and bunches of the fruit were hanging in the sun, which is the usual practice before proceeding to boil them. Each native marks his own tree, though sometimes one plant may have several owners, who work in concert. We observed many palms which had not been touched for years, and were now entirely covered with climbers. The oil-palms are sought after partly for the exuded juice, or palm-wine, and partly for the fruit, which is eaten as food, as well as used for the manufacture of oil. I saw many most interesting plants, of which I intended to have secured specimens during our return; among others one known as "Malaghetta," probably the "Bastard Malaghetta." When about three-fourths of our way, our path was crossed by a gushing mountain-stream, over which we passed on large stepping-stones, when, resting for a few minutes, we were refreshed by a draught of most deliciously cold water, one of the highest treats in tropical regions. A little farther on and we reached an elevated plateau, where the ground had been partially cleared, and where was situated the town of Basipú, of which we had been in quest. The distance from the landing-place was only three miles, but the shocking state of the *road* made it appear, to judge at least from the fatigue it occasioned, as fully double. As I mentioned, no European had been at Basipú for several years, on account of a quarrel with the natives, so that the first people who met us were alarmed, and rushed away from us; but on walking into the town Mr. Richards was recognized, and so we all became good friends. We went into the hut of the chief, and there sat down. It was a sorry affair, but it sheltered us from the sun, which was now getting very powerful. The huts are all oblong, and constructed in an exceedingly slim manner, consisting of upright sticks, with the intervening spaces badly closed, and with a very poor thatch, so that in wet weather they cannot afford much shelter. The chief was very civil to us, but not at all communicative, and though much pressed, would not tell me any of the traditions of his race, or what was their native name. He said if I wished to know more of them, that he would some day call a meeting of chiefs of villages, and ask them to take the matter into consideration.

The Fernandians are commonly known by the title of *Búbi*, which, however, is only taken from their mode of address, *Búbi* meaning friend. Their true appellation has been said to be *Adíya* (Adeeyah),* but on asking the chief if this were correct, he said it was not, but that Adíya was the name they gave either to Clarence, or to the white people residing in it. I had previously asked Mr. Richards and some others at Clarence, who spoke the Fernandian language fluently, and who had been much among the people, if they knew the term Adíya, but not one of them knew it. I therefore am inclined to hold, that for the present the native designation of the Fernandians must be considered as doubtful. Their language

* The chief authority for this name is Dr. Thomson, R.N., in one of the volumes of the Philological Transactions; and also in the second volume of the Narrative of the Niger Expedition of 1841. In a communication with which I have been kindly favoured by this gentleman, he has stated his reasons for considering *Adíya* as authentic, and they are certainly of considerable weight. But further enquiry is necessary to decide the matter.

is quite peculiar, and its affinities, though with some South African tongues, are not very decided. These people in appearance are unlike any other tribes I have met with, being in person rarely above the middle stature, and of a spare frame. In colour they are seldom black, but they delight in staining their skins of a brick-red. Their habiliments are extremely scanty, and it is said, that in the more remote parts of the island they go about unclad. Their appearance is much more savage than their behaviour, as they are a mild and inoffensive race. Their chiefs and headmen wear large, wide, rudely-fashioned grass-hats, ornamented with feathers; round the wrists are numerous beads, as also strings of small shells, which form their currency, and which are also worn round the leg, below the knee, so that a man carries about all his riches along with him. Some rude ornaments are suspended round the waist, while inserted under a piece of string encircling the upper left arm, is carried an unsheathed knife, and though the blade is laid along the arm, and is in close contact with the skin, accidents are said never to occur. Similarly secured on the upper right arm is often seen a short clay-pipe, both sexes being passionately fond of smoking; the women, however, often carry about their pipes in their hair. A most singular custom prevails of dressing the hair with red clay and palm-oil, until it becomes one entire, solid mass, with an irregular or nodulated surface. On certain festivals or if they have had any strange dream, they frequently appear with the face covered with chalk, or with some yellow powder. I saw a newly-married couple, and, according to the customs of the race, the bride must remain in her hut for twelve months, or for longer if she does not then evidence her intention of being fruitful and multiplying. Their faces are much tatooed, but I regret not having at the time taken a description of the markings; different markings are employed in different localities, and though their island is small, several very distinct dialects are spoken in the various districts. The total population of Fernando Po is estimated at from 20,000 to 30,000. Near Clarence they bring in palm-oil, yams, bananas, plantains, fowls, &c., which they barter for cloth, tobacco, hardware, and guns. Those near the sea have good canoes, and are great fishermen. They are said to be quick at learning anything, and those in the neighbourhood of Clarence speak a little English. Mr. Crowther asked the chief if his people would allow their children to come to school and be taught; to which he replied, "Certainly, if it did not make them become idle." Formerly missionaries were labouring among them, and had several stations around their villages; but since Spain has reclaimed the island, their endeavours have been prohibited, as that philanthropic country has, with what good taste or feeling towards the Fernandians I leave it to the judgment of my readers, restricted missionary efforts strictly to the town of Clarence. During our visit Mr. Snape and I became unwell, with a febrile accession. Mr. Snape had long been subject to ague, but it was my first attack, and I have no doubt whatever that I imbibed the malaria poison the morning I visited Angiáma, thus showing a period of ten days as the duration of incubation of the disease. I managed, though with difficulty, to retrace my steps, and being well sheltered from the sun by the trees arching over the pathway, at length reached our boat. I was not at all sorry when I found myself back at Clarence, only regretting that I had been unable to secure my promised botanical specimens, among which was a species of *Kóla*.

Among the persons with whom I had conversations, was a Baión man, from whom I got specimens of his native language, which with a few Báti words will appear in the Appendix. I also found among the residents at Clarence, a native of a country named Yála, called by the I'gbo Amáni, while the inhabitants they term Olalipíde. Amáni is derived from the town of Amán, on the west side of the Cross river, a little beyond Akúna-kúna; it is on the borders of Yála, but not in it; Yála is often called Atám, its language resembles the I'gbo. The town of Omún is called by the Yálas, Okré, but by its own people Idrága. To the northward of Yála is a country named Agányi, and the inhabitants are in Yála known as A'kpa. Isuáma is in Yála termed Iswáma, and Isiélu is called Isiólu. During the dry season the Cross river at Yála is easily fordable, the water being not more than from eighteen to twenty-four inches in depth. Many people from the Cameroons and from Bímbia reside at Clarence; the former are the Diwálla, and of late they have adopted a mark much resembling that of the Krúmen.

During our stay at Clarence the weather varied much, sometimes heavy rain and violent tornadoes, at others hot, burning weather, while just before our departure, symptoms of the "smokes" began to show themselves. This fine island is at present almost running to waste, its capabilities disregarded, and its soil uncultivated, and it is sad to think, that under the rule of its present possessors no improvement is likely to take place. How our government was ever advised to so mad an action as to give up Fernando Po, I cannot imagine; but it is said on the Coast, that among other influences at work, was the fear of those interested in Sierra Leone, who dreading a rival, thus sacrificed public interest to private jealousy. Whenever trade is established by the Kwóra with Central Africa, as must happen ere long, the value of this despised place will then be more easily estimated. Situated within a convenient distance of the mouths of the rivers, with good harbours, and easy of access, it must become the grand depot of trade for the Bight of Biafra, and a great emporium of commerce. Comparatively healthy, too, compared with the coast opposite, it will prove an excellent station for sick and for convalescents, as by means of the mountain any desirable climate may be commanded. Clarence is finely placed on a height upwards of a hundred feet above the sea, with a gentle slope which would permit of an easy drainage, with fine harbours on either side of it, where boats may land without trouble all the year round, with ample space for commodious storehouses along the beach, and withal with a good tropical climate. Behind it is every variety of hill and dale, and thousands upon thousands of acres of a rich fertile soil. The small yams of North-west Bay are considered as the finest in Africa, nor are the much larger ones of Melville Bay at all to be despised. Many hundred tons of palm-oil and palm-kernel-oil might annually be produced, and the forests teem with excellent timber. Such an island would be considered an acquisition anywhere, but situated as it is, it must be looked on as destined by Providence to play a very important part in the great work of African Regeneration. Clarence is just now but indifferently supplied with provisions, as the demand is not sufficient to raise an adequate supply. A curious epidemic annually commits ravages among the domestic fowls, ducks, and turkeys, numbers of which die during November and December, but I am not aware that this disease is general throughout the island. In the neighbourhood of Clarence finely flavoured oranges and limes grow in abundance, papaws are numerous, and a solitary bread-fruit tree seemed to be progressing favourably. We remained at Clarence three weeks, and on every Sunday Mr. Crowther performed Divine Service in a large and commodious house, built by the late Mr. Beecroft,* but now belonging to Governor Lynslager. A large and very attentive congregation regularly assembled, the numbers varying from 100 to 150. The missionaries resident at Clarence are of the Baptist persuasion, but one of them now remains nearly constantly at Bímbia and the Cameroons, where he has a printing press, and where he prints works in the Diwálla language. This excellent gentleman had for many years to divide his attention between Clarence and the Cameroons, and was in the constant habit of crossing from the one place to the other in an open boat.†

* I omitted previously to note that Mr. Beecroft's death took place at Clarence on the 10th of June, 1854.

† Intelligence has just (May 7th) reached this country that a Spanish colonizing party, including among others fifty priests, has left Vera Cruz for Fernando Po. This, if correct, is greatly to be regretted, as we are aware, from past experience, that expeditions setting forth under such auspices, are much more likely to be productive of harm than of good. It is a great pity that this fine island and its interesting inhabitants cannot be placed under the guidance of persons of more enlightened tendencies and more practical views.

CHAPTER XII.

THE VOYAGE HOME.

On Sunday, the 26th of November, while we were attending evening service, the "Bacchante," Captain Dring, arrived from England, bringing us fresh supplies of letters and of news. All our effects being shipped, we took our leave of Governor Lynslager, and our other kind and hospitable friends who had rendered our stay so comfortable and so pleasant, and sailed from Clarence Cove at half-past eleven on the night of the 28th. The "Pleiad" was to follow the next day, under the charge of the chief mate of the "Bacchante," who was put on board her for that purpose. The next day our pilot ran us aground in the mouth of the Cameroons river, so that we had to send the mails up by boat some dozen miles while we were getting afloat again. On the afternoon of the 1st of December, we got to Duke Town in Old Kalabár river, and in the evening I went on shore and called on Mr. Anderson, the resident missionary, whose acquaintance I had made when here on a former occasion. On inquiring about the place called Egbo-shári, this gentleman informed me that its I'gbo name is Uményi, while the E'fik call it "Ibíbio." From this place the E'fik derive their origin. The native name for Duke Town is Atákpa. The E'fik are emigrants, the land on which they are settled belonging to the Kwá people, whom they style Abákpa, and to whom they yet pay tribute. The Kwá people are quite distinct, and speak a totally different language; their country extends far inland, and they bring some very good oil to market. I could not ascertain their native name, but one designation is A'kwa, and from a letter I received a few months ago from the Rev. W. Thomson, I find that from the interior of their country are brought long swords, and other articles, of very superior workmanship, and all of native iron. Some of this tribe live on the west side of the mouth of the river, and trade both at Duke Town and at Bonny. People from a tribe named Mbrúkim come to E'fik occasionally to trade. They pass through the Kwá country, and the journey from their own land, which they say is near the Arabs, occupies from two to three months. The E'fik mark was formerly the same as that used by some of the I'gbos, but more recently they have adopted another, viz., three round spots, each about the size of a pea, on their temple, opposite the eye. Móko people do not come to the E'fik, they are believed to be connected with the Baióṅ. A case of poisoning with the ordeal bean had occurred near Duke Town on the Sunday previous to our arrival, being the first instance for a long period, as (thanks to the exertions of the missionaries) this shocking custom has nearly fallen into entire disuse. Since my visit to Old Kalabár many serious occurrences have taken place. Old Town has very properly been punished by order of the British Consul, for a glaring disregard of treaty, by which the natives undertook to give up human sacrifices; and I understand, also, that Mr. Anderson's comfortable residence has been entirely destroyed by fire. Much as I may differ from Mr. Anderson and his friends on many minor points, and much as I may believe that their usefulness would be increased, and their great designs furthered by some modifications of their views, I cannot but entertain a sincere respect for those who truly and entirely devote themselves to the holy end of opening the eyes of these benighted creatures, who laying aside thoughts of home and of friends, banish themselves from the world, sacrificing comfort, health, often life itself, in their earnest endeavour to supplant the horrid rites of Paganism by the mild, the beautiful doctrines of enlightened Christianity.

Most of the palm-oil sold at Old Kalabár is brought from the markets in the I'gbo country, but some also comes from districts to the eastward, and, as I have mentioned, from Kwá. The trust system still prevails in Old Kalabár, and when a man dies his debts are held to expire with him, a not over-comfortable practice for the white traders. In the morning, Captain Lewis, whom I have before alluded to as being so thoroughly acquainted with the pilotage of the river, came down with us, rather to the disgust of John Bull our pilot for the rivers generally, but much to the satisfaction of all else on board. He told me that along the mouths of the rivers in the Bight of Biafra, high water at full and change is about six o'clock, which differs from Captain Denham's statement, who fixes it at about four. At Duketown, it is about seven hours and thirty minutes, and the rise with spring tides is seven feet, and from four to four-and-a-half feet with neaps. The water begins to fall at the last quarter flood, and to rise at the last quarter ebb. The Kwá river has three fathoms water at its entrance, but it deepens and widens further up. Across the bar of the Old Kalabár are several good but winding passages. There is a very dangerous knoll, with two fathoms of water on it, about two miles right out to sea from the east end of the breakers. It is very circumscribed, and the sea does not break on it. A ship going in that direction will first have five fathoms, then two-and-a-half, and before the lead can be hove again she will strike.

The first river between the Old Kalabár and Bonny is not named in any modern chart, but in some old ones I find it marked as the Rio San Pedro, while at Bonny I heard it called the Kantóro, and the water in it is said to be beautifully clear, which, if correct, would indicate a different source from all the other streams, of which the water is extremely muddy, almost opaque. Next to it is the Andóni or St. Do-

A A

mingo river, with about nine feet of water across the bar, and which communicates with Bonny by a large creek. We arrived at Bonny on the 3rd of December, and as our boilers required some repair, did not leave until the 5th. During this time, as I was much annoyed with ague, I took up my quarters on board a large and airy vessel, in which Mr. Glanville, one of my fellow-passengers in the "Forerunner," was carrying on an extensive and lucrative trade. Poor fellow, by one of the last mails, I have heard of his death, which occurred in October last, though when I left him he looked strong, healthy, and acclimatized. He took me ashore to Okúloma or Bonny-town, where I met all the grandees of the place. I was introduced to the King Dáppa, a heavy, unintellectual looking man, and had the honour of drinking some bitter ale with him. I also visited A'ní Peppel, a shrewd, but rather too influential man, who was beginning to be troublesome, and who insisted on my drinking some palm-wine with him. I saw also King Peppel's first wife, the legitimate Queen of Bonny, who is of a pale copper colour, and was then living in a very poor way. During the war with Andóni, about 1848, the Bonny people brought many of the bodies of their enemies home with them, for the purpose of eating them, and some Europeans, one of whom was my informant, went ashore, and actually with their own hands rolled several casks filled with human flesh into the sea. There is a communication by creeks with the district to the westward where the Kwá people live, as they bring much oil to Bonny, and they take readily as money, a bad or inferior kind of Manilla (the currency of Bonny), which will not go elsewhere. I was anxious to go over to New Kalabár, but was too unwell to attempt it, and was therefore disappointed in getting much information about this people. Their King, Amakrí, had a year previously been visited by Captain Macdonald of H.M.S. "Ferret," and made to deliver up a number of doubloons he had received from a slaving ship. The people differ in appearance and in manner from those of Bonny. In New Kalabár circumcision is universal, in Bonny it is only practised on slaves. In Bonny the breasts of the women very soon become loose, flaccid, and pendulous, while in New Kalabár they keep plump and firm; the men, too, of New Kalabár are more determined and warlike. The trust system has been abolished, with much advantage, in New Kalabár, but in Bonny it still hangs like a millstone round the necks of the supercargoes. Among others whom I met, were Captain Edward Wyllie, a well-known trader, shrewd, successful, and much respected, and Captain Witt, a most intelligent man, who seemed better acquainted with the resources of the country, and with the wants and requirements of trade, than any one whom I saw in the Bights. At Bonny everything seemed to go on with greater regularity and with more smoothness than elsewhere, and this can only be accounted for by the English traders acting so far in concert.

A commercial or mercantile association was, by the exertions of Captain Witt and others, formed, the members being the chief white and black traders in the place, and the chair is occupied by the white supercargoes in monthly rotation. All disputes are brought before this court, the merits of opponents are determined, and with the consent of the King, fines are levied on defaulters. If any one refuses to submit to the decision of the court, or ignores its jurisdiction, he is tabooed, and no one trades with him. The natives stand in much awe of it, and readily pay their debts when threatened with it. A new court-house of brick is being erected, the former one of wood being old and crumbling. Here every Sunday the people assemble from the ships, while the church-service is read by one of the number. They have a code of rules for their guidance, by which all men must be off the beach by a certain hour, and no trading or work is permitted, as a general rule, on Sundays. Mr. Glanville told me that he had once gone by boat, through the creeks, to Nímbe or Brass-town, and that he found abundant water. The currency of Bonny is in Manillas, small horse-shoe-shaped pieces of copper, but accounts are reckoned in bars. Every river has its own mode of reckoning. Bonny counts in bars, equal to about sevenpence each. Benin river employs prawns, one being about fourpence. In Old Kalabár, coppers are used, one copper being about fourpence halfpenny, and in the Cameroon river they reckon by krus, which are a measure, one kru being properly twelve gallons, but often twelve-and-a-half or thirteen. In the Cameroon river and Bimbia, imperial measure is employed, but in the other rivers old wine measure. A matchet or large knife is about sixpence halfpenny in all these places. I inquired about King Peppel, and from what I heard, I came to the conclusion, that though treated perhaps not according to strict justice, yet he was well away from the place. He had become exceedingly cruel and tyrannical, had with his own hands shot one of his wives who had displeased him, and had inveigled a headman, named Manilla Peppel, who was obnoxious to him, into his house, and had him seized and murdered; and finally he had, for no reason but to gratify his own ambition, nearly involved Bonny in a war with New Kalabár. At Bonny since my visit there have been great disturbances. Dáppa the King died suddenly, and some one spread a report of poison, which roused party strife to a great extent. All trade was stopped, and fighting was daily going on, when at last 300 of King Peppel's supporters blew themselves up with gunpowder, and I believe since this awful tragedy that matters have been more peaceable.

At Lagos we parted with Mr. Crowther, who returned to Abbeokúta, to resume those labours which have been so simply, yet so charmingly described by Miss Tucker. Since that time Mr. Crowther has left Abbeokúta and taken up his abode at Lagos, a very important, but less pleasant station.

It was with a feeling almost of regret that I separated from this excellent and upright clergyman, who by his amiability, and the unostentatious yet conscientious manner in which he performed his duties, had endeared himself to all on board the "Pleiad." Personally I was greatly indebted to him for his sound advice and ready assistance, both ever ready when required. To my mind he typically represents the true African missionary, and were there only plenty of Mr. Crowthers, the work of regeneration and improvement would doubtless progress, for it is to the efforts of such single-minded, yet earnest and sensible men, that we must humanly trust for success. At Lagos we were joined by the Bishop of Sierra Leone and Archdeacon Graf, returning from a visitation to the missionary stations in the Yóruba country; the latter gentleman was so exceedingly ill that he had to be lifted on board, and when I first saw him I entertained great fears for his ultimate recovery. Bishop Vidal's widely spread diocese extended several thousand miles, entailing a responsibility and an amount of labour which would have been undertaken by none, but those like him, who with great, but quiet energy, could throw their whole heart and soul into the business.

Lagos is, by the Portuguese, often called Onín, but by the natives is styled E'ko. It is inhabited by the E'gba tribe of Yórubans, but the population is much mixed, and the language spoken extremely corrupt. The word Yóruba (Yo-ru-ba) means "I go meet," and it comprehends numerous tribes speaking distinct dialects of one common language. The Muhammadan population of Yóruba congregates chiefly around the large city of Ilọ́rin, and it is there that the language is spoken in its greatest purity. The Yóruba name for Bórgu, a country to the northward, near the Kwóra, is Ibárba. To the westward of Lagos, along the coast stands the town of Badágry, the name most probably corrupted from Agbáda ági, or from the Yóruban Agbādayígi. Not far from the site of Badágry, in former times, a man named Agbáda had a farm, and people when asked where they were going used to reply "Agbáda ági," i.e. "to Agbáda's farm," and this, by process of corruption, gradually assumed its present form of Badágry. Near to this place the Portuguese had a small settlement, named, after the owner of the spot, Aʹkpa. But this, not being near the sea, became inconvenient, so that they inquired after a more suitable locality, and hearing of Agbáda's farm, which was close to the water, they established themselves there. A slave-ship, believed to have been French, was wrecked off Agbáda ági, and as, according to custom, the slaves could not be re-shipped, they remained, and so increased the number of inhabitants. After a period a dispute arose between the coloured population and the Portuguese, which ended in a general massacre of the latter, and since that time the Portuguese have, fortunately, deserted Badágry. The caboceers of the old slaving times still nominally exist, and when, in 1839, the first liberated slaves from Sierra Leone arrived, after their unsuccessful attempt to land at Lagos, they were put under the charge of the English caboceer. Badágry has sent out several small colonies on both sides, towards Lagos, and also beyond Hwidá. The original town of A'kpa still stands, and gives its name to the Badágry and Porto Nuovo district, and all the towns still pay tribute to the King of A'kpa. Badágry is also called Bakagú, but I do not know why, or by whom. Porto Nuovo is by the natives termed Hágbonu, by the Yórubans Ajéshe, and it is also known as Zém. The dialects of Badágry and Porto Nuovo closely resemble each other. The dialects of Hwidá (Whydah) and of Pópo are analogous, belonging to the Dahomian language. The people of Pópo were originally from Dahómi proper, having been driven out during some revolution. Pópo is by the natives termed Adého, and by the Akrá people Tóm, which is more correctly applied to the adjoining river. Hwidá is the native Gréwhe, but by Dahomians is called Fó. It is a large and busy town, and is very well supplied with provisions of all kinds. It is at present the principal remaining seat of slave exportation. An excellent place for vessels wishing to procure stock is Kitá or Kwitá, a little to the eastward of Cape St. Paul, and where there is an English fort. The inhabitants are Awóna, and are somewhat allied to Dahomians. By some tribes this place is named Adjá and Djinikófi.

At Lagos had also embarked the Rev. T. Freeman,

the energetic and indefatigable Wesleyan missionary of the Gold and Slave Coasts, who was now returning, after a visit to the Yóruba country, to his head-quarters at Cape Coast Castle. With him was another gentleman, resident at Akrá, who had visited Ashánti, and had been in Kumássi, the capital, which, he told me, is now easily within the reach of Europeans. While there he once saw sixty human beings sacrificed at once, to the manes of some chief. The king is reported to be immensely wealthy, and to possess large quantities of gold; the property of all his subjects who die without heirs falls to him. The present king is a sensible quiet man, but his heir is a restless warlike person. The son is never the heir, the succession devolving on a nephew, namely, the eldest sister's eldest son. The kingdom of Ashánti is more powerful than that of Dahómi, and the customs and rites are fully as barbarous, if not more so. The Fantí district extends from beyond Cape Coast Castle to Akrá, being a belt of country from fifty to eighty miles in breadth. The language is allied to the Ashánti, and the people are the canoemen of this line of coast, extending their migrations as far as Lagos. Akwapím is to the north and north-east of Akrá, and Akím is north-east from Akwapím; the language is Otshí, allied to Ashánti. Asín is north and north-east from Cape Coast Castle; it is a small territory, and the language resembles the Fantí.

I had several interesting conversations with Bishop Vidal, who had been much pleased with his visit to

Abbeokúta and the other stations, and was now full of plans for future progress. An ardent and a distinguished philologist, no one could have been more adapted for an African see, where every few miles introduce the traveller to a new dialect, and where most of the languages are yet unstudied and unwritten. To the Yóruba the Bishop had paid considerable attention, and he had been inspecting and revising translations of portions of the Scriptures into that tongue. He told me that at Sierra Leone he had several advanced I'gbo scholars, now ready for ordination, and who would, were there a return of these people to their native lands, accompany them as teachers and missionaries. Aware that the Bishop had been more lately studying the I'gbo, I had, partly at Mr. Crowther's suggestion, taken with me Simon Jonas, whom I had intended to show to the Bishop as a man well versed in the principal I'gbo dialects, and able to give much information towards framing grammars or vocabularies. The Bishop, having had some conversation with him, was much pleased with his intelligence, and said that on reaching Sierra Leone he would at once set the matter on foot. The Bishop mentioned to me one day that he was inclined to trace the word "barbarian" to the Berber tribe, as he looked on their name as one of the most ancient in Northern Africa, and of course known to the Egyptians, from whom the Greeks borrowed both the word itself and the idea connected with it; whence, again, it passed into other European languages.

I must now refer to my little Mítshi boy, who, since I last referred to him, had made rapid progress. For some days after leaving Igbégbe he was rather timid, but that soon passed away, and whenever he saw me preparing to go ashore he always cleaned himself and went with me, behaving himself in a very quiet and orderly manner. On board he now and then got into trifling scrapes with the men, and I had once or twice to punish him, but he very soon quite understood when he was doing wrong. Being of a warm temper he used to break out into fits of passion, when I used to place him in some quiet corner to compose himself, and he remained there until he was cool enough to come and make friends with me, and so our differences always ended. He was fond of imitating those whom he saw at work, and soon began to insist on assisting the steward, and at Fernando Po always did his best to wait at table. When he first went to sea he could not comprehend the motion of the ship, and he felt rather uncomfortable, but he wonderfully soon became reconciled to it, and in the "Bacchante," even when she was rolling heavily, he learnt to carry a dish from the galley to the saloon; all these offices were voluntary, as I made him do nothing except keep himself clean, and he added to his other duties that of superintending the feeding of my little dog, my monkeys, and my parrot. He had a great love for finery, and whenever he could collect a few beads or brass ornaments, he would string them and make necklaces of them, and was greatly delighted when he got a bright-looking piece of calico, or a showy shirt. The Bishop was greatly interested in him, and undertook to superintend his education, and I was only too glad to be able to leave him in such excellent hands.

Since I had last been at Akrá sad havoc had been committed, the inhabitants of Christianborg or Danish Akrá having rebelled, and having had in consequence their town knocked to pieces, and many of themselves killed. The Akrá territory is isolated, and extends about twenty miles west, and about thirty-five to forty miles east, from the town, and about ten to twenty miles inland. The inhabitants are but remotely connected with the adjoining races, and their language, differing entirely from those of the neighbouring tribes, has been considered by Mr. Hanson, himself a native of Akrá, to have affinities with that of Tumbuktú. By the inhabitants, who call themselves Ghá or Gá, Danish Akrá is styled Osú, Dutch Akrá is called Kínka, while British Akrá is the real Akrá. The Fantí use Nkrán to designate the three towns. In Akrá are many Fantí, Ashánti, and Pópo, and all the natives speak Fantí as well as their own tongue. The women when at work are fond of singing extemporaneous songs, suggested generally by some passer-by, or by something occurring at the moment, but they always sing in Fantí, and not in Gá.

Owing to several of the boiler tubes leaking, there was a great waste of coals, and by the time that we arrived at Cape Coast Castle our fuel was nearly expended. Fortunately at this place there is abundance of a hard red wood, which burns capitally, and of this we got a good supply. Here we received on board Governor Hill, on his way to assume the chief rule at Sierra Leone, one of the few instances in Africa of the right man being put into the right place. Among other passengers was a former fellow-passenger of mine, the lady to whose marriage I formerly alluded, and who was now with her husband returning to England. Owing to the excessive leakage our red wood burnt as fast as the coals or faster, and as we had to put in at Cape Palmas to land a number of Krúmen, the opportunity was taken of laying in a fresh stock. We had to take in another supply of wood at the river Sestos, where we were supplied with good, dry mangrove billets. The coast from Cape Palmas, westward, is known as the Krú coast, and is the native land of that hardy and valuable race of men, who are the true sailors of Western Africa. They comprise several distinct tribes, which differ much among themselves, though agreeing in general appearance, in manners, and to a great extent in dialect. Two races are always distinguished, the true Krúmen and the Fishmen, the latter perhaps the more available for civilized purposes. Though in feature typically negro, they are generally above middle stature, often tall, beautifully proportioned, and with muscles splendidly developed, enabling them to stand great fatigue, and to perform feats of almost Herculean strength. They begin to go to sea when young, at first under a headman, until they advance in years, &c., when they in turn become headmen, and take charge of others. A Krûman works until he can purchase a sufficient number of wives to look after him, labour for him, and so keep him independent. They are much attached to their country, and if long away from it, pine extremely. When a vessel wants Krûmen she lies-to off one of their towns, and is in a very short time surrounded by canoes, which are brought off with the greatest neatness and dexterity in the roughest weather. A crew is soon selected, the pay arranged, a month's wages allowed in advance, and all is settled. The names of Krûmen being rather unpronounceable to a European mouth, the practice is to give them other designations, often exceedingly absurd, but still more easily remembered; thus, among a gang of them may be found, George, Tom, Black Will, Yellow Will, Prince of Wales, Prince Albert, Liverpool, Friday, Bottle-of-Beer, Razor, Flat-nose, John Bull, &c. Krûmen allow no slavery among themselves; their domestic slaves they purchase from the Bása people, who procure them from the interior. They will only buy children, and are very kind to their slaves, who are often hardly to be distinguished from free men. There are only five true Krû towns along the coast from Sinû to Piccaniny Krû, and to the eastward of this live the Fishmen. The names of the Krû towns are Little Krû, Settra Krû, Krû-bar, Nanna Krû, and

King Will's Town, these being the names by which they are known to navigators; their native designations will appear afterwards. At Grand Sestos the inhabitants are a kind of mixed breed, and are a very troublesome set. The little Sess men are typical Fishmen, and at the river Sestos is a Fish colony; many of the villages, too, along the Bása shore, are inhabited by Fishmen, as the Bása people seldom live near the coast. Near Cape Palmas the language again slightly differs, but the people are more nearly allied to the Fishmen. The native name of Cape Palmas is "Baine-lú," and of the village near it "Baine," the American settlement being Harper. The natives call Fish-town "Wá," and Garraway "Wiágbo." The river Sestos is "Nipúa." The best canoes along this part of the coast are made at Fishtown. Bása, which is to the north-west of the Krú coast, has a population with a different language, and different marks. Krúmen call themselves Krábo, the singular being Krábe. They are all Heathens, believing in fetishes, and wearing gréegrees or charms, a very favourite one being the claw of a leopard. The whole country, as far as Cape Palmas, is in connection with the Republic of Liberia, or as I heard it explained in Monrovia, the "Republic claims territorial jurisdiction," which right has been acquired by purchase, by treaty, &c.

At Monrovia our detention was sufficiently long to allow me to spend some time ashore, and through the kindness and attention of Mr. Newnham, our

Consul, I saw all that was to be seen. I met many of the principal people of the place. With Monrovia I was agreeably disappointed, for from previous accounts I had expected to find a very so-so place, rather on the decline than otherwise. But, on the contrary, within two or three years new vigour seems to have infused itself, and it is now progressing favourably. Liberia has many natural advantages, and its future success must depend principally on good management, and sound policy. I was introduced to the highly-intelligent and clear-headed chief of the republic, President Roberts, under whose rule, though some affect to be sceptical about it, it cannot be doubted that the country has advanced greatly. When I was there it was said, that at the next election he would be thrown out of the Presidential chair, as some acts of his had not been popular, he having been too prudent to please a number of the people. I do not know whether this has occurred, as I have seen no late Liberian intelligence, but if so it is, I think, to be regretted. Two, if not three, newspapers are published in Monrovia, which I look upon as a healthy and promising sign. The first appearance of a newspaper in a new country, let the attempt be ever so feeble, or the contents ever so paltry, is to be hailed with satisfaction, as it marks an era in the literary intelligence and public feeling of the place. Feeble commencements often lead to important results, and let an unfettered press once be introduced and it will firmly secure its footing, and powerfully conduce to independence of thought and action in its readers, besides tending to create a community of feeling and of political action. From what I have observed I have great faith in this young republic, which will some day, when the worn-out dynasties of savage tribes are forgotten, and when advancing civilization and Christianity have smoothed the asperities of barbarous customs and bloody rites, strongly assert the claims of the African to be admitted into the fellowship of his more fortunate brethren, and assist him in substantiating his rights as an integral, a free member of the vast human family. As might be expected, the Liberians are very American in their manners and mode of expression, but are, at the same time, anything but deficient in Yankee shrewdness and energy.

On Sunday, the 17th of December, when at Cape Palmas, Bishop Vidal, though rather indisposed, performed Divine Service, but at the conclusion he felt very faint and unwell, and had to retire early to rest. His symptoms, at first rather anomalous and obscure, soon indicated an attack of endemic fever of a severe type. I then learnt, for the first time, that whilst on his return from Abbeokúta, the Bishop had unfortunately travelled by canoe late at night, along a pestiferous mangrove creek near Lagos, as one of his travelling companions had been desirous of pushing on, and the good-natured, obliging Bishop would offer no obstacle on his part. He had then evidently contracted the seeds of the baneful malaria, which now had got the upper hand, and was telling heavily on a constitution not naturally strong. We had to attend to him and nurse him in a confined cabin, when much depended on his being in a free, well-ventilated chamber. We thought of getting him on deck, but the torrents of rain which were daily falling, would have soaked through any covering we could have placed over him. In a few days I became very apprehensive for him, his strength was failing, and he was not able to contend against this powerful and dangerous enemy. The Bishop had a few months previously been in England, and on his return to Africa had proceeded at once to Yóruba; his wife was to have followed him to Sierra Leone by the mail-steamer next to the one in which he sailed, and as she was in very delicate health, he was naturally most anxious to hear of her safe arrival. But of this he was destined never to learn. When at Monrovia the news reached the ship, but by that time the Bishop was too insensible to comprehend what was told him. In spite of all which could be done, the disease could not be controlled, and on the forenoon of Sunday, the 24th of December, he expired quietly, and without a struggle. During the voyage we had on board upwards of twenty cases of remittent fever, but the only fatal one deprived us of one whom we could ill spare. By the death of Bishop Vidal, which took place ere he had well reached the prime of life, Africa lost a firm and zealous friend, one never weary of well-doing, and who never spared himself where the thought that the welfare of her people was concerned. Had he been longer spared, it cannot be doubted but that signal advances would have taken place in the right direction, and that the tenure of the occupant of our first episcopal see in Western Africa would have corresponded with an important era in the history of its civilization. His ideas were not those of a lordly prelate, surrounded by pomp, and seeking for worldly renown, but he was in very deed a true Missionary Bishop, into whose hands had been committed the care and guidance of an important yet struggling section of the church, and his heartfelt desire was, that he might be enabled to render the highest account of his stewardship. His example is before us, and may his successors closely follow in his footsteps. During a very brief acquaintance I never met any one for whom I sooner acquired a more sincere respect, and though it may appear that I have dwelt rather long on his character, and his untimely end, I feel that my feeble efforts are quite inadequate to do justice to this Christian prelate. How truly it has been said, that "Man proposes but God disposes." When at Lagos the Bishop joined us in the full enjoyment of his ordinary health, while Mr. Graf was considered to be in a highly critical condition. Two short weeks had elapsed and the strong had passed away from among us, while the sick man walked with renewed strength. A death at sea is always a sad occurrence. In such a small community as on board ship all are acquaintances, and the disappearance of one of the number leaves a sad blank. No one can be ignorant of the solemn event; death in all its gloom, in all its horrors, is present to each. It is felt that this dread enemy is in the closest proximity, and none can tell who may be the next victim.

The day following was Christmas, we could not call it a merry one, yet as we were now nearing Sierra Leone, the thought of meeting with former acquaintances, and to many the prospect of getting completed one half of a dreary voyage, somewhat cheered our minds. During the afternoon a large water-spout passed about a mile to the eastward of us. Its appearance differed much from what is often represented; there was no conical mass of water, towering upwards from the surface of the ocean to meet the descending torrent, but the spout poured steadily down, throwing up, like a huge cascade, thick clouds of spray. Its hollow centre was plain to the naked eye, and it commenced to abate from below upwards, the spout gradually contracting and receding until it reached its cloudy origin.

On the 26th of December, we anchored at Sierra Leone, our ensign flying ominously but half hoisted. The melancholy tidings quickly spread, producing throughout Freetown, where the deceased had been greatly beloved, a profound sensation of grief. Two years before, almost on the same day, Bishop Vidal had landed from the "Propontis," full of hope, and with a cheering, and inspiriting prospect before him.

Now how changed, his remains, a mere inanimate mass of clay, were quietly removed to the shore, in the afternoon to be interred, earth to earth, and dust to dust, the spirit having fled to the God who gave it.

Our voyage from Fernando Po had been extremely protracted. By the time of our arrival at Sierra Leone, we ought, properly, to have been as far advanced as Vera Cruz or Madeira. But the engines were very defective, and sadly in need of repair. A survey was held on them, directed by the chief engineer of H.M.S. "Prometheus," when it was declared unsafe to proceed further without extensive alterations. This caused a delay of ten days, at which I cannot say that I was altogether sorry, as I was able to turn my time to some advantage among the representatives of the numerous tribes who are to be found in this vicinity. The hospitality of many friends, who did their utmost to render our stay comfortable, enabled Mr. May and myself to pass the time very pleasantly. To Mr. Heddle I stand especially indebted; his house was during the whole time my home, a large and airy apartment was set aside for me for writing in, and for receiving deputations from the coloured population, and all my enquiries were most kindly furthered. To Mr. Thensted, also, and to Mr. Mallard our warm thanks are due, as owing to them our reminiscences of Sierra Leone are of a very pleasant description.

It soon became known that the officers who had

been on the expedition up the "great river," had returned, and many of the natives called, partly to hear the news, partly to enquire what prospect there was of another expedition, and of their being enabled to return to their own countries. First and foremost there arrived a body, forty-three strong, from the I'gbo race, who are in Freetown both numerous and wealthy. This was followed by two from the Núpe tribe, one of twenty, the other of thirty-eight individuals, a smaller one of nine from the I'gbira-Pánda, and one of nineteen from the Bássa (Kukánda), but the crowning one was from the Háusa people, who came in upon me to the number of seventy-two. Smaller in appearance, but equally earnest, were the deputations I received from the Kanúri (Bornú), Kanembú, Djúku, Bonú, Ishábe, Orú, Igára, and Adó. I have by me the lists of names of all these, and I ascertained that they represented the desires of from 1500 to 2000 persons. The tenor of conversation was much the same with all; they were most desirous of re-visiting and settling in the lands of their birth, carrying with them civilized habits and Christian doctrines. They said they wished to have with them teachers to instruct their children, as they themselves had been instructed, and they concluded by asking if the "land was good," meaning thereby if peace prevailed, and if they would be well received. I had also conversations with people from I'gbira-Síma or I'gbira-Sáima, Zaría, Zánfara, Marádi, Bérber, &c. Two men called on me, who came from a place

I had never before heard of, called "Grímsa," said to be situated on a river named Mói, near a Púlo town, and distant from Búsa three to four days' journey. They said, too, that the dialect spoken there was peculiar. The Bérber was from a town named Wása, and he spoke both his own tongue and Púlo. Among the Háusas, was a man from Marádi (not Mariadi), who had, as a mark, a long line along the cheek, and he told me that in Gobír the mark is a line across the lower part of the cheek, opposite the mouth. In these two countries the language is entirely Háusa, the religion is mixed, but chiefly Pagan, and the people bear an intense hatred to the Púlbe. I believe that now they are the only remaining independent Háusa states. A man from Zaría informed me that the last Háusa king of Zaría was named Abdokarú, and that, when expelled by the Púlo invasion, he fled to Korórofa; he also set me right about Gwándawa or Gbándawa, which I have previously mentioned, and which is a district between Zaría and Dóma, the language and the mark agreeing with the latter. Among others were a Djúku, from Wákpa, a town west or south-west from Wukári, and a Mándara, who had been taken in war by the Púlbe of Adamáwa. The mark of the latter somewhat resembled that of Bornú, and consisted of some curved lines along the angle of the jaw, and some fainter ones along the cheek. From a Bagírmi man I learnt that the languages of Bagírmi, of Wádai, and of Bornú differ widely, and that the dialect, also, of

Músgo is quite distinct. The people of Loggóne and the Kanúri speak much alike, and they resemble each other in appearance and in marking. But in Bornú the former is often pronounced Lokóne. Among my Kanúri or Bornuese visitors, one was from Zínder, one from Birni-Bornú or Birnim-Bornú, and one from Mináu (Minyo). They said that Kánem, north of Lake Tsád or Tsádi, is a bush country, with but few towns, and that the Búduma are short, very black, and with thick legs. Kanúri is generally applied to the people and the language, and Bornú to the country, but one man said that strictly speaking Kanúri referred to the districts towards Mináu, while to the southward and eastward was Bornú proper. Zínder and Dámagram have been united into one province, the distance between these two chief towns being from three to four days. From Zínder to Katshína (pronounced Kátshina or Kátshna by the Bornuese), it is eight or nine days. The capital of Bornú is properly Kukáwa, and not Kúka: it was founded after the destruction, in a civil war, of Birni-Bornú the former capital, from which it is distant three or four days. Mináu is often called Mánga, and Koyám is also named Kuyáni. Southwest from Mináu is a place named Kárda. Many of the people of Damergú are light-coloured; they have plenty of camels. Músgo is usually known in Bornú as Mútshgo. The Bornuese buy guns and powder in exchange for slaves, at a place called Zéila, where caravans halt, and where much Arabic is spoken, and where some people come with light-coloured skins, whom the Bornuese term *Wâsilí*, nearly equivalent to the Háusa *Batúri*. The slaves are mostly girls and boys, forming part of the tribute paid to Kukáwa from the provinces, whence they are sent across the desert. These people brought with them a man from a district named Absináwa, said to be past Damergú and towards Zéila, where a different dialect was spoken. Absináwa is the Háusa name, Kandín is the Bornuese, while the native title is Imajága. In appearance he looked exactly like a Bornuese. The Bornuese have much more marked negro features than any of the nations to the westward of them, so much so as to be sub-typical. In the Púlo province of Dáura the population is Háusa, Púlo, and Bornuese, and in Hadéja, Háusa, and Púlo; in the former the natives are distinguished by two horizontal cuts opposite the mouth.

As to the countries near the Kwóra and Bínue, I gave these people all the information I could, but as to whether they could be assisted in returning to these regions, I could, of course, give no reply. All I could do was to promise to represent their wishes in England, and to endeavour to promote them as far as possible. And I sincerely trust that the small boon they crave may be accorded to them, as in helping them to settle in Central Africa, we should not be merely benefitting them, but the entire continent, and by thus introducing superior intelligence, we might, possibly, be laying the germ of a new nation, to be distinguished by its civilized rule and mild sway contrasting most strongly with present tyranny and oppression.

Sierra Leone is a thriving place, and of considerable commercial importance. The anchorage is safe, commodious, of easy access, and with ordinary precautions should be quite healthy. The exports of timber, ground-nuts, palm-nuts, palm-oil, pepper, gum, ginger, coffee, arrow-root, cam-wood, bees-wax hides, ivory, &c., are of great value. The coffee is very good and well flavoured, the bean being small, like that from Mocha. The quantity of ground-nuts shipped annually is immense, being upwards of a million bushels; these are sent almost entirely to France, where ground-nut oil is largely manufactured, a clear, excellent article, which I cannot imagine being so little valued in this country. Palm-nuts are now also largely shipped, and are likewise sent to France, where they appear more fully to appreciate the commercial importance and economical value of these oleaginous seeds than we do on this side the channel. A new oil-yielding fruit is now coming into repute, viz., that of the *Carapa Guineensis*, the product of which has long been in esteem among the natives. Like the *C. Guianensis*, it bears an irregularly triangular, chocolate-coloured nut, the kernel of which, when bruised and heated, yields a fine vegetable oil. A small specimen in my possession, is nearly colourless, without smell, and even in the tropical heat of Sierra Leone, was solid and firm, much more so than shea-butter. When better known this must become a most important article of commerce. Of arrow-root from 50,000 to 60,000 pounds are exported, it is of excellent quality, and is obtained at Sierra Leone for about three-pence per pound. Lastly, I may allude to hides, which are brought to Freetown partly from inland districts, partly by coasting vessels from the neighbouring rivers; of these nearly 400,000 are every year sent principally to markets in the United States.

Previous to the time of my visit the native population had been much troubled with vexatious Customs regulations, or by the undue strictness with which these had been carried out. I can better illustrate my meaning by an example. Some Yóruba men bought a little schooner to trade in with Lagos, and accordingly shipped at Sierra Leone a cargo which included amongst other things a quantity of white rum. This article was, however, found unsuitable, and on their return they wished to have it exchanged for an equal quantity of coloured rum, to ship which they got the usual permission at the Custom-house, mentioning their reason for doing so. They then landed the white rum, quite openly, probably thinking that as it was a mere exchange nothing else was required. But some of the authorities heard of their landing spirits without paying duty, on which the whole was seized, and a heavy fine was inflicted. Even little canoes coming down the river with fruit or some other trifling produce, are ordered to be entered at the Custom-house, and any neglect of this injunction is punished by confiscation of the property. Now in the case of these Yóruba men I cannot see that there was any real breach of law. There may have been an error in judgment, but they acted as they did without any concealment, not in premeditated violation of a Custom-house order, but according to principles of simple fair dealing, which regulate the transactions even of the most savage tribes. How easy would it have been in this case to have pointed out the error, or rather the informality committed, and caution against a repetition, such a course would have had infinitely more effect than the severest punishment. And so in respect to the canoe-men, what folly to expect people who know only perhaps a dozen words of English, to comprehend the nature of such regulations. It can hardly be expected that a Tímne or a Súsu, or even a Mandénga or a Púlo, can be versed in commercial jurisprudence or political economy, or that they can understand the advanced routine of a modern Custom-house. Justice, as well as common sense, demand that before punishing a person for violating a law of this nature, care be taken to explain its nature, and to point out its necessity. An undue observance of the very letter of the law in all cases, except in crimes against society and public order, produces not a stricter observance, but induces men to find out means of evasion. And in a colony, or a new country, where the people to be dealt with are uncivilized or ignorant, a most liberal mode of administering law and dispensing justice is absolutely requisite. Such a course will secure the affections of those governed, while an opposite method, as we have too often seen, disgusts and alienates. Such oppressive proceedings are, by this time, probably modified or stopped, but they were in full force little more than a year ago, at which time, also, any person in the colony could be seized and lodged in prison, without knowing what his offence was.

After the Bishop's death, Mr. Graf very kindly undertook to look after my little Mítshi friend, so accordingly I took him ashore and left him, after a hearty cry, with no little difficulty at Mr. Graf's house, and he has since been placed at school under the care of the Rev. Edward Jones. There being no person now to undertake the study of the I′gbo language, Simon Jonas had to be sent back to Fernando Po, but since that time the Rev. Mr. Venn, on the part of the Church Missionary Society, has directed Mr. Crowther to commence the task, and by my last letters from that gentleman Simon Jonas was with him at Lagos.

We sailed from Sierra Leone on the 6th of January, having embarked several fresh passengers, among whom was Captain Macdonald, R.N., whose constant good humour, and unceasing fund of amusement, tended greatly to allay the tedium of our lengthened voyage.

Of the remaining part of the passage I have but little to relate. One evening the usual phosphorescence of the sea mysteriously disappeared, but in its place were seen rolling by the ship large luminous balls, which I ascertained to be large *Acalephæ*, but where the usual more minute animals had stowed themselves away for that night, I cannot imagine. At Bathurst we were put to some inconvenience by the behaviour of a Custom-house official, whose laws, unchangeable as those of the Medes or Persians, were not to be shaken by the arrival of a paltry mail-packet, and whose colonial consequence far outweighed the interests of the owners of the vessel, the proprietors of the cargo, and the comfort of the passengers. We spent several hours at Gorée, where we were received with true French politeness, after which we bade adieu to the African coast.

Our incidents were very few, and of the usual nature, meeting the huge "Great Britain" on her outward voyage, and one dark night being very nearly run into by a large brig. The Peak of Tencriffe was now covered with snow, presenting a very striking spectacle, but the climate at Vera Cruz was not at all affected, the sun being nearly as powerful there as it was at the Gambia. Not being in quarantine we landed, visiting among other places the Cathedral, and seeing the British ensigns kept there as trophies. I do not know whether it was suspected that we intended, as some silly midshipmen once did, to try and abstract them, but while we were near them, our conductor kept a most watchful eye on us, and objected to our getting too close to them. The weather, hitherto, had been so fine, that we felt the first approach of European winter very much. We passed a very unpleasant night between Teneriffe and Madeira, as, in addition to its blowing hard, three seas met from opposite directions, producing in the middle, just where we were, such a commotion as to set everything on board not securely fixed in violent motion; while sleeping on a locker in the saloon, and carefully guarding myself from a leak in the skylight overhead, through which a stream poured down within about eighteen inches of me, I had a narrow escape from being squashed under a huge portmanteau which had been stowed away right over my head, and which now getting way on, seriously threatened my personal comfort. Luckily, at this moment the ship gave a roll in the right direction, and the portmanteau acquired sufficient impetus to take a flying leap and to clear my head. At Funchal so much sea was on that at first it was thought that we should not be able to communicate with the shore, but have to run to Lisbon; the gale, however, was on the decline, and next day the water was fine and smooth.

During the earlier part of our voyage, both Mr. May and I suffered much from frequent accessions of remittent fever, but our stay at Sierra Leone had a very beneficial effect on us. It seemed quite to cure him, but I had a fresh seizure at Gorée and during the remainder of the time had repeated paroxysms. Even after my arrival in England they continued, and to this day I am liable to troublesome ague, keeping me well in mind of my morning visit to the swamp at Angiáma.

We left Madeira on the 24th of January, and during the remainder of the passage had various weather. When close to the Lizard, a gale of wind obliged us to heave to with our head off shore, and with a very heavy sea running the "Bacchante" showed herself to be extremely easy and steady. A short interval of repose enabled us to reach Plymouth Sound, where we anchored on the night of the 3rd of February, after a voyage, from Fernando Po, of sixty-seven days. The following day we left by train for London to report ourselves at the Admiralty.

CHAPTER XIII.

CONCLUSION.

IN an age so highly practical as the present one, the question may possibly be asked, what has your expedition already done—and what future good do you anticipate? To such inquiries I should wish to offer a short reply. A detailed account of the immediate results has been already given, but here I am desirous of speaking in more general terms. Our voyage had points of interest for the utilitarian, the commercial man, the man of science, and the philanthropist. To the two former I would reply, we have discovered a navigable river, an available highway, conducting us into the very heart of a large continent, and by means of its branches and ramifications we are brought into immediate contact with many thousand miles of country. We have found these regions to be highly favoured by nature, teeming with animal life, and with fertile soils abounding in valuable vegetable products, and adapted by diversity of position, of elevation, and of character, for all the varied purposes of tropical agriculture. We have met on friendly terms with numerous tribes, all endowed by nature with what I may term the "commercial faculty," ready and anxious to trade with us, and to supply us from their inexhaustible stores, with immense quantities of highly-prized articles, most valuable for various economical appliances. We can likewise indicate a most important outlet for home manufactures, as the unclad millions of Central Africa must absorb thousands of cargoes of soft goods, eagerly bartering their raw cotton, their vegetable oils, and their ivory, for our calicoes and cloths. Thus we can confidently point out for those who follow a fresh field for energy and activity, an unbroken ground, where both honour and riches may be reaped.

To the man of science we would enumerate the additions made to our geographical knowledge, to the extent of new country examined and laid down, to the survey of a new river, and the determination of the erroneousness of the theory which derived the Bínue from Lake Tsád. How, the course of the Kwóra being known to be easterly, and that of the Bínue being now ascertained to be westerly, the accounts of ancient geographers may be reconciled, the descriptions of some evidently referring to the main river, of others to the confluent. We could also allude to the new tribes discovered, the definitions of the boundaries of various districts, and the additions to ethnology, philology, and natural history, which, though by no means extensive, will be found not to be wholly uninteresting. And to the medical philosopher we would mention the results of our experience of the climate, our opinions on the hitherto much dreaded "African fever," and the confirmation of the views of those who have recommended to prevent rather than to cure, but, when attacked by disease, to employ a rational instead of an empirical treatment.

And finally, we would address the philanthropist, by telling him of multitudes of human beings to whom he might well turn his attention. That they are organized like ourselves, have similar affections and desires, but that, unlike the inhabitants of our happier clime, they have been for ages a prey to the strong, ground down by ruthless oppression and savage passions. That naturally they are mild and friendly, apt to learn, and desirous of being taught, ready to receive first impressions, whether of good or of evil. That these people are, alas! mostly the slaves of degrading superstitions and of heathen practices, and totally ignorant of those blessed truths with which we have been favoured and which were instilled into our minds in infancy. And lastly, that gifted as we have been with a revelation from on high, it is only our duty to attempt to impart its doctrines to our less favoured brethren, and that a great—a noble task is in store for those who will pioneer the way of civilization and Christianity.

To one topic I must especially allude,—namely, to that horrid, that unnatural traffic in human beings, known as the slave-trade. Why the poor African should have been solely selected as the victim of the cupidity of his brother man might form a curious subject of enquiry: his intellect, when duly cultivated, will rank with that of the white man, and he is infinitely superior to many other races, such, for instance, as the aboriginal Australian. In appearance and construction he is certainly not more removed from the Japetic nations than is the Mongolian, and he has been shown to be in every respect made like ourselves in the image of the Creator. I do not intend to refer to domestic slavery, which, although highly repugnant to our notions of freedom of action and equality of rights, is yet a very different thing from foreign slavery, domestic slaves being, in countries where the rights of labour are unknown, the representatives of our servants. They are usually treated with kindness, and do not in general seem to have much to complain of except their original forcible abduction. It is an institution, too, so completely and so intimately mixed up with the state of society in Africa, that many years will not serve to uproot it, nor would we be justified in employing any but mild and persuasive means for stopping it. But of the other, who can ever think for a moment without feelings of acute horror, mingled with sensations of disgust, that our fellow-men can be so base, so degraded, so hardened as to pursue and to defend this dreadful commerce? Who, even the most callous amongst us, can meditate without intense emotion on the scenes daily enacted by the slave-hunter, on the husband separated from the wife, the mother torn from her child, brothers and sisters, whole families scattered, never again to meet on this side of the grave? But worse than all is the conduct of the man who ships these wretched creatures, and, stowing them with less care than he would horses or cattle, transports them to far distant lands.

The only real method of effectually checking this detestable trade is by striking at the root of the supply, by going directly to the fountain-head. It is by doing our utmost to improve the natives, by softening their feelings, and by showing them how much more advantageous it would be for them to retain their countrymen at home, even as hewers of wood and drawers of water, than to depopulate the land, that we shall succeed in our efforts. For these purposes no auxiliary is more effectual than commerce, which, to minds constituted like those of the Africans, is highly intelligible. Prove to them that they can derive more benefit by cultivating the ground, and by selling their grain, their cam-wood, their palm-oil, their shea-butter, than by living in a state of perpetual warfare. Convince them how much happier it would be for all to be able to rest quietly under their own vines and fig-trees, when there would be none to make them afraid, than, as at present, being in daily, nay hourly dread of being carried off into captivity by some one more powerful than themselves. And lastly offer them, as long as they abide by our wishes and directions, whatever advantages it may be in our power to present to them. Thus a promise of regular trade, of commercial establishments, of an uninterrupted supply of European goods, would form legitimate bribes for good behaviour, and one which would exercise great influence. Let but these tribes once experience, even for a short time, the comfort of such a new mode of life, and I hardly think that they would again return to their former ways. These are the commencing steps, and when missionary exertions are also brought to bear upon them, I can have no fear for the future.

As to the African squadron, I cannot but look on it as a very valuable agent, but its influence is only temporary and local. As long as we closely blockade the known slaving-ports, the traffic will be for the time knocked up in them; but as soon as the ships are withdrawn, slavers again appear. Besides, for such a lucrative trade other outlets are soon formed. But one means remains, which, though it has been long ago recommended, we have not yet adopted, namely, to declare slave-ships pirates, and to punish the officers and crews accordingly. Why this has never been done I cannot well imagine. No sensible mind can hesitate to pronounce foreign slavery to be piracy, yet we shrink from making a public avowal. It is but little punishment for a slave-captain to lose his vessel, he can easily get another, and the remuneration is too great not to tempt a man to risk anything except his life. But further, I have no hesitation in declaring, that there is no captain who has carried slaves, who has not been, either directly or indirectly, guilty of murder. Take even the mildest case: when slaves are shipped, they are stowed in a confined space, where they have no air to breathe, their food is stinted, and in this unwholesome, pestilential hole they are kept for weeks; a certain number of deaths is always allowed for, and I hold that he who for mere caprice, or contrary to the fundamental laws of humanity, confines human beings in such a manner that some must die, must be considered as the cause of their decease. And now to consider the opposite extreme; how often have we heard of captains of slavers, during a hard chase, throwing part or the whole of their human cargo overboard, thus consigning these wretches to the deep or to the jaws of hungry sharks, and hurrying hundreds of immortal souls into eternity! Who will be bold enough to say that such a one is not a murderer, and, if so, why not let him receive the just reward of his deeds? Nay, so complaisant were our slaving regulations, that a slave-captain could thus commit wholesale destruction of his species, be seen to do so, and yet, if, when overtaken, no slaves were found on board, he could not be seized. Such characters, such man-stealers, man-destroyers, deserve no mercy, and should, according to every principle of justice, be effectually prevented from again pursuing their unlawful calling. Instead of puzzling questions about nationalities and national flags, and ship's papers and clearances, let every such vessel be looked on as piratical, and without inquiring for the birthplace of the master, let him be treated as a pirate-captain. What does it matter whether he is a Spaniard or a Portuguese? he is equally an enemy to the rights of mankind, and the interests of society demand his punishment. He follows his vocation on the high seas, but does that render him the less dangerous, the less culpable? By no means; locality does not mitigate the guilt of abstract crime, and he who attempts the lives or the liberties of his fellows, equally requires arrest, whether in the crowded city or in the middle of the Atlantic. Let but this course, therefore, be adopted, and doubtless the number of those who would run their heads into a noose will soon dwindle away. The professed criminal, though he may be hardened, is seldom brave, and will not, except when rendered desperate, willingly face the prospect of death.

It is absurd to hear the defences of slavery which are from time to time offered to the public. It cannot clear what is in itself wrong, to tell how kind certain masters are to their slaves, or to say that negroes are better off in Brazil or in Cuba than they could be at home. No art, no ingenuity can palliate the original offence. It is very fine to see or hear persons sitting in comfort and luxury at home, breathe forth a sickly sentimentalism and utter commonplace vapidities on such an important topic. Let them place themselves in the position of an African,—let them imagine themselves torn from house, home, and everything dear to them,—let them picture themselves encased in heavy irons, driven from place to place at the point of the lash, sold, bartered for some idle trinkets or an old red-coat, put on board ship, chained in a space where there is not room to turn, deprived of food and drink, landed, again re-sold, and obliged to slave out a wretched existence at the commands of a brutal master. Let them fancy and mentally realize such horrors, and then let them say whether they can approve of this traffic. Whatever fine folks may think to the contrary, colour of skin constitutes no real difference. Under it is the same flesh and blood, a similar brain works, and a like heart beats. However refinement may be shocked with the idea, it is nevertheless true, that the black is indeed " a man and a brother; " and it should be remembered as a solemn truth, that the veriest negro on Africa's shore is of as much value in the eyes of his Maker, as the proudest peer or the mightiest warrior of our land.

I believe that for the promotion of commerce and of civilization in Central Africa, it is essential to cultivate the friendship of the Púlo nation as being exceedingly powerful and influential, and therefore likely, under good management, to be useful. For this purpose I have proposed that the expedition shall be renewed, and that the steamer shall proceed up the Kwóra as far as Rábba, from which place a deputation should proceed by land to Sókoto, to wait on the Púlo Sultan, and to endeavour to form with him a definite commercial treaty, and to persuade him to further our plans. Such a step gained would be of infinite importance, and would greatly facilitate future progress. I have also proposed that means be adopted to assist the civilized natives in Sierra Leone in returning to their homes, and in forming settlements. And lastly, I would recommend that regular intercourse be kept up for several years with the interior, after which time it will be so established as to follow as a matter of course. I am no advocate for endeavouring to acquire new territory; on the contrary, I think such a proceeding would be prejudicial to our views. We should go to Africa as we would to other foreign countries, as visitors, as traders, or as settlers, doing what we could to improve the race by precept and by practice, but avoiding any violent interference or physical demonstration. If attacked, we should be prepared to defend ourselves, but we should be careful not to give cause for offence.

Though the languages of Central Africa are very numerous, there are a few, which if known, are sufficient for the purposes of all ordinary intercourse. There are the Háusa,* the I'gbo, and the I'gbira; and I have placed them according to their relative value. The Háusa is smooth and easily acquired, and will carry the traveller almost from the sea to Bornú, or from Adamáwa in one direction to Timbuktú in the other. Further to the northward

---

* At present the Rev. Mr. Crowther, at Lagos, is engaged in the study of the I'gbo Language; and in this country the Rev. Mr. Schön is revising and expanding his Háusa grammar.

others will prove useful, such as Púlo, Kanúri, and Arabic.

During the last five or six years much has been added to our knowledge of the African continent. The travels of Richardson, of Barth, of Overweg, and of Vogel have told us much of Bornú, and of the Háusa and Púlo countries; and one of these enterprising men has even penetrated to the almost mythical city of Timbuktú. In the extreme south, Galton and Andersson have successfully explored vast regions previously unknown, while between these the adventurous Livingston is even now pursuing his unparalleled journey. The extent of country marked "unexplored" on the maps is annually lessening, and before many years it is to be hoped that such blots will be totally expunged. The time has, I believe, at length arrived when the inmost recesses of this ancient continent are to be laid open, its people made known, and its resources manifested. The cruel ills heaped for ages on the heads of its unfortunate inhabitants loudly demand reparation, and the neglect of ages has yet to be atoned for. England has always taken the lead in African exploration, hers has been the expense, hers many of the valuable lives lost in its prosecution. And now that she has sheathed the sword which she drew in a righteous and a just cause, let her afford a moment to think of other and not less noble purposes. Time is all-important, and every season allowed to pass away only further complicates the business, and may injuriously affect the result.

Already two years have elapsed, during which the natives have been anxiously on the outlook for our wished-for return, and, when the next expedition actually does take place, numerous will be the allusions to the want of faith and of punctuality on the part of white men, and many will be the enquiries why they do not practise what they are so ready to inculcate. The country is promising, the people are favourable, and the way, though not absolutely free from danger, is open and not difficult. Thousands will hail our advent, and in after-ages our first attempts to visit and to improve these regions will occupy a bright page in African history. Seeing these things, why should we further delay? I am not indulging in chimerical expectations, but am recording the impressions of actual personal experience. The requisite expense for renewing and continuing our explorations is very trifling, and when compared with the benefit which will be conferred on myriads of our fellow-creatures, it is absolutely nothing. Nor will we be without our share of temporal rewards, as a widely extended field will be opened to our commerce, and for years to come the demands for our manufactured goods will steadily increase, while in return we shall receive abundant supplies of rich tropical produce. Be it England's, then, to follow up the good work, commenced so long ago, and consecrated by the blood of Mungo Park, of Martyn, of Laing, of Clapperton, of Richardson, and of many others of her own sons, as well as by the lives of

Hornemann, of Belzoni, of Overweg, and other enthusiasts travelling on her behalf. Let her not leave to other nations to finish what she has begun, but let her pursue her labour of love, and aim at acquiring and retaining the glorious title of the Friend of Africa.

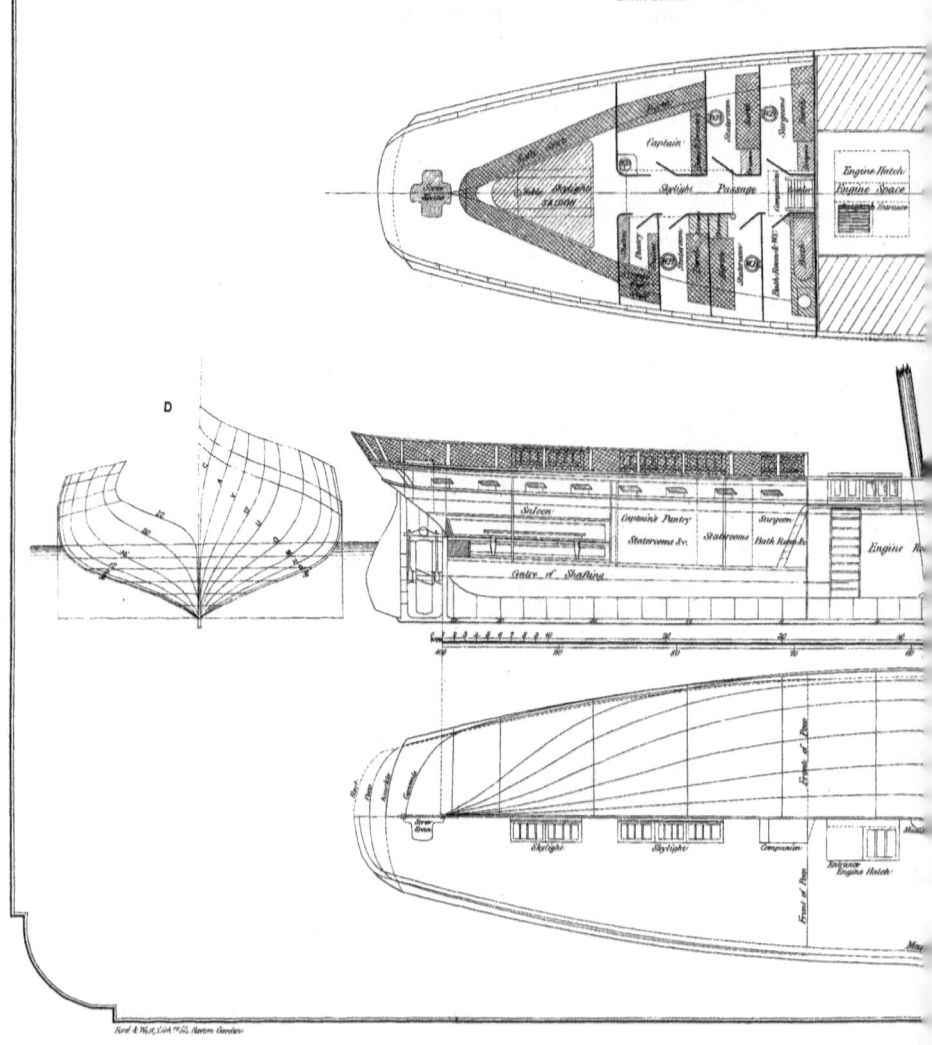

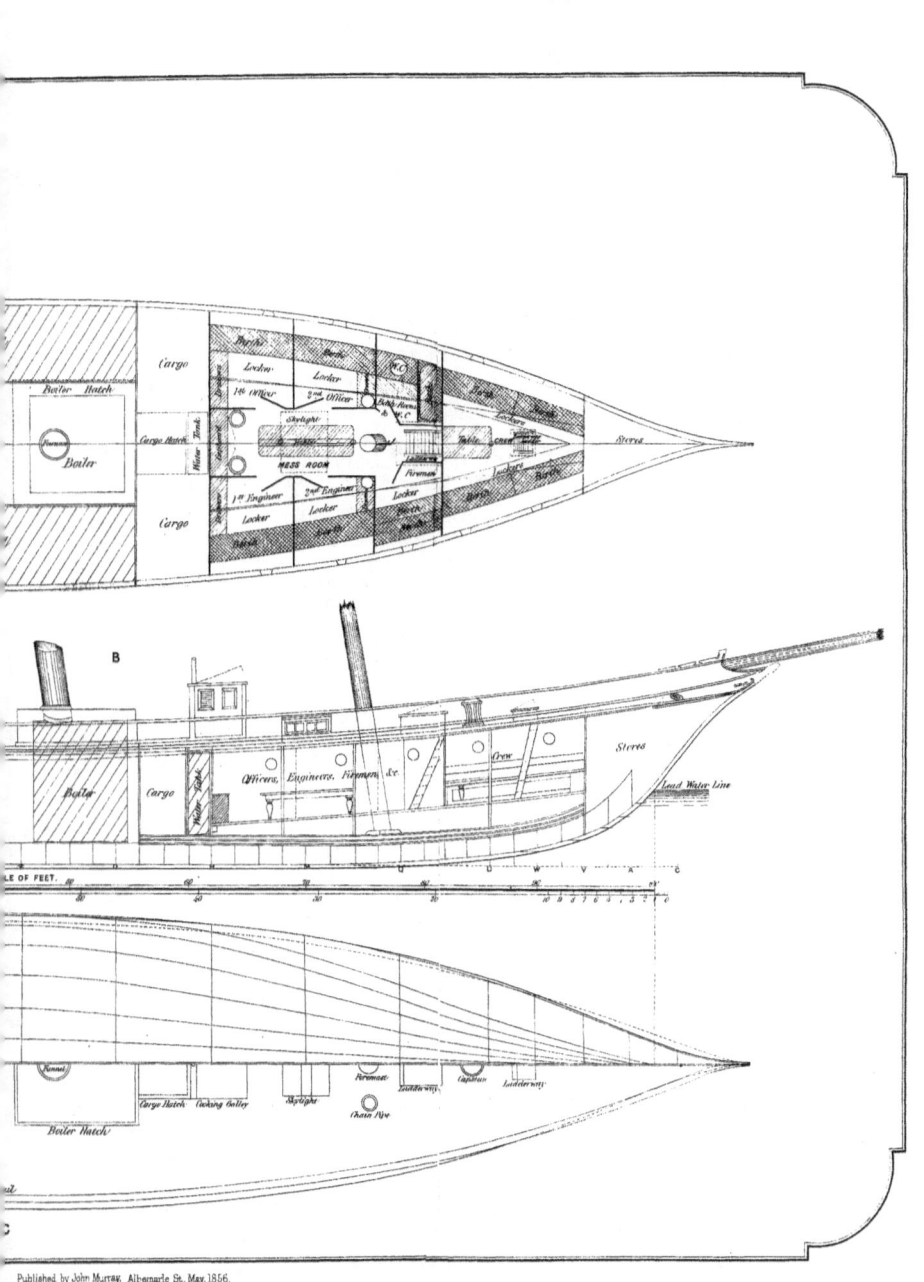

APPENDIX.

A.

The dimensions of the "Pleiad" have already been given at page 5; the accompanying lithographic plans are so complete as hardly to require any description.

Figure A is a section along the level of the lower deck, showing her internal arrangements and the abundant cabin accommodation.

Figure B is a longitudinal section, which particularly exhibits the angle and shape of the stem, the rake of the masts, the line of the shaft, and the draught of water. The ample height between decks, from six and a half to nearly eight feet is very striking.

Figure C is a section, principally exhibiting the upper deck plan, and also displaying well her great beam.

Figure D is a horizontal section, showing the shape of her bottom, and giving a foreshortened view of half the bow.

Not only was the "Pleiad" admirably adapted for her work, but the extreme beauty of her model must at once be perceived. She sailed very well indeed, was very stiff and dry, and the only fault which could be found with her was that she was rather slow in staying. She had a shifting fan, which was found very useful and convenient, as it could be unshipped, hoisted on deck, and again shipped within five minutes.

COPY.

ADMIRALTY INSTRUCTIONS, ADDRESSED TO THE LATE
MR. CONSUL BEECROFT.

ADMIRALTY, 23rd *May*, 1854.

SIR,—Her Majesty's Government having determined to send an expedition to the river Chadda, in Central Africa, and understanding that you have expressed your willingness to be the leader of such an expedition, and H.M. Secretary of State for Foreign Affairs having granted permission for you to be absent from your Consulate, I am commanded by my Lords Commissioners of the Admiralty to acquaint you that they have accepted your offer, and you are hereby directed to take charge of the expedition for exploring the river Chadda, and all those forming a part of the said expedition are required to obey your orders.

You will be accompanied by Dr. Baikie, a medical officer of the Royal Navy, who is a naturalist, and has been preparing himself during the past year with this object. Possibly also Dr. Bleek, Ph.D., of Bonn, an ethnologist, will be of the party. It is further understood that the Rev. Mr. Crowther, from Sierra Leone,* will avail himself of this opportunity of ascending the river.

The vessel prepared for this expedition is the "Pleiad," an iron screw steamer of 260 tons burthen, rigged as a schooner. She is 100 feet in length, 24 feet beam, engines of 60 horse power, and having 7 feet draught of water, with three months provisions and stores on board, and twenty days' coal of twelve hours each. She is officially reported on her trial of speed, at Liverpool, to have made ten knots an hour in smooth water. There will be, in addition to this vessel, two 50 feet sectional iron trade boats, and the consular boat, all three of which will be towed from Fernando Po, as far as the entrance of the Chadda, or farther if necessary.

* This is an error, Mr. Crowther having for several years been stationed at Abbeokúta in the Yóruba country, and more lately at Lagos.

The Expedition has two main objects.

One is to explore the river Chadda, or Benueh, the eastern branch of the Kawára from Dagbó, the highest point reached by Oldfield and Allen in 1833, to the country of Adamauá, a distance of about 400 miles, where the river was crossed at the junction of the Benueh and Faro, by Dr. Barth, in June 1851; and thence again, if the season permits and the waters are still rising, to the limit of navigation.

The other is to endeavour to meet and afford assistance to that excellent traveller Dr. Barth, who left England for Africa towards the close of the year 1849, and who, from the latest accounts received from him, would, after reaching Tumbuktu, make his way to the banks of the Benueh. On all occasions every possible enquiry is to be made for Dr. Barth, and no presents spared in endeavouring to obtain information respecting him. The same instructions hold good respecting Dr. Vogel, who left England in 1853, and who may have succeeded in penetrating to the banks of the Chadda.

In carrying out these two objects it is the desire of Her Majesty's Government, for the benefit of commerce and civilization, to take advantage of every opportunity for opening trade with the natives at each large town on the banks of the river, and within a moderate distance on either side. One hundred pounds' worth of suitable presents and samples of goods have been supplied by Government for this purpose, to be delivered to you by the sailing-master of the "Pleiad," and a list of which is enclosed. These are to be freely given on all occasions; it is left to your judgment to limit the amount, but the practice is always to be observed in conformity with the custom of the country. It is further desirable to make careful enquiries as to the political power of the several chiefs, as to the state of civilization among them, as to the existence of foreign slave-trade, and if so, whether they would consent to put an end to it, if lawful trade could be ensured to them, and a market opened for ivory and other products of the country. Mr. Crowther will naturally enquire into the apparent disposition, willingness, or aptitude of the natives to receive religious or secular instruction.

From your experience as a traveller in Central Africa, it is almost unnecessary to give you any detailed instructions, yet it is right to call your attention to the most recent and best map of Central Africa, accompanied by a memorandum compiled by Mr. Petermann from the papers of Messrs. Richardson, Barth, Overweg, and Vogel, placed at his disposal by the Earl of Clarendon, H.M. Secretary of State for Foreign Affairs. A copy of this work is supplied for your use. In it you will see that the town of Doma on the north of the Chadda, Wukári the capital of Korórrofa on the south, Juggum a settlement of the Kóana, Hamárrua, and Yola the capital of Adamaua, are places of importance. Wukári is described as a very large town lying eight miles south of the river, and the capital of the populous country of Korórrofa, with the chief of which it is hoped an extensive trade may be established. Within 30 miles of Yola Mount Alantika is said to reach an altitude of 10,000 feet; if the highest point could be attained it would be an admirable position for a round of angles or bearings, as on a clear day in that climate the radius of vision from it would be fully 100 miles.

It is essential, as you ascend the Chadda, to make a rapid survey of the windings of the river, noting the depths of water and width of stream, with the character and height of its banks, laying the work down at once on prepared sheets of paper by careful compass bearings, and measured or estimated distances, checking the whole by astronomical observations at every halt for the night. For this latter purpose you will be provided with three chronometers and the necessary instruments. In using the compass it must not be forgotten that the observations are made on board an iron ship; all bearings should therefore be taken from the standard compass and carefully corrected for local deviation, which should be ascertained by swinging the vessel at Fernando Po, before starting, and testing it every evening by bearings of the pole star, which, in those latitudes, will be always within 7° or 8° of the horizon.

On all occasions you will endeavour to ascertain the height of any hill or mountain which may be in sight; if no means are afforded of measuring it by angles or by barometer, never omit to estimate its altitude and mark down its position and height while on the spot. Trust nothing to memory.

In the Admiralty "Manual of Scientific Enquiry," a copy of which is supplied, you will find useful suggestions in geography, hydrography, and in all other departments of science.

Dr. Baikie is to act as medical adviser to your party. He has been supplied with all the necessary medicines, and a sufficient stock also to enable him to prescribe for the natives, whose goodwill is readily obtained by medical advice and assistance, more so perhaps than by any other means. It will, therefore, be politic to offer his services on many occasions. Dr. Baikie will also act as naturalist to the expedition; he is so well acquainted with the branches of zoology and botany that no special instructions are required, but a few suggestions are offered by Professor Edward Forbes, as well as some hints on geology by Sir Roderick Murchison, on ethnology by Dr. Latham, and on terrestrial magnetism by Col. Sabine, with instruments, instructions and blank forms for meteorological observations. You will see that Dr. Baikie is provided with boats or the necessary means for facilitating his researches, and that every care be taken of any collections he may make.

The Commander of the "Pleiad" is engaged to comply with all your requisitions, as you will observe by a copy of the Contract, and of his Instructions from his owners, which are annexed.

The "Pleiad" being armed with a 12-pounder pivot-gun, four swivels, Minié rifles and double-barrelled guns for the officers, muskets for the crew, and with boarding nettings of wire, it is not probable that she will meet with any opposition in the lower parts of the river where there may be danger. But you will remember that the best security from attack consists in the natives seeing and knowing you are well prepared to meet it. At the same time you are strictly enjoined to use the greatest forbearance towards the people, and, while retaining proper firmness in the event of any misunderstanding, to endeavour to conciliate as far as can possibly be admitted with safety to your party. You will, on all occasions, enforce the strictest justice, and never, on any account, permit one of your party to ill-treat, insult, or cheat the natives.

You will comply with the first Article of War in Her Majesty's naval service, in causing Divine Worship to be celebrated on board on Sundays, and allow no unnecessary work to be done, or trading operations to be carried on, on that day. At the same time you will be careful to observe the spirit rather than the letter of the law, and never allow the vessel or your party to remain in a dangerous or unhealthy position, or risk being caught in a falling river, or defer any work of positive necessity on that day.

You should not delay your departure from Fernando Po beyond the 1st July at latest; if the vessel can be ready it would be better to leave earlier, as this late period will only leave you two months for your ascent of the river, since you must commence your return voyage as soon as the river ceases to rise, probably about the beginning of September.

In the possible, but, it is trusted, most improbable, loss of the "Pleiad," on any of the numerous rocks and banks which may be expected in an unexplored river, the consular boat and two trade-boats will ensure you the means of a safe return to the sea; and their Lordships will direct the mail-packets to call off the mouth of the river each voyage from the middle of September to the end of the year, to make enquiries as to your safety, and to afford you assistance in case of need.

During the whole of the expedition you will keep a full journal of your proceedings, and, if an opportunity offers of sending home despatches from time to time, you will not fail to avail yourself of it, transmitting, at the same time, a tracing, however rough, of the chart of the river, as far as you may have advanced, so that, in case of an accident to your papers, the results of the expedition, so far, will be recorded.

On reaching Fernando Po, you will of course resume your consular duties; Dr. Baikie will return to England in one of the contract packets, on board of which a free passage is provided for him, bringing with him the journal, plans, and collections connected with the expedition, and report himself to the Admiralty on his arrival.

Finally, you are strictly enjoined to be careful of the health of the party entrusted to your charge, and to afford them the benefit of your experience as to the best mode of maintaining health in African rivers; and should, unfortunately, fever break out and assume a threatening appearance, you are to remember that you are not called upon to persevere in the ascent of the river, but that your first care is the safety of your people.

     (Signed)   R. OSBORNE.

(COPY.)

MR. LAIRD'S INSTRUCTIONS TO MR. T. C. TAYLOR, SAILING-MASTER OF THE "PLEIAD."

LONDON, 3, MINCING LANE, *May* 8, 1854.

SIR,—Having appointed you to command the screw steamer "Pleiad," about to proceed under a contract with the Lords Commissioners of the Admiralty (a copy of which is handed you herewith) on an exploring voyage up the river Niger and its tributaries, I have now to state the manner in which you will carry out the contract, your relation to the government passengers who are appointed to accompany you, and the principles which will guide you in your intercourse and trading operations with the natives.

2. You will consider all trading operations subsidiary and auxiliary to the main design of the voyage, which is to ascend the river Chadda, the eastern branch of the Niger, as high as possible during the rise of the river.

3. The Admiralty appoint three gentlemen to accompany the expedition,—Captain Beecroft, Her Majesty's Consul at Fernando Po, Dr. Baikie, R.N., and a third, for the purpose of laying down the course of the river, and making observations on the character of the people and the productions of the country.

Their relation to you is that of first-class passengers in a contract steam-packet, found and provided in everything by the ship; to whom you will afford every facility, by stopping, proceeding, or delaying your voyage, and supplying them with boats, men, and provisions, whenever required for their scientific pursuits.

In case of any difference of opinion, you will require an order in writing from the senior present, and that order you will *obey*. You are to supply them with any articles of merchandise, cowries, or dollars at the market value at the time of such supply. These gentlemen will join the "Pleiad" at Fernando Po.

4. In your intercourse with the natives you are not to assume any other character than that of a trader, which they will at once recognize and understand. You are not to mix yourself up with their local disputes; and, when they exist, change your location as quickly as possible, deal with them firmly and justly, and on no account allow the slightest insult or the smallest theft offered or committed on board your vessel to pass unnoticed or unpunished.

You will conform to the customs of the country in making the usual presents to the chiefs and leading men in the villages and towns you visit, using your judgment as to the amount, but never omitting the practice, which corresponds to the Custom-House charges of civilized countries.

5. You will enforce strict discipline with your officers and crew, and severely punish any of them who ill-treat, insult, or cheat the natives, and you will not permit women to remain on board on any pretence.

6. The "Pleiad" being armed with a 12-pounder pivot-gun, four swivels, Minió rifles and double-barrelled guns for the officers, and muskets for the coast negroes employed as crew, and with boarding nettings of wire, it is not probable she will meet with any opposition in the lower parts of the river where *there is danger*. But you will remember the only security from attack is the natives seeing and knowing you are well prepared to meet it, and if you are attacked that you forfeit all your advantages if you allow them to make a hand-to-hand fight of it.

Your superiority is in your arms, and a few rounds of canister from your pivot-gun will be sufficient to show them that, after which you will have no more trouble. The cause of any collision is generally misunderstanding. As a rule the natives are well disposed, but in the lower parts of the river they cannot resist the temptation to plunder, if they think

APPENDIX.   407

it can be done with impunity. Above Eboe there is no
danger.

7. The Rev. Mr. Crowther, to whom I have offered a passage
in the "Pleiad," will join at Fernando Po from Lagos. It is
my desire that he has every opportunity given him of seeing
the country and the people. His position on board is that of
my guest, and you will see that he is treated with deference
and respect.

8. You will have Divine Service on Sundays, and allow no
unnecessary work to be done, or trading operations to be carried
on; but you will draw a broad line between the Jewish observance of the Sabbath and the Christian one, and never allow
your ship or ship's company to remain in a dangerous or unhealthy position, or defer any work of necessity on that day.

9. The mail-packet "Bacchante" took out on the 25th of
April to Fernando Po the cargo, provisions, and stores for the
"Pleiad," and two iron sectional boats, 50 feet long by 8 feet
beam; and by the mail-packet of the 24th of May three inter-
preters, selected from the liberated Africans at Sierra Leone by
Mr. Oldfield, will join you. They will be of Eboe, Haussa, and
Yariba tribes, the three languages, dialects of which are spoken
as far as you will proceed.

10. You will follow, with as little deviation as possible, the
following plan of proceedings:—

On your arrival at Fernando Po, and assuming command of
the "Pleiad," which vessel will be delivered to you there by
Captain Johnston, who takes her out, you will receive your
provisions, stores, and cargo—shipped per "Bacchante"—
together with the two 50-feet canoes. These canoes and the
consular boat are to be towed by the "Pleiad" to the main
branch of the Niger, and up that stream when needful; you
are to load them with coal and such parts of the cargo of the
"Pleiad" as you may deem best, taking care to leave Fernando
Po with twenty days' coal of twelve hours for your engines,
which, if no accident occur, should carry you to the limit of
navigation in the Chadda. The departure from Fernando Po
must be as soon after the 1st July as possible.

The Admiralty Charts of the main branch of the Niger, the
accounts of former ascents, and the presence of Captain Bee-

croft, will be sufficient guides to you in the ascent of the river from the sea.

You will proceed as rapidly as possible from the mouth of the river to the confluence of the Niger and Chadda, where you will leave one or both of your 50-feet boats, in charge of such of your supercargoes as you may think fit, and proceed without delay up the Chadda, making every exertion to reach "Yola," the capital of Adamowa. This, either in the "Pleiad" or the boats, ought to be done before the 1st of September.

In your ascent of the river, in order to secure a safe return to the sea, in case of the loss of the "Pleiad," trade of some sort must be carried on with every large town, and at the two great market-places below the Confluence, and you will use your discretion either to push on with the steamer, or to leave one of the trade-boats to follow you, so as to keep up your mercantile character with the natives.

In the extreme case of the loss of your vessel on any of the numerous rocks and banks of both rivers, the consular boat and two trade-boats will ensure you a safe return to the sea, and I will move the Lords of the Admiralty to order the mail-packets to call off the river every voyage.

On your return down the Chadda, if the river Niger is still rising, it will depend on the state of your ship and crew, and the wishes of the Government officer, declared in writing, whether you ascend that stream to Rabbah or beyond it.

Before leaving for the coast you will offer to leave in charge of any of your supercargoes, who shall volunteer for the service, both the trade-boats and what merchandise you have left, to remain in the river until the next season—say July, 1855—and you will leave with them a sufficient crew for both boats.

On your arrival at Fernando Po you will take passages for yourself and the Government passengers in the first contract-packet for England, sending the "Pleiad" home under canvass in charge of a suitable officer.

    (Signed) MACGREGOR LAIRD.

LIST OF EUROPEANS ON BOARD THE PLEIAD.

William Balfour Baikie, M.D.,	in charge of the expedition.
Daniel John May,	Second Master, R.N.
John T. Dalton,	Zoological Assistant.

Thomas C. Taylor,	Sailing-master and Supercargo.
Thomas J. Hutchinson,	Surgeon and Supercargo.
John Harcus,	Chief-mate.
John Kirkpatrick,	Second-mate.
Charles Johnson (a Prussian),	Third-mate.
William Guthrie,	Chief-Engineer.
Richard Gower,	Second-Engineer.
Samuel R. Crawford,	Supercargo.
John J. Elvege,	Steward.

Europeans   12
Persons of Colour 54

Total 66

A slight numerical error has crept into the text at page 30.

To do proper justice to the share taken by Mr. May in the proceedings of the expedition, and the assistance he constantly rendered, I think it right to publish the official certificate given to him on his return to England:—

"It affords me more than ordinary satisfaction to testify to the general conduct of Mr. D. J. May during the late exploring voyage up the rivers Kwóra and Tsádda, and to the great assistance he afforded in carrying out the designs of the expedition. Mr. May had been serving on the coast of Africa for three years previously in H.M.S. "Crane," but hearing, on the arrival of the "Pleiad" at Fernando Po in June last, that the numbers of the Government party were much reduced, he at once volunteered his services, and from the excellent character given him by his commanding officer, was at once entrusted with the superintendence of the surveying duties.

"From the very limited period during which our explorations could be carried on, there was necessarily the closest application required. The labour of laying down, within four months, 700 miles of river, with careful soundings, besides inspecting tributary branches, examining innumerable islands, taking constant observations for latitude, longitude, and variation of the compass, frequently re-rating chronometers, &c., in a tropical climate, can hardly be understood except by those who have shared or witnessed such exertions.

"Whenever I required help of any kind, I had invariably a most willing and able assistant in Mr. May, who most readily undertook to aid in any branch of enquiry. His intimate acquaintance with and love for nautical astronomy and the other scientific branches of his profession, peculiarly fitted him for that most important division of our pursuits to which he more particularly devoted himself.

"His charts, the results of his labours, with his work-book, showing the observations and other *data* on which our geographical positions are based, being now in the Admiralty, will at once show that in what I have now written I have done but scant justice to his diligence, his perseverance, and his acquirements.

(Signed) "W. B. B."

"LONDON, *April 5,* 1854."

The following letter, which, at the conclusion of the voyage, I felt it my duty to address to Mr. Crowther, has already, with the exception of one paragraph, been published with that gentleman's journal, but his characteristic and modest reply has not been printed :—

CLARENCE, *November* 28, 1854.

MY DEAR MR. CROWTHER,—After having been together for upwards of four months, closely engaged in exploring Central Africa, I cannot allow you to depart without expressing to you, in the warmest manner, the pleasure I derived from your company, and acknowledging the information I have reaped from you.

Your long and intimate acquaintance with native tribes, with your general knowledge of their customs, peculiarly fit you for a journey such as we have now returned from, and I cannot but feel that your advice was always readily granted to me, nor had I ever the smallest reason to repent having followed it. It is nothing more than a simple fact, that no slight portion of the success we met with in our intercourse with the tribes is due to you.

Our voyage has providentially terminated so far favourably and without loss of life. As to the unhappy differences which existed on board the "Pleiad," I can only say, I regret deeply the constant part I was obliged to take in them. I need not further allude to them; they must frequently have disturbed your comfort, and the very remembrance of them must be unpleasant.

You are now about to return to the scene of your past labours, and to resume your share of the work for civilizing and regenerating a vast territory. That your labours may continue to meet with success, and that you may be spared to see your exertions bearing good fruit, is the sincere wish of

Yours, very faithfully,
WM. BALFOUR BAIKIE.

THE REV. SAMUEL CROWTHER.

THE REV. S. CROWTHER TO DR. BAIKIE.

CLARENCE, FERNANDO PO, *November* 28, 1854.

MY DEAR SIR,—I have received your kind letter of this day's date, and I thank you very much for the sentiment therein expressed.

I have always thought, and do think the same still, that the praise and honour of the success which has attended the expedition to explore the Tshádda, and which you had the honour to head, on the part of Government, is due to God, who has thus mercifully preserved the health of all the Europeans therein engaged, in so singular a manner; and in the enjoyment of such health, nothing could deter you from carrying out the wishes of Government in that noble object.

May we be led from this to resign ourselves to God's all-wise disposal, who can continue or dispense with our services, as seems good in his sight.

(Signed) SAM. CROWTHER.

The following correspondence took place at Fernando Po on the removal of the various instruments from the "Pleiad," preparatory to their being sent by the mail-packet to England:—

No. 1.

MR. T. C. TAYLOR TO DR. BAIKIE.

S. S. Pleiad, Clarence Cove, *November* 10, 1854.

Sir,—Seeing that Mr. May has removed the chronometers from the "Pleiad" this morning, I beg to say that, although I have no writing concerning them, I consider the fact of its having been arranged between Mr. Laird and the Admiralty, for them to come out in the vessel, implies that they should also return in her. And I hereby inform you, that the vessel will be disabled, unless supplied with at least two of them, with an authenticated certificate of their error and rate.

(Signed)   Thos. C. Taylor.

Dr. Baikie, R.N.

No. 2.

DR. BAIKIE TO MR. TAYLOR.

Clarence, *November* 10, 1854.

Sir,—In consequence of your representation to me, of this morning's date, of the inefficiency of the screw-steamer "Pleiad," from the want of a chronometer for the navigation of the ship to England, I have to inform you that I will take upon myself the responsibility of supplying you, for that purpose, with one of the Admiralty chronometers in my charge.

One chronometer is the number usually supplied to her Majesty's ships and vessels of war of a much larger size than the "Pleiad," and is esteemed better than two.

The instrument with which I intend to supply you is "Young, 110," which will be delivered to you, or to a careful messenger, by Mr. May, who will take a receipt for the same.

The error and rate of this instrument, determined in a comparatively doubtful locality, and under very disadvantageous circumstances, cannot be nearly so correct or so satisfactory to yourself as those which you will have ample time and opportunity for ascertaining before the "Pleiad" can leave this port.

(Signed)   W. B. B.

MR. T. C. TAYLOR.

No. 3.

MR. TAYLOR TO DR. BAIKIE.

S. S. PLEIAD, FERNANDO PO, *November* 10, 1854.

SIR,—I have to acknowledge your letter of this date respecting the chronometers, and beg to say I am so busy just now winding up the affairs of the expedition, and making arrangements for getting the "Pleiad" to England, that it is very little time I could spare to finding the error and rate of a chronometer; but if Mr. May could spare time, and would take the trouble to do it for me, it would oblige me; and if not, he will please to let me have the present error and rate, so far as he knows it, with which whosoever I take as sailing-master of the "Pleiad" home must do as well as he can.

(Signed)   THOS. C. TAYLOR.

DR. BAIKIE, R.N.

The "Pleiad" did not leave Fernando Po for England until the 29th of November.

The following document may be looked on as a diplomatic curiosity. The original, from which I copied this, is in the possession of King Pepple, and it contains the terms of a treaty made between the people of Bonny and of Andóni, between whom a fierce and bloody war was waged about ten years ago:—

(COPY.)

TREATY BETWEEN KING PEPPLE OF BONNY AND THE CHIEFS OF ANDONY.

From the date of this document the natives of Andony shall be considered as subjects of King Pepple, and shall be entitled to the same rights and privileges as the Bonny men.

2nd. The Andony men bind themselves not to have any communication whatever with Young Calabar or Creeka country; if on the contrary such communication is held, the person or persons so offending shall be subject to such punishment as King Pepple shall choose to inflict. But should Young Calabar or Creeka men bring provisions to Andony for sale, the Andony men shall be allowed to buy the same; but under no circumstances or pretence whatever shall Young Calabar or Creeka men *retail* spirits in the Andony.

3rd. No marriages between Andony, Young Calabar, and Creeka country will be allowed.

4th. When the Andony men make their great Jewjew, the natives of Bonny promise to give them hip-cloths, caps, rum, &c.; and when the Andony men come to receive the above, they promise to present the Bonny men with some dried fish.

5th. The Andony men further promise, that when desired by the King of Bonny to catch fish for the public feasts, they will do it.

6th. They, the Andony men, also promise not to destroy the Guano, but allow the animal liberty the same as in Bonny.

7th. Should there be war between Bonny and any other power, the Andony men promise to supply war-canoes, well fitted out and ready-manned, in order to assist the Bonny men. If the Andony men should be short of canoes, guns, or ammunition, the Bonny men will supply them with the same.

Further, if any other country should in any wise molest the Andony men, the Bonny men bind themselves to interfere and act in the same manner as they would were it their own country.

8th. Each party,—viz., the Andony and Bonny men,—

mutually agree and bind themselves, that for the future they will not eat human flesh.

9th. The Andony men also promise to supply Bonny canoes with men to assist in pulling to the fair.

10th. That in case of any dispute arising between any two parties, natives of Andony, King Pepple is to be informed of the same, and that he (the King) will send a competent person (without charge) to settle the matter.

11th. The Andony men bind themselves to pay Jewjew Guano 800 manillas.

12th. Should the Andony men kill any elephants, they are to present the teeth thereof to King Pepple; and should the Andony men at any time be short of muskets or powder, King Pepple will supply them.

13th. In case of any shipwrecks, and should any white men, under whatever circumstances, get into the power of the Andony men, they (the Andony men) are immediately to transfer them over to King Pepple without injury.

SIGNATURES (ANDONY)   SIGNATURES (BONNY).

Chiefs' Names.	Towns.		
Oto Aboloocana	} Aganda.	*Pepple*	*Rey*
Breya		Anna Pepple	his **X** mark.
Aberedam	} Ungo.	Manilla Pepple	do.
Eborilla		Jack Brown	do.
Obalacoo	Aperama.	Amatacca or Dappa	do.
Soocoo	Ereyama.	Allison	do.
Amaberaa	} Corro.	Captain Hart	do.
Atrongballa		Black Foobra	do.
Eparacong	Ayangala.	Jewjew Tiger	do.
Ooroonee	} Egoolé.	John Africa	do.
Inkie		William Pepple	do.
Ayaga	} Allabea.	Jewjew Telefar	do.
Acacca		Indian Queen	do.
Enutto	} Elletoombé.	Tom-Tom	do.
Obolum			
Ecreequebo	Okenda.		

The forenamed chiefs have sent representatives, whose marks are affixed below, to ratify to the above-named treaty:—

APPENDIX.

Representatives' Names.

Otebong	his **X** mark.	Egoo	his **X** mark.
Sanga	do.	Ogbolotoo	do.
Amabarra	do.		

Witnesses.

John Angus Ward,	Princess Royal.
Chas. Calvert,	William Batsford.
Wm. Kelly,	Huskison.
G. W. S. Witt,	Swiftsure.
G. W. W. Bond,	Fanny.
Wm. Owens,	B. Packet.
Arthur J. P. Cutting,	
Peter Jacobson,	Warwick.

Dated this 22nd December, 1846, in the Jewjew House, or Parliament House, Grand Bonny.

B.

In the various districts on the Delta of the Kwóra, in Yóruba, Bíni, I'gbo, Igára, I'gbira, Núpe, and the Háusa and Púlo countries, the principal currency consists of cowries. These are almost all originally exported from England, and vary in price according to the supply and demand. They are sold in bulk, the average price being from about 4*l.* 4*s.* to 5*l.* 5*s.* a cwt. Their equivalent in English money in Africa ranges from a shilling to a dollar a thousand, the average being from 1*s.* 6*d.* to 2*s.* Attempts are being made by the missionaries in the Yóruba countries to introduce dollars as a medium of exchange, which would be a vast improvement. I have at pp. 114 and 220 alluded to two forms of iron money which we met with. This currency, far from being of recent introduction, is most probably of indigenous origin, and certainly anterior to the employment of cowries. I find the following notices regarding an analogous form:—

"In *Moko* they have Coin'd Money, made of Iron in the form of a Roach, the Rundle as big as the Palm of a Hand, with a Handle about an Inch long."—*Ogilby's Africa*, fol., 1670, p. 482.

"The money of *Moko* is of iron, in the shape and figure of a thornback, flat and as broad as the palm of the hand, having a tail of the same metal, of the length of the hand."—*Barbot's Description of the Coasts of South Guinea*, in *Churchill's Collection of Voyages and Travels*, 1732, vol. v. p. 380.

The various media of exchange now established in the trading rivers in the Bights, as brass-rods at Old Kalabar, and manillas at Bonny, have been introduced by European commerce. The use of cowries extends far into the interior, reaching even to Timbuktú. The coined money along the coast is to a great extent English, but other forms are also commonly met with, principally French five-franc pieces and Spanish doubloons and dollars; the rate of exchange of the latter varying from 4*s*. to 4*s*. 4*d*. In 1854-5 coin was so scarce, that along the Gold-Coast the chief circulating medium was gold-dust, and, of course, in weighing and transferring small quantities, considerable loss was incurred.

C.

In reducing previously unwritten languages,—under which category have been included, until very lately, nearly all African tongues,—great difficulty has been experienced from the want of a uniform system of orthography, and much confusion has thereby been caused. Until a very recent date, each writer transcribed words in accordance with the genius of his own language, or to agree with some pet phonetic theory, and thus his labours were often comparatively unintelligible to scholars belonging to other nations. In endeavouring to introduce alphabetical writing, the great aim should be to employ a system which assigns one simple power to each letter, and which represents similar sounds and combinations of sounds by the same letters. English philologists ought to remember, that when so engaged they should not write merely for their own countrymen, but that their transcripts should be able to be read and to be *pronounced* easily by continental students, whether French, Italian, or German. A few years ago several of the Foreign Missionary Societies having experienced the evil results of such discrepancies, proposed the adoption of a uniform standard, to comprehend all such vocal sounds as were then known among African tribes, or such as were likely to occur. The system then determined on has, with some improvements, been pursued ever since, and has been productive of the best results. At present the plan almost universally in use is that of Professor Lepsius of Berlin, with a few modifications, it being the most comprehensive and the most philosophical yet proposed.

The following is, therefore, the alphabet which I have employed, and which is the one recommended by the Church Missionary Society. In it the vowels are used with the powers given to them by the Italians—examples of their sounds being added in English words :—

VOWELS.

i	as in	*ravine.*		*o̦*	as in	*saw.*
i̦	,,	*it.*		*ǫ*	,,	*König* (German), or *peu* (French).
e	,,	*prey.*				
e̦	,,	*affect.*		*u*	,,	*foot.*
a	,,	*cat.*		*u̦*	,,	*güte* (German), or *une* (French).
a̦	,,	*but.*				
o	,,	*dome.*				

DIPHTHONGS.

ai as in *tide.* | *au* as in *now.* | *oi* as in *noise.*

CONSONANTS.

b	as in	*bay.*		*p*	as in	*pan.*
d	,,	*den.*		*r*	,,	*run.*
f	,,	*fan.*		*s*	,,	*sun.*
g	,,	*got.*		*ș*	,,	*she.*
h	,,	*hot.*		*t*	,,	*tan.*
ḵ	,,	*loch* (Scotch).		*ț*	,,	*thin.*
j	,,	*join.*		*d̦*	,,	*that.*
k	,,	*keep.*		*v*	,,	*vail.*
l	,,	*let.*		*w*	,,	*will.*
m	,,	*man.*		*y*	,,	*yet.*
n	,,	*not.*		*z*	,,	*amaze* or *noise.*
ṇ	,,	*English* (nasal).				

APPENDIX. 419

DOUBLE CONSONANTS.

ts like the German *z*.
dz is a modified *ts*.
gb is a hard sound of *b*, found in many African languages.

kp is the hard co-relative of *gb*.
c is always expressed by *s* or *k*.
q   ,,   ,,   ,, *kw*.
x   ,,   ,,   ,, *ks*.

THE LANGUAGES OF THE COUNTRIES BORDERING ON THE KWO'RA AND BÍNUE.

To the westward of the Rio Formoso the language spoken is the Ijebú dialect of Yóruba, while more inland, towards the north-east, is found the Bíni (Benin) tongue. From the Rio Formoso to the Nun, including all the western portion of the Delta, the natives speak Orú or Ejó, and to the westward of Abó a distinct dialect is used, namely the Sóbo. Nímbe or Brass is very nearly related to the Orú, and I believe that from the Brass River to the New Kalabár, the natives dwelling on the banks of each of the intervening rivers all talk differently. At the Sombréiro I know positively that this is the case, but here the dialect closely approaches that of New Kalabár. Between the last-mentioned place and Ebáne or Bonny there are well-marked differences, and I have been told that the language spoken in the intervening district of Okríka is distinct from either, while beyond Okúloma a fresh language is to be found at Andǫ́ni. Along both sides of the mouth of the Old Kalabár the Kwá language will, I believe, be found prevalent, but about fifty miles up this river, around Duke-Town, Old Town, and Creek Town, it is replaced by E'fik. From Old Kalabár to the Cameroons little, if anything, is known of the languages, but that spoken up this latter river is the Diwálla.

Ascending the Kwóra, from the mouth of Wári affluent to the borders of Igára, the languages on either side are dialects of I'gbo, namely Abó, Isuáma, and E'lugu. Beyond this to the eastward we find Igára, which is related to the Yóruba, while opposite to Iddá Bíni is spoken. The people of I'gbira-Síma do not quite reach the river, and beyond them on the right bank are heard Bonú, Bássa, and Ishábe. Núpe, though well known, does not properly reach so far down as the Confluence.

On entering the Bínue, on the right side is heard the I'gbira-Pánda dialect of I'gbira, which also prevails in Igbégbe and in the various I'gbira settlements along the southern shore. Further up, to the northward, are the Bása and Dóma languages, and on the south the Mítshi. In Báutshi and Hamarúwa, Háusa is always spoken, though Púlo is also understood by many. In Korórofa and among the Báibai to the eastward, the language comprises different forms of Djúku.

The lower part of the Kwóra and the Bínue, though they do not form quite an absolute barrier, yet constitute a well-marked line of distinction between the tribes living on the opposite sides. Those to the eastward and southward are in most respects closely allied to the South African races, while to the westward and northward the resemblances are much less marked, and intermixture with more northern tribes and with Arabs show themselves. All the coast dialects from Orú to Old Kalabár, are either directly or indirectly connected with I'gbo, which latter Dr. Latham informs me is certainly related to the Káfir class, and I have but little doubt that, when critically examined, Mítshi and Djúku will prove to be members of the same extensive family.

With regard to other tongues, Igára, I'gbira, and Kakánda are all related to the Yóruba, which, though not the centre of a distinct group, yet may be regarded as forming what would be termed in natural history, a sub-family. Bása is connected both with Yóruba and Núpe, and the affinities of Háusa and of Púlo, though not entirely distinctive, yet show them to be very considerably removed from the true South African type.

I'GBO WORDS.

Éso	King (Abó).	Orísa	God the Creator (Abó).
óko	fire.		
mó	spirit.	Tshúku-okéke	God the Creator (Isuáma).
ókomo	hell.		
nólu	heaven.	Ófu	an image.
úti	a grave.	Ófum	my image.
Tshúku	the Deity.	Tshúkum	my God.

APPENDIX. 421

Ófu Tshúku	God's image.	eríse-náo	he cuts on both sides.
Ọ́mo Tshúku	God's children.	móma Tshúku	angel.
mọ́ ndjọ́, or	⎱ a demon, an evil	tshí	soul.
mọ̀ djó	⎰ spirit, or the devil.	anyámwo	sun.
Kamállo	Satan?	ómwa	moon.
Igwik	⎧ one who lived above ⎨ before coming ⎩ down.	akpopándo or bankpódo	⎱ star.
		ágega	north.
álla	ground.	ágega-káni	south.
Igwikálla	⎰ the name of an evil ⎱ spirit.	ezínhir-anyámwo	east.
		ogwéri	west.
máwo	⎧ a country fashion ⎨ for raising an ⎩ evil spirit.	mínyi	rain or water.
		mínyi edó	rain comes.
		uféri	⎱ wind.
ọ́mo	child or children.	uwhéri (Ọzuzu)	
né	mother.	tshiabatshána	light.
néin	my mother.	itriába	darkness.
ótutu	morning.	menínu (Ọzuzu)	sea, i.e. salt water.
djí	yam.	osímori	river or great water.
ágba	pig.	imú or ií	lake.
ágba-ézhi	pig's jaw.	ebeigwe or ebélu	thunder.
óno	cloth, baff.	amúm-ígwi	lightning.
zhí	blue, black.	égrugu	rainbow.
osí, odjí (Isuáma)	blue, black.	igrígi or idrígi	dew.
úndji	dark	amúm	⎰ smoke, used thus,
óno-zhí	blue baff.		⎱ amúm-ọ́kọ
akwásha	white baff.	elúgwe	cloud.
únyi	charcoal.	enyúnyo	shadow.
ókri	a wedder goat.	ndó	shade.
íhe	thing or something.	ógro	fog, mist.
ókwa	a wooden basin.	ohó mínyi	spring of water.
ógbo	a calabash.	ólili	⎱ well of water.
ítshi	cut-face.	ólulu (Ọzuzu)	
keín	mine.	mbá	country.

English.	E'lugu.	Isuáma.	Abó.
how do ye do? (salutation)	⎱ mamáo	mamáo	ná.
cock	okógba	okógba	ókpa.
cockcrow	okógba-'mbó	okógba-'mbó	ókpa-íbe.
daylight	tshí-'nwhó or tshí abóa	do.	do.
sunrise	anyámwo-aftána	ámo-awá	ámo-awá.
mid-day	etite-ehínhe	do.	do.
sunset	tshí-fíle	tshí-fíle	ámo-adó.
evening	anyás	do.	do.
night	tshí-djí	tshí-djí	utshís.
day	ehínhe or tshí *	do.	do.

* Both are equally correct.

APPENDIX.

English.	Igbo.	Ebáne.	New Kalabar.	Nímbe.	Orú.
water	mínyi	míngi	mínzi or mínji	míndi or mígi	mégi.
fire	óko	féne		féndi	fíni.
firewood	únyi			fíngia	féndia.
God	Orísa	Támono *		Orísa	Orísa.
idol	djú-dju	djú-dju		ówu,	ówu.
house	úlo	wári		wále	wále.
mat	úte	bíle		úte	úte.

The comparisons of these words shew tolerably the relations of the above dialects with the I'gbo.

The following numbers were given to Mr. Crowther and myself by King Peppel; as they were very carefully taken down, they may be considered as tolerably authentic.

English.	Ebáne.	I'gbo.
one	ngé	óte.
two	nmé	ábo.
three	tére	áto.
four	éni	áwo.
five	sónna	ése.
six	súniu	isín.
seven	soniáma	ása.
eight	ínine	asáto.
nine	esóni	tóili.
ten	atí and oyí	íri.

A'ti is used for "ten" in counting up or in reckoning, but when it is employed to designate a specific number, as "ten men," oyí is selected. These numbers of King Peppel's correspond pretty closely with those given by Koelle. The I'gbo numbers all belong to the Isuáma dialect, except tóili, which appears to resemble that of A'ro. For "thirty-six," Bonny people say "forty without four."

English.	Háusa.	Púlo.
cockcrow	asubá	fajíri.
daybreak	dasáfe	
about 8 A.M.	anthín	lúha, wóluha.
noon	rána-sáka	náge-tsháka.
about 2 P.M.	azahár	zúra.
,, 4 ,,	la úser	alazára.
sunset	almurú	magáriba.
about 8 P.M.	lísha	esháí.

* This seems to correspond with Orisa rather than with Tshúku.

APPENDIX. 423

The following was given to me by Mr. Crowther as the best division of the dialects of Yóruba.

1. Yóruba, including Ífe.
2. Égba.
3. Ijebú.
4. Ijésha, including Yágba. (This might go with No. 2.)
5. Óta.
6. Kétu, spoken on the borders of Dahómi.
7. Igbóma, near Núpe.

The purest Yóruba is spoken by the Muhammadans of Ilọ́rin. The dialect of Lagos is very impure. Abbeokúta is E'gba.

DIALECTS OF HÁUSA.

1. Katshína, the purest and best.
2. Káno.
3. Gobír.
4. Dáura.
5. Zámfara.
6. Zúzu.
7. Biránta Góbaz.
8. Kábi.
9. Shíra or Shúra.

Specimens of the Mítshi, and of the Dóma or Arago languages have been published in the Appendix to Crowther's Journal.

BAIÓN WORDS.

The following, which have also been published by Dr. Latham, in the "Proceedings of the Philological Society," I procured from a man a native of Baión, whom I met at Clarence.

one	ntshí.	seventeen	tshabsámba.
two	iba.	eighteen	tshámfam.
three	ité.	nineteen	tshúbu.
four	íkwa.	twenty	gúmba.
five	íta.	one hundred	{ ikúmbo or nkúmbo.
six	ntówa or ntóko.		
seven	sámba.	a thousand	ndúmbo.
eight	fám or mfám.	God	nsi.
nine	bú or mbú.	man	múla.
ten	wúm.	woman	múngwe.
eleven	tshámtshi.	boy	món.
twelve	tshákpa.	girl	gongói.
thirteen	tshúpte.	father	taiám.
fourteen	tshámkwa.	mother	máwa.
fifteen	tshábta.	head	tú.
sixteen	tshamtóko.	eye	djigedá.

APPENDIX.

hair	nú.	sword	nyí.
mouth	ntshú.	bow	ntshét.
nose	ntshadína.	arrow	ṇkóṇtshet.
ear	tokodjám.	hat	tshátu.
arm	bú.	cloth	ndí.
hand	léṇbo.	river	montshíṇkọ.
finger	ofúmbo.	town	lá.
thumb	melógwa.	road	mándji.
leg	démku.	mountain	kokolónji.
foot	ntshéku.	rain	béṇ.
King	mfóṇ.	wind	fulmbú.
master	tawón.	thunder	mfámbe.
slave	nkwám.	lightning	ndjím.
house	ndá.	good	bónke.
war	bí.	bad	kalóṇ.
salt	ngwá.	hungry	ndjí.
water	ntshí.	thirsty	faminyú mákwe?
bread	ntshán.	tired	mafúm.
fish	ntshá.	tree	gúm.
bird	mọsín.	white	efúko.
fowl	ngú.	black or blue	súe.
goat	mbí.	red	ibáṇ.
wood	nkwí.	yes	nụ́.
spear	nkón.	no	gáṇya.

On comparing these words with Koelle's Báyọṇ specimens in the "Polyglotta Africanæ," there can be no doubt of their belonging to one common language, but representing different dialects.

BÁTÍ WORDS.

The following I procured also at Fernando Po from a Báti man, through a Baióṇ interpreter. The number of words is very few, but I only saw the man for a quarter of an hour before I left the place, and I had barely time to secure and correct what are here given.

one	bankále.	nine	bantámba.
two	basámgu.	ten	bambánta.
three	báshit.	eleven	baliṇsa.
four	bangúbia.	twelve	bánjiwo.
five	badumbóṇsọṇ.	thirteen	balamfénsọ.
six	bandóṇ.	fourteen	bánkit.
seven	bándo.	fifteen	banwúrkam.
eight	bafúlim.	sixteen	búkwa.

APPENDIX. 425

seventeen	búngola.	*sun*	nyó.
eighteen	bága.	*moon*	ndjémtshi.
nineteen	bába.	*river*	mónki ntshí.
twenty	bámandjo.	*house*	ndáp.
God	minbúa.	*water*	fawánkí.
father	téia.	*yam*	kó.
mother	má.		

These numerals must at once strike as being peculiar and elaborate, but I am certain of their being correct. A few of the words resemble the Baióṇ, which is very probable, as Báti and Baióṇ border on each other. Under the head of Báyoṇ, Koelle gives a Páti dialect, which, however, does *not* at all correspond with what are given above. In Petermann's Atlas it is said that the Báti people are white; but this is erroneous, as the man I saw had a very black skin, and he told me all his countrymen were the same.

D.

A fertile source of confusion and difficulty has arisen from different travellers and writers having described the same place or the same tribe by various appellatives, which, to the reader not previously versed in African geography, must be productive of endless trouble and mystery. Thus the Púlo race is known in Bornú as Fuláta, and in Háusa as Fuláni; English writers often style them Fúlo, and the French call them Peul. The town of Lagos is by the natives known as E'ko, and by the Portuguese as Onín; and Abó is variously entitled Eboe, Abé, Opú and Abo 'ntá. To endeavour to clear up these points, I have drawn up, partly from my own enquiries, partly from such authorities as have been within my reach, the following lists of synonymes, which catalogue the various names given to the same spot or race by different people, and also the numerous designations employed by travellers to denote the same place. I have been careful to distinguish native and original names; and I trust the lists, which are necessarily rather long, may assist the researches of geographers and philologists.

The Kwóra or Niger is known at different parts of its course by many distinct names, but the meaning of the greater number appears to be "great river." It is very difficult to select from these one general one, but perhaps Kwóra is the most advisable, as being more generally known. The spelling I have adopted is that which accords most closely with the pronunciation I heard from the natives, and it likewise corresponds best with its derivation, which is either from the Kanúri word *Kúra*, pl. *wúra*, signifying "great," or else from its flowing through a district named *Kúra*. It is sometimes styled Kwóra-bá, but chiefly among Muhammadan tribes, most of whom have a smattering of Arabic, the word *ba* being the Arabic *bahr*, sea or river, as *Bahr el abiad*, the White Nile. For convenience sake I have divided the river into two portions, the one above the Confluence of the Bínue, and the the other from the Confluence to the sea.

The Kwóra (below the Confluence) is called—

Osímini, Osímini, Osímiri, Osímiri,	} in Abó and Orú.	Ujímini,	in Igára.
		Quórra,	„ Allen's Chart.
Anyím,	in some parts of Ígbo.	Akássa-tǫ́rǫ,	„ Nímbe.
Úzie,	„ Sóbo.		

The mouth is known as the Nun, Non, or First Brass River.

The Kwóra (above the Confluence) is called—

Nigeir (Νίγειρ),	by Ptolemy.	Joliba,	by Park.
Niger,	by ancient writers.	Dhioliba,	{ by De Caillie and Jomard.
Nile of the Negroes,	by Edrisi.		
Quórra, Quólla, Kowára, Kewára, Kowára-ba,	} by modern writers and travellers.	Tembie *and* Bâ,	by Jomard.
		Dsene,	in Timbuktú.
		Óya *and* Odóya,	„ Yóruba.
Couara,	by Jomard.	Fúrodi,	„ Núpe.
Guliba 'n Kowara, Fári 'n rúa,	} in Háusa.	F̨du,	in Bássa *and* Bonú.
		Ehulobá,	in Ígbira.
Dsélba,	„ Bambara.	Ujímini fúfu,	„ Igára.
Dsóriba,	„ Geriwa.	Koara *and* Ghulby,	by Dupuis.
Bahr Sudán,	„ the Arabs.		

The Bínue is called—

Benueh *and* Chadda-Benueh,	} by Petermann.	Dsáde,	by Koelle.
Tshádda (Tsádda),	„ Lander.	Tchadda, Chadda,	{ „ Allen and Oldfield.

APPENDIX. 427

Shary,	by Laird.	Ilihú, Irihú, Lihú,	} in Ígbira.
Shadderbah,	„ Macqueen.	Ehulogi,	
Etshi,	in Bonú.	Nú,	„ Korórofa.
Fároji,	„ Núpe.	Ujimini dúdu,	„ Igára.
Báki 'n rúa,	„ Háusa.	Chadee *and* Shady, by Dupuis.	

I never could hear the name Zanfira mentioned by Barth.

Mouths of the Kwóra.

1. Rio Formoso,
   Benin River.
2. Rio dos Escravos, Esclavos, Escrados, Escardos, El Bróder, Brodero, Bródi, Slaves River.
3. Rio dos Forcados, Galley-Slaves River.
4. Rio Ramos, Bough River.
5. Rio Dodo.
6. Pennington River.
7. Middleton River.
8. Winstanley Outfalls.
9. Sengána *or* Segma, Angána.
10. Rio Nun *or* Non, First Brass River.
11. Brass River *or* Second Brass River, St. John, Rio Bento, Malfonsa, Oddy, Fonsoady.
12. Rio di San Nicolas, Rio di Filana *or* Tilana, Rio di Juan Diaz, Sempta *or* Leupta.
13. Rio di Santa Barbara, Rio Meas.
14. Rio di San Bartolomeo, Rio dos tres Irmãos *or* Jermaus.
15. Rio Sombreiro, Sambreiro, Sombrero.
16. New Kalabár, Kalebar, *or* Calabar, New Calbary or Calebare, Calbarine, Rio Real.
17. Bonny, Bani, Bandy.
18. Andóni, Andoney, Rio di San Domingo, Loitomba *or* Laitomba.
19. Kantóro, Rio di Conde, Rio San Pedro.

The Old Kalabár is also called—

Old Calebare or Calabar, Old Kalborgh and Oude Calborgh.

Púlo (pl. Púlbe) is called—

Fuláni, Filáni, Fuládsi, in Háusa.		Tebáre,	in Ndób or Burúkem.
Fúlani, Fílani,	„ Yóruba.	Tíbār,	„ Bálu.
Fuláta, Filáta,	„ Bornú.	Agói *and* Gói,	„ Dsúmu *and* Ébe.
Angóye, Angbóye,	„ Ígbira.	Poula *and* Fula,	by Clark.
Silmíra,	„ Móre.	Foulahs, Foules, Poules, by Mollien.	
Kambumána,	„ Gurép.	Fulahs, Peuls,	by Golberry.
Tebále & Gáyi, in Bákum, Baióṇ, &c.		Falitahs,	„ Lauder.
Abáte,	in Korórofa.	Fullans,	„ Richardson.
Futo,	„ Dsáham.	Foolāh *and* Felarney	„ Oldfield.
Búle,	„ Mfút.	Falatíya *and* Felatah	„ Prichard.
Adínyi,	„ Bórītsu.	Fallatah	„ Macqueen.

APPENDIX.

The following list of states under Púlo rule applies only to the Western Púlbe, or to those countries which are tributary to Sókoto. It is correct so far as it goes, but I cannot say whether it is quite complete, most probably not quite so.

Katshína,	Shíra,	Márma,
Káno,	Katagúm,	Dóma,
Zánfara,	Boberú,	Korórofa (*part*),
Dáura,	Hamarúwa,	Núpe?
Zózo,	Adamáwa,	Yäúri?
Báutshi,	Hadéja,	Búsa?
Mesáu,		

Háusa is one of the divisions of Arab geographers, and originally its extent was much more limited than at present, when it is held to comprehend all countries where the Háusa tongue is spoken, namely :—

Katshína,	Marádi,	Dáura,
Káno,	Báutshi,	Zózo,
Gobír,	Zánfara,	Zína.

Háusa is called—

Abákpa,	{ in Igára, Ígbira, and Dóma.	Afúno,	in Bornú.
		Habédso,	by the Púlbe.
Amógba,	„ Korórofa.	Abebére,	in Kóro.
Mbágba,	„ Mítshi and Borítsu.	Pára,	„ Dṣáham.
Zangwáda,	„ Gureṇ.	Óza,	„ Yasgúa.
Asíndṣi,	„ Kiámba.	Houssa, Housa, }	by various
Kéndṣi,	„ Ébe.	Howssa, }	writers.
Adṣébi,	„ Goúli.	Haoussa,	„ Macqueen.
Abúno,	„ Kánem.		

The early Arab geographers divided Central Africa into various regions, some of them defined in a more or less arbitrary manner; but as many of their designations are still retained, it is of some importance to be able to recognize them, with their varied orthographical forms and synonymes. Some of these countries, as Háusa, have in modern times greatly expanded; others, as Takrúr, have contracted; and a few, like Ghána, have nearly disappeared. With these are associated certain other names introduced by the modern Muhammadans, of which the following are the principal:

APPENDIX. 429

Ghána, Ghánah,	Tocrúr.
Ghánat, Ghanáta,	Filláni, Fillany.
Gualáta? Waláta?	Marroa.
Magharáwa, Maghráwah,	Háusa, Houssa,
Magraoa,	Haoussa, Haowssa,
Magaraoa, Magaráua,	Afnu.
Magraua, Magaraba,	Bámbara.
Magarawa, Machurebii.	Ungúra,
Inkizár,	Oonghór, Oongóoroo,
Kissour?	Guángara, Gángara,
Kúku, Kaukau,	Owencára, Vancára,
Kágho, Gágo,	Ougornou.
Kúghah, Kárkar,	Kánem.
Cochia, Cáuga?	Yémyem,*
Kóuka, Ghow,	Lémlem, Lámlem,
Gáro.	Nyémnyem, N'yémn'yem,
Kúra.	Rémrem, Démdem,
Dámlu, Dámloo.	Al-Límiyin, N'yúmnyum,
Mali, Meli,	Gnúmgnum, Námnam,
Meli, Melli, Maly.	Temiam?
Gunjá, Ghunjáh.	Wángara, Wánkara.
Saróm.	Genéwah,
Dagómba.	Gheneoa, Ghinéa,
Intá, Intáa.	Chinóia, Génni,
Takrúr, Tekrúr,	Gúinea.
Takróur, Tak-roor,	

* Yémyem or N'yémnyem is not, strictly speaking, the name of a country, but was applied to a supposed race of cannibals, believed to live on the southern borders of Háusa. The name is now confined to a district situated between Báutshi and Bornú, or, more correctly, to its inhabitants. The "Umburm, near Jacoba," mentioned by Sultan Bello, is probably the district of Mbúla or Umbúla, east from Báutshi.

Timbuktú, or Tumbuktú, is called—

Tumbutum,	by Leo.	Tumbactu,	by Professor Lee.
Tanbaktu,	„ Ibn Batuta.	Temboctou,	„ Caillie.
Tonbaktoo,	„ Bello.	Tymboctou,	„ Jomard.
Timbuctoo,	„ Authors.	Teenbuktu,	„ Richardson.

Agádez, or Aghádez, is called—

Agdas in Sultan Bello's Map.

This place has been supposed, but on insufficient grounds, to be the A'udaghost of Edrisi, which was more probably situated to the northward of Ghána.

Ahír, Ahéer, or Aïr, is also called—

Asbén, Azbén, Asóuty, Asóuda, or Blad es-Sultán.

Ghádames, or Ghádamis, is called—

Gadamáwa in Háusa. Ghodémis by Cooley.
Ardamas by De Caillie.

Tuárik, Tawárik, Touarik, pl. Touarghee, is called—

Azgher by Richardson. Tawarák by Bello.

Sudán, Soudan, is called—

Dar Sudán } by Arabs. Soodan by Bello.
Belad el Sudan Nigritia } by older writers.
  Negroland

Imajága is called—

Kandín in Háusa. Absináwa in Bornú.

This last title is probably derived from a town named A'bsen, situated towards Agádez.

Sókoto is called—

Sackatu in Bello's Map. Soccatoo by Clapperton & Oldfield.
Sokkattoo by Sir R. Donkin. Succatou } by Richardson.
Saccatoo by Macqueen. Sakkatou

Káno or Kánu is called—

Cano by Barbot. Kanou by Richardson.
Kanoo by Bello.

Leo Africanus seems to confound this city with Ghána.

Katshíua, or Kadzína, is called—

Kátshina in Bornú. Catsheenah by Lander.
Chesona and Kasena by Leo. Kotshina and Cashna by Clark.
Kassene and Kasene ,, Ogilly. Kashna by Clapperton & Macqueen.
Cassena and Chana ,, Barbot. Kasnah ,, Bello.
Kachenah ,, Cooley. Katshna ,, Barth & Petermann.
Kásína ,, Koelle. Kassína ,, Dupuis.

Hadéja, or Hadéji, is called—

Hadega by Clapperton. Khadedsha in Petermann's Atlas.

APPENDIX. 431

Gobír is called—

Ghoobér, by Bello.
Ghouber, ,, Richardson.
Goober, ,, Macqueen.

Gobur, by Clark.
Guber ,, Petermann and Overweg.

Marádi is called—

Mariadi, by Overweg.
Maladi, by Koelle.

Gobír and Marádi are the only Háusa provinces which remain independent.

Katagúm is called—

Katakúma by Ibn S'aíd.
Caancouma, by Hamaker.

Báutshi, Báushi, or Bóshi, is called—

Bowsher, in Bello's Map.
Boushy & Beetchee, by Clapperton.
Bowchee, ,, Lander.

Jacoba district, by Clark.
Bolobolo and Bolewa, ,, Barth.

Zúzu, Zózo, or Zéze, is called—

Saria, Zaría, and Zalía, } from its chief town.
Zégzeg and Zegizégi, in Háusa.
Zágzag, by Bello.

Zára, by Clark.
Za-ri-ya, ,, Bello, (map).
Zari, ,, Clapperton.

Zína is called—

Sina, in Petermann's Atlas.

Hamarúwa is called—

Hamarrua, by Barth and Petermann.
Kúndi, by the Djúku.

Adamáwa is the

Adamowa of the maps.
Adamáa of Koelle.

Adamaua of Barth, Petermann, and Richardson.

It has also been conjectured to be the Haúdama of Ibn S'aid, but this is very doubtful.

Yákuba is the

Yacoba of Macqueen.
Yakoba ,, Richardson, &c.

Jacoba of Oldfield.

Búla, or Mbúla, is the

Umbŭla of Petermann, possibly the Umburm of Bello and the Rábúmú of Ibn S'aíd.

Bak'n dútshi of Háusa is Morinú of the Djúku.

Bundú	is the	Bundang of Petermann's Atlas.		
Kwóntsha	,, ,,	Kontsha	,,	,, ,,
Kwóna	,, ,,	Kóana	,,	,, ,,
Tángale	,, ,,	Tangare	,,	,, ,,
Bátshama	,, ,,	Batshamba ,,		,, ,,

Bagírmi is called—

Bugármi, at Hamarúwa. Ibkarem by Ibn S'aíd.
Begharmí, by Clark. Bekarmí ,, Cooley.
Bāgrmi, ,, Kölle. Baghermi ,, Macqueen.

Fumbina is the Foobena of Macqueen.

Loggóne, or Loggéne, is called—

Loggun, by Denham & Macqueen. Lókone, in Bornú. Lagun, by Richardson.

Zánfara, or Zánfira, is the

Zamfra of Clapperton. Zanfarah of Bello.
Zumfra ,, Lander. Zanfara, or Pharan, of Barbot.
Zamfari ,, Clark. Zeffra of Mohammed Masini.
Zamfara ,, Koelle.

Dáura is the

Dowry, or Dor, of Bello. Doura of Clark.
Doúla ,, Koelle.

Tsád, or Tshád, is the

Tsāde of Bornú. Shad of Macqueen.
Tsáde ,, Munio. Dsháde of Koelle.
Tchad ,, Denham. Chad and Tschad of writers.

Kanúri is the Kanowry of Clark.

Bornú is the

Burno, Borno, & Burney of Ogilby. Bino of Núpe.
Barnou of Bello. Kániki of Yóruba, Sierra Leone.
Birebíre, Balebálo of Háusa.

APPENDIX. 433

Mináu is the Manga or Minyo of Petermann's Atlas, also called Múnio.

Kuyámi is the Koyám of Petermann's Atlas.

Gándiko is the Gánako of the Djúku.

Zhibú, Gándiko, Gankéra, and I'bi, are the Katshára of the Djúku.

Kurórofa, or Korórofa, is the

Kororrofa of Barth.	Gbàgban of the Bóritṣu.
Kornorfa „ Bello's Map.	Akpa „ „ Igára and I'gbira.
Kora-raffa „ Bello's Narrative.	Dṣûku „ „ Koelle.
Ke, or Wiki, of the Tíwi.	

Wukári is the Okári of W. Allen.

Mítshi, or Mútshi, is the

Mísi and Míṣi of Dóma & Ákpoto.	Béṣi of Afúdu.
Tíwi, Mídṣi, & Mbídṣí of Koelle.	Ákpa of Igára, Ígbo, Sierra Leone.
Gbàlọu of Agáya.	

Dóma, or Arago, is the Dauma of Ogilby.

Núpe is the

Nufe and Nyffee	of writers.	Tàkpa	of Háusa.
Noofee	„ Bello.	Tágba	„ Yóruba.
Noufee	„ Richardson.	Tapa, Tapua, & Nuffi,	„ Clark.
Nufie & Núpāysee	„ Oldfield.	Tacwa and Nouffie	„ Lander.
Nife	„ the Góali.	Tapua	„ Latham.
Anupéri	„ Ébe.	Yowí or Yúfí	„ Ibn S'aíd.

E'be is the Anúpe of Háusa and Bárba, the Agaláti of the Kambálè.

E'gga is also called E'ga and I'gọ.

Yaúri or Yawúri is the

Ya-ori	of Bello.	Youri of Clapperton.
Yoouri	„ Clark.	Yaoori „ Macqueen.
Yaoorie	„ Lander.	Yaouri „ Mohammed Masini.

Líver is the

Lever of Lander and Beecroft.   Layaba of its inhabitants.

Búsa is the

Boosa of Lander.   Boussa of Clapperton.
Boossa „ Mohammed Masini.

F F

APPENDIX.

Mandénga is the Mandingo of authors.

Jólof is the

Gelofe, or Jalofe, of Barbot.   Jalaf of Ogilby.
Also Wolof, Woloff, Ouolloff.

Bárba, or Ibárba, is the

Bargú of Háusa.   Bargho of Bello.
Bíso „ Ébe.

Yóruba is called—

Yáriba   by Háusa.   Yekoo   by Dupuis.
Yarriba „ Latham.   Ayáji   „ Núpe.
Oyeo   „ Barbot.   Anagónu or Inágo „ Pópọ.
Akú   in Sierra Leone. Ayọnu   „ Dahómi.

E'ko is the

Lagos of the maps.   Onín of the Portuguese.

Kakánda is also pronounced Kakándi, Kakúnda, and Kakúndya.

Bonú is probably the Puna of Clark.

Ishábe is the Shabi and Shabee of Clark.

Bása (at the Confluence) with Akúya is the Akándsa or Kakándsa of Igára.

Dsúmu, or Idsúmu, is the

Akúya of Bása.   Abínu of Anúpe.

Owọ́rọ is called—

Eyági by Núpe.   Égbe by Yóruba.
Akandsa „ Igára.

Kí, or Ekí, with Dsúmu, and Owọ́rọ, is the

Akúya of Bása.   Kakánda *and* ⎫
Bonú „ Núpe.   Ganagána   ⎬ of Háusa.
Ishábe „ Ígbira and Igára.   Kakándsa   „ Ígbo.

Abítshi is the

Abushi *or* Bishi of W. Allen.   Beeshee of Oldfield.

APPENDIX. 435

Ajéwon-Ígbira is the

Rógan-Kóto of Háusa.   Djáshi-Ágbira of Djúku.
Pumávo   „ Mítshi.

A'kpa is the Akbah of W. Allen.
Okétta is the Aketo of W. Allen.

Ikéreku is the

Cheraku *or* Karuko of W. Allen.   Corracu of Oldfield.

Yimahá is called—

Yimasha in Háusa.   Immoshah by W. Allen.
Yimmahah by Laird.

Odokódo is the

Addakudda *and* } of Laird.   Adda-Kuddu of Allen and Thomson.
Addah-Kuddah
                                      Addacoodah „ Oldfield.

I'gbira-Pánda, also

Ígbira-Ihí, Ígbira-Odó, *and* Ígbira-Igú *or* Egú, or simply Ígbira, is the

Igbála   of Mítshi.   Égbira, Égūra, }
Igberra   „ Clark.   Égbīra-Pandẹ, } of Koelle.
Birrah   „ W. Allen.   *and* Opánda, }
Kotoonfauda „ Bello's Map.

Pánda is the

Fundah   of Laird.   Opánda of Koelle.
Fandah   „ W. Allen.

Ẹ'kpe (Ẹpe) is the A'fo of Dóma and Háusa.

Egú or Igú is the

Koto'n Kárifi of Háusa.   Cuttum Curafee { of Laird and Lander.
Kotun Karfee „ Bello.
Kuttum Karifi „ Allen's Chart.   Egòh   { „ Allen and Thomson.
Kattam Karifi „ W. Allen.

I'gbira-Síma, also

Igbira-Shíma, Ígbira-Sáima, *and* Ígbira-Iddá, is the Ígbira-Híma of Kölle.

Mount Páte is the

Patteh of Allen's Chart.   Lukósa of Kakánda.

Mount Sorácte is also named E'tse.
Beaufort Island is also named Barrága.

Okíri, or Ikíri, is the

Iccory of Oldfield.	Bocqua of Lander.
Ikóri „ McWilliam.	Bokweh „ Allen's Chart.

A'kpoto is the Akwottia of Allen's Chart.

Igára, Igála, or Igána is the

Atagarra of Bello's Map.	Egarra, Igarra, } of Clark.
Eggarah „ W. Allen.	and Igalla,
	Eggarra „ McWilliam.

Iddá is the

Attá and Attah { of Laird and Oldfield.   Iddah of Allen and Thomson.

Wífa is the Wappa of Allen and Thomson.

Ada-mugú is the

Damuggoo of Laird.	Damagu of McWilliam.

Adó or Edó is the Edú or Idú of Abó.
I'gbo (I'bo) is the Hackbous of old writers.
I'tshi, or Mbrítshi, is the Bretshi of Clark.

Asabá is the

Kirree of Lander and Oldfield.	Kirri of McWilliam.
Kíri Market of Allen's Chart.	Asabaa of Hutchinson.

Ossamaré is the

Atchimary of Oldfield.	Asamarae of Allen & Thomson.

E'lugu, E'nugu, or I'lugu, is the Olugu of Clark.
Isiélu is the Isiólu of Yála.

Isuáma, or Isú, is the

Isoama of Koelle.	Iswáma of Yála and of Clark.

Ogóne is called Egáne in Okúloma.
A'ro or A'no is the Aaru of Clark.

APPENDIX. 437

Abó is the

Eboe of Laird, Lander, & Oldfield.	Abé	of Nímbe, Orú, & Bíni.
Ibu and Eboe of Allen's Chart.	Ébbe	„ Okúloma.
Abóh „ Schön.	Abo 'bá and }	„ Orú & Okúloma.
Opú „ Igára.	Abo 'kú. }	

Mbóhia is the

Ikpófia of Okúloma.   Akpófia of Orú.

Korotúmbi (Allen and Thomson) is the

Little Ibu of Lander, Laird, & Allen.   Abo 'ntá of Okúloma *and* Orú.

Wári is the

Warree of Beecroft.   Dowerre, Awerri, ⎫
Ouwerre „ Ogilby.   Ouwerri, Oveiro, ⎬ of Barbot.
                    Forcados, ⎭

Angiáma is the

Ingiamah of Allen's Chart.   Hyammah of Lander & Oldfield.

Orú is called—

Ejó & Esó, by Nímbe, Bíni, & Ebáne.   Udṣo *and* Utṣo, by Koelle.
Aru *and* 'Njo, by Clark.

Bíni.

Oedo of Barbot and old authors.   Benin of maps.
Benyn of Ogilby.

Ijebú is the

Jaboe of Barbot and Ogilby.   Jaboo of traders.
Dṣẹ́bu „ Koelle.

Agáton is the

Gotton, Agatton, & Hugato of Barbot.   Gatto of traders.

Tshẹ́keri is the

Senáma of Nímbe.   Dṣẹ́kiri of Koelle.
Iwíni „ Abó.

Tuwón is the

Brass-town of charts.   Twa of English traders.

Nímbe is the

Némbe or Démbe of Orú. Itebú of Abó.
Numbe of Clark. Brass „ traders.

New Kalabár is called—

Anán and Bóm in Ígbo. Kanibári, Kalabári, in Ọzuzu.
Karabár „ Orú. Okulubur by Clark.
Karabári „ Ebane. New Calabar, and ⎱ by traders.
  Young Calabar ⎰

Ebáne is the

Obáne of Ígbo. Bandy, Bany, of Barbot.
Ibáne „ New Kalabár. Bonny „ traders.
Bani „ Ogilby.

Okúloma (town) is the

Okúloba of Nímbe. Kuleba of Ogilby.
Osimini-ku „ Abó. Okulome „ Clark.
Culebo „ Barbot. Grand Bonny-town „ traders.

Okríka is the

Krike of Ogilby. Akrika, Egriki, of Clark.
Cricke „ Barbot. Creeka and Young Creeka „ traders.

Ndọ́ki is the

Mina of Ebáne. Oqua of Clark.
Ókwa „ Ígbo. Ŏkūa „ Koelle.

Ogobéndo is the Bénde of Okúloma.

E′fik is called—

Éfi, by Igbo. Karaba by Clark.
Efiki „ Ebáne. Old Kalabár, ⎱ „ traders.
Bíe and Bíbīe? ⎱ „ Koelle. or Calabár, ⎰
and Ibibīa, ⎰

Akúna-Kúna is also pronounced Akúra-Kúra.

Egbo-Shári is called—

Uményi in Igbo. Ibíbio in Éfik.

Omún is the

Okré of Yála. Idrága of its inhabitants.

APPENDIX. 439

Yála is called—

Amúni in Ígbo.   Ọla in Akám.

Its people are called Olalapíde in I'gbo.
The people of Agányi are called A'kpa in Yála.

Baión is the

Bayung of Clark.   Báyoṇ of Koelle.

Ndób is the

Burúkem of Korórofa & Mítshi.   Mbrúkim ? of Éfik.

Cameroon is the

Diwálla of the Natives.   Ehála of Ngóten and Nhålemōe.
Niwára „ Moménya.

The Fernandians are the

Adeeyah (Adíya) of Thomson.   Búbi (Boobi) of traders.

Badagry is called—

Agbádayígi in Yóruba, *also* Bakagú.

Porto Nuovo is the

Ajéshe of Yóruba, Hagbonú of its people, and also Zém.

Pópo is the

Adého of its inhabitants.   Egún of Yóruba.

Hwída is the

Gréwhe *and* Grefe, } of its people.   Fida, Ouidah, Juida, *and* Juyda, } of Barbot.
Greghwee ? of Macqueen.   Whida, Whidah, *and* Whydah, } of traders.

Akrá is the

Accra of charts.   Nkrán of the Fantí.

Aṣánti is the

Ashantee of maps.   Kambóṇ (pl. Kambenza) } of Guréṇ.
Kambuse „ Móre.

440   APPENDIX.

Krábe (pl. Krábo) is the

Grébo of Clark.
Grebo, Cru, *and* ⎫ of Latham.
Cruman, ⎭

Krébo of Koelle.
Krumen *and* ⎫ of traders.
Fishmen ⎭

Native names of the Krú towns.

Little Krú,	Irúfa.	Grand Cestos,	Segléo.
Settra Krú,	Wóte.	Rock-Town,	Táke.
Krú-bar,	Nimbéo.	Fish-Town,	Wá.
Nanna Krú,	Maláo.	Garaway,	Wiágbo.
King Will's Town,	Wiáo.	Cavalley,	Báwo.
River Cestos,	{ Nipúa *or* Nipóe.	Cape Palmas,	{ Báine-lu *or* Gbúmle.
Town at its Mouth,	Nigbáe.	Native Town there, Báine.	
Little *or* Piganino Cestos,	Bitáo.		

Several places along the Krú coast have a name variously spelt, Cestos, Sestos, Sesters, or Cess. I have been unable to satisfy myself which is the correct one. Barbot says they got the designation from Cestos, a Portuguese word, meaning a kind of pepper, which was plentiful, but I have not been able to trace the word. Mr. Norris suggests that the word may be "Sestro," the left, an old Portuguese word, derived from the Latin *sinister*. If so, they were probably named by navigators because these places were situated on the left hand while sailing southwards; but they may have been named from baskets (cestos) of pepper, which is not improbable.

Names of places between the Confluence of the Bínue and Páro, and Zhibú, from a Púlo trader.

Bundú.	Búla.
Adamáwa.	Bátshama.
Kenmi.	Háma, *i. e.* Hamarúwa.
Tambul.	Káfi (the Chief of Érima.)
Garin (probably Górin, in Adamáwa).	Djanduróde.
	Belal.
Dámsa.	Zhibú.

Towns between Zhibú and Añyishi.

Zhibú.	Pia.	Ayakú.
Wukári.	Arúfu.	Akwóna.

APPENDIX. 441

Names of places between Zhibú and Wukári.

Zhibú.	Gankéra.	Mítshi.
Íbi.	Wuzhíri.	Fagúnke.
Gándiko.	Húnue.	Báibai.

Short route from Hamarúwa to Yola, five long days.

Hamarúwa.
1. Wurabéli, a Púlo village behind Láu.
2. Gowói.
3. Zéna, passed during the night on account of the natives.
4. Tahíru, a village belonging to Lawal.
5. Wúro-Alaháji, close to
6. Yóla.

Long route, Hamarúwa to Yóla, fourteen days.

1. Zhirú,
2. Érima,
3. Zóngo'n Káwo, } Under the direct rule of the Sultan of Hamarúwa.
4. Akám,
5. Zóngo'n Kengi,
6. Gangúme.
7. Zóngo'n dóka.
8. Kógi'n babá.
9. Zhán garigári.
10. Kwóntsha : the Governor is Muháma 'Ngabído, a Púlo.
11. Láro.
12. Dardío.
13. Hamedú, governed by Lawal's brother.
14. Yóla.

Hamarúwa to Yákuba, five days, first halt at Jébjeb.

The route from Dáli to Yákuba leads through Dámpara and Wázai.

Route from Zhibú	to Érima,	2 days.
,, ,, ,,	,, Gómkoi,	4—5 days.
,, ,, ,,	,, Súntai,	2½ days.
,, ,, Gómkoi	,, Alúnge,	3 days.
,, ,, Zhibú	,, Wukári,	1 long day, halt at Zú.
,, ,, Gándiko	,, ,,	5—6 hours.
,, ,, Ányishi	,, Kwóta,	2 days.
,, ,, ,,	,, Keána,	{ a day and a half, halt at Mágidi.
,, ,, ,,	,, Wukári,	{ 3—4 days' route through Akwóna, Arúfo, and Afiái.
,, ,, Rógan-kóto	,, Keána,	{ a day and a half, halt at Tufíye.

APPENDIX.

Rout from Ikéreku to	Pánda,	4 days.
,, ,, ,,	,, Dóma,	10 days.
,, ,, Erúku	,, Ikéreku (new),	1 hour.
,, ,, ,,	,, Ikéreku (old),	6—7 hours.
,, ,, Amarán	,, Iddá,	6 days.
,, ,, Old Ikéreku to	Ákpata,	1 day, NNW.
,, ,, Pánda to	Abáshi,	1 day, NW.
,, ,, ,, ,,	Ékpe,	half a day.
,, ,, Abáshi	,, Tóto,	1 day, NNE.

Towns between O'jogo and Dóma.

Túnga.   Kiréyi.
Keána (').   Kadoróko (').
Kéndoko.   Kowára.
Kaláshi.   Dóma (').
Gíza (').

Those marked (') are large towns.

Slave routes to the coast.

1.

Omodióko (in Élugu).   Ngwá.
Abája.   Ndóki.
Esómeran.   Ebáne.
Ogobéndo.

2.

Ogú (in Isuáma).   Ngwá.
Íngulu.   Ndóki.
Nivése.   Ebáne.
Lánkwo.

Route of a slave from Baión to the Cameroon river.

James Líloben (Támunku), native of Baión, caught when a boy in a war with 'Ngólam, a contiguous country, but speaking a different dialect. Sold in Bandém, distant a day's journey, thence sent half-a-day's journey to Dokáte, and again a long day's journey to Bám. Next sold at Yágbasi, half-a-day's journey off, and sent a day and a half to Bónkoi, where he escaped and ran two long days to Bidéma, from which place he came five or six hours by canoe to E'gbo or A'gbo, and, finally, one day more by canoe to 'Nfái or Cameroon. 'Nfái is the E'gbo name for the Cameroon: the language of E'gbo resembles the Diwálla.

APPENDIX. 443

In Baión and Báti the people are warlike. Cloth is woven by the inhabitants, but some use coverings of leaves; the houses are all round. The Baión people are not cannibals, but in war they cut off the heads of their slain enemies and dry them.

Names of Baión towns.

Basánga, Basánkte, Bánka, Bàsi, Balé$_n$, Bátya, Búua, Búlon, Bámanu, Bándebla, Bándem, Bándyo, Bawún, Balenyo, Bámoko, Bándesa, Bánem, Bákobi, Balíkem, Bafán, Ibuénto, Bábadi, Bámunjo, Báti, Bagán, Bágbo, Bandjíndjo, Igbógba, Bákom, Báwo, each of which towns has its own chief.

These were all my informant could remember; it will be observed that with hardly an exception the initial letter in all is the same.

Names of towns in E′lugu.

Onitshá, Obúnkar, Mbo-ája or Mbája (meaning large country), U′bri, Upóm, Opóse, Akéyza, Isiágum, Adelúgbo, Opánka, A′da, Ihúe, Lópa, Utrú, Isuótshi, Ndáwa, Loyán, Abája, Agóro, Obóye, Esu-ukún, Mbrumbú, Abáyan, Lofúja, Isupuáto, 'Ngódo, Omodióko, Esomerán, and Omiúnsi, of which last the inhabitants are said to be very short and very stout.

Towns in Isuáma.

Ossamaré, Míma, A′wo, Mohinú, Osuniriána, Ogù, Nivése, I′ngulu, A′wo, Amuzúri, Mbédi, Ubágo ? Umanóha, Amís.

Towns in Abó.

Óko-ála, a day's journey up the Abó creek, I′buku, O′ko, Asáka, Utágba (large), A′fo, Ibrédi, Anyáma.

Kings of Pánda.

1. Malegedú, the founder.
2. Idóko, about 1819 or 1820.
3. Akòsa.
4. Mamaláfia, about 1825 or 1827.
5. Itódo.
6. Abúha, during Laird's visit in 1832; a bad ruler.
7. Adéke.
8. Oyigú, slain by the Púlbe in 1854: unpopular.
9. Ogára, or Mohamma, grandson of the first king; succeeded in 1854.

Malegedú was a native of Kóto 'n Kárifi, whence he emigrated to Tóto, before commencing to build Pánda.

Muhammadan States in Central Africa, and their rulers.

1. Bagírmi	. . . .	Saraki 'n Bagírmi.
2. Adamúwa	. . .	Láwal.
3. Hamarúwa	. . .	Mohámma.
4. Gómbe	. . . .	Koiránga.
5. Bornú	. . . .	Sumanú.
6. Shíra	. . . .	Abduramáni.
7. Katagú	. . . .	Daukaówa.
8. Márma	. . . .	Mohámma.
9. Hadéji	. . . .	Bohári.
10. Káno	. . . .	Sumanú.
11. Awóyo	. . . .	Sámbo.
12. Kasawurái	. . .	Démbo.
13. Dáura	. . . .	Zuheíru.
14. Katshína	. . .	Mohámma Bello.
15. Zánfira	. . . .	Mamadú.
16. Gobíri	. . .	Áli.
17. Báutshi	. . . .	Ibrahíma.
18. Zózo	. . . .	Sídi.
19. Damudú	. . . .	Bája.
20. Núpe	. . . .	Dásaba.
21. Ilórin	. . . .	Abdusalámi.
22. Yaúri	. . . .	Thíta.
23. Kábi	. . . .	Sáraki 'n Kábi.
24. Sókoto	. . .	} Alihú, Sáraki 'n Musulmin, or Sultan of the Faithful.

This list was taken verbatim from the mouth of our friend Ibrahim or Saraki'n Háusa at Hamarúwa. In two instances his memory failed him, but rather than leave a blank he desired me to write down *Sáraki* with the name of the state, *Sáraki* meaning king. These names differ somewhat from those of Richardson in "A Mission to Central Africa," vol. ii. p. 189, and also from those of Dr. Barth, in Petermann's Atlas.

Kings of Ebáne.

1. Pápa.
2. Zhídie, his son.
3. Pelíkoli, his son,   the 1st King Péppel.
4. Fumára   „ „   „ 2nd „   „
5. Opúbu   „ „   „ 3rd „   „
6. Bríbo   „ cousin   „ 4th „   „
7. Dáppa, son of Opúbu   „ 5th „   „

APPENDIX.   445

He succeeded on April 9th, 1847, and was deposed in February, 1854; when he was temporarily replaced by another Dáppa, who died suddenly in 1855.

By late letters from Fernando Po, I learn that King Péppel or Dáppa has been freed from all restraint, and is at liberty to go where he chooses.

The Old Ebáne Week.

1st day,	Esen-íniadi.	5th day,	Eséne-Níuadi.
2nd „	Eséne-sónadi.	6th „	?
3rd „	Eséne-Suniádi.	7th „	?
4th „	Eséne-Sunaniádi.	8th „	?

I got these names from King Peppel, but he gave them with some hesitation, and he could not recollect the last three.

The Map which accompanies this volume has been very carefully reduced by Mr. Arrowsmith, from the large chart which he has prepared for the Admiralty from Mr. May's drawings. The large chart gives, on a scale of half-an-inch to a mile, merely the courses of the river as far as we went, with the countries immediately adjoining, but in the smaller one the upper part of the Kwóra, as far as Rábba, has been adapted from Allen's Survey, and the coast line and mouths of the rivers have been inserted from Denham. The mouth of the Cameroon river is from Capt. W. Allen, and Fernando Po from the most recent Admiralty Charts. The principal difficulty experienced was with regard to the Old Kalabár, of which there has been no actual survey. The Cross river was ascended by Beecroft, and the river was laid down by Dr. King, and we have employed his latitude for Duke Town as being the only available one. Consequently we have had somewhat to adapt the estuary of the river to this latitude. In the Kwóra itself Capt. Denham's position of the mouth, which differs considerably from Allen's, has been assumed as correct, but above that all the points were ascertained for ourselves. The principal alterations made in the lower parts of the river are moving Abó eight miles further south, as several meridian altitudes of the sun taken by Mr. May invariably gave the same result. The position of the

Confluence has been altered a good deal from that originally assigned to it; in the Map it approaches much more nearly to that given to it by the expedition in 1841, but is not quite so far west. In the Bínue everything beyond Dágbo is of course quite new. The furthest good observation was taken at Djín, in latitude 9° 22' north, and longitude 11° 25' 7" east; our last point, namely Dúlti, is not perfectly fixed, as the observations taken there were interrupted and consequently imperfect, still it cannot be very far out. All the positions determined during the ascent were checked by fresh observations during the return voyage, when, however, very few alterations seemed to be required. The positions of places near the upper Bínue, differ about a degree and a half from those given in Petermann's Atlas, but these changes correspond very well with the corrections in the longitude of lake Tsád, recently determined by Vogel. Dr. Barth has informed me that the positions of places towards Yóla, sent home by him, were assigned by bearings, starting originally from places which have since been proved to have been very incorrectly fixed. I am glad, however, to have referred to this Atlas, that I may mention of what service it proved to us, and that I may record my testimony as to the amount and general correctness of the information it contains. During July, August, and September, all the meridian altitudes taken were of the moon, of planets or of stars, as all the observations being taken with an artificial horizon, during these months the sun was too high to be within the scope of the sextant. The first occasion on which Mr. May was able to obtain a sun's meridian altitude, was on the 18th of October, at Okétta, not far above the Confluence. A list of the principal latitudes and longitudes determined will be subjoined in a tabular form.

Throughout the I'gbo country, every place has been noted for which a probable locality could be given, but, of course, such positions are only inserted provisionally. I have discarded a supposed connecting branch of the river from above Abó to Bonny, as I can find no evidence for it, and the testimony of the natives I examined gave no grounds for believing in its existence. I am perfectly certain that there is no direct communication there. All places marked without absolute authority have after them a note of interrogation. On the western side of the river there is certainly no affluent higher up than the Wári branch, and Abó may be looked as situated at the extreme apex of the Delta. Yákuba has been placed on the evidence of Dr. Vogel, who visited it last year. From Dr. Petermann I have just learnt that this traveller has recently sent some further important geographical results, including the following latitudes and longitudes, which may, he considers, be depended on, the former within two minutes, and the latter within five minutes:

Gujéba (in Bornú) . . .	11° 29′ 40″ N.	11° 39′ 0″ E.
Gábbei (on the frontier of Bornú, the Gebbeh of Barth) . . }	11° 4′ 10″ ,,	11° 20′ 0″ ,,
Gómbe (in Boberú) . . .	10° 49′ 0″ ,,	10° 16′ 0″ ,,

The only other point to which I wish to allude is the position of Cape Formoso. I was somewhat puzzled by the discrepancies of the various published maps and charts, some placing this much to the eastward, others to the westward of the Nun. Not being able to satisfy myself otherwise, I began to search the earlier records, and finding them pretty unanimous in favour of the western locality, I determined to follow their decision. In this I differ from several persons whom I have consulted, and in particular from one whose opinion is so deservedly of authority as Mr. Arrowsmith, who holds, as the older charts were not laid down from actual survey, and as the most projecting portion of the coast is to the eastward of the river, that the name ought to be retained for that spot. But, again, as the projection there is far from decided, and I find some of the voyagers actually naming the coast between the Nun and the Sengána as being the Cape, I believe that the land in that direction has the right of priority, and ought not therefore to be deprived of its title. Besides, the question is what was originally called the Cape, and not what ought geographically to have borne the name. The "Brass-Town" of charts, Mr. May ascertained during his visit there to be properly called "Tuwón;" it is merely a small village, the true " Brass Town" or Nímbe being from 30 to 35 miles from the sea.

Table of Latitudes and Longitudes.

Places.	Lat. N.	Long. E.
Agbéri	5° 14′ 41″	
Abó	5° 31′ 16″	6° 29′ 11″
Asabá	6° 11′ 16″	
Adu-mugú	6° 31′ 12″	6° 39′ 23″
Iddá	7° 6′ 2″	6° 42′ 14″
South end of Shuter Island	7° 17′ 45″	
Içbégbe	7° 44′ 33″	6° 44′ 27″·5
Átipo	7° 50′ 53″	6° 49′ 1″·5
Little Harriet Island	7° 55′ 30″	7° 2′ 56″·5
Yimahá	7° 59′ 14″	7° 9′ 47″
Okétta	8° 2′ 34″	
West end of Bay Islands	8° 1′ 15″	7° 29′ 5″·5
Ábatsho	8° 1′ 0″	7° 35′ 23″
Dágbo	7° 59′ 30″	7° 53′ 41″
Ákpoko	7° 55′ 34″	8° 5′ 22″·5
Ójogo	7° 45′ 8″	8° 28′ 31″·5
Rógan-Kóto	7° 45′ 45″	8° 40′ 12″·5
Ányishi	7° 52′ 46″	9° 4′ 51″·5
Gándiko	8° 10′ 39″	9° 42′ 7″·5
Zhibú	8° 18′ 32″	9° 56′ 17″
Point Lynslager	8° 43′ 17″	10° 32′ 27″·7
Gúrowa	9° 8′ 36″	11° 0′ 37″·4
Djín	9° 22′ 0″	11° 25′ 7″·4
Dúlti	9° 27′ 0″ ?	11° 30′ 0″ ?

I had intended to have added a list of observations for variation of the compass, but unfortunately the paper containing these has been mislaid, and Mr. May, who possibly may have a copy of the document, has been obliged to leave for the East Indies.

I was furnished with "Barrow's Circle," for ascertaining the dip of the needle, but unfortunately was not able to make many complete series of observations, several having been interrupted by the curiosity, &c. of the natives, by heavy rain, and other unforeseen accidents. The only sets on which I can place much confidence are the following :

1. Opposite Kénde, lower Bínuc, on a sand-bank, 12th August, 1854. between 10·30 and 11·25 A.M., and 12·50 and 1·50 P.M. Wind S.S.W. 1—3. Therm. 84°—94° F. Barom. (aneroid) 29·86—29·95. Weather *b, c.* Dip, 6° 6′ 58″.

APPENDIX. 449

2. On the sandy shore at Ójogo, 25th August, between 6·30 and 8·15 A.M. Wind 0. Therm. 73°—77° F. Barom. (aner.) 29·79—29·845. Weather *b, c*. Dip, 4° 37′ 8″.
3. At Zhíbú, on a grassy bank, 9th September, between 6·45 and 8 A.M. Wind W. 2. Dip, 5° 59′ 22″.

This last I place but little confidence in. It is the result only of a partial set of observations, and the dip was doubtless increased by the interruption which compelled me to stop, which was being surrounded by from sixty to eighty natives, each of them carrying iron weapons. I tried to make them lay down their arms at a considerable distance, but being by myself, was only partially successful, as fresh arrivals were constantly taking place : the vibration of the needles was so great and so varied, that it became impossible to obtain a reading.

During the greater of the river voyage, meteorological observations were taken every three hours during the twenty-four, the only interruptions being when I was on shore. These included registers of *pressure, temperature of air, moisture, temperature of water, wind, clouds, weather, and general or remarkable phenomena, rapidity of the current, &c.* I was furnished with two marine barometers by Adie, which proved to be excellent instruments. I had also two Aneroids, which though always more sensitive, yet generally corresponded well with the mercurial instruments. *Moisture* was ascertained by the wet and dry bulb thermometer. On the 21st of September, 1854, I took a series of twenty-five hourly observations. I have as yet found it impossible to go over and check the whole series, and so can now only state the general results. The barometers seemed to be very little affected by change of weather, the difference between rainy and dry days being but slight, and the occurrence of a tornado appeared to exercise hardly any influence. Two daily *maxima* and *minima* were invariable and well marked. The *maxima* occurred at from 9 to 10 A.M. and P.M., and the *minima* about 4 or 4·30 A.M. and P.M., the morning *minimum* being generally rather earlier than the afternoon one. The daily range of the barometers was about ·05 to ·07 of an inch on the mercurial barometers, and from ·07 to ·09 on the Aneroids. The extreme range of the barometers was from 30·23 at the mouth of the river, to 29·77 at the upper part of the Bínue, both these being *maxima* readings. This would tend to show that the river has no great descent, but flows along nearly level country, which is also to be inferred from other appearances. Working by a rule given in one of the volumes of the "Journal of the Geographical Society" for the Aneroid barometer, I could only find an elevation of 119 feet at the Confluence, and 268 feet at O'jogo; but these results are, I should suppose, too low, yet there can be no question that the Bínue and the lower part of the united rivers flow along a very level valley.

The extremes of temperature were from 69° to 97° F., the former being the morning temperature, in October, and the latter the extreme in the shade during the commencement of the dry season. The average mid-day temperature was from 82° to 84°. The coldest period during the day was from 4 to 5 A.M. The temperature of the surface water of the river varied from 79° to 84°, the average being 81°.

E.

Distinguishing marks of different tribes.

Tatooing, or marks on various parts of the body, is used chiefly by the Pagan races, the Muhammadans generally avoiding this practice, which they term "Shushúa."

Tribe.	Marks.
Orú.	A straight, very prominent line along centre of forehead, and upper part of nose; three lines extending diagonally across the cheek from inner angle of eye; other varied marks on chest and arms.
Nimbe.	Six short perpendicular incisions between eye and ear.
Abó.	*Males.*—Three short perpendicular cuts on each temple, and three short horizontal lines across upper part of

APPENDIX.

Tribe.	Marks.
	nose, between the eyebrows. *Females*—the same on the nose, but with six perpendicular lines on the temples.
Élugu.	Six perpendicular lines in front of the ear.
Áro.	From ten to twelve short horizontal lines just before the ear.
Ọzuzu.	Three rows of minute lines from ear to angle of eye, the middle row straight, the two others curving towards it; two curved lines of small incisions from lobe of ear, curving along cheek to end of lines at eye; two short rows of similar lines under eyes towards nose; a line of similar incisions down forehead and nose.
Itshi, or Mbrítshi }	Numerous extensive but varied cicatrices on forehead.
Asabá	Three perpendicular lines along breast and belly, centre one straight, the others curved; one line behind, following curve of armpit, and going downwards; seven short perpendicular incisions on forehead; curved row of small lines under each eye.
Agáto.	Three spots, arranged triangularly, with base upwards, on temple.
Yóruba.	Markings only partially in use; some have several rows of fine lines along the cheeks.
Básn (Confluence) }	Two or three broad curved lines from temple to chin.
Bonú.	Same as Básn, but crossed by several fine lines.
Ishábe.	Four broad lines along each cheek.
Igára.	Marking not practised.
Ígbira.	No distinctive mark.
Núpe.	Markings partial; a short line, slightly curved, from near inner angle of eye, proceeding diagonally about two-thirds across cheek.
Bása (on the Bínue). }	No particular mark.
Dóma.	Markings vary. Some employ ten or twelve fine curved lines along the cheek. In Keána, many, especially among the females, have two rows of fine perpendicular lines under each eye.
Mítshi.	Short perpendicular cuts over each eyebrow; a curved incision on each cheek; and various devises on breast and arms.
Koróroſa.	Ear-lobes pierced with large holes; among Báibai far up the river, numerous irregular cuts on upper arm.
Bornú and Loggóne. }	Numerous curved lines along cheeks.
Mándara.	Curved lines along angle of jaw; fainter lines along cheek.
Dáura.	Two horizontal cuts opposite mouth.

Tribe.	Marks.
Marádi.	A long line along cheek.
Gobír.	One horizontal line opposite mouth.
Éfik.	Three round spots on each temple.
Krábo.	One broad line down centre of forehead and nose; arrow-head on each temple, with point towards eye.
Cameroon.	A mark adopted of late resembling that of Krúmen.

The marks which I have here given for Marádi and Gobír differ from those mentioned by Richardson in the "Mission to Central Africa," vol. ii. p. 222.

F.

The collections of natural history made during the voyage though not very extensive, have as yet been but very partially examined, my time having been fully occupied by other matters. A brief notice of them was read at the meeting of the British Association at Glasgow, by Andrew Murray, Esq., as an Appendix to his paper on the Natural History of Central Africa. Numerous specimens of raw products, and of the cereals, have been sent to the Crystal Palace at Sydenham, and some others to the Museum at Kew and to Edinburgh; but of the zoological and botanical specimens most yet remain for future investigation.

G.

As I intend shortly to discuss at some length the question of African fever, I shall touch but very lightly on it here. It has been hitherto a great bugbear, and until very recently has been regarded and treated in an empirical and unscientific manner. More sound and common-sense views are now beginning to spread, and to few persons are medical men more indebted for this reformation than to Dr. Bryson, R.N., in whose "Reports" is to be found much sound and valuable information. It will be sufficient here to say that African fever has nothing specific about it; that it is certainly not *sui generis*, and that it is merely an aggravated form of the disease known in this country as ague. The various divisions into continued, remittent, and intermittent are only calculated to puzzle and to mislead; they refer to degrees and not to actual differences, and these forms gradually, but surely, merge into each other. In its mildest form the fever is intermittent, that is to say, between the paroxysms intervals of health occur: more aggravated, the complaint becomes remittent, meaning, that between the febrile accessions the symptoms only remit, but do not altogether disappear: in its greatest intensity the disease is quasi-continued, or to the unpractised eye seems to be devoid of paroxysmal changes, but to proceed with an undeviating deadly career. But in all these the poison, the original cause of the malady, is essentially the same, and the results depend partly on constitutional causes, partly on the amount and virulence of the poison imbibed. The same amount of poison will, as is the case with alcohol, affect two persons inhaling it in very different degrees. The disease is what is termed by medical men *periodic*, and the remedies required are called *anti-periodics*, of which the best known and the most efficacious is quinine. This may be given as soon as the complaint shows itself, and the sooner the better, as it is the main-stay of the sufferer; of course, various occasional symptoms may occur during its progress, which will require to be treated according to circumstances. But the great modern improvement is the discovery that quinine not only cures, but that it actually prevents, and that by taking this invaluable drug while in unhealthy localities, persons may escape total'y unscathed. The best form for use for this purpose is *quinine wine*, of which half a glass should be taken early in the morning, and repeated if requisite in the afternoon. Experience likewise proves, that if endemic fever seizes a person who has been using quinine as a prophylactic, he will escape much more easily, and have a milder and more manageable attack than another who has not been so employing it. The other means of avoiding disease are such as reason and common sense would

suggest—namely, avoiding night exposure, sleeping in the open
air, or delay in sickly spots, &c., and for Europeans a rather
generous diet, with the frequent use of the shower-bath. Drugs
should be avoided as much as possible, especially calomel and
other mercurials, which are not only unnecessary, but have
actually killed far more people than ever fever has. Calomel
has no real or curative effect on malarious poisons, but only
adds fuel to the fire, as the unfortunate to whom it is administered has to contend against two poisons rather than one.

Much ingenuity has been displayed by those who believe in
the specific nature of African fever in endeavouring to discover
causes for its supposed malignity. At one time sulphuretted
hydrogen was pronounced to be the *origo mali*, the theorists
forgetting that if so, Harrowgate and Strathpeffer would be
highly dangerous spots. Then putrid matters, moisture, vegetable decay, &c., each had their supporters, as well as many
other hypotheses; but at present we only know that the poison,
of the nature of which we are as yet ignorant, may arise from a
dry soil. It is certainly more abundant where there is moisture,
and generally more intense; but all that is really required for
its production are a certain amount of heat and *previous*
moisture. These conditions are widely spread, and therefore
we find *malaria* also nearly ubiquitous, though more prevalent
in warm climates. But in no *essential* does African endemic
fever differ from the fever of Hindustán, of Borneo, of the
Spanish Main, of the West Indies, or of fenny and marshy
countries in Europe. The treatment required is the same;
only as the symptoms are more violent, so should the remedies
be more decided and more quickly pushed. It has been stated
as an inexplicable paradox, that fever often does not make its
appearance while travellers are actually in malarious regions,
but that it breaks out, as in the case of the expedition of 1841,
after reaching healthy regions. But this is easily explained,
as the miasmata seldom or never lay men prostrate at once,
but the poison—like in this respect that of small-pox or of
typhus—has a period of incubation, as it is termed, varying
from five or six to sixteen or eighteen days, but usually from
nine to twelve; so that before the primary symptoms are
evidenced, the swampy district where the seeds of illness

were sown may have been left far behind. Lastly, let it be always borne in mind, that this disease is strictly and inherently non-infectious.

H.

To pursue trade to advantage along the Kwóra and Bínue, it will be necessary to establish at various suitable places along their banks depôts or stations, from which the products of the country can be shipped and carried away. With the natives trade will be carried on in a petty manner; therefore the most advantageous method of pursuing it will be by the intervention and employment of civilized natives, such as those of Sierra Leone, who will manage the retail business, and then deal on the larger scale with the white trader. Though the climate will not be so dreaded as it has been hitherto, still it can never prove adapted for Europeans, so that much must be effected by coloured agency. These people would reside in the country, would collect the products, and store them up until the rainy season, when steamers would ascend to bring fresh supplies of manufactured goods, and to carry off the products collected during the year. Before long not only would the trade of the immediate vicinity of the river be thus concentrated, but that of the countries as far as the borders of the Sahara would flow in the same direction, as I see in one of Dr. Barth's despatches that various chiefs stated, that were ships to ascend the Kwóra, they and their people would bring their goods for disposal towards the river, in preference to the dangerous march across the Desert.

The staple articles of trade would be palm-oil, shea-butter, cam-wood, and ivory, but other articles would also be easily procurable, as ground-nuts, indigo, peppers, cotton, croton-oil seeds, hides, ostrich-feathers, &c.; and probably an internal trade would spring up in rice, corn, yams, provisions, native cloths, &c. Gold-dust would also be obtained, but not in any quantity. With the advance of civilization other articles would be introduced, and other crops cultivated, especially coffee and sugar-canes. In exchange the principal demand on us would be for soft goods, and in a smaller degree for stoneware, hardware, arms, and gunpowder.

Most of our African colonies have availed themselves of the recent postal reductions; but it would be a great boon if the same could be extended to the trading rivers, which are, practically speaking, floating colonies, inhabited almost exclusively by natives of Britain. Having no functionaries, I suppose the request has never been made; but it would be, doubtless, of much service to those interested in the prosperity of these places. To Sierra Leone, Cape Coast Castle, and Akrá the postage now is sixpence, while to the rivers it is a shilling. But if we wish to write to Madeira or Teneriffe, places much nearer England, the postal expense is more than three times the amount of a letter to Tasmania—so considerate to us are our allies, who depend for the welfare, almost for the existence, of these dependencies on our support. It certainly is preposterous, that writing to a sick friend at Madeira we must pay for the lightest letter one shilling and eightpence, while we may send one three or four times the weight, and more than treble the distance, for sixpence. Were it not for its English visitors and English residents, what would Madeira be? yet, with its uncalled-for quarantine expenses, and its high rate of postage, undue restrictions are wantonly heaped on its best friends.

THE END.

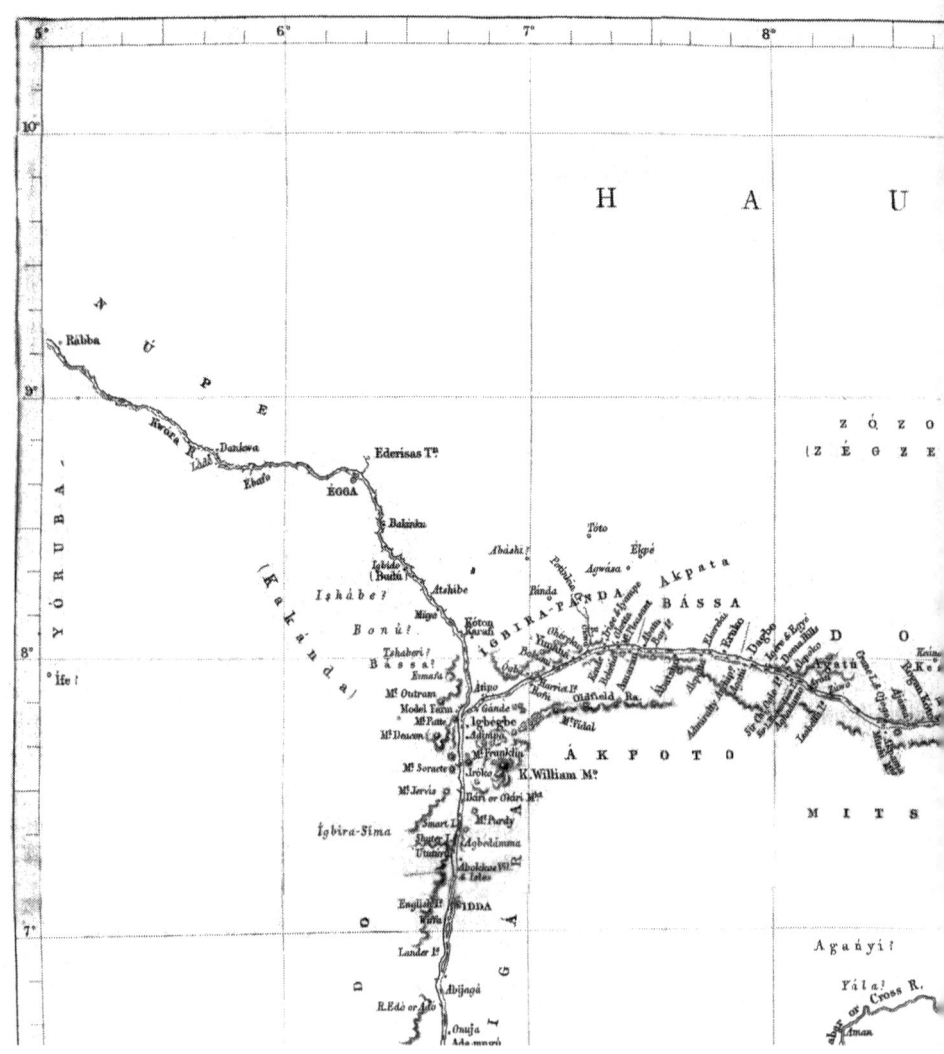

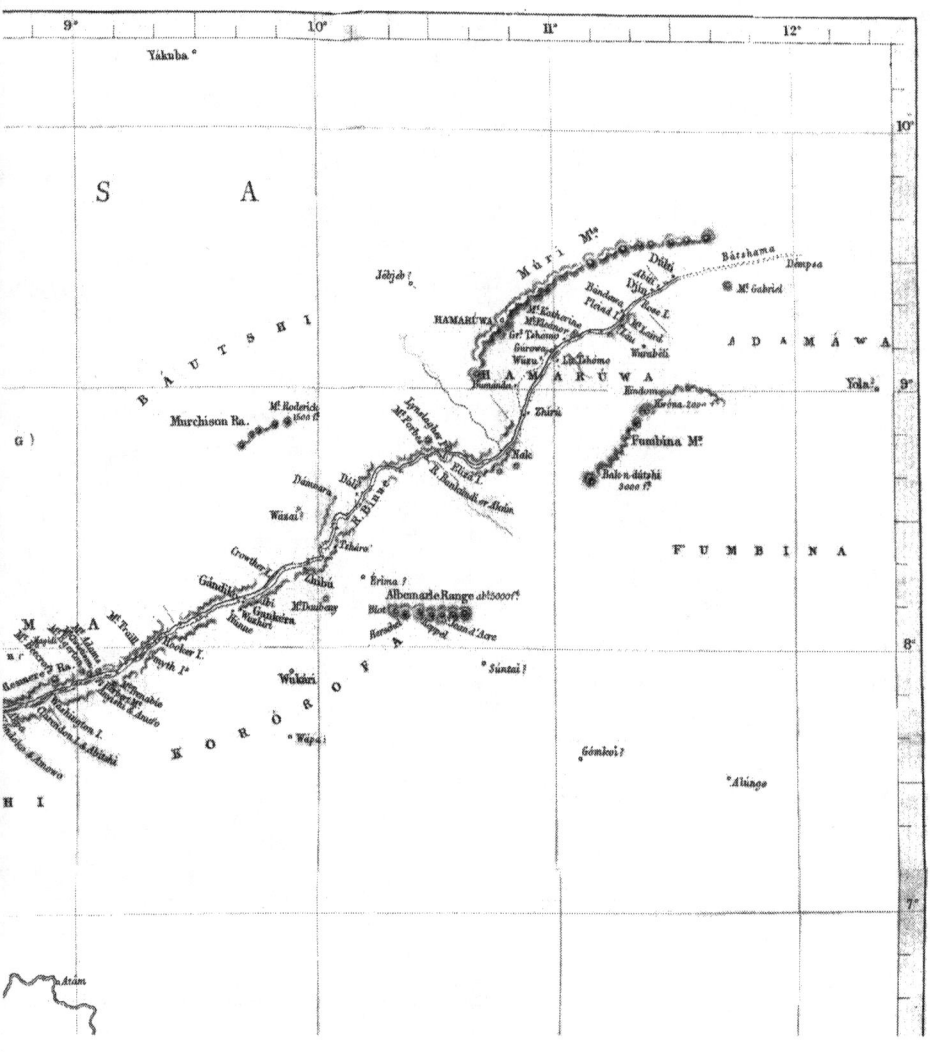

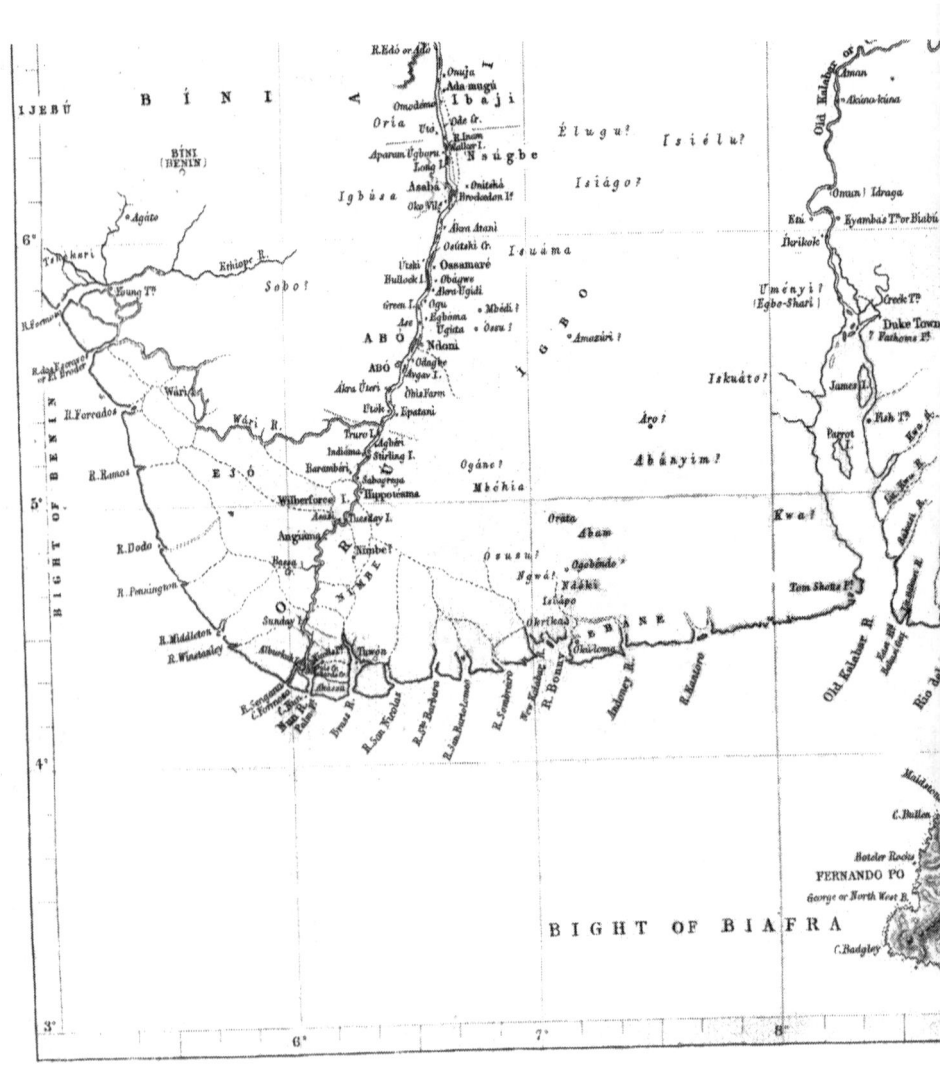

www.ingramcontent.com/pod-product-compliance
Lightning Source LLC
Chambersburg PA
CBHW021825220426
43663CB00005B/134